Trajectory Analysis, Positioning and Control of Mobile Robots

Trajectory Analysis, Positioning and Control of Mobile Robots

Guest Editors

Juan Ernesto Solanes Galbis
Luis Gracia

Basel • Beijing • Wuhan • Barcelona • Belgrade • Novi Sad • Cluj • Manchester

Guest Editors

Juan Ernesto Solanes Galbis
Instituto de Diseño y
Fabricación
Universitat Politècnica de
València
València
Spain

Luis Gracia
Instituto de Diseño y
Fabricación
Universitat Politècnica de
València
València
Spain

Editorial Office
MDPI AG
Grosspeteranlage 5
4052 Basel, Switzerland

This is a reprint of the Special Issue, published open access by the journal *Applied Sciences* (ISSN 2076-3417), freely accessible at: https://www.mdpi.com/journal/applsci/special_issues/positioning_and_control_of_mobile_robots.

For citation purposes, cite each article independently as indicated on the article page online and as indicated below:

Lastname, A.A.; Lastname, B.B. Article Title. *Journal Name* **Year**, *Volume Number*, Page Range.

ISBN 978-3-7258-3245-3 (Hbk)
ISBN 978-3-7258-3246-0 (PDF)
https://doi.org/10.3390/books978-3-7258-3246-0

© 2025 by the authors. Articles in this book are Open Access and distributed under the Creative Commons Attribution (CC BY) license. The book as a whole is distributed by MDPI under the terms and conditions of the Creative Commons Attribution-NonCommercial-NoDerivs (CC BY-NC-ND) license (https://creativecommons.org/licenses/by-nc-nd/4.0/).

Contents

About the Editors vii

Preface ix

J. Ernesto Solanes, and Luis Gracia
Mobile Robots: Trajectory Analysis, Positioning and Control
Reprinted from: *Appl. Sci.* 2025, 15, 355, https://doi.org/10.3390/app15010355 1

Zhiguo Lu, Guangda He, Ruchao Wang, Shixiong Wang, Yichen Zhang, Chong Liu, et al.
An Orthogonal Wheel Odometer for Positioning in a Relative Coordinate System on a Floating Ground
Reprinted from: *Appl. Sci.* 2021, 11, 11340, https://doi.org/10.3390/app112311340 9

Jordi Palacín, Elena Rubies and Eduard Clotet
Systematic Odometry Error Evaluation and Correction in a Human-Sized Three-Wheeled Omnidirectional Mobile Robot Using Flower-Shaped Calibration Trajectories
Reprinted from: *Appl. Sci.* 2022, 12, 2606, https://doi.org/10.3390/app12052606 33

J. Ernesto Solanes, Adolfo Muñoz, Luis Gracia and Josep Tornero
Virtual Reality-Based Interface for Advanced Assisted Mobile Robot Teleoperation
Reprinted from: *Appl. Sci.* 2022, 12, 6071, https://doi.org/10.3390/app12126071 56

Radim Hercik, Radek Byrtus, Rene Jaros, Jiri Koziorek
Implementation of Autonomous Mobile Robot in SmartFactory
Reprinted from: *Appl. Sci.* 2022, 12, 8912, https://doi.org/10.3390/app12178912 78

Albina Kamalova, Suk Gyu Lee and Soon Hak Kwon
Occupancy Reward-Driven Exploration with Deep Reinforcement Learning for Mobile Robot System
Reprinted from: *Appl. Sci.* 2022, 12, 9249, https://doi.org/10.3390/app12189249 96

Tanzeela Shakeel, Jehangir Arshad, Mujtaba Hussain Jaffery, Ateeq Ur Rehman, Elsayed Tag Eldin, Nivin A. Ghamry and Muhammad Shafiq
A Comparative Study of Control Methods for X3D Quadrotor Feedback Trajectory Control
Reprinted from: *Appl. Sci.* 2022, 12, 9254, https://doi.org/10.3390/app12189254 116

Guangzhi Guo, Zuoxiao Dai and Yuanfeng Dai
Real-Time Stereo Visual Odometry Based on an Improved KLT Method
Reprinted from: *Appl. Sci.* 2022, 12, 12124, https://doi.org/10.3390/app122312124 135

Yuanfeng Lian, Hao Sun and Shaohua Dong
Point–Line-Aware Heterogeneous Graph Attention Network for Visual SLAM System
Reprinted from: *Appl. Sci.* 2023, 13, 3816, https://doi.org/10.3390/app13063816 148

Hui Jiang and Yukun Zhang
A Spatial Location Representation Method Incorporating Boundary Information
Reprinted from: *Appl. Sci.* 2023, 13, 7929, https://doi.org/10.3390/app13137929 170

Pingguo Huang and Yutaka Ishibashi
Enhancement of Robot Position Control for Dual-User Operation of Remote Robot System with Force Feedback
Reprinted from: *Appl. Sci.* 2024, 14, 9376, https://doi.org/10.3390/app14209376 189

Hongchao Zhuang, Jiaju Wang, Ning Wang, Weihua Li, Nan Li, Bo Li and Lei Dong
A Review of Foot–Terrain Interaction Mechanics for Heavy-Duty Legged Robots
Reprinted from: *Appl. Sci.* **2024**, *14*, 6541, https://doi.org/10.3390/app14156541 . . . . **203**

About the Editors

Juan Ernesto Solanes Galbis

Juan Ernesto Solanes Galbis received a B.S. degree in Industrial Electronics Engineering, a B.S. degree in Industrial Automatics, an M.S. degree in Automatics and industrial informatics, and a Ph.D. in Robotics, Automatics, and Industrial informatics from the Universitat Politècnica de València (UPV), Spain, in 2007, 2009, 2011, and 2015, respectively. He is currently an Associate Professor with the Department of Systems Engineering and Control (DISA), UPV. His research interests include nonlinear and robust control, extended reality, human–machine interaction, and robotics.

Luis Gracia

Luis Gracia received a B.Sc. degree in Electronic Engineering, an M.Sc. degree in Control Systems Engineering, and a Ph.D. in Automation and Industrial Computer Science from the Universitat Politècnica de València (UPV), Spain, in 1998, 2000, and 2006, respectively. He is currently a Professor at the Department of Systems Engineering and Control (DISA) of UPV, where he has worked since 2001. His research interests include mobile robots, robotic manipulators, sliding-mode control, collaborative robots, and system modeling and control.

Preface

This reprint brings together a collection of groundbreaking research articles that delve into the latest advancements in mobile robotics, focusing on trajectory analysis, positioning, and control. The contributions featured in this Special Issue showcase innovative solutions developed by leading experts from around the globe, pushing the boundaries of what is achievable in the field. From advancing SLAM technologies and deep reinforcement learning for autonomous navigation to integrating augmented and virtual reality for intuitive robot teleoperation, these studies provide a comprehensive view of how cutting-edge technologies are reshaping the role of mobile robots. By addressing challenges in diverse environments and applications, this collection envisions a future where mobile robotics enhances human capabilities with precision, efficiency, and inclusivity.

Juan Ernesto Solanes Galbis and Luis Gracia
Guest Editors

Editorial

Mobile Robots: Trajectory Analysis, Positioning and Control

Juan Ernesto Solanes * and Luis Gracia

Instituto de Diseño y Fabricación, Universitat Politècnica de València, 46022 València, Spain
* Correspondence: esolanes@idf.upv.es

1. Introduction

The rapid evolution of mobile robotics over the last decade has reshaped the landscape of technology and its applications in society [1–3]. From autonomous vehicles revolutionizing urban mobility to drones transforming delivery systems and robots performing tasks in extreme or hazardous environments, mobile robotics have transcended experimental boundaries to become a tangible part of our daily lives [4–7]. These advancements are driven by an interplay of disciplines, including artificial intelligence (AI), robotics, computer vision, and control theory, which continue to push the limits of what mobile robots can achieve in terms of autonomy, efficiency, and adaptability [8–10].

One of the most significant challenges in mobile robotics lies in trajectory analysis, positioning, and control. Accurate trajectory planning and execution are critical for robots to navigate dynamic environments, avoid obstacles, and operate effectively alongside humans. Simultaneous Localization and Mapping (SLAM) technologies [11,12], coupled with robust navigation algorithms [13,14], have advanced significantly, enabling robots to construct detailed maps of their surroundings while localizing themselves in real time. These developments are essential for the deployment of mobile robots in unstructured and unpredictable environments, such as urban settings or disaster-stricken areas [15].

Control systems also play a pivotal role in ensuring the reliability and stability of mobile robots. Advances in control theory have enabled the creation of sophisticated models that adapt to uncertainties and dynamic conditions. Techniques such as model predictive control (MPC), adaptive control, and reinforcement learning-based controllers are empowering robots with the capability to make intelligent decisions in complex scenarios [9,16–21]. These innovations ensure precision in tasks ranging from trajectory tracking to collaborative operations with other robots or humans.

Another layer of complexity arises from the increasing presence of mobile robots in human-centric environments. This integration introduces the challenge of human–robot interaction (HRI), which requires robots to not only perform tasks autonomously but also communicate, cooperate, and adapt to human behavior [22–25]. Designing intuitive and safe HRI systems is a critical research area, especially as robots become more involved in healthcare, logistics, and personal assistance. Tools such as natural language processing, gesture recognition, and emotion detection are being integrated into robotic systems to make interactions more seamless and user-friendly [26–28].

Emerging technologies such as augmented reality (AR) and virtual reality (VR) are opening up new frontiers in the field of mobile robotics [29–31]. These tools provide enhanced visualization and interaction capabilities, enabling humans to better understand and control robotic systems. AR and VR also offer new possibilities for training robots, simulating complex environments, and improving remote operations, particularly in scenarios where direct human presence is challenging or impossible.

The integration of these advancements in mobile robotics highlights the interdisciplinary nature of this field. It requires collaboration between AI researchers, control engineers, computer scientists, and human–machine interaction specialists to address the multifaceted challenges and opportunities it presents [10]. This Special Issue brings together cutting-edge research and methodologies from these domains, providing a comprehensive overview of current trends and fostering innovation in this vibrant area.

2. The Present Issue

This Special Issue received a total of 17 submissions, each of which was meticulously assessed by at least one Guest Editor to ensure alignment with the core themes of mobile robotics. Submissions that matched the scope were subjected to a comprehensive review process, which included evaluation by at least two external reviewers, while those outside the thematic focus were declined. Following this rigorous peer review process, 10 articles and 1 review were ultimately selected for publication. A detailed summary of the key findings and contributions of each article is provided in the following.

The authors of Contribution 1 introduce an orthogonal wheel odometer system designed for the precise positioning of mobile robots on floating surfaces such as ship decks. This innovative system utilizes four orthogonal wheels equipped with encoders to achieve centimeter-level accuracy in determining position and orientation in a relative coordinate system, overcoming the limitations of traditional gyroscope-based methods.

Their experimental results demonstrate the system's effectiveness in mitigating errors caused by the irregular movements of floating surfaces. Their system consistently delivered accurate results across various motion scenarios, including linear, curved, and rotational movements. Notably, in tests conducted on a simulated floating platform, the maximum recorded error was 2.43 cm, with a root mean square error (RMSE) of 1.51 cm. These findings underscore the system's potential for applications in challenging environments where conventional positioning systems struggle.

The authors of Contribution 2 propose a systematic method for evaluating and correcting odometry errors in a human-sized, three-wheeled omnidirectional mobile robot. Using a novel flower-shaped calibration trajectory consisting of 36 individual paths, the study iteratively adjusts the robot's kinematic parameters to minimize discrepancies between odometry data and ground truth trajectories obtained via a 2D LIDAR sensor.

The experimental results demonstrate significant improvements in the robot's positional accuracy, with an average reduction of 82.14% in the error of final position and orientation after calibration. This approach highlights the effectiveness of using both straight and curved trajectories for comprehensive calibration, offering a robust solution for improving odometry in omnidirectional robots designed for diverse indoor applications.

The authors of Contribution 3 present a virtual reality (VR)-based interface designed to enhance the teleoperation of mobile robots in unknown environments. The interface aims to provide an intuitive and immersive user experience, enabling seamless interaction between the operator and the robot. Unlike traditional approaches, this system focuses on simplifying the control process by including essential virtual elements, such as a real-time 3D map of the environment, the robot's position, and any detected obstacles, rather than prioritizing hyper-realistic visuals.

The VR interface leverages a potential field-based navigation method to assist the user in guiding the robot while automatically avoiding obstacles. Using a Turtlebot3 Burger robot (which is manufactured by the ROBOTIS company, located in Seoul, Korea) equipped with a LiDAR sensor, the system demonstrated its ability to ensure collision-free navigation in both simulated and real-world scenarios. The researchers also incorporated a gamepad for interaction, prioritizing user ergonomics and long-term usability over conventional VR controllers.

User studies involving participants of various ages and backgrounds highlighted the system's usability and effectiveness. Feedback showed high levels of immersion and user satisfaction, with participants finding the interface easy to learn and operate. The authors conclude that the VR-based interface successfully combines the adaptability of human guidance with the precision of automated navigation, making it suitable for tasks such as search and rescue or industrial inspection.

The authors of Contribution 4 describe the implementation of an autonomous mobile robot (AMR), specifically the MiR100, within the SmartFactory production line environment. The study focuses on integrating the AMR for tasks such as transporting and presenting products produced on the line. Key objectives included establishing effective communication between the robot and the production line, ensuring precise navigation in confined spaces, and testing various positioning markers for optimal accuracy.

The results highlighted the system's ability to achieve a high degree of accuracy, with the L-marker proving to be the most reliable for repeated precise positioning and yielding an error margin of ±3 mm. This precision was crucial for enabling seamless interaction with robotic arms during product transfers. The study demonstrates the potential of AMRs in enhancing automation in manufacturing processes, offering insights into the challenges of integrating navigation and communication systems in constrained industrial environments.

The authors of Contribution 5 tackle the challenge of autonomous exploration for mobile robots in unknown environments using a deep reinforcement learning (DRL) approach. Specifically, they employ the Deep Deterministic Policy Gradient (DDPG) algorithm to guide a robot equipped with a laser sensor as it navigates and maps indoor spaces. Their custom-designed environment models the mapping process with real-time visualization, allowing the DDPG agent to make decisions based on laser sensor input, producing linear and angular velocities as outputs.

The study demonstrates the effectiveness of occupancy reward-driven exploration, where the reward function incentivizes the robot to prioritize unexplored areas while penalizing actions leading to collisions or inefficiencies. The results show that the DDPG algorithm successfully optimizes the robot's motion, enabling efficient mapping with fewer collisions and smoother trajectories compared to alternative strategies. This work underscores the potential of DRL in addressing complex navigation and mapping tasks in robotics.

The authors of Contribution 6 perform a comparative study of linear and nonlinear control methods for the feedback trajectory control of an X3D quadrotor. Their research focuses on evaluating four different control strategies: two linear methods (Proportional-Integral-Derivative (PID) and Linear Quadratic Regulator (LQR)) and two nonlinear methods (Fuzzy Logic Controller and Model Reference Adaptive PID Controller based on the MIT Rule). Their study aims to assess the transient performance of these controllers in terms of rise, settling, and peak times and overshoot.

Using a Simulink model of the X3D quadrotor, the authors found that the LQR controller outperformed the other methods, offering robust stability and minimal overshoot. While the PID controller showed simplicity in implementation, it lacked robustness against disturbances. Nonlinear controllers, such as the Fuzzy Logic and Adaptive PID Controller, demonstrated better handling of system nonlinearities but required complex parameter tuning. These findings provide a comprehensive analysis of control strategies for quadrotors, emphasizing the balance between performance and complexity for different application scenarios.

The authors of Contribution 7 propose an advanced real-time stereo visual odometry (SVO) system using an improved Kanade–Lucas–Tomasi (KLT) method. Their work addresses the computational challenges inherent in traditional SVO approaches by introducing novel techniques, including feature inheritance, an adaptive KLT tracker, and a simplified KLT matcher. These innovations minimize the time-consuming processes of feature detection and stereo matching while maintaining localization accuracy.

The adaptive KLT tracker optimizes tracking by dynamically adjusting the feature window size based on average disparity, translation velocity, and yaw angle, thereby mitigating scale distortion and affine transformations. Furthermore, a veer chain matching scheme effectively corrects drift errors during turning maneuvers. Experimental evaluations on the KITTI odometry dataset demonstrate that this method achieves a balance between high computational efficiency and localization accuracy, with a real-time processing capability of 15 Hz on a single-thread CPU. The results underscore the potential of this approach in advancing robust and efficient visual odometry systems for mobile platforms.

The authors of Contribution 8 present an advanced visual SLAM system that addresses the challenges of weak textures and complex geometries that are often encountered in industrial environments. The authors introduce a novel point–line-aware heterogeneous graph attention network (HAGNN) to improve the robustness and accuracy of feature extraction and matching. Their system integrates a point–line geometric feature extraction network (PL-Net) with an attention mechanism that aggregates the contextual features of points and lines for enhanced SLAM performance.

To optimize feature matching, the study transforms the matching process into an optimal transport problem, solved using a Greedy Inexact Proximal Point Method (GIPOT). This approach reduces computational complexity while achieving optimal feature assignments. Experiments conducted on the KITTI dataset and a custom industrial dataset demonstrated significant improvements in pose estimation accuracy and robustness compared to state-of-the-art SLAM algorithms like ORB-SLAM2. Additionally, the system's performance was validated in real-world scenarios, such as a virtual simulation of oil and gas station inspections, where it achieved high consistency with ground truth trajectories.

The authors conclude that the integration of point–line features with advanced attention mechanisms significantly enhances SLAM system reliability in challenging environments. They also highlight the potential for future improvements, such as by incorporating semantic information to handle dynamic objects.

The authors of Contribution 9 propose a novel spatial location representation method for mobile robots inspired by mammalian spatial cognition mechanisms. This approach addresses the challenges of low localization accuracy and large cumulative errors in long-term navigation within unknown environments. The authors introduce a system that integrates boundary, grid, and place cells, modeled after the navigation cells in mammalian brains, to improve environmental perception and localization accuracy.

The method incorporates boundary information by modeling the firing characteristics of boundary cells based on direction- and distance-aware data relative to environmental boundaries. These boundary cell responses are input into a Location-Adaptive Hierarchical Network (LAHN), which generates grid cells and updates their distribution to better align with environmental boundaries. The system also utilizes competitive Hebbian learning to produce place cells, ensuring precise location representation.

The experimental results demonstrate that the proposed method effectively reduces localization errors by correcting cumulative drift through boundary cell activation. The spatial representation maps generated show high accuracy in dynamic and complex environments, highlighting the method's potential for enhancing mobile robot navigation and environmental cognition.

The authors of Contribution 10 address the challenge of dual-user operation in remote robot systems equipped with force feedback, where two users collaboratively control a single robot to perform tasks such as object transportation. Their work focuses on clarifying the mechanisms by which a user with lower network delay can assist another user with higher delay, as well as proposing enhanced robot position control to improve efficiency and reduce the force exerted on objects during operation.

The authors conducted experiments to analyze the effects of network delays on collaborative operations, finding that the average and maximum force applied to objects increases as delays grow. However, they also observed that when the total network delay between the two users remains constant, the applied force remains nearly identical, regardless of individual delay distributions. This highlights the supportive role of the user with the lower delay in mitigating the challenges faced by the user with the higher delay.

To address these issues, they proposed an enhanced robot position control method that adjusts the contribution ratio of each user's input based on their respective network delays. The experimental results demonstrated that this approach effectively reduced the applied force compared to conventional methods, particularly in scenarios with high network delay disparities. The findings emphasize the importance of incorporating adaptive delay-based control strategies to improve operability and accuracy in dual-user remote robot systems, making the proposed method applicable in scenarios such as remote medical surgery and deep-sea exploration.

The authors of Contribution 11 provide a comprehensive review of foot–terrain interaction mechanics for heavy-duty legged robots, which are critical for navigating and performing tasks in complex and harsh environments. The authors focus on analyzing the mechanical behavior of foot–terrain interactions to address challenges such as the instability caused by dynamic interactions with uneven terrains. They examine various foot-supporting structures, including cylindrical, semi-cylindrical, and spherical configurations, and evaluate their impact on the robots' mobility and stability.

The review also discusses the development of mechanical models for foot–terrain interactions, including pressure-sinkage and tangential force models, which are essential for predicting and optimizing robot performance on soft or slippery surfaces. The authors highlight key technologies, such as biomimetic foot designs inspired by natural systems, and the integration of multimodal information fusion to enhance terrain recognition and adaptability.

The study identifies unresolved issues, such as improving foot design for diverse terrains and refining control strategies to reduce sinkage and slipping. The authors conclude by emphasizing the importance of advancing foot–terrain interaction research to enhance the mobility and functionality of heavy-duty legged robots in applications ranging from planetary exploration to industrial operations.

3. Further Directions

Rapid advances in mobile robotics, while groundbreaking, highlight the need for continued exploration in several pivotal areas. As the field progresses, researchers are tasked with addressing unresolved challenges, pushing the boundaries of robotic capabilities, and ensuring seamless integration into complex environments that demand adaptability, intelligence, and safety.

One of the most critical areas for future development is enhanced autonomy and learning. Although our current robotic systems exhibit impressive capabilities, many still depend on predefined models or significant human intervention for decision-making. To address this, research must focus on advanced machine learning techniques, including reinforcement learning and unsupervised approaches, which enable robots to dynamically adapt to novel and unpredictable scenarios. Furthermore, the implementation of lifelong learning paradigms, in which robots continuously refine and expand their knowledge base without the need to retrain from scratch, could significantly improve their ability to operate autonomously over extended periods and in diverse settings.

Another promising direction lies in the evolution of SLAM and perception technologies. Despite notable advancements, robust SLAM solutions for highly dynamic, unstructured, or GPS-denied environments remain a challenge. Future research should explore algorithms that enable more efficient large-scale and real-time mapping, with a focus on reducing computational demands while maintaining accuracy. The integration of multi-modal sensor inputs, such as visual data, LiDAR, and radar, along with state-of-the-art AI-driven perception techniques, has the potential to elevate the robustness and versatility of SLAM systems, paving the way for their use in increasingly demanding applications.

Human–robot collaboration also stands out as a pivotal area for growth. As robots become more prevalent in human-centered environments, the dynamics of interaction between humans and robots require significant refinement. This entails the development of intuitive and accessible interfaces that facilitate seamless communication, such as natural language processing systems and advanced gesture recognition. Equally important is designing robots capable of perceiving and responding to human emotions, behaviors, and intentions, creating interactions that are not only functional, but also empathetic and user-friendly. These advances are essential for mobile robots to effectively support humans in areas such as healthcare, logistics, and education.

Another frontier in mobile robotics involves the integration of AR and VR technologies. These tools offer immense potential for improving interaction, training, and operational capabilities. AR can provide users with enhanced visualization and control over robotic systems, enabling more intuitive and effective management. Simultaneously, VR facilitates the simulation of complex and hazardous environments, allowing for safer testing and the remote operation of robots in situations where direct human involvement is impractical. The synergy between these technologies and robotics presents exciting opportunities for innovation across multiple sectors.

In addition to technical advancements, addressing ethical, social, and regulatory concerns will be a vital component of future research. The deployment of mobile robots in public and private spaces raises questions about safety, privacy, and the societal implications of widespread automation. Developing frameworks that ensure the responsible design, deployment, and management of robotic systems will be critical in fostering public trust and ensuring the long-term success of this technology.

Ultimately, the future of mobile robotics lies in interdisciplinary collaboration. By combining expertise from artificial intelligence, control systems, human–machine interactions, and ethical design, researchers can create mobile robotic systems that are not only intelligent and autonomous but also safe, adaptable, and deeply integrated into human life. These efforts will pave the way for robots to become invaluable partners in addressing some of the most pressing challenges of our time.

Author Contributions: Conceptualization, J.E.S. and L.G.; Methodology, J.E.S. and L.G.; Formal analysis, J.E.S.; Investigation, J.E.S. and L.G.; Writing—original draft, J.E.S.; Writing—review & editing, J.E.S.; Supervision, L.G.; Funding acquisition, L.G. All authors have read and agreed to the published version of the manuscript.

Funding: This work was funded by the Spanish Government (grant PID2020-117421RB-C21 funded by MCIN/AEI/10.13039/501100011033).

Acknowledgments: We extend our heartfelt appreciation to all the researchers who submitted their work to this Special Issue. We commend the authors whose papers were selected for publication, acknowledging their valuable contributions and dedication to advancing knowledge in this field. Our sincere thanks go to the reviewers, whose thoughtful and constructive feedback played a key role in maintaining the high standard of the articles included. We are also deeply grateful to the Editorial Board of *Applied Sciences* for entrusting us with the opportunity to serve as Guest Editors, and to the Editorial Office for their outstanding support and efficient management, which were instrumental in the successful and timely completion of this Special Issue.

Conflicts of Interest: The authors declare no conflicts of interest.

List of Contributions

1. Lu, Z.; He, G.; Wang, R.; Wang, S.; Zhang, Y.; Liu, C.; Chen, D.; Hou, T. An Orthogonal Wheel Odometer for Positioning in a Relative Coordinate System on a Floating Ground. *Appl. Sci.* **2021**, *11*, 11340. https://doi.org/10.3390/app112311340.
2. Palacín, J.; Rubies, E.; Clotet, E. Systematic Odometry Error Evaluation and Correction in a Human-Sized Three-Wheeled Omnidirectional Mobile Robot Using Flower-Shaped Calibration Trajectories. *Appl. Sci.* **2022**, *12*, 2606. https://doi.org/10.3390/app12052606.
3. Solanes, J.E.; Muñoz, A.; Gracia, L.; Tornero, J. Virtual Reality-Based Interface for Advanced Assisted Mobile Robot Teleoperation. *Appl. Sci.* **2022**, *12*, 6071. https://doi.org/10.3390/app12126071.
4. Hercik, R.; Byrtus, R.; Jaros, R.; Koziorek, J. Implementation of Autonomous Mobile Robot in SmartFactory. *Appl. Sci.* **2022**, *12*, 8912. https://doi.org/10.3390/app12178912.
5. Kamalova, A.; Lee, S.G.; Kwon, S.H. Occupancy Reward-Driven Exploration with Deep Reinforcement Learning for Mobile Robot System. *Appl. Sci.* **2022**, *12*, 9249. https://doi.org/10.3390/app12189249.
6. Shakeel, T.; Arshad, J.; Jaffery, M.H.; Rehman, A.U.; Eldin, E.T.; Ghamry, N.A.; Shafiq, M. A Comparative Study of Control Methods for X3D Quadrotor Feedback Trajectory Control. *Appl. Sci.* **2022**, *12*, 9254. https://doi.org/10.3390/app12189254.
7. Guo, G.; Dai, Z.; Dai, Y. Real-Time Stereo Visual Odometry Based on an Improved KLT Method. *Appl. Sci.* **2022**, *12*, 12124. https://doi.org/10.3390/app122312124.
8. Lian, Y.; Sun, H.; Dong, S. Point–Line-Aware Heterogeneous Graph Attention Network for Visual SLAM System. *Appl. Sci.* **2023**, *13*, 3816. https://doi.org/10.3390/app13063816.
9. Jiang, H.; Zhang, Y. A Spatial Location Representation Method Incorporating Boundary Information. *Appl. Sci.* **2023**, *13*, 7929. https://doi.org/10.3390/app13137929.
10. Huang, P.; Ishibashi, Y. Enhancement of Robot Position Control for Dual-User Operation of Remote Robot System with Force Feedback. *Appl. Sci.* **2024**, *14*, 9376. https://doi.org/10.3390/app14209376.
11. Zhuang, H.; Wang, J.; Wang, N.; Li, W.; Li, N.; Li, B.; Dong, L. A Review of Foot–Terrain Interaction Mechanics for Heavy-Duty Legged Robots. *Appl. Sci.* **2024**, *14*, 6541. https://doi.org/10.3390/app14156541.

References

1. Sahoo, S.K.; Choudhury, B.B. Challenges and opportunities for enhanced patient care with mobile robots in healthcare. *J. Mechatron. Artif. Intell. Eng.* **2023**, *4*, 83–103. [CrossRef]
2. Yu, J.; Wu, J.; Xu, J.; Wang, X.; Cui, X.; Wang, B.; Zhao, Z. A Novel Planning and Tracking Approach for Mobile Robotic Arm in Obstacle Environment. *Machines* **2024**, *12*, 19. [CrossRef]
3. Peng, G.; Fan, Z. Recent Advances in Trajectory Planning and Object Recognition for Robot Sensing and Control. *Sensors* **2024**, *24*, 4509. [CrossRef]
4. Bernhard, L.; Schwingenschloegl, P.; Hofmann, J.; Wilhelm, D.; Knoll, A. Boosting the hospital by integrating mobile robotic assistance systems: A comprehensive classification of the risks to be addressed. *Auton. Robot.* **2024**, *48*, 1. [CrossRef]
5. Hou, X.; Guan, Y.; Han, T.; Wang, C. Towards real-time embodied AI agent: A bionic visual encoding framework for mobile robotics. *Int. J. Intell. Robot. Appl.* **2024**, *8*, 1038–1056. [CrossRef]
6. Goncalves, R.S.; Souza, F.C.; Souza, C.C.; Sudbrack, D.E.T.; Trautmann, P.V.; Clasen, B.C.; Homma, R.Z. Semi-autonomous mobile robot coupled to a drone for debris removal from high-voltage power lines. *Robot. Auton. Syst.* **2024**, *177*, 104697. [CrossRef]

7. Lin, X.; Gao, F.; Bian, W. A high-effective swarm intelligence-based multi-robot cooperation method for target searching in unknown hazardous environments. *Expert Syst. Appl.* **2025**, *262*, 125609. [CrossRef]
8. Hua, Y.; Wang, X.; Wang, Y.; Chen, S.; Lin, Z. A novel trajectory planning method for mobile robotic grinding wind turbine blade. *J. Manuf. Process.* **2024**, *132*, 142–158. [CrossRef]
9. Prasuna, R.G.; Potturu, S.R. Deep reinforcement learning in mobile robotics—A concise review. *Multimed. Tools Appl.* **2024**, *83*, 70815–70836. [CrossRef]
10. Licardo, J.T.; Domjan, M.; Orehovački, T. Intelligent Robotics—A Systematic Review of Emerging Technologies and Trends. *Electronics* **2024**, *13*, 542. [CrossRef]
11. Zhao, Y.L.; Hong, Y.T.; Huang, H.P. Comprehensive Performance Evaluation between Visual SLAM and LiDAR SLAM for Mobile Robots: Theories and Experiments. *Appl. Sci.* **2024**, *14*, 3945. [CrossRef]
12. Yue, X.; Zhang, Y.; Chen, J.; Chen, J.; Zhou, X.; He, M. LiDAR-based SLAM for robotic mapping: State of the art and new frontiers. *Ind. Robot. Int. J. Robot. Res. Appl.* **2024**, *51*, 196–205. [CrossRef]
13. Zhao, L.; Deng, X.; Li, R.; Gui, X.; Sun, J.; Li, T.; Zhang, B. Graph-Based Robust Localization of Object-Level Map for Mobile Robotic Navigation. *IEEE Trans. Ind. Electron.* **2024**, *71*, 697–707. [CrossRef]
14. Shamshiri, R.R.; Azimi, A.; Behjati, M.; Ghasemzadeh, A.; Dworak, V.; Weltzien, C.; Karydis, K.; Cheein, F.A.A. Online path tracking with an integrated H-robust adaptive controller for a double-Ackermann steering robot for orchard waypoint navigation. *Int. J. Intell. Robot. Appl.* **2024**, 1–21. [CrossRef]
15. Tolenov, S.; Joldasbekov, B.O. Real-Time Self-Localization and Mapping for Autonomous Navigation of Mobile Robots in Unknown Environments. *Int. J. Adv. Comput. Sci. Appl.* **2024**, *15*, 882–893. [CrossRef]
16. Muñoz-Benavent, P.; Gracia, L.; Solanes, J.E.; Esparza, A.; Tornero, J. Sliding mode control for robust and smooth reference tracking in robot visual servoing. *Int. J. Robust Nonlinear Control* **2018**, *28*, 1728–1756. [CrossRef]
17. Xu, J.Z.; Liu, Z.W.; Ge, M.F.; Wang, Y.W.; He, D.X. Self-Triggered MPC for Teleoperation of Networked Mobile Robotic System via High-Order Estimation. *IEEE Trans. Autom. Sci. Eng.* **2024**, 1–13. [CrossRef]
18. Vangasse, A.d.; Freitas, E.J.R.; Raffo, G.V.; Pimenta, L.C.A. Safe Navigation on Path-Following Tasks: A Study of MPC-based Collision Avoidance Schemes in Distributed Robot Systems. *J. Intell. Robot. Syst.* **2024**, *110*, 166. [CrossRef]
19. Zeng, Y.; Zhang, D.; Chien, S.Y.; Tju, H.S.; Wiesse, C.; Cao, F.; Zhou, J.; Li, X.; Chen, I.M. Task Sensing and Adaptive Control for Mobile Manipulator in Indoor Painting Application. *IEEE-ASME Trans. Mechatron.* **2024**, *29*, 2956–2963. [CrossRef]
20. Wu, H.; Wang, S.; Xie, Y.; Li, H.; Zheng, S.; Jiang, L. Adaptive Abrupt Disturbance Rejection Tracking Control for Wheeled Mobile Robots. *IEEE Robot. Autom. Lett.* **2024**, *9*, 7787–7794. [CrossRef]
21. Haider, Z.; Sardar, M.Z.; Azar, A.T.; Ahmed, S.; Kamal, N.A. Exploring reinforcement learning techniques in the realm of mobile robotics. *Int. J. Autom. Control* **2024**, *18*, 655–697. [CrossRef]
22. Gracia, L.; Solanes, J.E.; Muñoz-Benavent, P.; Miro, J.V.; Perez-Vidal, C.; Tornero, J. Human-robot collaboration for surface treatment tasks. *Interact. Stud.* **2019**, *20*, 148–184. [CrossRef]
23. Coronado, E.; Itadera, S.; Ramirez-Alpizar, I.G. Integrating Virtual, Mixed, and Augmented Reality to Human–Robot Interaction Applications Using Game Engines: A Brief Review of Accessible Software Tools and Frameworks. *Appl. Sci.* **2023**, *13*, 1292. [CrossRef]
24. Wang, D.; Zhang, B.; Zhou, J.; Xiong, Y.; Liu, L.; Tan, Q. Three-dimensional mapping and immersive human-robot interfacing utilize Kinect-style depth cameras and virtual reality for agricultural mobile robots. *J. Field Robot.* **2024**, *41*, 2413–2426. [CrossRef]
25. Reardon, C.; Gregory, J.M.; Haring, K.S.; Dossett, B.; Miller, O.; Inyang, A. Augmented Reality Visualization of Autonomous Mobile Robot Change Detection in Uninstrumented Environments. *ACM Trans. Hum.-Robot. Interact.* **2024**, *13*, 1–30. [CrossRef]
26. Koubaa, A.; Ammar, A.; Boulila, W. Next-generation human-robot interaction with ChatGPT and robot operating system. *Softw.-Pract. Exp.* **2024**, 1–28. [CrossRef]
27. Mogahed, H.S.; Ibrahim, M.M. Development of a Motion Controller for the Electric Wheelchair of Quadriplegic Patients Using Head Movements Recognition. *IEEE Embed. Syst. Lett.* **2024**, *16*, 154–157. [CrossRef]
28. Lu, S.R.; Lo, J.H.; Hong, Y.T.; Huang, H.P. Implementation of Engagement Detection for Human-Robot Interaction in Complex Environments. *Sensors* **2024**, *24*, 3311. [CrossRef]
29. García, A.; Solanes, J.E.; Muñoz, A.; Gracia, L.; Tornero, J. Augmented Reality-Based Interface for Bimanual Robot Teleoperation. *Appl. Sci.* **2022**, *12*, 4379. [CrossRef]
30. Costa, G.d.M.; Petry, M.R.; Moreira, A.P. Augmented Reality for Human–Robot Collaboration and Cooperation in Industrial Applications: A Systematic Literature Review. *Sensors* **2022**, *22*, 2725. [CrossRef]
31. Walker, M.; Phung, T.; Chakraborti, T.; Williams, T.; Szafir, D. Virtual, Augmented, and Mixed Reality for Human-robot Interaction: A Survey and Virtual Design Element Taxonomy. *J. Hum.-Robot. Interact.* **2023**, *12*, 1–39. [CrossRef]

Disclaimer/Publisher's Note: The statements, opinions and data contained in all publications are solely those of the individual author(s) and contributor(s) and not of MDPI and/or the editor(s). MDPI and/or the editor(s) disclaim responsibility for any injury to people or property resulting from any ideas, methods, instructions or products referred to in the content.

Article

An Orthogonal Wheel Odometer for Positioning in a Relative Coordinate System on a Floating Ground

Zhiguo Lu [1,†], Guangda He [1,*,†], Ruchao Wang [1], Shixiong Wang [1], Yichen Zhang [2], Chong Liu [1] and Ding Chen [3] and Teng Hou [3]

1. School of Mechanical Engineering and Automation, Northeastern University, Shenyang 110819, China; zglu@me.neu.edu.cn (Z.L.); 2110099@stu.neu.edu.cn (R.W.); neuwsx@126.com (S.W.); congliu@me.neu.edu.cn (C.L.)
2. Research Institute of Mico/Nano Science and Technology, Shanghai Jiao Tong University, Shanghai 200240, China; zhangyic@sjtu.edu.cn
3. System Engineering Research Institute, China State Ship Building Corporation, No. 1 Fengxian East Road, Beijing 100094, China; chending1986@163.com (D.C.); lxuanyun@126.com (T.H.)
* Correspondence: 1970102@stu.neu.edu.cn; Tel.: +86-130-4240-1336
† These authors contributed equally to this work.

Abstract: This paper introduces a planar positioning sensing system based on orthogonal wheels and encoders for some surfaces that may float (such as ship decks). The positioning sensing system can obtain the desired position and angle information on any such ground that floats. In view of the current method of using the IMU gyroscope for positioning, the odometer data on these floating grounds are not consistent with the real-time data in the world coordinate system. The system takes advantage of the characteristic of the orthogonal wheel, using four vertical omnidirectional wheels and encoders to position on the floating ground. We design a new structure and obtain the position and angle information of a mobile robot by solving the encoder installed on four sets of omnidirectional wheels. Each orthogonal wheel is provided with a sliding mechanism. This is a good solution to the problem of irregular motion of the system facing the floating grounds. In the experiment, it is found that under the condition that the parameters of the four omnidirectional wheels are obtained by the encoder, the influence of the angle change of the robot in the world coordinate system caused by the flotation of the ground can be ignored, and the position and pose of the robot on the fluctuating ground can be well obtained. Regardless of straight or curved motion, the error can reach the centimeter level. In the mobile floating platform experiment, the maximum error of irregular movement process is 2.43 (±0.075) cm and the RMSE is 1.51 cm.

Keywords: positioning; orthogonal wheel; mobile robot; encoder; floating ground; relative coordinate system

1. Introduction

Robots have been a hot topic ever since the idea of artificial intelligence was raised. The concept of "robot" was first mentioned in the 1920s by Czech writer Karel Capek in his novel, *Rossum's Universal Robot* [1]. Among them, the mobile robot is a kind of early development in the field of robot research. In the early 1960s, research on mobile robots was carried out abroad [2]. As the birthplace of robots [3], the United States first realized the first generation of industrial robots and put them into production, for example, Google's earliest driverless car [4], Da Vinci's surgical robot [5], and Atlas [6], which represents the most advanced humanoid robot technology in the world.

With the development of robotic research, many robot-related technologies are mature. However, for mobile robots, there are still several aspects worth studying further: First, the mobile robot full-field positioning system. Based on a certain reference position, the mobile robot can obtain the real-time position and attitude of the robot through the data measured by one or more of its own sensors when considering the changes of the environment where the robot is located [7]. The second is the study of path planning. In the known map environment, the mobile robot can dynamically plan a safe and reliable accurate route to reach the feasible target point according to the requirements. Finally, the motion control of mobile robot is studied. On the premise of feasible path planning for the robot, the control robot can reach the target point automatically and safely [8]. All these aspects enable the robot to complete the task. The positioning system of mobile robots is to determine the real-time pose of robots in the environment, which is the basis for the development and application of mobile robots [9]. For mobile robots, posture recognition is the foundation of path planning and motion control. High-precision sensors are needed to detect the pose of mobile robots. Therefore, how to make mobile robot pose detection in a variety of complex environment has become a problem of concern.

At present, there are some mature methods for the study of plane localization: the global navigation satellite system (GNSS) [10,11] and China's BeiDou navigation satellite system (BDS) [12], which play a major role in outdoor positioning; the pseudolite indoor positioning [13,14] and the indoor positioning system using the beacon [15,16] and Bluetooth [17]; in order to achieve seamless indoor and outdoor positioning services, Chinese researchers are developing a BDS/GPS indoor positioning pseudo-satellite system; precise positioning technology using real-time kinematics (RTK) [18]; using natural or artificial landmarks for positioning, such as two-dimensional code positioning [19]; signal guidance and positioning based on the sensor signals of visual camera [20], RFID [21], ultrasonic [22] and LiDAR [23]; positioning systems using Wi-Fi [24,25] such as (OS-ELM) [26]; inertial navigation and positioning (MEMS) [27]; odometer positioning [28]; etc.

When the robot is on a floating ground (such as the deck of a ship), these positioning methods may not be as effective in obtaining its own posture. When the robot is on the deck, as the ship floats along with the water, the deck is in an irregular motion in both horizontal and vertical directions. In this case, the accuracy of the robot's positioning is a challenge. For positioning methods such as GPS, GNSS and BDS, which are mainly used for outdoor positioning, signals are blocked when there are obstacles around [29]. In addition to the positioning method mentioned above, the most commonly used positioning system at present is odometer positioning using gyroscopes and orthogonal wheels; although orthogonal wheels are both adopted, the use of gyroscopes has its own limitations in the face of such floating ground. In the following article, we prove the limitations based on experiments.

To solve this problem, we propose a planar positioning sensing system. Figure 1 shows the physical picture of the positioning system. We design a kind of orthogonal wheel structure, which uses four vertical omnidirectional wheels to position on the floating ground. Each driven wheel is equipped with a magnetically coded sensor. Figure 2a shows the installation of the encoder and omnidirectional wheel. The four omnidirectional wheels placed vertically are provided with a sliding mechanism, as shown in Figure 2b, which can move up and down. The range of up and down movement is 6 cm. Every sliding mechanism supports the amount of ground unevenness at ±3 cm. Springs on both sides always provide downward force to the wheels. When the chassis is mounted above the positioning system, it provides downward load to the positioning system so that the wheels can fully contact the ground. In this way, the influence caused by the ground fluctuation on the angle of the robot in the world coordinate system can be ignored, and the motion parameters of the robot in the relative coordinate system relative to the fluctuating ground can be obtained. Finally, the parameters of the four omnidirectional wheels obtained by the sensor can be solved to obtain the pose.

The organization of this paper is as follows. The first part mainly introduces the structure and calculation method of the planar positioning sensor system. The second part proves the limitations of the gyroscope through experiments and analyzes the experimental data of our design of this positioning system. Finally, the experimental results are analyzed and summarized.

Figure 1. Physical picture of the positioning system.

Figure 2. (**a**) Physical picture of encoder and slave wheel installation. (**b**) Physical drawing of sliding mechanism. The range of up and down movement is 6 cm. Every sliding mechanism supports the amount of ground unevenness at ±3 cm.

2. Materials and Methods

The positioning system is the basic part of an intelligent mobile robot, and it is also one of the key research directions in the field of mobile robots. The orthogonal positioning sensor system introduced in this paper is designed based on the positioning principle of the orthogonal wheel and magnetic encoder. Due to the sudden acceleration of the driving wheel, such as acceleration and emergency stop, the phenomenon of the wheel slipping increases the error of the sensor data. In order to solve the influence of this error, the positioning system designed in this paper adopts the driven way to obtain the position coordinates and rotation angle of the robot relative to the initial pose. The positioning system consists of orthogonal wheels, magnetic encoders and a main frame. Figure 3 shows a three-dimensional diagram of the system.

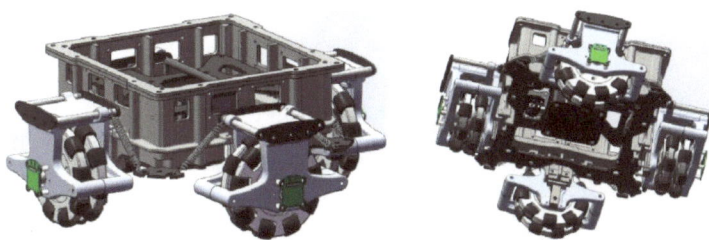

Figure 3. A 3D diagram of positioning sensing system.

An orthogonal wheel adopts two identical omnidirectional wheels fixed on the same mechanism. A single orthogonal omnidirectional wheel is shown in Figure 4. Each wheel stand has two degrees of freedom: one is the movement of the axis of the wheel vertically, and the other is the rotation of the axis around the wheel.

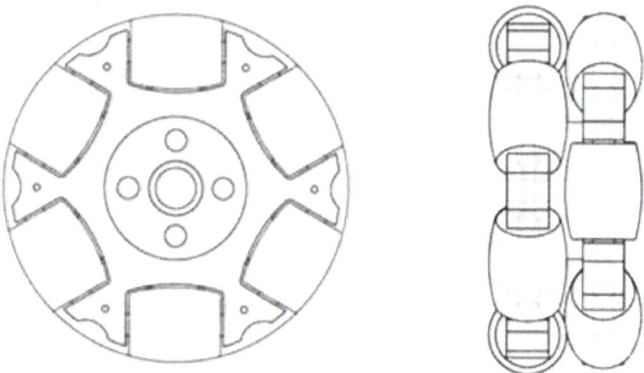

Figure 4. Main view and left view of a single orthogonal omnidirectional wheel.

The orthogonal wheels assembly includes a bracket and four omnidirectional wheels. The four orthogonal wheels are fixed on the bracket, and the axes of the four orthogonal wheels are perpendicular to each other. Four orthogonal wheels fixed on the bracket can rotate at the same time to achieve any direction of movement. Each driven wheel group includes a sliding mechanism in addition to a bracket and an orthogonal wheel. By designing the sliding mechanism on the bracket of each orthogonal wheel, it is connected with the driven wheel bracket and the whole frame so that the driven wheel group can keep rolling in contact with the ground when sliding in the vertical direction perpendicular to the orthogonal driven wheel shaft. The sliding mechanism consists of a slider, a slide track and a spring. On the floating plane, four orthogonal wheels interact with each other through vertical sliders and slide up and down according to the conditions of the road so that the wheels can always contact the ground, reducing the possibility of wheel slipping and improving the positioning accuracy of the positioning device. Figure 5 shows the tolerance of the positioning system for floating ground.

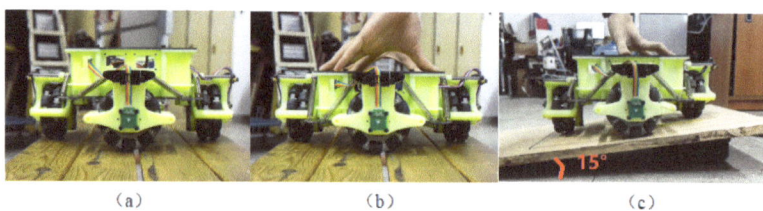

Figure 5. (a,b) The status of the sliding mechanism of the positioning system before and after complete pressure, respectively, which can withstand a movement of approximately 6 cm up and down. (c) The positioning system can still maintain contact with the ground under the plane simulating the inclined ground. From the positioning system structure, the maximum allowable slope is approximately 15°.

2.1. The Motion Model of a Single Orthogonal Wheel

Counting in the X and Y directions of the orthogonal wheel depends on a magnetic encoder to complete. The dividing value of magnetic encoder is 16,384, that is, one turn corresponds to 16,384. The radius of the orthogonal wheel is 25.4 mm. The displacement of the robot in the X and Y directions can be obtained by integrating the short distance. To determine the real-time accurate pose of the robot in the constructed map, the scheme adopts the relative positioning method. The positioning sensor system is installed on the bottom of the car, and the orthogonal wheels sense the prior position of the robot. For the algorithm of orthogonal wheel odometer, Figure 6 shows the odometer motion model in the X and Y directions of a single orthogonal wheel.

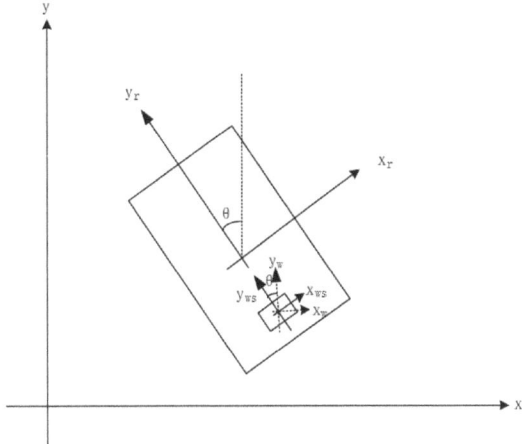

Figure 6. The motion model of single omnidirectional wheel in world coordinate system and self coordinate system.

The displacement of the car in the world coordinates and the speed v_{xws} and v_{yws} of the car's own coordinate system are calculated with the counting of the orthogonal code plate. The coordinate axis X_{ws}-O-Y_{ws} shown in the diagram is the coordinate system of the orthogonal wheel group and records the velocity and displacement of the orthogonal wheel group. The angle between the two frames is θ. The distance from the center of the trolley to the installation of the orthogonal wheels is l, and the velocity v_{xw} and v_{yw} of the orthogonal wheel set in the X-O-Y coordinate system is:

$$v_{xw} = v_{xws}\cos(\theta) - v_{yws}\sin(\theta) \tag{1}$$

$$v_{yw} = v_{yws}\cos(\theta) - v_{xws}\sin(\theta) \tag{2}$$

The displacement s_{xw} and s_{yw} of the orthogonal wheels in the X-O-Y coordinate system can be calculated by (1) and (2):

$$s_{xw} = \int v_{xw} dt \tag{3}$$

$$s_{yw} = \int v_{yw} dt \tag{4}$$

Through (3) and (4), the displacement s_{xr} and s_{yr} of the trolley in the X-O-Y coordinate system can be calculated:

$$s_{xr} = s_{xw} + l\cos(\theta) \tag{5}$$

$$s_{yr} = s_{yw} + l\sin(\theta) \tag{6}$$

By differentiating both sides of (5) and (6), the velocity v_{xr} and v_{yr} of the car in the X-O-Y coordinate system can be calculated, where ω is the angular velocity of the car:

$$v_{xr} = v_{xw} - \omega l\sin(\theta) \tag{7}$$

$$v_{yr} = v_{yw} + \omega l \cos(\theta) \tag{8}$$

Through (7) and (8), the velocity v_{xrs} and v_{yrs} of the car in the coordinate system of the car itself can be obtained:

$$v_{xrs} = v_{xr} \cos(\theta) + v_{yr} \sin(\theta) \tag{9}$$

$$v_{yrs} = v_{yr} \cos(\theta) - v_{xr} \sin(\theta) \tag{10}$$

From the above, the data received through the magnetic encoders on the orthogonal wheels can be converted into the position and velocity information in the world coordinate system. In other words, the velocity and the displacement of the moving chassis in the X-O-Y coordinate system are obtained.

In a simpler sense, the use of two vertically positioned omni-wheels and encoders results in accurate coordinate information relative to the world's coordinate system, rather than four. In this case, the angle information of the robot can be obtained by using a gyroscope. However, the disadvantages of such positioning systems can be shown when gyroscopes are exposed to floating ground. In subsequent chapters, we prove the defect through experiment.

2.2. The Motion Model of Four Orthogonal Wheels

Based on a single wheel, the positioning system we designed uses four orthogonal wheels to solve and obtain accurate coordinate information and angle information. Figure 7 shows the odometer motion model in the X and Y directions of four orthogonal wheels.

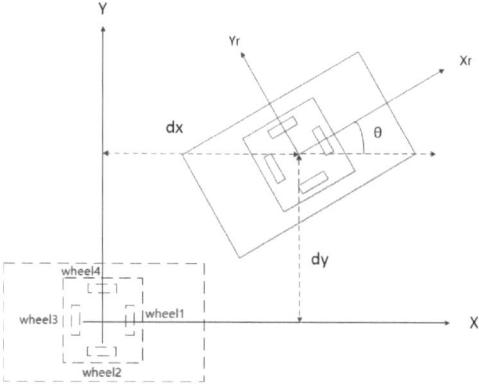

Figure 7. The motion model of four omnidirectional wheels in world and its own coordinates. The horizontal plane body coordinate system XOY: the center of the body is the center point O, OX direction is the direction of the moving robot, OY direction is the vertical direction of the moving robot. The initial position coordinates of the mobile robot (x, y) are the origin of the world coordinate system.

Through the linear velocity acquisition module–magnetic encoder, we can obtain the rotation angle θ_1, θ_2, θ_3 and θ_4 of each omnidirection from the driving wheel. Given that the radius of each omnidirectional driven wheel is R, the distance l_1, l_2, l_3, l_4 of the omnidirectional driven wheel can be calculated. The wheel in the front direction is 1, and clockwise is 2, 3, and 4, as shown in Figure 7:

The wheel axes of the adjacent omnidirectional driven wheels are perpendicular to each other. Through (11), the rotation angle θ of the mobile robot relative to itself can be calculated:

$$l_n = \theta_n R (n = 1, 2, 3, 4) \tag{11}$$

$$\theta = \frac{l_1 + l_2 - l_3 - l_4}{4L} \tag{12}$$

By differentiating Equations (11) and (12), we can obtain the distance d_{l_1}, d_{l_2}, d_{l_3} and d_{l_4} of the omnidirectional rotation from the driving wheel under each instantaneous moment. Then, the displacement dX and dY of the mobile robot in the direction of OX and OY relative to the coordinate system XOY with itself as the origin is obtained at every instantaneous moment:

$$dX = \frac{d_{l_2} - d_{l_4}}{2} \cos(\theta) - \frac{d_{l_1} - d_{l_3}}{2} \sin(\theta) \tag{13}$$

$$dY = \frac{d_{l_1} - d_{l_3}}{2} \cos(\theta) - \frac{d_{l_2} - d_{l_4}}{2} \sin(\theta) \tag{14}$$

By integrating the displacement dX and dY in the direction of OX and OY at every instantaneous moment, the displacement ΔX and ΔY in the direction of OX and OY relative to the origin position of the mobile robot can be obtained:

$$\Delta X = \int dX dt \tag{15}$$

$$\Delta Y = \int dY dt \tag{16}$$

Thus, the data received by the magnetic encoders on the orthogonal wheels can be converted into position and velocity information in the world coordinate system. That is, the displacement of ΔX and ΔY relative to the origin position of the mobile robot and the rotation angle relative to itself are obtained.

In the next chapter, the positioning module using an orthogonal wheel and gyroscope is compared with the positioning sensor system we designed to illustrate the disadvantages of using a gyroscope in some specific situations and the advantages of the positioning sensor system introduced in this paper. The positioning sensor system mainly collects and processes the encoder data on the orthogonal wheels to calculate the real-time position and pose state of the positioning system. Through the acquisition of encoder data, the data are transferred to the central processing unit, and then the central processing unit calculates the pose state of the mobile robot and transmits it to the upper computer through the serial port.

3. Experiments

Figure 8 shows the system flow chart of the positioning system we designed. The positioning system using gyroscope mainly collects and processes the data of gyroscope and encoder, and then transfers it to the central processing unit for processing and uploading to the upper computer. Figure 9 shows a system flow chart for a positioning system using a gyroscope.

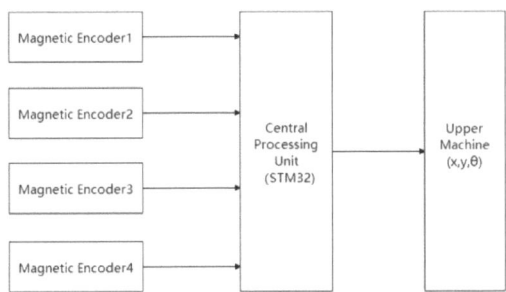

Figure 8. The magnetic encoders on the four omnidirectional wheels transmit the data to the CPU respectively. After data processing by the central processor, the position information is transmitted to the upper computer through serial port.

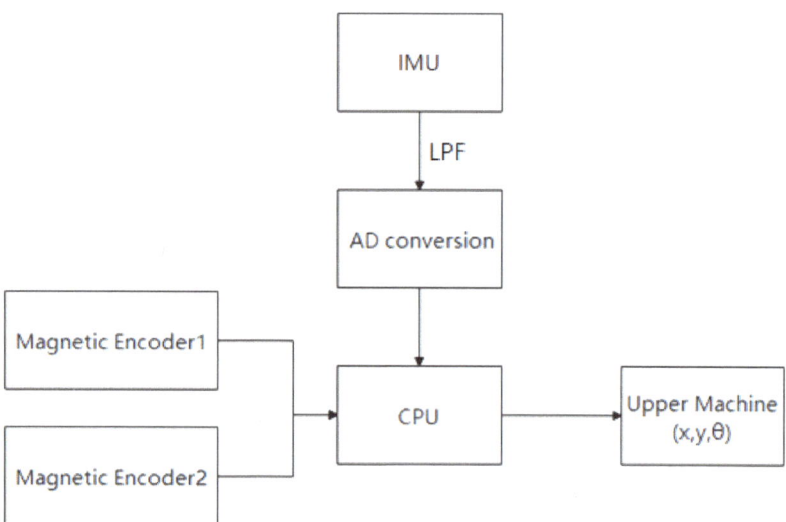

Figure 9. Data from the encoders on the two orthogonal wheels and a gyroscope converted by AD are transmitted to the CPU respectively. After data processing by the CPU, the position information is transmitted to the upper computer through serial port.

3.1. The Experiment Equipment

This section discusses the positioning device developed on the mobile robot chassis platform. Figure 10 shows the chassis platform of the mobile robot in this experiment. The data collected by the chassis platform are used to analyze the positioning effect. The experiment involves linear motion, curved motion, and rotation around the center of the robot. The positioning system transmits the output position information to the upper computer and draws the time displacement curve of the mobile robot.

Figure 10. (**a**) The mobile chassis platform used in this experiment. (**b**) The self-developed positioning system is mounted under the mobile chassis.

Figure 11 shows the chassis coordinate diagram of mobile robot.

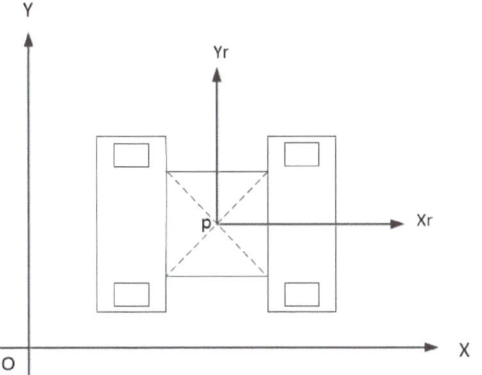

Figure 11. The chassis coordinate diagram of mobile robot. In the figure, P is the origin of the vehicle's own coordinate system, and O is the origin of the world coordinate system.

3.2. The Experiment of Linear Motion

In order to simulate the floating ground, we built a floating platform with a size of 5.4 m × 1.3 m, as shown in Figure 12. During the movement of the moving chassis, the platform is disturbed by the irregular up and down movement, artificially. The platform floats mainly by artificial up and down motion. The floating platform can have six degrees of freedom because it has multiple universal wheels under it. The wheels under the platform are locked, and the platform is only artificially pitched and rolled. In addition, the floating degree of platform can be obtained by installing IMU on the moving chassis. Through IMU and the position system, the six degrees of freedom of moving chassis can be obtained, so the floating degree of the simulated platform can be reflected by the angle of chassis coiling around the pitch and roll axis. For pitch and roll angles, we mainly limit them to 15°.

Figure 12. Simulation floating experimental platform, size of 5.4 m × 1.3 m.

3.2.1. The Chassis Moves in the X Direction

In the initial case, the front of the chassis is oriented in the positive direction of the X axis. The chassis moves in the X direction from point P to point P_1 with a motion distance of 5 m. Figure 13 shows the movement track of the moving chassis. During the movement, the floating platform is artificially disturbed by moving up and down. The actual motion scene in the X direction is shown in the Figure 14.

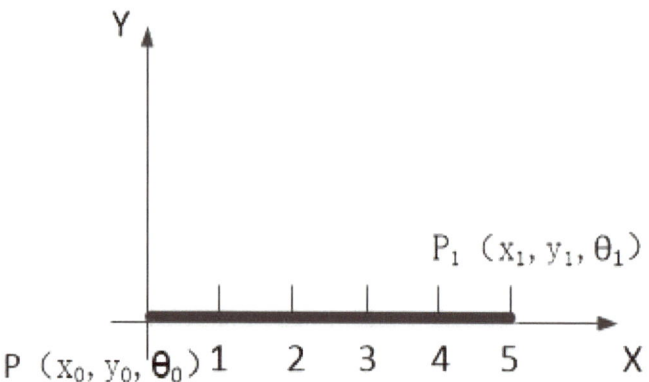

Figure 13. The motion of the chassis in the X direction. The motion distance is 5 m.

The travel displacement transformation curve of the mobile robot chassis is shown in Figure 15. In the process of motion, due to the linear motion along the X axis, the displacement of the Y axis and the angle of the Z axis basically do not fluctuate. The floating degree of the simulated platform can be reflected by the angle of chassis coiling around pitch and roll axis, as shown in Figure 16.

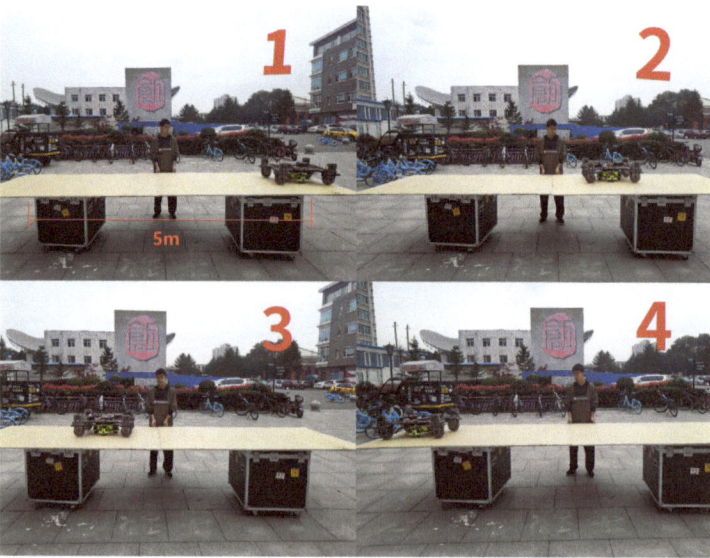

Figure 14. The actual motion scene in the X direction. In the figure, 1, 2, 3 and 4 are the four stages of the movement process respectively.

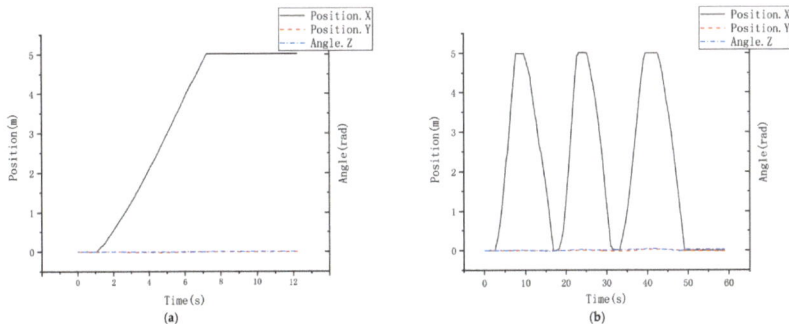

Figure 15. (**a**) The change curve of displacement when the mobile robot travels once along the X direction. (**b**) The displacement curve of the mobile robot when it repeats three times along the Y axis.

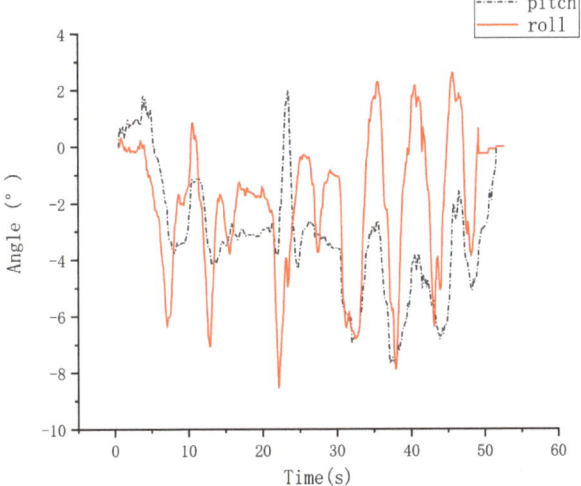

Figure 16. The angle of chassis coiling around pitch and roll axis.

Table 1 records the actual movement value and error of the positioning system for each movement of 5 m along the X axis. It can be seen from Table 1 the positioning value after each movement of 5 m. In addition, the cumulative error of the positioning system is approximately 1.1 cm after it moves a distance of 5 m continuously for four times in the X direction. The experiment shows that the positioning system can meet the requirements in the short distance.

Table 1. The actual movement value and error of the positioning system for each movement of 5 m along the X axis.

The Theoretical Movement Value (cm)	The Actual Movement Value (cm)	Error (cm)
500	500.5	0.5
500	500.3	0.3
500	500.8	0.8
500	501.1	1.1

3.2.2. The Chassis Moves in the Y Direction

The moving chassis uses the Mecanum wheel, which provides freedom of movement in the Y direction. Therefore, this chassis can be used to detect the positioning error of our self-developed positioning system in the Y direction. The actual motion scene in the X direction is shown in the Figure 17.

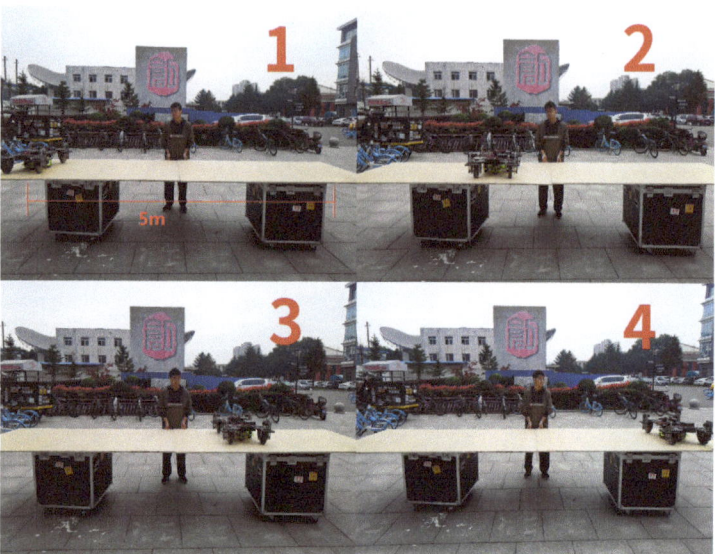

Figure 17. The actual motion scene in the Y direction. The motion distance is 5 m. In the figure, 1, 2, 3 and 4 are the four stages of the movement process respectively.

The travel displacement transformation curve of the mobile robot chassis is shown in Figure 18. In the process of motion, due to the linear motion along the Y axis, the displacement of the X axis and the angle of the Z axis basically do not fluctuate. Figure 19 shows that the angle of chassis coiling around pitch and roll axis.

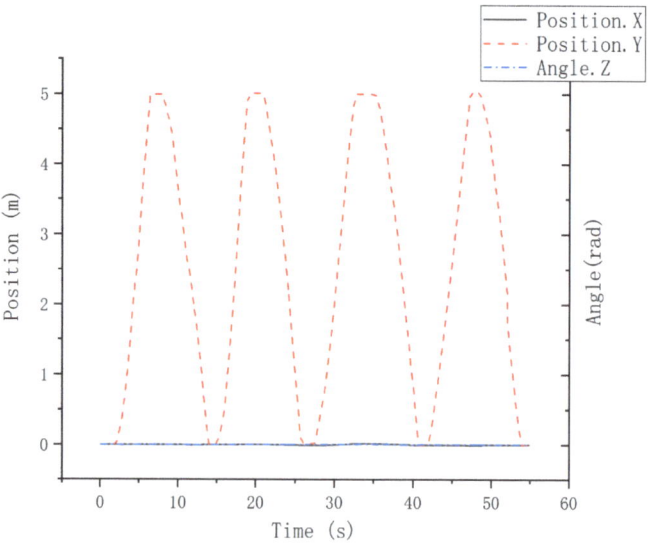

Figure 18. The displacement curve of the mobile robot when it repeats four times along the Y axis.

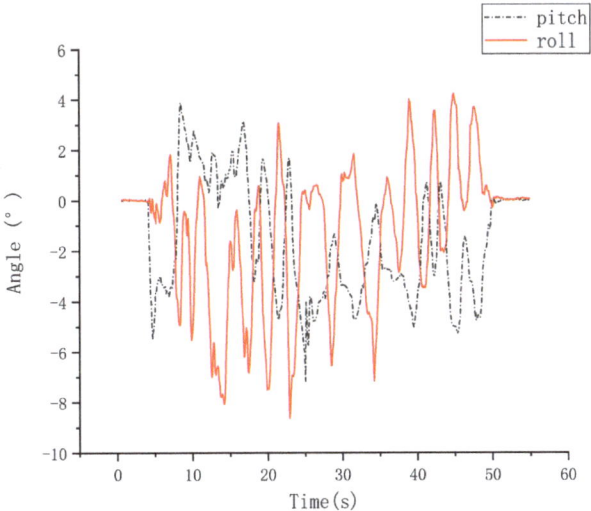

Figure 19. The angle of chassis coiling around pitch and roll axis.

Table 2 records the actual movement value and error of the positioning system for each movement of 5 m along the Y axis. It can be seen from Table 2 the positioning value after each movement of 5 m. In addition, the cumulative error of the positioning system is approximately 1.0 cm after it moves a distance of 5 m continuously for four times in the Y direction. The experiment shows that the positioning system can meet the requirements in the short distance.

Table 2. The actual movement value and error of the positioning system for each movement of 5 m along the Y axis.

The Theoretical Movement Value (cm)	The Actual Movement Value (cm)	Error (cm)
500	500.1	0.1
500	500.3	0.3
500	500.7	0.7
500	501.0	1.0

3.2.3. The Experiment of Rotational Motion

In order to verify the accuracy of the angle of the orthogonal wheel positioning system, the chassis of the mobile robot rotates around the center of the body and stops once every 180° for two consecutive turns. The actual motion scene of the chassis rotation is shown in the Figure 20. Figure 21 shows the angle curve of the moving chassis as it rotates in situ. During the rotation of the moving chassis, the displacement along the X and Y directions appears very small fluctuations because the center of the chassis and the center of the orthogonal wheels do not coincide completely. Figure 22 shows that the angle of chassis coiling around pitch and roll axis.

Table 3 shows the actual angle value and error of the positioning system for each rotation of 180° around the Z axis. Table 3 shows the positioning values after each rotation of 180°. In addition, the cumulative error of the positioning system is approximately 1.15° after continuous rotation of 720° around the Z axis. The experiment shows that the precision of rotation angle of the positioning system is satisfactory.

Figure 20. The actual motion scene of the chassis rotation. In the figure, 1, 2, 3 and 4 are the four stages of the movement process respectively.

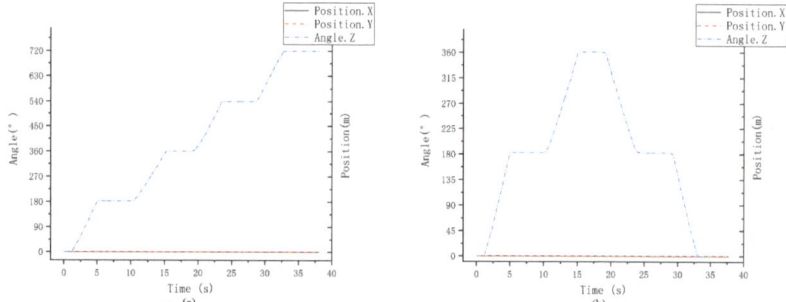

Figure 21. (**a**) The angle change curve of the mobile robot when it rotates continuously for two turns along the Z axis. (**b**) The angle change curve when the mobile robot rotates one circle counterclockwise and one circle clockwise along the Z axis.

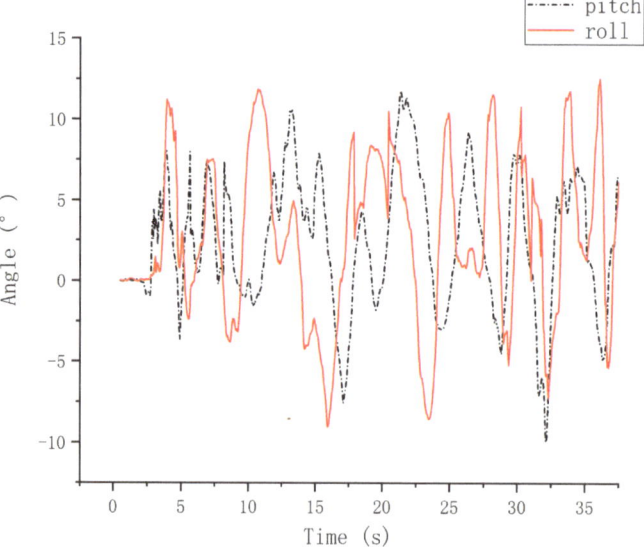

Figure 22. The angle of chassis coiling around pitch and roll axis.

Table 3. The actual movement value and error of the positioning system for each movement of 180° along the Z axis.

The Theoretical Angle Value (°)	The Actual Angle Value (°)	Error (°)
180.00	180.12	0.12
360.00	360.42	0.42
540.00	540.62	0.62
720.00	721.15	1.15

3.2.4. The Experiment of Moving along a Square

The mobile robot chassis moves in a square counterclockwise direction along the simulated floating platform as shown in Figure 23.

Figure 23. Simulation floating experimental platform, size of 2.4 m × 2.4 m.

Due to the size limitation of the floating platform, we choose the side length of the square to be 1.8 m. Figure 24 shows the movement track of the mobile chassis. The positioning effect of the positioning module is verified by the movement of the chassis along the square. The four points of the square are set to P_0, P_1, P_2, and P_3. The actual motion scene is shown in Figure 25.

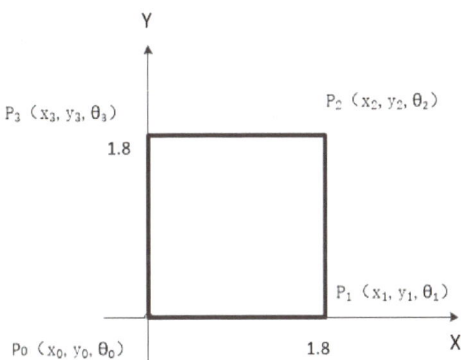

Figure 24. The movement track of the mobile chassis. The length of the square side is 1.8 m. The four points of the square are set to P_0, P_1, P_2, and P_3. In the horizontal plane coordinate system XOY, the center of the chassis is center point O, OX direction is the initial motion direction of the mobile chassis, and OY direction is the vertical direction of moving robot. The initial position coordinates of the mobile robot (x, y) are the origin of the world coordinate system.

Figure 25. The actual motion scene. In the figure, 1, 2, 3 and 4 are the four stages of the movement process respectively.

The displacement transformation curve and angle change curve of the mobile robot chassis are shown in Figure 26. In the process of movement, the actual motion curve is basically consistent with the theoretical motion curve, with only a little fluctuation. The floating degree of the simulated platform can be reflected by the angle of chassis coiling around pitch and roll axis, as shown in the Figure 27.

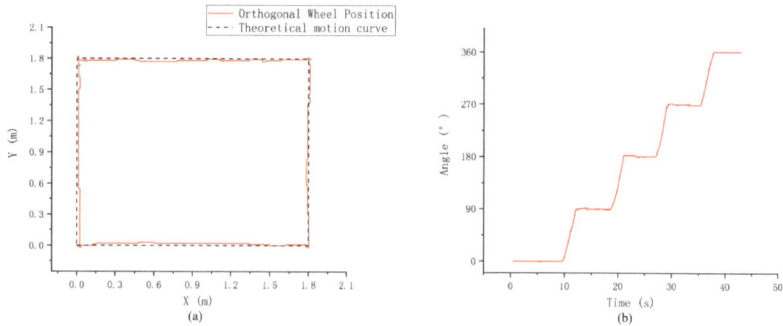

Figure 26. (**a**) Comparison diagram of actual motion curve and theoretical motion curve. The actual motion curve is basically consistent with the preset motion path. (**b**) The angle change curve of the mobile robot when it moves in a counterclockwise direction along a square.

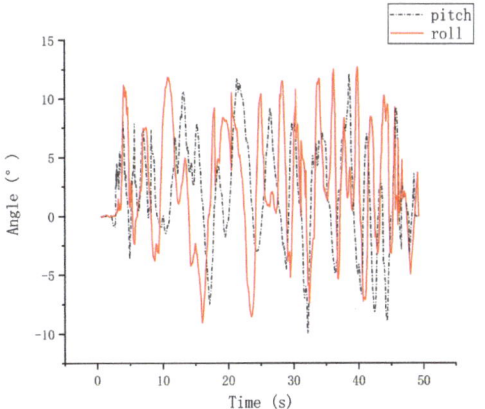

Figure 27. The angle of chassis coiling around pitch and roll axis.

Table 4 records the actual movement value and error of the positioning system for each point along the square. It can be seen from Table 4 the positioning value after moving to each point along the square. In addition, after the positioning system returns to the origin after four points, the distance cumulative error is approximately 1.6 cm, and the angle cumulative error is approximately 1.42°. The experiment shows that the positioning system can meet the requirements in the short distance.

Table 4. The actual movement value and error of the positioning system for each point along the square.

	Theoretical Movement Value			Actual Movement Value			Error	
	x(m)	y(m)	$\theta(°)$	x(m)	y(m)	$\theta(°)$	$\Delta d(m)$	$\Delta\theta(°)$
P_0	0	0	0	0	0	0	0	0
P_1	1.80	0	90	1.802	−0.008	90.02	0.008	0.02
P_2	1.80	1.80	180	1.808	1.795	181.45	0.009	0.45
P_3	0	1.80	270	0.011	1.805	270.87	0.012	0.87
P'_0	0	0	360	0.013	−0.010	361.42	0.016	1.42

3.3. The Experiment of Random Curve Motion

Before we talk about the experiment, let us first introduce the Steam VR tracking system based on HTC VIVE used in the experiment [30]. This system has long been used in VR motion-sensing games. It is equipped with STEAM tracking technology that allows accurate positioning within a space area of 6 m × 6 m, with an accuracy of less than 1 mm. It includes two HTC VIVE2.0 location base stations and a tracker. By installing the tracking device used in the joystick in the motion sensing game on the chassis of the mobile robot, we can obtain the most accurate actual curve in the random curve movement so as to carry out comparative experiments with the orthogonal wheels positioning system and gyro positioning system designed by us.

First, we introduce the experimental site of random curve motion experiment. Figure 28 shows the site layout of the laboratory. The HTC VIVE2.0 base stations are placed on both sides. The base station is placed on the same axis with a height of one meter. The tracker as shown in Figure 29 is mounted on the mobile chassis, which is fixed in the center of the mobile chassis, that is, the center of the orthogonal wheels system. The mobile robot is randomly moved, S-shaped, by the remote control.

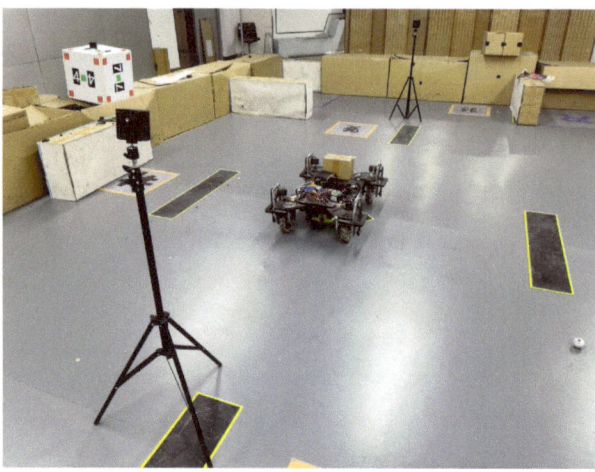

Figure 28. The site layout of the laboratory. HTC VIVE2.0 base stations are placed on both sides of the site, and the base stations are placed on the same axis with a height of one meter.

Figure 29. The tracker is fixed in the center of the moving chassis, which is the center of the orthogonal wheels system.

In this experiment, we conducted a comparative experiment on our own positioning system, the gyroscope positioning system and the HTC VIVE positioning system. In the experiment, the gyroscope positioning system can obtain the rotation angle in the movement process by itself, and at the same time, the data of two mutually perpendicular wheels of the four wheels in the orthogonal wheel system serve as the data of X and Y. According to the solution method mentioned in Section 2.1, coordinate information of gyroscope positioning can be obtained. In the process of random S-shaped motion, the upper computer can obtain the data of orthogonal wheel positioning and gyroscope positioning at the same time for comparison test. In combination with the data obtained by HTC VIVE, three experimental curves can be obtained at the same time in one movement for comparison. Figure 30 shows the gyroscope position curve, orthogonal wheels position curve, HTC VIVE position curve and the error curve of orthogonal wheels relative to HTC VIVE, respectively.

As can be seen from the comparison curve, the positioning curve of the orthogonal wheels positioning system is basically consistent with that of HTC VIVE in the random S-shaped motion, and the maximum error is 1.18 (±0.075) cm in the process of moving. As for the positioning curve of the positioning system using a gyroscope, the deviation degree of the curve is increasing with the progress of the motion, due to the accumulated error of gyroscope rotation during the traveling process. This is due to the orthogonal wheel positioning system, which does not have the same sudden or continuous rotation as a gyroscope, resulting in a large deviation in the angle acquisition.

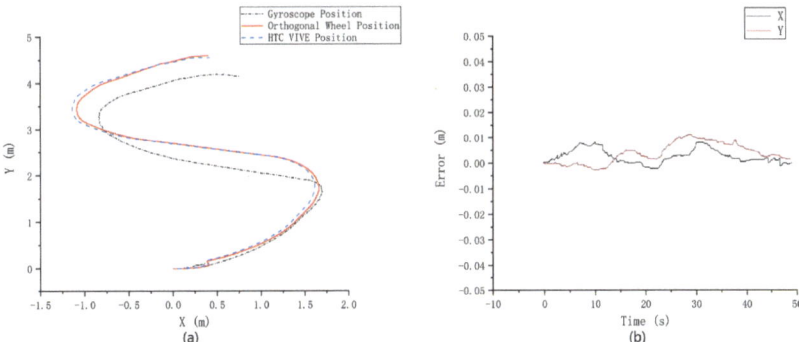

Figure 30. (**a**) Comparison diagram of the gyroscope position curve, orthogonal wheels position curve and HTC VIVE position curve. (**b**) The error curve of orthogonal wheel relative to HTC VIVE.

3.4. Simulated Floating Deck Experiment

The orthogonal wheels positioning system is designed at the beginning to deal with the common positioning methods, such as a gyroscope on the ship deck and other floating carriers, which do not have a good positioning effect. The environment of the above experiments is a fixed world coordinate system. In the world coordinate system, through the above experiments, we can verify the positioning accuracy and robustness of the orthogonal wheel positioning system in the absolute coordinate system. Next, the relative coordinate system experiment is carried out on the simulated floating deck experimental platform. Because the experimental scenes, such as the hull deck, are not convenient to obtain, the platform as shown in Figure 31 is adopted as the floating platform for this experiment. The floating hull is simulated by people lifting the plank and walking around at random. The floating platform is fitted with universal wheels to simulate the movement of the deck at sea.

On the floating test platform, the desired motion curve should be the actual curve of the positioning system relative to the floating test platform, not the actual curve in the world coordinate system. The tracker reflects the x, y, z coordinates and yaw, pitch, roll angles of the current moment relative to the world coordinate system. So we put a tracker on the moving chassis and a tracker on the corner of the platform. Through the tracker on the chassis, we can obtain the coordinates (x, y) of the chassis in the world coordinate system at every moment. Through the tracker fixed in the corner of the platform, we can obtain the coordinates (x_T, y_T) of the origin of the floating platform coordinate system in the world coordinate system and the rotation angle θ of the floating platform coordinate system in the world coordinate system at every moment. The position of a point (x, y) in world coordinates in relative coordinates (x', y') is:

$$\begin{bmatrix} x' \\ y' \end{bmatrix} = \begin{bmatrix} \cos\theta & \sin\theta \\ -\sin\theta & \cos\theta \end{bmatrix} \begin{bmatrix} x \\ y \end{bmatrix} + \begin{bmatrix} x_T \\ y_T \end{bmatrix}$$

The actual curve of the moving chassis relative to the floating platform can be obtained by the above method. Then the positioning curve is compared with that of the orthogonal wheel positioning system developed by ourselves. Figure 32 shows the actual process of this floating platform experiment. Two students control the floating platform to move irregularly, during which they shake the floating platform up and down to produce a floating effect. Another student remotely controls the chassis, moving around the floating platform in an irregular circle.

Figure 31. Simulated floating deck experimental platform. The size of the experimental platform is 2.4 m × 2.4 m. Place a tracker in the center of the chassis and in the corner of the platform.

Figure 33a shows the motion track of the orthogonal wheel positioning system and HTC VIVE positioning system on the mobile floating platform. Figure 33b reflects the trajectory of the gyroscope positioning in this case.

As can be seen from the figure, the positioning curve of the orthogonal wheel positioning system tends to be consistent with the real curve of HTC VIVE. In the process of floating motion, the angle read by the gyroscope is not that of the orthogonal wheels relative to the floating platform, but that of the world coordinate system. As a result, the curve of the gyroscope positioning is unpredictable and inconsistent with the actual motion curve.

Figure 34 shows that the floating degree of the mobile floating platform and the error curve of the orthogonal wheel positioning system relative to HTC VIVE in the process of movement. On the mobile floating platform used in this experiment, the maximum error is 2.43 (±0.075) cm. According to the experimental data, the RMSE of the positioning system on the floating platform is 1.51 cm.

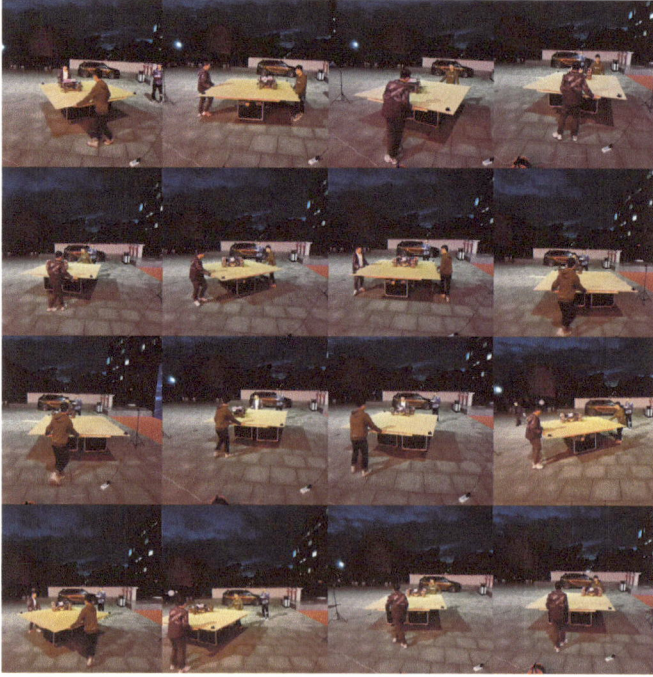

Figure 32. The actual process of this floating platform experiment.

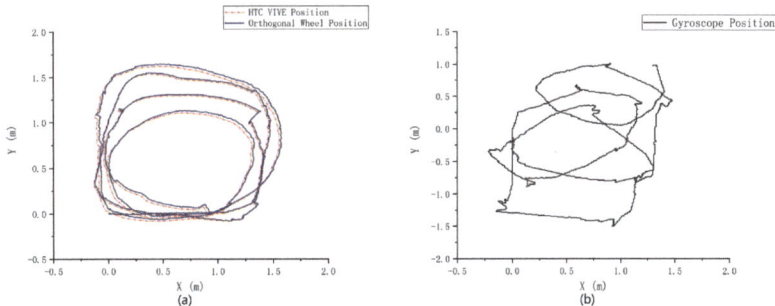

Figure 33. (**a**) The motion curve of the orthogonal wheels in irregular motion with the mobile floating platform. Compared with the actual curve, the orthogonal wheel positioning system has a good positioning effect relative to the moving path of the mobile floating platform. (**b**) Motion curve of gyroscope positioning along with irregular movement of the floating experimental platform. With the accumulation of angle errors in the process of motion, the obtained motion curve becomes more and more yaw.

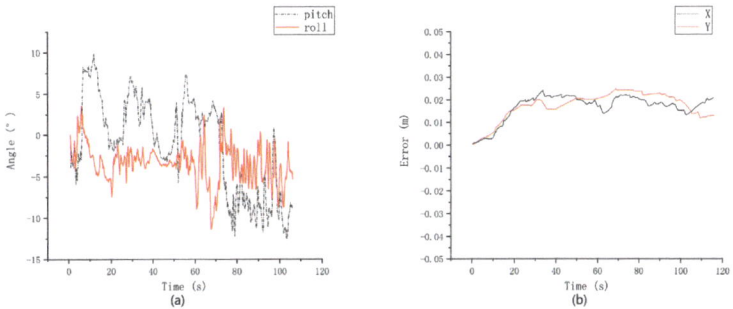

Figure 34. (**a**) The angle of chassis coiling around pitch and roll axis. (**b**) The error curve of orthogonal wheel relative to HTC VIVE.

4. Discussion

As far as we know, previous studies have not focused much on floating surfaces, such as decks. For the wheeled positioning of robots, a gyroscope is the current, preferred method used for the angle measurement in terms of economy and practicality. The usual odometer system does have the biggest problems with turns and orientation changes. However, our positioning system is a mechanical structure design, and the calculation of the position when turning is mainly dependent on the radius of rotation of the structure. This is a fixed value, and as long as the radius of rotation is accurate, the error tends to zero. There is no sensor like the gyroscope: the more turns, the greater the angle deviation. Different from other commonly used odometers, the error of self-developed orthogonal wheel odometers fundamentally depends on whether the rotation radius and our orthogonal wheel radius are accurate, as well as the accuracy of the encoder to read the orthogonal wheel mileage.

Compared with the orthogonal wheel positioning system developed by ourselves, both LiDAR and gyroscopes have their drawbacks. The use of gyroscope is usually limited to the fixed plane based on the world coordinate system. With the increase in the gyroscope angle, the error also increases. In order to ignore the angle cumulative error of the gyroscope, the influence on the positioning error is minimal only in the case of a small number of turns. Laser positioning of LiDAR [23] is similar to the positioning mode of HTC VIVE used in the experiment. Although it has very high positioning accuracy, it has high requirements for the environment. In the process of LiDAR positioning, it is necessary to scan the surrounding environment and then match the boundary on the map to achieve the positioning effect. However, on a wide deck, it is hard to scan the boundaries we want, and it is even harder to locate them when there are dynamic obstacles. So LiDAR has its drawbacks, especially in the case of wide decks with unclear boundaries or sea fog. This new positioning technology needs to have accurate positioning accuracy and adaptability to floating environment. In view of the floating motion environment and the desired positioning task, the orthogonal wheels positioning sensor system designed by us can achieve a satisfactory positioning effect in this kind of environment.

According to the experiment in the third chapter, we can understand that the positioning effect of the orthogonal wheels positioning system can achieve a very high positioning accuracy during the movement of a certain distance, and the positioning error can reach within 0.025 m. It can be seen from the random comparison curve that the positioning curve of the orthogonal wheel positioning system is basically consistent with that of HTC VIVE, and the maximum error is 2.43 (±0.075) cm in the process of moving. The RMSE of the positioning system on the floating platform is 1.51 cm. However, the positioning curve of the positioning system using gyroscope deviates more and more with the progress of the movement. This is because the orthogonal wheels are driven by design, and the positioning mode of the orthogonal wheel positioning system is not affected by the error caused by rotation like the gyroscope. Additionally, the orthogonal wheel structure is equipped with a sliding structure so that the positioning system can easily ignore the irregular movement of the system caused by the floating ground. The experimental results show that the errors of the orthogonal wheel positioning system are within the acceptable range (±3 cm) under the conditions of linear motion, curvilinear motion and floating environment, and the expected effect of the centimeter-level positioning system is achieved. The experimental results highlight the potential application of the positioning system in a complex environment. In the case of subsequent use of other positioning calibrations, the accuracy may be even higher.

5. Conclusions and Future Work

This paper introduces a plane positioning sensor system based on orthogonal wheels and encoders. By using the characteristics of the orthogonal wheels of the system, we designed a new structure. The position and angle information of the mobile robot is obtained by solving the encoder installed on four sets of omnidirectional wheels. The system is designed to be an independent, economical, and easy-to-use customized solution for a ground that may be floating. It can obtain the desired position information that we want on any surface where floating occurs (such as ship decks, jolting cars or trains). In view of the current use of the IMU gyroscope positioning method, we use the experiment to prove its limitations. Due to the vertical sliding mechanism on each orthogonal wheel, the positioning system can easily face the irregular up and down movement of the system caused by the floating ground. In addition, it can solve the mismatch between the positioning data of the IMU odometer and the data in the world coordinate system under the floating ground condition. The experiment shows that the error of the positioning system is within the allowable range under the condition of linear and curved motion, and the expected effect is achieved.

In future work, on the basis of using the positioning system, we will continue to study the fusion of multi-sensor positioning, such as RFID, visual tags and so on, to make the positioning effect more obvious. In addition, we will consider using the fused localization sensor system to realize the functions of SLAM mapping and navigation. Using the positioning system as an odometer for map navigation in different environments should have better results.

Author Contributions: Z.L. put forward the research topic of orthogonal wheels positioning and designed the whole experimental scheme. G.H. carried out the experiments, and worked on the data collection and the writing of the paper. S.W. was responsible for the structural design of the orthogonal wheel positioning sensor system. R.W. developed the hardware for the orthogonal wheel positioning system, as well as the development of embedded programs. C.L. improved the experimental process and the design of the program. Y.Z. participated in the development of the positioning system and the development of the 3D structure diagram. D.C. and T.H. participated in the experiment and supervised the safety of the experiment. All authors have read and agreed to the published version of the manuscript.

Funding: This document is the result of the research project funded by the National Key R&D Program of China (2018YFB1304504), National Natural Science Foundation of China (51505069), together with Fundamental Research Funds for the Central Universities (N182410007-05).

Institutional Review Board Statement: Not applicable.

Informed Consent Statement: Not applicable.

Data Availability Statement: Not applicable.

Acknowledgments: We would like to thank all participants for helping us with data acquisitions.

Conflicts of Interest: The authors declare no conflict of interest.

References

1. Graham, J.D. An Audience of the Scientific Age: Rossumś Universal Robots and the Production of an Economic Conscience. *Grey Room* **2013**, *50*, 112–142. [CrossRef]
2. Minsky, M.L. The emotion machine: Commonsense thinking, artificial intelligence, and the future of the human mind. *Encycl. Neurol. Sci.* **2008**, *11*, 15–17.
3. Tabarelli, D.; Vilardi, A. A Statistically robust evidence of stochastic resonance in human auditory perceptual system. *Eur. Phys. J. B* **2009**, *1*, 155–159. [CrossRef]
4. Kube, C.R.; Vilardi, A. Task Modelling in Collective Robotics. *Auton. Robot.* **1997**, *4*, 53–72. [CrossRef]
5. Rosenberg, L.B. Virtual fixtures: Perceptual tools for telerobotic manipulation. In Proceedings of the IEEE Virtual Reality International Symposium, Seattle, WA, USA, 18–22 September 1993; pp. 76–82.
6. Wilson, A.R. Boston Dynamics introduces next generation humanoid robot. *Vis. Syst. Des.* **2016**, *21*, 53–72.
7. Zhang, S.; Xie, L.; Adams, M. An efficient data association approach to simultaneous localization and map building. In Proceedings of the IEEE International Conference on Robotics & Automation, Barcelona, Spain, 18–22 April 2005; Volume 24, pp. 49–60.
8. Cheng, Y.H.; Zhang, C.L. Mobile Robot Obstacle Avoidance Based on Multi-Sensor Information Fusion Technology. *Appl. Mech. Mater.* **2014**, *2958*, 490–491. [CrossRef]
9. Sugihara, K.; Smith, J. Genetic algorithms for adaptive motion planning of an autonomous mobile robot. In Proceedings of the IEEE International Symposium on Computational Intelligence in Robotics & Automation, Monterey, CA, USA, 10–11 July 1997.
10. Borio, D.; Closas, P. Robust transform domain signal processing for GNSS. *Navigation* **2019**, *66*, 305–323. [CrossRef]
11. Borio, D.; Closas, P. A Pseudolite-Based Positioning System for Legacy GNSS Receivers. *Sensors* **2014**, *4*, 6104–6123.
12. Tu, R.; Zhang, R. Real-time detection of BDS orbit manoeuvres based on the combination of GPS and BDS observations. *IET Radar Sonar Navig.* **2020**, *10*, 1603–1609. [CrossRef]
13. Fujii, K.; Sakamoto, Y. Hyperbolic Positioning with Antenna Arrays and Multi-Channel Pseudolite for Indoor Localization. *Sensors* **2015**, *10*, 25157–25175. [CrossRef]
14. Zhao, Y.; Peng, Z. A New Method of High-Precision Positioning for an Indoor Pseudolite without Using the Known Point Initialization. *Sensors* **2018**, *18*, 1977. [CrossRef]
15. Stavrou, V.; Bardaki, C.; Papakyriakopoulos, D.; Pramatari, K. An Ensemble Filter for Indoor Positioning in a Retail Store Using Bluetooth Low Energy Beacons. *Sensors* **2019**, *19*, 4550. [CrossRef]
16. Kwangjae, S.; Dong, L.; Hwangnam, K. Indoor Pedestrian Localization Using iBeacon and Improved Kalman Filter. *Sensors* **2018**, *18*, 1722.
17. Xin, L.; Jian, W.; Liu, C. A Bluetooth/PDR Integration Algorithm for an Indoor Positioning System. *Sensors* **2015**, *15*, 24862–24885.
18. Ferreira, A.; Matias, B.; Almeida, J.; Silva, E. Real-time GNSS precise positioning: RTKLIB for ROS. *Int. J. Adv. Robot. Syst.* **2020**, *17*, 1729881420904526. [CrossRef]
19. Zhang, H.; Zhang, C.; Wei, Y.; Chen, C.Y. Localization and navigation using QR code for mobile robot in indoor environment. In Proceedings of the IEEE International Conference on Robotics & Biomimetics, Zhuhai, China, 6–9 December 2015.
20. Duque Domingo, J.; Cerrada, C.; Valero, E.; Cerrada, J.A. An Improved Indoor Positioning System Using RGB-D Cameras and Wireless Networks for Use in Complex Environments. *Sensors* **2017**, *17*, 2391. [CrossRef]
21. Xu, H.; Ding, Y.; Li, P.; Wang, R.; Li, Y. An RFID Indoor Positioning Algorithm Based on Bayesian Probability and K-Nearest Neighbor. *Sensors* **2017**, *17*, 1806. [CrossRef]
22. Guarato, F.; Laudan, V.; Windmill, J.F.C. Ultrasonic sonar system for target localization with one emitter and four receivers: Ultrasonic 3D localization. In Proceedings of the 2017 IEEE SENSORS, Glasgow, Scotland, 29 October–1 November 2017.

23. Kim, H.; Liu, B.; Myung, H. Road-feature extraction using point cloud and 3D LiDAR sensor for vehicle localization. In Proceedings of the 2017 14th International Conference on Ubiquitous Robots and Ambient Intelligence (URAI), Jeju, Korea, 28 June–1 July 2017.
24. Wang, B.; Liu, X.; Yu, B.; Jia, R.; Gan, X. An Improved WiFi Positioning Method Based on Fingerprint Clustering and Signal Weighted Euclidean Distance. *Sensors* **2019**, *19*, 2300. [CrossRef]
25. Chen, G.; Meng, X.; Wang, Y.; Zhang, Y.; Tian, P.; Yang, H. Integrated WiFi/PDR/Smartphone Using an Unscented Kalman Filter Algorithm for 3D Indoor Localization. *Sensors* **2015**, *15*, 24595–24614. [CrossRef] [PubMed]
26. Zou, H.; Lu, X.; Jiang, H.; Xie, L. A Fast and Precise Indoor Localization Algorithm Based on an Online Sequential Extreme Learning Machine. *Sensors* **2015**, *15*, 1804. [CrossRef] [PubMed]
27. Willemsen, T.; Keller, F.; Sternberg, H. Concept for building a MEMS based indoor localization system. In Proceedings of the International Conference on Indoor Positioning & Indoor Navigation, Busan, Korea, 27–30 October 2014.
28. Eyobu, O.S.; Poulose, A.; Han, D.S. An Accuracy Generalization Benchmark for Wireless Indoor Localization based on IMU Sensor Data. In Proceedings of the 2018 IEEE 8th International Conference on Consumer Electronics, Berlin, Germany, 2–5 September 2018.
29. Gan, X.; Yu, B.; Huang, L.; Jia, R.; Zhang, H.; Sheng, C.; Fan, G.; Wang, B. Doppler Differential Positioning Technology Using the BDS/GPS Indoor Array Pseudolite System. *Sensors* **2019**, *19*, 4580. [CrossRef] [PubMed]
30. HTC Vive. China Releases First Self-Developed Group Standard for the VR Industry. *Electronics Newsweekly*, 25 April 2017; p. 74.

Article

Systematic Odometry Error Evaluation and Correction in a Human-Sized Three-Wheeled Omnidirectional Mobile Robot Using Flower-Shaped Calibration Trajectories

Jordi Palacín *, Elena Rubies and Eduard Clotet

Robotics Laboratory, Universitat de Lleida, 25001 Lleida, Spain; helenarubies@gmail.com (E.R.); eduard.clotet@udl.cat (E.C.)
* Correspondence: palacin@diei.udl.cat

Abstract: Odometry is a simple and practical method that provides a periodic real-time estimation of the relative displacement of a mobile robot based on the measurement of the angular rotational speed of its wheels. The main disadvantage of odometry is its unbounded accumulation of errors, a factor that reduces the accuracy of the estimation of the absolute position and orientation of a mobile robot. This paper proposes a general procedure to evaluate and correct the systematic odometry errors of a human-sized three-wheeled omnidirectional mobile robot designed as a versatile personal assistant tool. The correction procedure is based on the definition of 36 individual calibration trajectories which together depict a flower-shaped figure, on the measurement of the odometry and ground truth trajectory of each calibration trajectory, and on the application of several strategies to iteratively adjust the effective value of the kinematic parameters of the mobile robot in order to match the estimated final position from these two trajectories. The results have shown an average improvement of 82.14% in the estimation of the final position and orientation of the mobile robot. Therefore, these results can be used for odometry calibration during the manufacturing of human-sized three-wheeled omnidirectional mobile robots.

Keywords: odometry; odometry calibration; omnidirectional mobile robot

Citation: Palacín, J.; Rubies, E.; Clotet, E. Systematic Odometry Error Evaluation and Correction in a Human-Sized Three-Wheeled Omnidirectional Mobile Robot Using Flower-Shaped Calibration Trajectories. *Appl. Sci.* **2022**, *12*, 2606. https://doi.org/10.3390/app12052606

Academic Editors: J. Ernesto Solanes and Luis Gracia

Received: 25 January 2022
Accepted: 28 February 2022
Published: 2 March 2022

Publisher's Note: MDPI stays neutral with regard to jurisdictional claims in published maps and institutional affiliations.

Copyright: © 2022 by the authors. Licensee MDPI, Basel, Switzerland. This article is an open access article distributed under the terms and conditions of the Creative Commons Attribution (CC BY) license (https:// creativecommons.org/licenses/by/ 4.0/).

1. Introduction

Mobile robots have a huge range of potential applications in industrial, office and home environments. Autonomous mobile robots must be able to perform localization, mapping and navigation with reasonable levels of accuracy in order to successfully develop and complete their tasks. Localization methods consist of absolute or relative positioning methods [1,2]. Borenstein et al. [2] reviewed the most relevant mobile robot relative positioning methods based on internal data gathered by the mobile robot: odometry and inertial navigation, and the most relevant absolute positioning methods based on gathering external surrounding data.

Odometry is usually defined as a relative positioning method that uses the measures of the velocities of the wheels to estimate the position of the robot. Compared to other techniques, odometry is simple, affordable, and can be used in real-time, but as a relative positioning method it cumulates errors that may lead to inaccurate results. The improvement of odometry through proper calibration reduces the position errors and can contribute to lowering the costs of mobile robots by avoiding the use of precise external sensors.

In 1996, Borenstein et al. [3] introduced a benchmark test to measure the odometric accuracy of a mobile robot. This test, called University of Michigan Benchmark (UMBmark), consists on a bidirectional square path experiment in which a differential drive mobile robot performs a squared path in the clockwise and counterclockwise directions to avoid the compensation of odometry errors that might occur in unidirectional squared path experiments. The method first computes the contribution of errors caused by incorrect wheelbase (distance from the wheel to the center of the mobile robot) and by unequal wheel diameters. These errors are evaluated separately and then superimposed. In the case of a differential drive mobile robot, a wheelbase error causes pure rotation errors, which can be corrected by applying a correction factor to the wheelbase distances. The unequal wheel diameters error causes the robot to move on curved paths instead of straight trajectories. The radius of curvature of the real path can be computed to determine the ratio between the two-wheel diameters and compensate this systematic error. The application of the UMBmark provides a quantitative measure and corrects the systematic odometry errors, which allows comparison between different mobile robots. In summary, the results presented by Borenstein et al. [3] allowed an improvement of one order of magnitude in odometry accuracy.

An alternative to direct odometry calibration from the information gathered from the wheels is the application of data fusion from different sensors. Gargiulo et al. [4] estimated the mobile robot position and orientation by fusing information gathered from the wheels and an Inertial Measurement Unit (IMU). Zwierzchowski et al. [5] used a similar approach and included the information gathered from a vision system that measures the distance between the robot and custom markers located in the surrounding space. Xue et al. [6] fuses the information gathered from the wheels, an IMU and a 2D LIDAR in order to operate in diverse outdoor environments without any prior information. In a different approach, Palacin et al. [7] directly estimates the position and orientation of the mobile robot using the information provided by an onboard precise 2D LIDAR processed with simultaneous location and mapping (SLAM) [8]. In this case, the odometry was used as an initial estimation of the relative motion in order to improve the computational efficiency of SLAM. More recently, Xiao et al. [9] fused the information gathered from one IMU and two low-precision 2D LIDARs placed transversally to estimate the position and orientation of a mobile robot. However, the main disadvantage of using LIDARs is the cost of the sensor that is proportional to its measurement accuracy.

In the specific case of omnidirectional mobile robots, the determination of the odometry from the velocity gathered from the wheels has similar error sources but more complexity because of having more degrees of freedom in the motion [10]. In this direction, Maddahi et al. [11] proposed a method for the calibration of small three-wheeled omnidirectional mobile robots in order to reduce positioning errors. The procedure was based on the determination of two corrective indices for the inverse kinematic matrix used by the odometry to estimate the position of the robot. This method consists of: (1) determining the kinematic equations of the robot; (2) registering of the motion of the non-calibrated robot moving along a straight line; (3) evaluating the longitudinal error (x_e), lateral error (y_e) and angular error (θ_e) between the target and real trajectory positions; and (4) the computation of some corrective indices. This method corrects the longitudinal (x_e) and lateral (y_e) errors separately. First, a lateral corrective matrix, which compensates the lateral position error of the robot (y_e), is computed from the angular error of the robot (θ_e). Secondly, a longitudinal corrective factor used to eliminate the longitudinal position error (x_e) is computed from the longitudinal (x_e) and lateral errors (y_e). Finally, both indices are multiplied with the Jacobian matrix used by the odometry to estimate the velocities of the wheels. The corrected Jacobian matrix is then used to compute the corrected angular velocities of the wheels. This proposal was experimentally validated with different trajectories, comparing the positioning errors before and after calibration. Results showed significant improvements: the root mean square (RMS) of the positioning error was reduced between 68% and 91% in double-squared, double-triangle and circular paths. In this case, the analysis of the trajectories and positioning errors evidenced that the improvement depends on the type of trajectory being accurate in straight trajectories and less accurate in the case of combined straight and curved trajectories.

Similarly, Lin et al. [12] presented an odometry calibration method for medium-size three-wheeled omnidirectional mobile robots based on the correction of its kinematic model. The method consists on gathering discrete position and orientation data and estimating the kinematic parameters by a least square method. The information required by this process is the initial and final positions of the mobile robot through N experiments (multiple data sets). This proposal is not limited by the relationship between the parameters used in the kinematic equations, so the obtained kinematic model may better describe the odometry of the mobile robot. Lin et al. [12] verify their calibration method by comparing the ideal trajectory and the trajectories before and after calibration.

In a similar direction, Li et al. [13] presented a method for the reduction of positioning errors of four-wheel omnidirectional mobile robots using Mecanum wheels. The main problem of four-wheel omnidirectional mobile robots is wheel slippage, so this method analyzed the kinematic model of the mobile robot and provides a velocity compensation matrix to reduce the errors of the robot motion caused by wheel slippage. This compensation matrix was validated using virtual simulations and experimental tests. Results showed that the compensation matrix reduces the errors of robot motions caused by wheel slippage, improving the motion accuracy of the system. However, Li et al. [13] concluded that this velocity compensation matrix must be adjusted according to the velocity of the mobile robot. Alternatively, Lu et al. [14] fused the information gathered from an IMU, a gyroscope and encoders to estimate the odometry of a mobile robot using four Mechanum wheels to estimate the estimated odometry on a floating ground.

More recently, Savaee et al. [15] proposed a simplification of the method presented by Maddahi et al. [11]. The new method uses the kinematic model of a three-wheeled mobile robot and computed a corrected Jacobian matrix to reduce the effects of systematic errors in the odometry. This method used a genetic algorithm to find the matrix elements of a corrected Jacobian matrix, which are called Effective Kinematic Parameters (EPKs). This new method consists of: (1) creating a model of the virtual robot and of the systematic errors; (2) performing simulation tests with the virtual robot; (3) performing experimental tests with a real robot; (4) comparing both results to estimate the EPKs and redefine the Jacobian matrix of the mobile robot. In this case, the simulation and experimental tests consist of two robot translations along straight paths and one rotation about itself, and the calculated EPKs are used to correct the angular velocities of the wheels. This procedure was verified with a three-wheeled omnidirectional mobile robot performing different paths. In general, the evaluation of tracking errors in offline analysis has the advantage of avoiding local minimum in complex parametric nonlinear systems [16].

New Contribution

The new contribution of this paper is the proposal of a combination of 36 straight and curved calibration trajectories for systematic odometry error evaluation and correction in a three-wheeled omnidirectional mobile robot. This procedure has been empirically applied and validated in a real human-sized three-wheeled omnidirectional mobile robot of 1.760 m and 30 kg (Figure 1). These 36 calibration trajectories have been proposed as a representative test-bench of the infinite trajectories that can be performed by an omnidirectional mobile robot, which together depict a characteristic flower-shaped figure. The calibration procedure implemented requires the registering of the real odometry and ground truth trajectories generated while performing each calibration trajectory. Finally, the odometry of each calibration trajectory is recomputed offline to iteratively adjust the effective values of the kinematic parameters of the mobile robot in order to match the odometry with the ground truth trajectory. This paper has evaluated different matching strategies using different sets of calibration trajectories. The best matching between the odometry and ground truth trajectories has been obtained using genetic algorithms and 5 repetitions of each one of the proposed 36 calibration trajectories. The fitting results of the kinematic parameters have been validated by performing 5 additional repetitions of the 36 calibration trajectories.

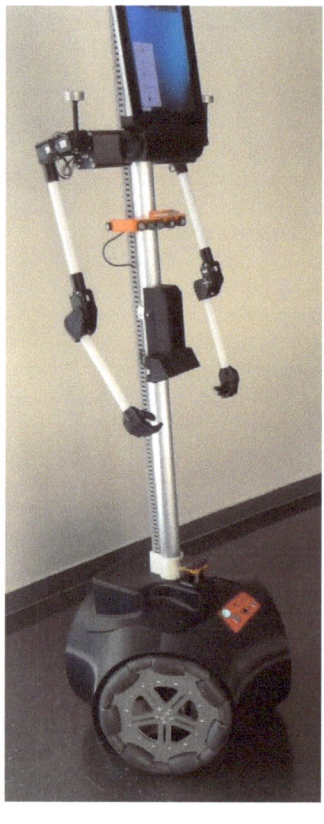 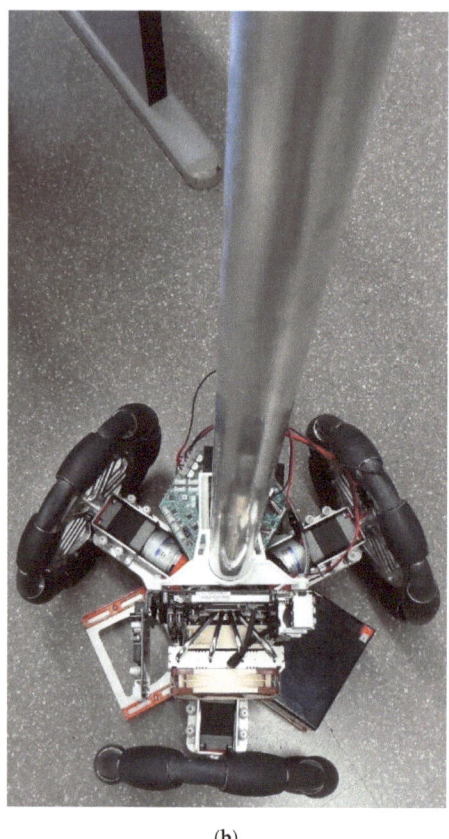

(a) (b)

Figure 1. Mobile robot APR-02: (**a**) general view of the mobile robot and (**b**) detail of its omnidirectional motion system.

This new contribution was inspired in Batlle et al. [17], who proposed the use of four curved calibration trajectories, and in Maddahi et al. [11], who calibrated the odometry with straight paths but concluded that the percentage of error correction depends on the type of the path. The new contribution is the proposal of a complete set of straight and curved calibration trajectories which together depict a characteristic flower-shaped figure. This new contribution is also inspired in the work of Savaee et al. [15] that used genetic algorithms to adjust the kinematic matrix of a three-wheeled mobile robot although without comparing the results obtained with other minimization alternatives. This proposal will apply the same methodology proposed by Lin et al. [12], based on the comparison of the initial and final positions of the mobile robot through N experiments to directly evaluate the odometry improvement achieved. Finally, as an alternative to Savaee et al. [15] and Lin et al. [12], this new proposal adjusts the value of the kinematic parameters of the mobile robot (radii of the wheels, distance from the wheel to the center of the mobile robot and angular orientation of the wheels) instead of directly adjusting the values of the kinematic matrix, allowing a direct physical interpretation of the fitting results obtained.

2. Materials and Methods

The material used in this paper is the omnidirectional mobile robot APR-02 (Figure 1). The methods used in this paper are the odometry of the mobile robot and two nonlinear minimization procedures based on gradient search and genetic algorithm. These two minimization methods will be applied to calibrate the odometry of the mobile robot.

2.1. Omnidirectional Mobile Robot APR-02

The omnidirectional mobile robot APR-02 is the second family prototype designed under the project concept titled Assistant Personal Robot (APR). The goal of the APR project is the final implementation of a versatile human-sized mobile robot that can be applied to develop different assistance services, for example, to supporting older people with mobility limitations [18]. The main difference of the APR concept with other comparative mobile robot designs [19] is the use of an omnidirectional motion system based on three omnidirectional wheels in which the free rollers are aligned with the rotation plane of the wheels. The main advantage of this design using three wheels is the minimization of wheel slippage regardless of the motion implemented by the mobile robot [20].

Figure 1a shows the omnidirectional mobile robot APR-02 and Figure 1b shows a detail of its omnidirectional motion system based on the use of three omnidirectional wheels. The main sensor of the APR-02 is a precise onboard 2D LIDAR Hokuyo UTM-30LX either placed horizontally or tilted down [7] to directly detect small obstacles laying on the ground or holes or stairs in front of the mobile robot, and for SLAM [8]. The APR-02 has been used as a research tool in some recent applications. In [21] an alternative omnidirectional wheel design was proposed to foster future outdoor applications. In [22] the motors and encoders of the mobile robot were analyzed in order to improve the measurement of the estimated angular velocity of the wheels.

The trajectory of the mobile robot APR-02 is established by its path-planning algorithm that continuously updates the target motion vector (v, α, ω, t_r) of the mobile robot [20] accordingly to a task or objective. This target motion vector is converted into individual target angular rotational velocities of the three wheels $(\omega_{Ma}, \omega_{Mb}, \omega_{Mc})$ which are then applied to the PID controllers of the DC motors driving these three wheels in order to implement the planned motion.

2.2. Odometry Trajectory

Odometry is a simple and practical method that provides a periodic real-time estimation of the relative displacement of a mobile robot based on the measurement of the angular rotational speed of its wheels. Odometry estimation is valid in the case of non-slippage wheel conditions in which wheel revolutions can be translated into linear displacement relative to the floor. The advantage of an omnidirectional mobile robot using three optimal omnidirectional wheels is that the wheels do not have motion constrains and do not require slippage in order to implement any motion trajectory [20].

The kinematics and the odometry of the mobile robot APR-02 are described in [20]. Figure 2 presents the parametric definition of the omnidirectional motion system based on three omnidirectional wheels (Figure 2a) and a detail of the parameters of one wheel (Figure 2b). The main parameters are: the position of the mobile robot (x, y, θ) referred to the fixed world frame (X_W, Y_W), the motion command of the robot (v, α, ω), the angular velocities of the wheels $(\omega_a, \omega_b, \omega_c)$, the linear velocities of the wheels (V_a, V_b, V_c), the radii of the wheels (r_a, r_b, r_c), the distance between the center of the robot and each wheel (R_a, R_b, R_c) and the angular orientation of each wheel $(\delta_a, \delta_b, \delta_c)$ referred to the mobile robot frame (X_R, Y_R).

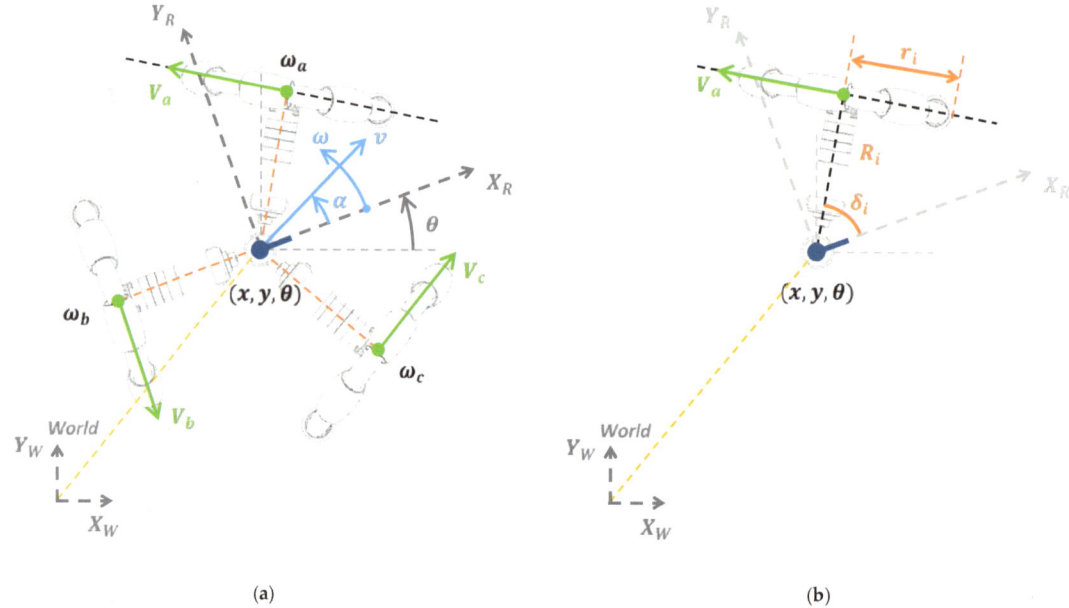

Figure 2. Parametric definition of the omnidirectional motion system of the mobile robot APR-02: (**a**) general representation of the three omnidirectional wheels and (**b**) detail of the parameters of one omnidirectional wheel. (X_R, Y_R) represents the mobile robot frame in which X_R is the front of the mobile robot.

The odometry procedure uses the instantaneous estimate of the current angular velocities of the three wheels, a, b, c, available as a vector sequence $(\omega_a(k), \omega_b(k), \omega_c(k))$ in order to estimate the instantaneous position of the mobile robot $(x(k), y(k), \theta(k))$ in the world frame (X_W, Y_W). The relation between the instantaneous estimation of the angular velocities of the wheels $(\omega_a(k), \omega_b(k), \omega_c(k))$ and the instantaneous robot velocity $(v_x(k), v_y(k), \omega(k))$ in the world frame (X_W, Y_W) can be summarized as [20]:

$$\begin{bmatrix} \omega_a(k) \\ \omega_b(k) \\ \omega_c(k) \end{bmatrix} = \begin{bmatrix} 1/r_a & 0 & 0 \\ 0 & 1/r_b & 0 \\ 0 & 0 & 1/r_c \end{bmatrix} \cdot \begin{bmatrix} -\sin(\delta_a) & \cos(\delta_a) & R_a \\ -\sin(\delta_b) & \cos(\delta_b) & R_b \\ -\sin(\delta_c) & \cos(\delta_c) & R_c \end{bmatrix} \cdot \begin{bmatrix} \cos(\theta(k-1)) & \sin(\theta(k-1)) & 0 \\ -\sin(\theta(k-1)) & \cos(\theta(k-1)) & 0 \\ 0 & 0 & 1 \end{bmatrix} \cdot \begin{bmatrix} v_X(k) \\ v_Y(k) \\ \omega(k) \end{bmatrix}_{World} \quad (1)$$

Which includes a rotation matrix $R(\theta)$ and a compact kinematic matrix M that defines the overall kinematics of the mobile robot:

$$R(\theta) = \begin{bmatrix} \cos(\theta) & \sin(\theta) & 0 \\ -\sin(\theta) & \cos(\theta) & 0 \\ 0 & 0 & 1 \end{bmatrix} \quad (2)$$

$$M = \begin{bmatrix} -\sin(\delta_a)/r_a & \cos(\delta_a)/r_a & R_a/r_a \\ -\sin(\delta_b)/r_b & \cos(\delta_b)/r_b & R_b/r_b \\ -\sin(\delta_c)/r_c & \cos(\delta_c)/r_c & R_c/r_c \end{bmatrix} \quad (3)$$

Equation (1) can be arranged to update the current position of the mobile robot $(x(k), y(k), \theta(k))$ in the world frame (X_W, Y_W) based on the new estimate of the current angular velocities of the three wheels of the mobile robot $(\omega_a(k), \omega_b(k), \omega_c(k))$ and the time lapse Δt between the samples $k-1$ and k, which in the mobile robot APR-02 coincides with the sampling time T of its proportional-integral-derivative (PID) motor controllers, $\Delta t = T = 10$ ms:

$$\begin{bmatrix} x(k) \\ y(k) \\ \theta(k) \end{bmatrix}_{World} = \begin{bmatrix} x(k-1) \\ y(k-1) \\ \theta(k-1) \end{bmatrix}_{World} + T \cdot R(\theta(k-1))^{-1} \cdot M^{-1} \cdot \begin{bmatrix} \omega_a(k) \\ \omega_b(k) \\ \omega_c(k) \end{bmatrix} \quad (4)$$

where $R^{-1}(\theta)$ is the inverse of the rotation matrix defined by the previous instantaneous angular orientation of the mobile robot $\theta(k-1)$:

$$R(\theta)^{-1} = \begin{bmatrix} \cos(\theta) & -\sin(\theta) & 0 \\ \sin(\theta) & \cos(\theta) & 0 \\ 0 & 0 & 1 \end{bmatrix} \quad (5)$$

And M^{-1} is the inverse of the compact kinematic matrix M:

$$M^{-1} = \frac{1}{R_a \sin(\delta_b - \delta_c) - R_b \sin(\delta_a - \delta_c) + R_c \sin(\delta_a - \delta_b)} \cdot \begin{bmatrix} r_a(R_b \cos(\delta_c) - R_c \cos(\delta_b)) & -r_b(R_a \cos(\delta_c) - R_c \cos(\delta_a)) & r_c(R_a \cos(\delta_b) - R_b \cos(\delta_a)) \\ r_a(R_b \sin(\delta_c) - R_c \sin(\delta_b)) & -r_b(R_a \sin(\delta_c) - R_c \sin(\delta_a)) & r_c(R_a \sin(\delta_b) - R_b \sin(\delta_a)) \\ r_a \sin(\delta_b - \delta_c) & -r_b \sin(\delta_a - \delta_c) & r_c \sin(\delta_a - \delta_b) \end{bmatrix} \quad (6)$$

2.3. Odometry Errors: Systematic and Non-Systematic

The main disadvantage of odometry is its unbounded accumulation of errors in the evaluation of the trajectory of a mobile robot (see Equation (4)). The error sources that cause inaccuracies in the determination of the odometry depend largely on the type of terrain practiced by the mobile robot [3], and are classified as systematic and non-systematic. In general, the concept of odometry calibration is focused on the minimization of systematic errors because they remain constant during the displacement. In general, the errors affecting the orientation of the mobile robot have the worst cumulative effects because once they are incurred they grow into lateral position errors [23,24].

2.3.1. Systematic Odometry Errors

Systematic odometry errors are usually invariant because they are caused by inaccuracies and imperfections in the mechanical implementation of the robot, such as mismatches between the nominal and effective parameters, or by limited sensors capabilities, resolution and sampling rate. Borenstein et al. [3] concluded that the systematic errors that have greater effects in the odometry are caused by unequal wheel diameters and placement accuracy in the wheelbase, which is the distance between the point of contact of the wheel with the floor and the center of the robot. Systematic errors accumulate constantly, so they are usually the main contributors to positioning errors in smooth indoor terrains.

2.3.2. Non-Systematic Odometry Errors

Non-systematic odometry errors are not possible to predict, because they are originated by unpredictable features of the environment such as terrain irregularities, terrain obstacles, structural wheel slippage during specific motions, wheel slippage originated by the terrain conditions, or the application of external forces to the mobile robot. However, this paper is applied to a mobile robot operating in perfect flat indoor terrains, so the assumption is that the motion will not be affected by non-systematic odometry errors.

2.4. Systematic Odometry Error Sources in a Three-Wheeled Omnidirectional Mobile Robot

The exact theoretical value of the inverse of the compact kinematic matrix M^{-1} computed with the nominal values of the kinematic parameters ($R_a = R_b = R_c = 0.195$ m, $r_a = r_b = r_c = 0.148$ m and $\delta_a = 60°$, $\delta_b = 180°$, $\delta_c = 300°$) evaluated using a standard double precision floating-point format (IEEE 754-1985: 4-bytes data or 64-bit data, precision 1.11×10^{-16} [25]) is:

$$M^{-1} = \begin{bmatrix} -0.0854478398400646 & 0.0000000000000000 & 0.0854478398400646 \\ 0.0493333333333333 & -0.0986666666666667 & 0.0493333333333333 \\ 0.2529914529914529 & 0.2529914529914529 & 0.2529914529914529 \end{bmatrix} \quad (7)$$

The simple numerical representation of the exact values of the coefficients of the inverse of the compact kinematic matrix M^{-1} of the mobile robot APR-02 intuitively indicates that any inaccuracy in the values of the kinematic parameters may cause a large impact in the generation of systematic errors during the cumulative evaluation of the odometry (see Equation (4)).

In a real mobile robot application, the effective values of the kinematic parameters R_a, R_b, R_c, r_a, r_b, r_c, δ_a, δ_b, δ_c can differ from the nominal values due to imprecisions in the manufacturing process and then originate systematic errors in the cumulative computation of the odometry of a mobile robot. The following figures are proposed to graphically illustrate the uncertainties that appear in the determination of the exact or effective value of the kinematic parameters of a real mobile robot. Figure 3 shows two views of one omnidirectional wheel of the motion system of the mobile robot APR-02 and a representation of its radius r_a. Even in this case in which the wheel cover is thin and smooth, the accurate determination of the radius of the wheel is very difficult and will have some uncertainty because of the difficulty in the estimation of the point of contact with the floor [26]. Similarly, Figure 4 shows two views of the representation of the distance to the center of the mobile robot. Figure 4a shows the effect of a vertical wheel misalignment (exaggerated in this case) and Figure 4b the effect caused by the point of contact with the floor. Finally, Figure 5 shows two views of the effect of angular wheel misalignment that can be caused by the application of non-uniform pressure to the screws that hold the motor to the wheelbase through a rubber piece designed to absorb vibrations. These figures clearly reveal that manufacturing inaccuracies and assembly imprecisions will originate crossed systematic errors in the odometry of the omnidirectional mobile robot.

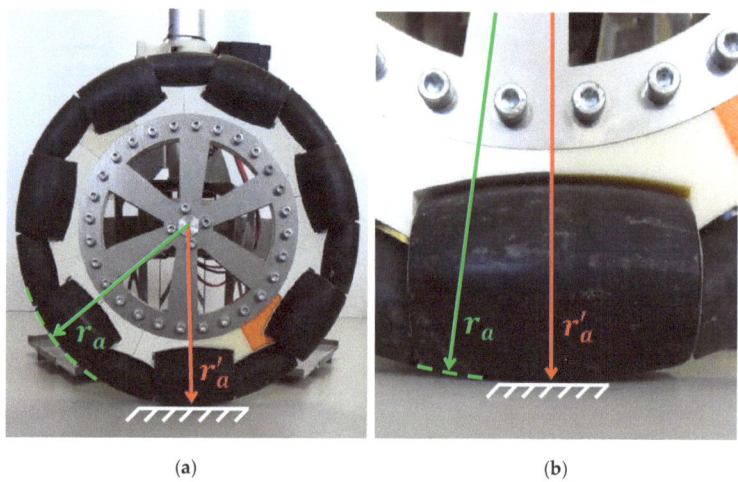

Figure 3. General view (**a**) and detail (**b**) of the wheel radius and the point of contact of the wheel with the floor: r_a depicts the nominal radius (green font and lines) and r'_a the real or effective radius (red font and lines).

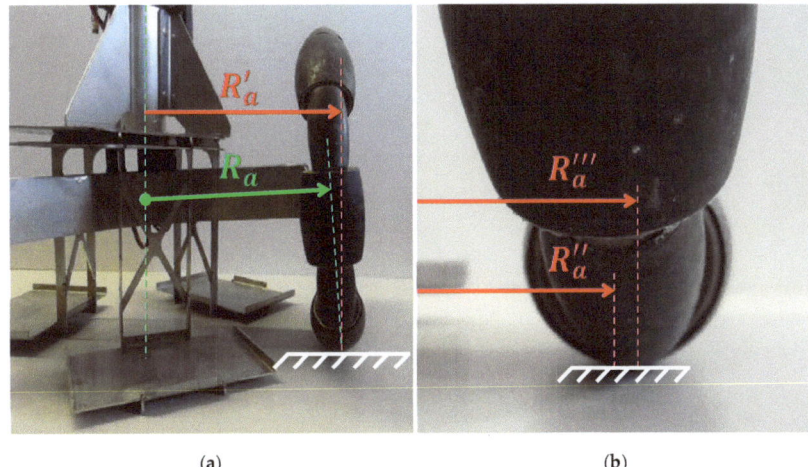

Figure 4. General view (**a**) and detail (**b**) of the point of contact with the floor and the distance from the wheel to the center of the mobile robot: R_a depicts the nominal or design value (green font and lines) and R'_a the real or effective value (representing R'_a as the average value of R''_a and R'''_a, red font and lines).

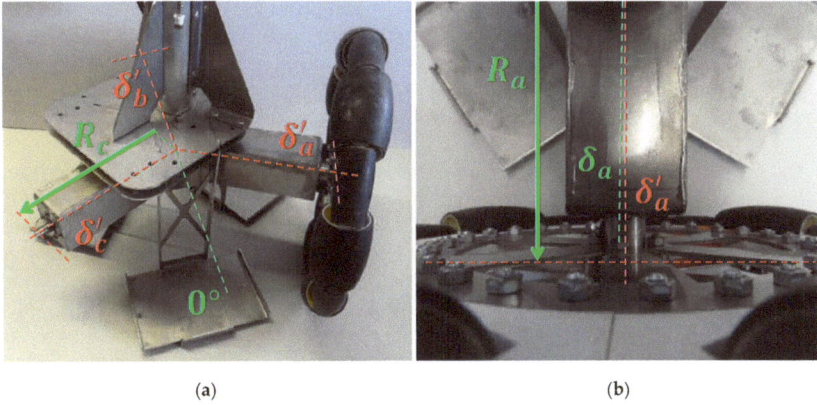

Figure 5. General view (**a**) and detail (**b**) of the angular orientation of the front-left wheel (wheel a) relative to the mobile robot frame: δ_a depicts the nominal or design value (green font and lines) and δ'_a is the real or effective value (red font and lines).

Finally, Tables 1–3 show the analytic determination of the sensitivity of the kinematic matrix M^{-1} to the kinematic parameters of the wheels, computed form Equation (6). These tables show very high sensitivities in the array values of M^{-1}, a matrix that is used to cumulatively update the position and location of the mobile robot 100 times per second (See Equation (4)). In the case of the distance from the center of the robot to each wheel, the maximum individual sensitivity of M^{-1} is as high as 0.43 mm/s for each millimeter of error in the determination of the real value of (R_a, R_b, R_c). In the case of the radii of the wheels, the maximum individual sensitivity of M^{-1} is as high as 1.70 mm/s for each millimeter of error in the determination of the real value of (r_a, r_b, r_c). Finally, in the case of the angular orientation of each wheel, the maximum individual sensitivity of M^{-1} is 0.14 mm/s for each angular arc degree error in the determination of the real value of $(\delta_a, \delta_b, \delta_c)$.

Table 1. Sensitivity of M^{-1} to the values of the nominal kinematic parameters of the wheel a.

$$\frac{\Delta M^{-1}}{\Delta R_a}\bigg|_{R_a=0.195\,m} \begin{bmatrix} 0.1461 & 0.1461 & 0.1461 \\ -0.0843 & -0.0843 & -0.0843 \\ -0.4325 & -0.4325 & -0.4325 \end{bmatrix} \quad \frac{\Delta M^{-1}}{\Delta r_a}\bigg|_{r_a=0.148\,m} \begin{bmatrix} -0.5774 & 0.0000 & 0.0000 \\ 0.3333 & 0.0000 & 0.0000 \\ 1.7094 & 0.0000 & 0.0000 \end{bmatrix} \quad \frac{\Delta M^{-1}}{\Delta \delta_a}\bigg|_{\delta_a=60°} \begin{bmatrix} 0.0000 & 0.0493 & -0.0493 \\ 0.0000 & -0.0285 & 0.0285 \\ 0.0000 & -0.1461 & 0.1461 \end{bmatrix}$$

Table 2. Sensitivity of M^{-1} to the values of the nominal kinematic parameters of the wheel b.

$$\frac{\Delta M^{-1}}{\Delta R_b}\bigg|_{R_b=0.195\,m} \begin{bmatrix} 0.0000 & 0.0000 & 0.0000 \\ 0.1687 & 0.1687 & 0.1687 \\ -0.4325 & -0.4325 & -0.4325 \end{bmatrix} \quad \frac{\Delta M^{-1}}{\Delta r_b}\bigg|_{r_b=0.148\,m} \begin{bmatrix} 0.0000 & 0.0000 & 0.0000 \\ 0.0000 & -0.6667 & 0.0000 \\ 0.0000 & 1.7094 & 0.0000 \end{bmatrix} \quad \frac{\Delta M^{-1}}{\Delta \delta_b}\bigg|_{\delta_b=180°} \begin{bmatrix} 0.0000 & 0.0000 & 0.0000 \\ -0.0570 & 0.0000 & 0.0570 \\ 0.1461 & 0.0000 & -0.1461 \end{bmatrix}$$

Table 3. Sensitivity of M^{-1} to the values of the nominal kinematic parameters of the wheel c.

$$\frac{\Delta M^{-1}}{\Delta R_c}\bigg|_{R_c=0.195\,m} \begin{bmatrix} -0.1461 & -0.1461 & -0.1461 \\ -0.0843 & -0.0843 & -0.0843 \\ -0.4325 & -0.4325 & -0.4325 \end{bmatrix} \quad \frac{\Delta M^{-1}}{\Delta r_c}\bigg|_{r_c=0.148\,m} \begin{bmatrix} 0.0000 & 0.0000 & 0.5774 \\ 0.0000 & 0.0000 & 0.3333 \\ 0.0000 & 0.0000 & 1.7094 \end{bmatrix} \quad \frac{\Delta M^{-1}}{\Delta \delta_c}\bigg|_{\delta_c=300°} \begin{bmatrix} -0.0493 & 0.0493 & 0.0000 \\ -0.0285 & 0.0285 & 0.0000 \\ -0.1461 & 0.1461 & 0.0000 \end{bmatrix}$$

2.5. Ground Truth Trajectory

The calibration procedure proposed in this work requires the development of several motion experiments conducted in a controlled, clean and structured area, without obstacles on the floor and with plain and clean surrounding walls. During these motion experiments the odometry and the ground truth (or real) trajectory of the mobile robot are registered for offline calibration analysis. The trajectory estimated with the odometry is based on relative onboard information that is prone to cumulative systematic errors (see Section 2.4). The trajectory estimated from the precise information provided by the onboard LIDAR (providing 1.081 points per scan and a radial distance range up to 30 m) and processed with SLAM [8] is assumed as the ground truth trajectory of the mobile robot [20] because the absolute LIDAR information gathered in this clean conditions is not prone to systematic errors. The trajectory estimated with the odometry is based on relative onboard information that is prone to cumulative systematic errors (see Section 2.4) while the ground truth trajectory estimated with the precise onboard LIDAR is based on an absolute description of the structured environment around the mobile robot that is not prone to systematic errors. This procedure to obtain the ground truth trajectory was used previously in [20]. In case an accurate onboard LIDAR is not available, it will be necessary to obtain the ground truth trajectory using other means such as an external laser tracker [27,28] or external cameras [29].

Figure 6a shows a representation of the odometry and ground truth trajectories, which are usually different because of the existence of systematic odometry errors. The values represented are: the starting point of the mobile robot (x_i, y_i, θ_i), the motion command applied $M = (v, \alpha, \omega, t_r)$, the true final position and orientation estimated with SLAM $(xgt_f, ygt_f, \theta gt_f)$, and the final position and orientation of the mobile robot estimated with the odometry (x_f, y_f, θ_f). In each motion experiment the mobile robot also registers all intermediate information needed to replicate the offline computation of the odometry and ground truth trajectories in order to perform the calibration of the odometry. The information registered is (see Figure 6b): a vector containing the sequence of instantaneous angular velocities of the three wheels and the elapsed time $E(k = 1 \ldots n) = [t(k), [\omega_a(k), \omega_b(k), \omega_c(k)]]$, where n is the number of velocity samples available; a vector containing the position of the mobile robot estimated by the odometry $O(k = 1 \ldots n) = [t(k), [x(k), y(k), \theta(k)]]$; and a vector containing the ground truth position $GT(p = 1 \ldots m) = [t(p), [xgt(p), ygt(p), \theta gt(p)]]$ estimated with SLAM. Please note that

$t(k)$ is the time in which a new estimation of the instantaneous angular velocities of the wheels $E(k)$ is provided by the encoder. This time can be computed as $t(k) = k \cdot T$ or $t(k) = t(k-1) + T$, where T is the sampling time of the PIDs; in the APR-02 this value is $T = 10$ ms. The odometry information $O(k)$ is computed from $E(k)$, so it is defined by the same time sequence $t(k)$. Alternatively, $t(p)$ is the time in which a new raw scan $L(p)$ is provided by the LIDAR. This time can be computed as $t(p) = t(p-1) + D_p$, where D_p ranges from 200 ms to 300 ms depending on the time required by the control system of the mobile robot to apply SLAM and estimate $GT(p)$. This variation is because the control system waits to request a new LIDAR scan until the SLAM procedure finishes, so this time lapse will be different depending on the time needed to apply SLAM from the raw LIDAR scans.

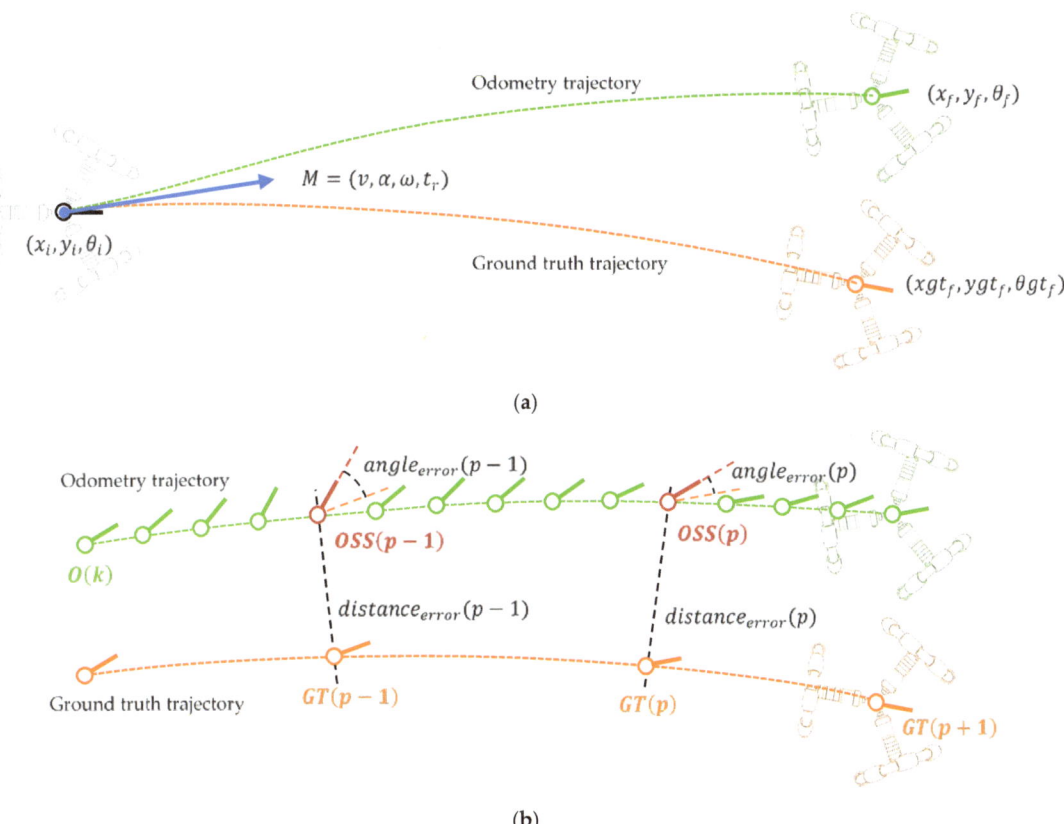

Figure 6. Representation of the ground truth trajectory of the mobile robot (orange line) and the trajectory estimated with the odometry (green line): (**a**) complete trajectories; (**b**) angle and distance differences between the trajectory positions estimated with the odometry and the SLAM procedure.

The hypothesis of this paper is then that the odometry trajectory will be correct and exact when this trajectory matches the ground truth (real) trajectory of the mobile robot.

Figure 7 shows the final position results obtained when the mobile robot APR-02 repeats the same calibration trajectory five times, starting each trajectory with the same initial position and angular orientation. Figure 7 represents the zoomed information of the planned final destination of the mobile robot (black dot and line) when the mobile robot completes a simple straight trajectory, the ground truth trajectory (orange dotted line) and ground truth final position and orientation of the mobile robot (orange circle and line), and the trajectory (green dotted line) and final mobile robot position and orientation estimated with the odometry (green square and line). The results of Figure 7 reveal the existence of systematic differences between the odometry and ground truth trajectories. This paper proposes the reduction of such differences by applying an iterative calibration procedure to the kinematic parameters used to estimate the odometry of the mobile robot APR-02.

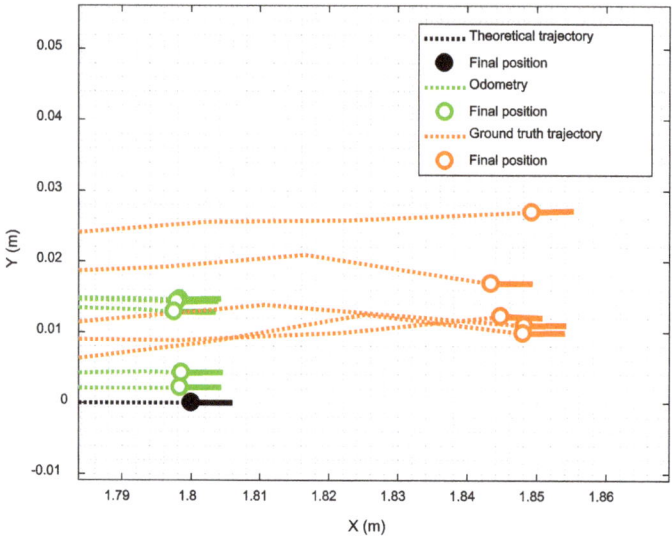

Figure 7. Planned trajectory (back dotted line) zoomed at the planned ending position and orientation of the mobile robot (black point and line); measured ground truth trajectories (orange dotted line) detailing the final position and orientation of the mobile robot (orange circle and line); and measured odometry trajectory (green dotted line) detailing the ending position and orientation of the mobile robot (green circle and line).

2.5.1. Distance and Angular Errors during a Trajectory

The determination of the distance and angular errors between the odometry trajectory points $O(k = 1 \ldots n)$ and the ground truth trajectory points $GT(p = 1 \ldots m)$ require the subsampling of the original odometry trajectory in order to have an odometry trajectory vector with the same length as the ground truth vector. The subsampled odometry trajectory vector $OSS(p = 1 \ldots m) = [t(p), [x(p), y(p), \theta(p)]]$ is then obtained by searching for the nearest $t(k)$ and $t(p)$ values (see Figure 6b). The distance and angle error vectors are then computed as:

$$distance_{error}(p) = \sqrt{(xgt(p) - x(p))^2 + (ygt(p) - y(p))^2} \tag{8}$$

$$angle_{error}(p) = \sqrt{(\theta gt(p) - \theta(p))^2} \tag{9}$$

2.5.2. Maximum Error in a Trajectory

The determination of the maximum distance and angular error between the odometry and ground truth trajectory is obtained from the distance error vector and the angle error vector, respectively, using:

$$MaximumError_{Distance} = \max(distance_{error}(p = 1 \ldots m)) \tag{10}$$

$$MaximumError_{Angle} = \max(angle_{error}(p = 1 \ldots m)) \tag{11}$$

2.5.3. RMS Error in a Trajectory

The determination of the Root Mean Square error (RMSE) that summarizes the differences between the odometry and ground truth trajectory are computed using:

$$RMSE_{distance} = \sqrt{\frac{\sum_{p=1}^{m}\left(distance_{error}(p)\right)^2}{m}} \qquad (12)$$

$$RMSE_{angle} = \sqrt{\frac{\sum_{p=1}^{m}\left(angle_{error}(p)\right)^2}{m}} \qquad (13)$$

2.5.4. Cost Function Summarizing Trajectory Differences

The cost function used in this paper to summarize in one single value CF the overall differences (position and angular orientation) between the odometry and ground truth trajectories is computed from the final position of the mobile robot using:

$$CF = \sqrt{\left(xgt_f - x_f\right)^2 + \left(ygt_f - y_f\right)^2 + \left(\theta gt_f - \theta_f\right)^2} \qquad (14)$$

This cost function value CF will be used to guide the iterative odometry calibration procedure in order to tune the effective kinematic parameters of the mobile robot. This cost function was also used by Savaee et al. [15] to calibrate the effective kinematic parameters of a comparable omnidirectional mobile robot. This cost function implicitly applies the same weights to a final positioning with a distance error of 1 m or an angular arch error of 1°. We have selected this cost function because a small angular error usually has a large cumulative effect in the odometry of an omnidirectional mobile robot.

2.6. Iterative odometry Calibration Procedure

This paper proposes the application of an iterative calibration procedure to tune or adjust the effective value of the kinematic parameters of the mobile robot: R_a, R_b, R_c, r_a, r_b, r_c, δ_a, δ_b, δ_c, used to compute the M^{-1} matrix. These kinematic parameters have been described in Section 2.2 and represented graphically in Figure 2. The planned result of the iterative calibration procedure is a better match between the odometry and ground truth mobile robot trajectories.

Figure 8 depicts the flowchart of the iterative odometry calibration procedure. The iterative process starts with the nominal or theoretical values of the kinematic parameters of the mobile robot (R_a, R_b, R_c, r_a, r_b, r_c, δ_a, δ_b, δ_c), which are used to compute a first estimation of the M^{-1} matrix. Then, the iterative process uses the initial position and orientation of the mobile robot (x_i, y_i, θ_i) and the sequence of angular rotational velocities of the wheels obtained from the encoders $E(k = 1 \ldots n) = [t(k), [\omega_a(k), \omega_b(k), \omega_c(k)]]$ to compute the odometry trajectory $O(k = 1 \ldots n)$ of the mobile robot and estimate the final position and angular orientation of the mobile robot $\left(x_f, y_f, \theta_f\right) = O(k = n)$. Then, the cost function is used to compare this estimate of final position and orientation of the mobile robot $\left(x_f, y_f, \theta_f\right)$ with its true position and orientation $\left(xgt_f, ygt_f, \theta gt_f\right) = GT(p = m)$.

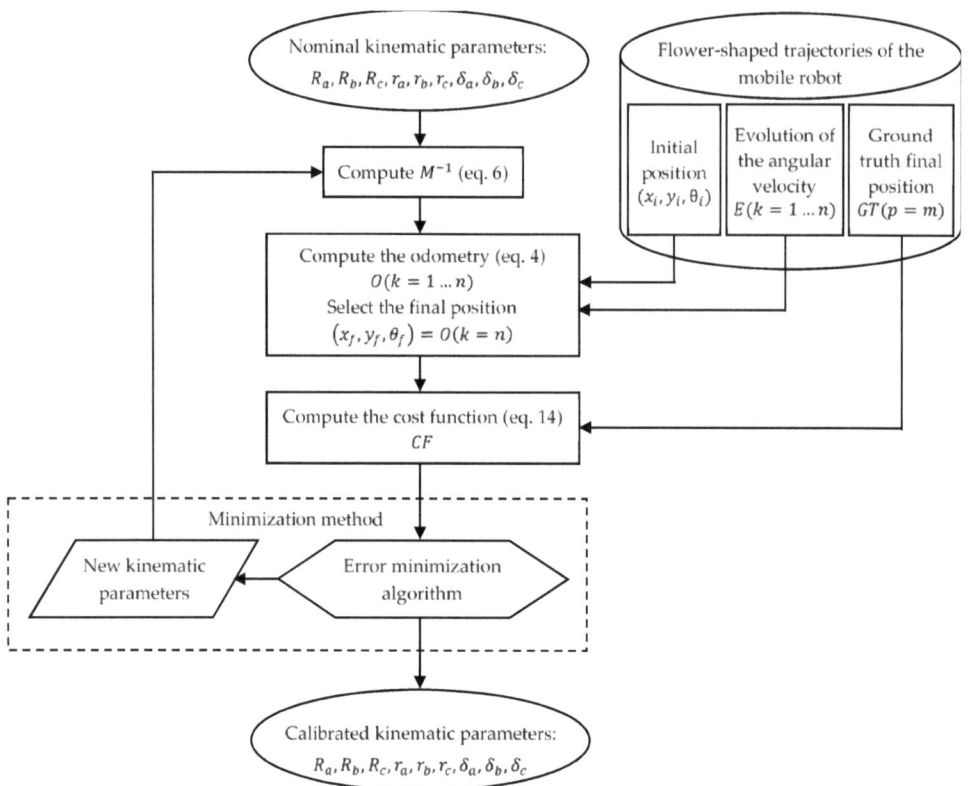

Figure 8. Flowchart of the complete calibration procedure.

The iterative minimization function evaluates the cost function and decides between repeating the loop with new values of the kinematic parameters or stopping the iterative minimization search. The final result of this iterative procedure is an improved or corrected M^{-1} matrix ready to better estimate the odometry of the mobile robot APR-02. The nonlinear minimization functions evaluated in this paper are based on gradient search and genetic algorithms (GA). In both cases, the inputs and genome of the minimization functions are the initial values of the kinematic parameters $param_i$ defined as:

$$param_i = (0.195,\ 0.195,\ 0.195,\ 0.148,\ 0.148,\ 0.148,\ 60.000,\ 180.000,\ 300.000) \quad (15)$$

And the upper ($param_{ub}$) and lower ($param_{lb}$) bounds proposed to guarantee the physical interpretation of the results:

$$param_{ub} = (0.220,\ 0.220,\ 0.220,\ 0.158,\ 0.158,\ 0.158,\ 62.000,\ 182.000,\ 302.000)$$
$$param_{lb} = (0.170,\ 0.170,\ 0.170,\ 0.138,\ 0.138,\ 0.138,\ 58.000,\ 178.000,\ 298.000) \quad (16)$$

The specific search functions used in this paper are:

Fmin search function. The implementation of a gradient search nonlinear minimization to calibrate the odometry is based on the Matlab function *fmincon.m*, which is a nonlinear multivariable function that attempts to iteratively find the local unconstrained minimum of an objective multivariate cost function summarized in a value *CF* evaluated within specific bounds. In this calibration application, the search will use $param_i$ as the initial population and $param_{lb}$ and $param_{ub}$ as the lower and upper bounds of the iterative search. The stopping criteria of this iterative search is a change in CF less than the default value of the parameter StepTolerance (10^{-10}) with a maximum constraint violation less than the default value of the parameter Constraint Tolerance (10^{-6}) before reaching the maximum number of iterations that is usually defined as the number of variables of $param_i$ multiplied by 100 (900).

GA search function. The implementation of a genetic algorithms (GA) minimization to calibrate the odometry is based on the Matlab function *ga.m*, which will attempt to iteratively find the local unconstrained minimum of an objective multivariate cost function summarized in a value CF evaluated within specific bounds. The inputs and outputs of the iterative search are the same as in the previous function. The initial population and bounds for the GA algorithm are defined using the Matlab function *gaoptimset.m* in the parameters InitialPopulation and PopInitRange. This iterative search stops if the average relative change in the best fitness of the cost function CF is less than or equal to the default value of the parameter FunctionTolerance (10^{-6}).

3. Systematic Odometry Error Evaluation and Correction

The procedure proposed in this paper to systematically evaluate and correct the systematic odometry errors of the omnidirectional mobile robot APR-02 is based on the definition of 36 individual calibration trajectories which together depict a flower-shaped figure, on the measurement of the odometry and ground truth trajectory in each calibration trajectory, and on the application of several strategies to iterative adjustment of the effective value of the kinematic parameters to match the odometry and the ground truth trajectories registered in these 36 calibration trajectories. The implementation of the 36 trajectories that define the flower-shaped figure is proposed as a representative test-bench of the infinite trajectories that can perform this omnidirectional mobile robot. In this paper, each calibration trajectory has been repeated 10 times; with a total of 360 registered trajectories. Five repetitions will be used to calibrate the effective value of the kinematic parameters and Five repetitions will be used to validate the results.

3.1. Calibration Trajectories Depicting a Characteristic Flower-Shaped Figure

This paper proposes the improvement of the odometry of the omnidirectional mobile robot APR-02 using a set of specific individual calibration trajectories that globally depict a characteristic flower-shaped figure. Figure 9 shows the proposed trajectories and Table A1 (listed in Appendix A) presents the motion command required to implement each calibration trajectory and the values of the corresponding target angular rotational velocities of the wheels required to implement each trajectory that will be specific for each mobile robot type.

The target angular velocities of the wheels shown in Table A1 (Appendix A) are in revolutions per minute (rpm) because this unit is normally used by the PIDs controlling the angular rotational velocity of the motors of the mobile robot. The calibration trajectories comprise straight displacements (Figure 9, red line labeled with an R followed with a number), clockwise displacements (blue line labeled with a B followed with a number), and counterclockwise displacements (green line labeled with a G followed with a number). These 36 combinations of angular rotational velocities of the wheels are a short representation of the infinite set of possible motion combinations. The linear displacement of all trajectories has been limited to 1 m in order to generate a characteristic and easy to remember flower-shaped figure. In this paper, each trajectory has been repeated and registered 10 times in a total of 360 trajectory experiments. Each trajectory register contains the sequence of instantaneous angular velocities of the three wheels $E(k = 1 \ldots n)$, where n is the number of samples available; the vector containing the position of the mobile robot estimated by the odometry $O(k = 1 \ldots n)$; and the vector containing the ground truth position $GT(p = 1 \ldots m)$ estimated by the SLAM procedure.

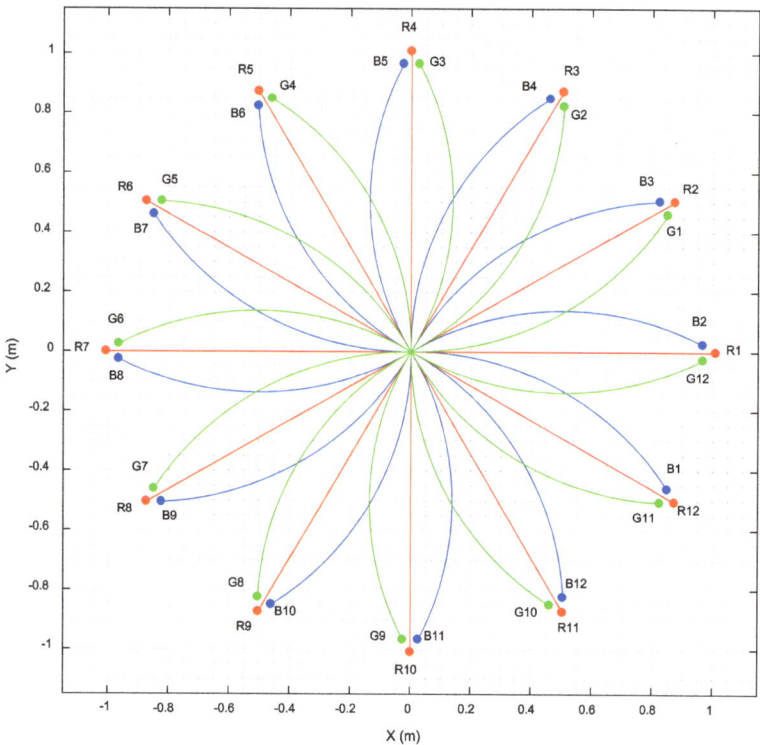

Figure 9. Representation of the ideal flower-shaped trajectories proposed to calibrate the odometry of the omnidirectional mobile robot APR-02.

The adequacy of the trajectories proposed in Figure 9 to the calibration of the odometry mobile robot APR-02 will be evaluated in the following section.

3.2. Odometry Calibration Strategies and Results

The odometry calibration strategies tested in this paper are based on analysis of the calibration trajectories proposed in Figure 9. The iterative calibration procedure used has been previously described in Section 2.6. In summary, this iterative calibration gets the registered calibration trajectories and iteratively adjusts the values of the effective kinematic parameters to globally match the odometry and ground truth trajectories.

Table 4 presents the results obtained: *Trajectories* depicts which trajectories have been used in the iterative search; *Strategy* shows the acronym of the calibration strategy applied; *Method* describes the iterative function used (GA or fmin) and the number of trajectory repetitions used in the iterative search: (1) one or (5) five repetitions; M^{-1} shows the value of the kinematic matrix obtained as a result of the iterative search; $CF_{CALIBRATION}$ is the value of the average cost function obtained during the iterative search or training; $CF_{VALIDATION}$ is the average value of the cost function obtained with five additional calibration trajectories (the complete flower-shape); *Improvement* depicts the relative improvement of $CF_{VALIDATION}$ relative to the uncalibrated case (*None* strategy).

Table 4. Trajectories, calibration strategies and results obtained.

Trajectories	Strategy	Method	M^{-1}			$CF_{CALIBRATION}$	$CF_{VALIDATION}$	Improvement
All	All	None	−0.0854 0.0493 0.2530	−0.0000 −0.0987 0.2530	0.0854 0.0493 0.2530	-	0.1242	-
R1, R5, R9	STA	GA1	−0.0866 0.0517 0.2567	0.0015 −0.1012 0.2552	0.0891 0.0536 0.2539	0.0214	0.1215	2.18%
		Fmin1	−0.0881 0.0497 0.2594	0.0009 −0.1024 0.2588	0.0876 0.0517 0.2565	0.0228	0.1386	−11.61%
		GA5	−0.0849 0.0503 0.2559	0.0043 −0.1014 0.2560	0.0909 0.0507 0.2561	0.0202	0.1267	−2.03%
		Fmin5	−0.0883 0.0505 0.2569	0.0007 −0.1015 0.2593	0.0874 0.0509 0.2598	0.0192	0.1436	−15.62%
B2, B6, B10, G12, G4, G8	STB	GA1	−0.0898 0.0533 0.2379	−0.0010 −0.1000 0.2340	0.0851 0.0567 0.2335	0.0170	0.0333	73.19%
		Fmin1	−0.0862 0.0479 0.2404	−0.0009 −0.0964 0.2352	0.0835 0.0496 0.2369	0.0503	0.0691	44.36%
		GA5	−0.0894 0.0525 0.2369	−0.0011 −0.0999 0.2340	0.0860 0.0539 0.2350	**0.0166**	0.0232	81.36%
		Fmin5	−0.0857 0.0477 0.2393	0.0003 −0.0966 0.2356	0.0844 0.0486 0.2376	0.0525	0.0677	45.52%
R1 ... R12	STC	GA1	−0.0907 0.0512 0.2579	−0.0030 −0.1014 0.2559	0.0844 0.0520 0.2567	0.0264	0.1278	−2.92%
		Fmin1	−0.0883 0.0515 0.2494	−0.0005 −0.1014 0.2472	0.0871 0.0524 0.2479	0.0258	0.0817	34.2%
		GA5	−0.0861 0.0511 0.2585	0.0018 −0.1015 0.2565	0.0891 0.0523 0.2573	0.0273	0.1308	−5.31%
		Fmin5	−0.0881 0.0512 0.2497	−0.0001 −0.1015 0.2475	0.0873 0.0524 0.2483	0.0264	0.0832	33.00%
B1 ... B12, G1 ... G12	STD	GA1	−0.0897 0.0524 0.2373	−0.0002 −0.1001 0.2346	0.0864 0.0530 0.2364	0.0199	0.0248	80.05%
		Fmin1	−0.0852 0.0490 0.2398	0.0009 −0.0968 0.2361	0.0844 0.0492 0.2383	0.0539	0.0660	46.89%
		GA5	−0.0892 0.0518 0.2365	−0.0004 −0.1027 0.2333	0.0874 0.0533 0.2358	0.0202	0.0261	78.98%
		Fmin5	−0.0851 0.0489 0.2393	0.0009 −0.0967 0.2358	0.0845 0.0490 0.2383	0.0554	0.0665	46.43%
All	STE	GA1	−0.0895 0.0528 0.2367	−0.0007 −0.1002 0.2346	0.0867 0.0537 0.2355	0.0212	0.0226	81.83%
		Fmin1	−0.0859 0.0497 0.2421	0.0008 −0.0983 0.2397	0.0851 0.0501 0.2408	0.0591	0.0636	48.82%
		GA5	−0.0893 0.0521 0.2364	−0.0006 −0.1010 0.2341	0.0867 0.0533 0.2354	0.0221	**0.0222**	**82.14%**
		Fmin5	−0.0859 0.0495 0.2418	0.0007 −0.0982 0.2394	0.0850 0.0501 0.2406	0.0603	0.0634	48.97%

The calibration strategies shown in Table 4 have been generally labeled as *STX-GAZ* and *STX-FminZ*, where *X* describes the group of trajectories considered (from *A* to *E*); *GA* refers to the use of the *ga.m* iterative function and *Fmin* to the *fmincon.m* iterative function; and *Z* is the number of repetitions of each calibration trajectory considered, a value that can be 1 or 5. The evaluation of each calibration strategy with one or five repetitions was proposed to compare the achievements obtained relative to the additional effort required to obtain 5 repetitions of each calibration trajectory. The calibration strategies evaluated in Table 4 are:

None. This strategy provides a reference evaluation result of the cost function $CF_{VALIDATION}$ using the uncalibrated kinematic parameters to compute the odometry of the 5 repetitions of all calibration trajectories registered to validate the results.

STA. This strategy uses only the straight calibration trajectories corresponding to a forward motion and two additional motions at $\pm 120°$ (Figure 9, trajectories: R1, R5 and R9). For example, STA-GA1 uses one repetition of the straight calibration trajectories and genetic algorithms, whereas STA-Fmin5 uses five repetitions of the straight calibration trajectories evaluated with the nonlinear multivariable function.

STB. This strategy uses only the curved clockwise and counterclockwise trajectories corresponding to a forward motion and two additional motions at $\pm 120°$ (Figure 9, trajectories: B2, B6, B10, G12, G4 and G8).

STC. This strategy uses only the straight trajectories corresponding to a forward motion and eleven additional motions at $\pm 30°$ (Figure 9, trajectories from R1 to R12).

STD. This strategy uses only the curved clockwise and counterclockwise trajectories corresponding to a forward motion and eleven additional motions at $\pm 30°$ (Figure 9, trajectories from B1 to B12 and from G1 to G12).

STE. This strategy uses all the straight and curved paths that depict the characteristic flower-shaped figure (Figure 9, all calibration trajectories).

3.3. Discussion of the Results Obtained with the Odometry Calibration Strategies

The results of the calibration strategies evaluated in Table 4 show that the evaluation of straight trajectories usually generates worse validation results than curved trajectories. It is likely that straight target trajectories (Table A1: R1 . . . R12) are less representative of the motion because they only use three different angular rotational velocities: ± 11.291, ± 19.557 and ± 22.583 rpm, while the curved trajectories cover six angular velocities (Table A1). In general, the best results of the iterative search are obtained with GA, probably because GA is less prone to local minimum converge.

The best calibration result ($CF_{CALIBRATION} = 0.0166$) was obtained with the strategy STB-GA5, using GA and five repetitions of only six curved calibration trajectories, also with very good validation results ($CF_{VALIDATION} = 0.0232$). A similar result was obtained with the strategy STB-GA1, using only one repetition of these six curved calibration trajectories ($CF_{CALIBRATION} = 0.0170$), confirming the representativeness of the curved calibration trajectories. The strategies STB-GA1 and STB-GA5 represent a huge improvement of 73.1% and 81.3% in the average validation of $CF_{VALIDATION}$ relative to the uncalibrated case.

The best validation result ($CF_{VALIDATION} = 0.0222$) was obtained with the strategy STE-GA5, using GA and 5 repetitions of all 36 calibration trajectories (180 training experiments). However, a very similar result was also obtained using GA and with only 1 repetition of all training trajectories (STE-GA1, 36 experiments, $CF_{VALIDATION} = 0.0226$). The improvements obtained in the validation of STE-GA1 and STE-GA5 were 81.8% and 82.1% respectively, so the conclusion is that both strategies are valid to calibrate the kinematic parameters of the mobile robot APR-02.

Table 5 compares the differences between the nominal and calibrated kinematic parameters obtained with STE-GA5. Unexpectedly, the differences between the nominal and calibrated values of the distance from the wheels to the center of the mobile robot (R_a, R_b, R_c) are higher than 10%, likely caused by the bending of the structure that supports the wheels (wheelbase). The differences in the effective values of the radii of the wheels (r_a, r_b, r_c) are in a range from 2 to 5%, probably caused by the complex assembly of the wheels. Finally, the values of the angular orientation of the wheels ($\delta_a, \delta_b, \delta_c$) vary within a very small range (0.18% and 0.52%), confirming the good alignment of the wheels and DC motors during the assembly of the mobile robot.

Table 5. Nominal and calibrated kinematic parameters (strategy STE-GA5) of the mobile robot.

	R_a (m)	R_b (m)	R_c (m)	r_a (m)	r_b (m)	r_c (m)	δ_a (°)	δ_b (°)	δ_c (°)
Nominal	0.195	0.195	0.195	0.148	0.148	0.148	60.0	180.0	300.0
Calibrated	0.218643	0.215735	0.216287	0.155068	0.151534	0.152728	59.7397	179.6820	301.5735
Difference	12.13%	10.63%	10.92%	4.78%	2.39%	3.19%	−0.43%	−0.18%	0.52%

The exact value of the best inverse of the compact kinematic matrix M^{-1} computed from the effective value of the kinematic parameters obtained with STE-GA5 is:

$$M_{STEGA5}^{-1} = \begin{bmatrix} -0.0892930568372762 & -0.0005606566978203 & 0.0867466159313470 \\ 0.0520955668635434 & -0.1010213675626970 & 0.0533117820461363 \\ 0.2364093797047320 & 0.2341358647406650 & 0.2353792947863630 \end{bmatrix} \quad (17)$$

Finally, Table 6 summarizes the average RMS errors and average maximum errors obtained with the uncalibrated and calibrated kinematic parameters. These validation results have been obtained with the five repetitions of the 36 calibration trajectories registered for validation (180 validation experiments). Table 6 shows that the improvement computed from the validation value of the cost function (82.1%) is representative of the trajectory improvements achieved. The application of the calibrated kinematic parameters showed an improvement of 67% in the evaluation of the RMS error distance between the odometry trajectory and the ground truth trajectory, and an improvement of 71% in the RMS error evaluation of the absolute difference between the angular orientation of the mobile robot during these trajectories. The application of the calibrated kinematic parameters also showed a reduction in the maximum absolute differences between the odometry and ground truth trajectories, which have been reduced from 76 mm to 23 mm and from 5.86° to 1.77°. Similar improvements have been obtained in the error in the determination of the final location and angular orientation of the mobile robot that has been reduced from 74 mm to 16 mm and from and from 5.32° to 0.73°. Figure 10 shows the application of the calibrated odometry to the trajectories shown previously in Figure 7, which correspond to five repetitions of the R1 calibration trajectory.

Table 6. Summary of the average trajectory errors obtained with the uncalibrated and calibrated kinematic parameters.

	RMS Error		Max Error		Final position error		$CF_{VALIDATION}$
	Distance (m)	Abs(angle) (°)	Distance (m)	Abs(angle) (°)	Distance (m)	Abs(angle) (°)	
Uncalibrated	0.040	3.00	0.076	5.86	0.074	5.32	0.1242
Calibrated (STE-GA5)	0.013	0.86	0.023	1.77	0.016	0.73	0.0222
Improvement	67.00%	71.22%	68.99%	69.82%	78.38%	86.24%	82.14%

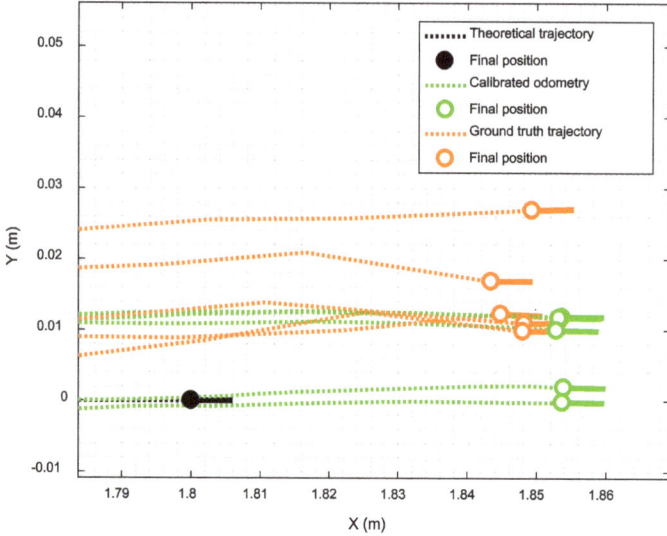

Figure 10. Planned trajectory (back dotted line) zoomed at the planned ending position and orientation of the mobile robot (black point and line); measured ground truth trajectories (orange dotted line) detailing the final position and orientation of the mobile robot (orange circle and line); and odometry trajectories measured after calibration (green dotted line) detailing the ending position and orientation of the mobile robot (green circle and line).

4. Discussion and Conclusions

This paper proposes a general procedure to evaluate and correct the systematic odometry errors of a real three-wheeled omnidirectional mobile robot (1.760 m, 30 kg) designed as a versatile personal assistant tool. This procedure is based on the definition of 36 representative straight and curved calibration trajectories which together depict a characteristic flower-shaped figure.

The odometry and ground truth trajectories measured while performing each one of these calibration trajectories are measured and registered for later offline fitting of the kinematic parameters of the mobile robot in order to match these two trajectories. This paper has evaluated the use of different trajectory subsets and the use of two iterative matching strategies based on gradient search minimization and genetic algorithms. The best matching between odometry and ground truth trajectories has been obtained using genetic algorithms and five repetitions of all calibration trajectories. The fitting of the kinematic parameters has shown differences higher than 10% in the distance from the wheels to the center of the mobile robot (R_a, R_b, R_c), and between 2 and 5% in the radii of the wheels (r_a, r_b, r_c). This approach has the advantage of the feasible physical interpretation of the fitting results in the omnidirectional mobile robot.

The fitting results have been validated with five new additional repetitions of all these measured trajectories, providing an average improvement of 82% in the evaluation of the multivariable cost function that compares the final position and orientation of the mobile robot. The best performances of the genetic algorithm agree with the results of Savaee et al. [15], and confirm that the mutation and combinations generated during the search based on genetic algorithms has the best chance to detect the global minimum of the multivariate function that summarizes the differences between the odometry and ground truth trajectories of the mobile robot. In this case, the genetic algorithm search (strategy STE-GA5) required 187 iterations and 37.545 function counts to meet the stopping criteria.

The final conclusion of the comparative calibration analysis performed in this work is that the use of curved calibration trajectories is more representative to calibrate the kinematic parameters of an omnidirectional mobile robot. This conclusion agrees with Batlle et al. [17], who proposed the use of four curved trajectories for general omnidirectional mobile robot calibration, and with Maddahi et al. [11], who concluded that the performance of a calibration procedure depends on the type of trajectory analyzed.

Future works will analyze the application of this procedure to different units of the same mobile robot type in order to validate its application in a general manufacturing stage.

Author Contributions: Conceptualization, J.P.; Investigation, E.R. and E.C.; Methodology, J.P. and E.R.; Software, E.C.; Writing—original draft, E.R.; Writing—review & editing, J.P. All authors have read and agreed to the published version of the manuscript.

Funding: This research received no external funding.

Institutional Review Board Statement: Not applicable.

Informed Consent Statement: Not applicable.

Data Availability Statement: Not applicable.

Conflicts of Interest: The authors declare that they have no conflict of interest.

Appendix A

Table A1. Description of the motion commands and the corresponding target angular velocities of the wheels corresponding to the calibration trajectories shown in Figure 9.

Trajectory	Motion Command				Target Angular Velocities (rpm)		
	v (m/s)	$\alpha(°)$	ω(rad/s)	d(m)	ω_{Ma}	ω_{Mb}	ω_{Mc}
R1	0.35	0	0	1.0	−19.557	0.000	19.557
R2	0.35	30	0	1.0	−11.291	−11.291	22.583
R3	0.35	60	0	1.0	0.000	−19.557	19.557
R4	0.35	90	0	1.0	11.291	−22.583	11.291
R5	0.35	120	0	1.0	19.557	−19.557	0.000
R6	0.35	150	0	1.0	22.583	−11.291	−11.291
R7	0.35	180	0	1.0	19.557	0.000	−19.557
R8	0.35	210	0	1.0	11.291	11.291	−22.583
R9	0.35	240	0	1.0	0.000	19.557	−19.557
R10	0.35	270	0	1.0	−11.291	22.583	−11.291
R11	0.35	300	0	1.0	−19.557	19.557	0.000
R12	0.35	330	0	1.0	−22.583	11.291	11.291
G1	0.35	0	0.35	1.0	−15.154	4.404	23.961
G2	0.35	30	0.35	1.0	−6.888	−6.888	26.986
G3	0.35	60	0.35	1.0	4.404	−15.154	23.961
G4	0.35	90	0.35	1.0	15.695	−18.179	15.695
G5	0.35	120	0.35	1.0	23.961	−15.154	4.404
G6	0.35	150	0.35	1.0	26.986	−6.888	−6.888
G7	0.35	180	0.35	1.0	23.961	4.404	−15.154
G8	0.35	210	0.35	1.0	15.695	15.695	−18.179
G9	0.35	240	0.35	1.0	4.404	23.961	−15.154
G10	0.35	270	0.35	1.0	−6.888	26.986	−6.888
G11	0.35	300	0.35	1.0	−15.154	23.961	4.404
G12	0.35	330	0.35	1.0	−18.179	15.695	15.695
B1	0.35	0	−0.35	1.0	−23.961	−4.404	15.154
B2	0.35	30	−0.35	1.0	−15.695	−15.695	18.179
B3	0.35	60	−0.35	1.0	−4.404	−23.961	15.154
B4	0.35	90	−0.35	1.0	6.888	−26.986	6.888
B5	0.35	120	−0.35	1.0	15.154	−23.961	−4.404
B6	0.35	150	−0.35	1.0	18.179	−15.695	−15.695
B7	0.35	180	−0.35	1.0	15.154	−4.404	−23.961
B8	0.35	210	−0.35	1.0	6.888	6.888	−26.986
B9	0.35	240	−0.35	1.0	−4.404	15.154	−23.961
B10	0.35	270	−0.35	1.0	−15.695	18.179	−15.695
B11	0.35	300	−0.35	1.0	−23.961	15.154	−4.404
B12	0.35	330	−0.35	1.0	−26.986	6.888	6.888

References

1. Borenstein, J.; Koren, Y. Motion Control Analysis of a Mobile Robot. *J. Dyn. Syst. Meas. Control* **1987**, *109*, 73–79. [CrossRef]
2. Borenstein, J.; Everett, H.R.; Feng, L.; Wehe, D. Mobile Robot Positioning: Sensors and Techniques. *J. Robot. Syst.* **1997**, *14*, 231–249. [CrossRef]
3. Borenstein, J.; Feng, L. Measurement and correction of systematic odometry errors in mobile robots. *IEEE Trans. Robot. Autom.* **1996**, *12*, 869–880. [CrossRef]
4. Gargiulo, A.M.; di Stefano, I.; Genova, A. Model-Based Slippage Estimation to Enhance Planetary Rover Localization with Wheel Odometry. *Appl. Sci.* **2021**, *11*, 5490. [CrossRef]
5. Zwierzchowski, J.; Pietrala, D.; Napieralski, J.; Napieralski, A. A Mobile Robot Position Adjustment as a Fusion of Vision System and Wheels Odometry in Autonomous Track Driving. *Appl. Sci.* **2021**, *11*, 4496. [CrossRef]
6. Xue, H.; Fu, H.; Dai, B. IMU-Aided High-Frequency Lidar Odometry for Autonomous Driving. *Appl. Sci.* **2019**, *9*, 1506. [CrossRef]
7. Palacín, J.; Martínez, D.; Rubies, E.; Clotet, E. Mobile Robot Self-Localization with 2D Push-Broom LIDAR in a 2D Map. *Sensors* **2020**, *20*, 2500. [CrossRef] [PubMed]
8. Lluvia, I.; Lazkano, E.; Ansuategi, A. Active Mapping and Robot Exploration: A Survey. *Sensors* **2021**, *21*, 2445. [CrossRef] [PubMed]
9. Xiao, K.; Yu, W.; Liu, W.; Qu, F.; Ma, Z. High-Precision SLAM Based on the Tight Coupling of Dual Lidar Inertial Odometry for Multi-Scene Applications. *Appl. Sci.* **2022**, *12*, 939. [CrossRef]
10. Sousa, R.B.; Petry, M.R.; Moreira, A.P. Evolution of Odometry Calibration Methods for Ground Mobile Robots. In Proceedings of the IEEE International Conference on Autonomous Robot Systems and Competitions (ICARSC), Ponta Delgada, Portugal, 15–17 April 2020; pp. 294–299. [CrossRef]
11. Maddahi, Y.; Maddahi, A.; Sepehri, N. Calibration of omnidirectional wheeled mobile robots: Method and experiments. *Robotica* **2013**, *31*, 969–980. [CrossRef]
12. Lin, P.; Liu, D.; Yang, D.; Zou, Q.; Du, Y.; Cong, M. Calibration for Odometry of Omnidirectional Mobile Robots Based on Kinematic Correction. In Proceedings of the 14th International Conference on Computer Science & Education (ICCSE), Toronto, ON, Canada, 19–21 August 2019; pp. 139–144. [CrossRef]
13. Li, Y.; Ge, S.; Dai, S.; Zhao, L.; Yan, X.; Zheng, Y.; Shi, Y. Kinematic Modeling of a Combined System of Multiple Mecanum-Wheeled Robots with Velocity Compensation. *Sensors* **2020**, *20*, 75. [CrossRef]
14. Lu, Z.; He, G.; Wang, R.; Wang, S.; Zhang, Y.; Liu, C.; Chen, D.; Hou, T. An Orthogonal Wheel Odometer for Positioning in a Relative Coordinate System on a Floating Ground. *Appl. Sci.* **2021**, *11*, 11340. [CrossRef]
15. Savaee, E.; Hanzaki, A.R. A New Algorithm for Calibration of an Omni-Directional Wheeled Mobile Robot Based on Effective Kinematic Parameters Estimation. *J. Intell. Robot. Syst.* **2021**, *101*, 28. [CrossRef]
16. Bożek, A. Discovering Stick-Slip-Resistant Servo Control Algorithm Using Genetic Programming. *Sensors* **2022**, *22*, 383. [CrossRef] [PubMed]
17. Batlle, J.A.; Font-Llagunes, J.M.; Barjau, A. Calibration for mobile robots with an invariant Jacobian. *Robot. Auton. Syst.* **2010**, *58*, 10–15. [CrossRef]
18. Palacín, J.; Clotet, E.; Martínez, D.; Martínez, D.; Moreno, J. Extending the Application of an Assistant Personal Robot as a Walk-Helper Tool. *Robotics* **2019**, *8*, 27. [CrossRef]
19. Penteridis, L.; D'Onofrio, G.; Sancarlo, D.; Giuliani, F.; Ricciardi, F.; Cavallo, F.; Greco, A.; Trochidis, I.; Gkiokas, A. Robotic and Sensor Technologies for Mobility in Older People. *Rejuvenation Res.* **2017**, *20*, 401–410. [CrossRef] [PubMed]
20. Palacín, J.; Rubies, E.; Clotet, E.; Martínez, D. Evaluation of the Path-Tracking Accuracy of a Three-Wheeled Omnidirectional Mobile Robot Designed as a Personal Assistant. *Sensors* **2021**, *21*, 7216. [CrossRef] [PubMed]
21. Palacín, J.; Martínez, D.; Rubies, E.; Clotet, E. Suboptimal Omnidirectional Wheel Design and Implementation. *Sensors* **2021**, *21*, 865. [CrossRef] [PubMed]
22. Palacín, J.; Martínez, D. Improving the Angular Velocity Measured with a Low-Cost Magnetic Rotary Encoder Attached to a Brushed DC Motor by Compensating Magnet and Hall-Effect Sensor Misalignments. *Sensors* **2021**, *21*, 4763. [CrossRef]
23. Crowley, J.L. Asynchronous Control of Orientation and Displacement in a Robot Vehicle. In Proceedings of the 1989 IEEE International Conference on Robotics and Automation, Scottsdale, AZ, USA, 14–19 May 1989; pp. 1277–1282. [CrossRef]
24. Feng, L.; Koren, Y.; Borenstein, J. Cross-Coupling Motion Controller for Mobile Robots. *IEEE J. Control. Syst.* **1993**, *13*, 35–43. [CrossRef]
25. Goldberg, D. What every computer scientist should know about floating-point arithmetic. *ACM Comput. Surv.* **1991**, *23*, 5–48. [CrossRef]
26. Smieszek, M.; Dobrzanska, M.; Dobrzanski, P. Measurement of Wheel Radius in an Automated Guided Vehicle. *Appl. Sci.* **2020**, *10*, 5490. [CrossRef]
27. Hess, D.; Kuenemund, F.; Roehrig, C. Simultaneous Calibration of Odometry and external Sensors of Omnidirectional Automated Guided Vehicles (AGVs). In Proceedings of the 47st International Symposium on Robotics, Munich, Germany, 21–22 June 2016; pp. 1–8.

28. Yagfarov, R.; Ivanou, M.; Afanasyev, I. Map Comparison of Lidar-based 2D SLAM Algorithms Using Precise Ground Truth. In Proceedings of the 15th International Conference on Control, Automation, Robotics and Vision (ICARCV), Singapore, 18–21 November 2018; pp. 1979–1983. [CrossRef]
29. Iaboni, C.; Patel, H.; Lobo, D.; Choi, J.W.; Abichandani, P. Event Camera Based Real-Time Detection and Tracking of Indoor Ground Robots. *IEEE Access* **2021**, *9*, 166588–166602. [CrossRef]

Article

Virtual Reality-Based Interface for Advanced Assisted Mobile Robot Teleoperation

J. Ernesto Solanes *, Adolfo Muñoz, Luis Gracia and Josep Tornero

Instituto de Diseño y Fabricación, Universitat Politècnica de València, 46022 Valencia, Spain; amunyoz@upvnet.upv.es (A.M.); luigraca@isa.upv.es (L.G.); jtornero@isa.upv.es (J.T.)
* Corresponding: esolanes@idf.upv.es

Abstract: This work proposes a new interface for the teleoperation of mobile robots based on virtual reality that allows a natural and intuitive interaction and cooperation between the human and the robot, which is useful for many situations, such as inspection tasks, the mapping of complex environments, etc. Contrary to previous works, the proposed interface does not seek the realism of the virtual environment but provides all the minimum necessary elements that allow the user to carry out the teleoperation task in a more natural and intuitive way. The teleoperation is carried out in such a way that the human user and the mobile robot cooperate in a synergistic way to properly accomplish the task: the user guides the robot through the environment in order to benefit from the intelligence and adaptability of the human, whereas the robot is able to automatically avoid collisions with the objects in the environment in order to benefit from its fast response. The latter is carried out using the well-known potential field-based navigation method. The efficacy of the proposed method is demonstrated through experimentation with the Turtlebot3 Burger mobile robot in both simulation and real-world scenarios. In addition, usability and presence questionnaires were also conducted with users of different ages and backgrounds to demonstrate the benefits of the proposed approach. In particular, the results of these questionnaires show that the proposed virtual reality based interface is intuitive, ergonomic and easy to use.

Keywords: virtual reality interface; mobile robot teleoperation; obstacle avoidance; mobile robot navigation; motion planning

Citation: Solanes, J.E.; Muñoz, A.; Gracia, L.;Tornero, J. Virtual Reality-Based Interface for Advanced Assisted Mobile Robot Teleoperation. *Appl. Sci.* **2022**, *12*, 6071. https:// doi.org/10.3390/app12126071

Academic Editor: Manuel Armada

Received: 12 May 2022
Accepted: 13 June 2022
Published: 15 June 2022

Publisher's Note: MDPI stays neutral with regard to jurisdictional claims in published maps and institutional affiliations.

Copyright: © 2022 by the authors. Licensee MDPI, Basel, Switzerland. This article is an open access article distributed under the terms and conditions of the Creative Commons Attribution (CC BY) license (https:// creativecommons.org/licenses/by/ 4.0/).

1. Introduction

1.1. Motivation

The main area of this work is mobile robots, which play an increasingly primary role in our society. Due to rapid development of AI, powerful lithium batteries, and low-power microchips, mobile robots are becoming cheaper, available to more people, and introduced in various areas of life, taking more significant roles in society and removing labor-intensive jobs in such areas as rescue operations [1–3], space exploration [4–6], military application [7,8] industrial use [9–11], underwater exploration [12–14], and healthcare applications [15–17], among others.

While many approaches can be found in the literature regarding the automatic control and navigation of this kind of robot, most of the mentioned applications imply the interaction between humans and robots. This collaboration is usually done in such a way that the human guides the robot remotely while the robot navigates in a hostile and/or dangerous environment for the human. However, many approaches do not develop a natural and intuitive interaction for the human [18–21] and, hence, the resulting human–robot cooperation may be dismissed.

This paper develops a new virtual reality-based interface for mobile robot navigation in unknown scenarios, providing an intuitive and natural interaction for the user.

1.2. Literature Review

The main object of this work is the teleoperation of robotic systems, in general, and mobile robots, in particular. The teleoperation or remote control of robotic systems by humans has been deeply studied in the past decades [22] and is still an ongoing tendency in research. Robot teleoperation is carried out for many reasons: to operate in hazardous environments (e.g., radioactive zones [23,24], aerial zones [25,26], underwater areas [27,28], or in space [29]); to conduct accurate surgeries [30–33]; to perform rescue operations [34], etc.

Recently, advanced artificial intelligence (AI) techniques have facilitated the automation of many complex operations that previously had to be conducted using robot teleoperation. Nevertheless, there are still many robot applications that cannot be completely automated due to their subjectivity or complexity. However, these partially automated tasks can significantly benefit from human–robot cooperation by means of shared-control architectures [35]. In this sense, many contributions have been developed focusing on the human–robot interaction in teleoperation tasks [21,36–42], as is the case of this work.

Telepresence [22] provides the user with an interface which makes the direct control task less dependent on his or her skills and concentration. Telepresence for direct control teleoperation is a strong trend in recent research developments due to the introduction of visual interfaces [30], virtual and augmented reality [39], haptic devices [43], or a combination of them [31,40,44]. For example, the authors in [22] provided the user with an interface which makes the direct control task less dependent on his or her skills and concentration. The authors in [37] proposed an approach where one arm of a bimanual robot is teleoperated to grasp a target object, while the other develops an automatic task of visual servoing to keep the object in sight of a camera and avoid occlusions, thus making the teleoperation easier.

The success of telepresence lies directly upon the skills of the user who performs the teleoperation [9,45]. For this reason, many current approaches propose to incorporate constraints to avoid the user commanding the robot in a wrong way. For instance, in [32] virtual fixtures (i.e., virtual barriers) were included to automatically modify the reference position provided by the user in order to confine it within the allowed area. In [24,43], haptic devices were used to prevent the user from commanding reference positions beyond certain limits.

However, assisted teleoperation with telepresence interfaces and virtual barriers is still an ongoing research field due to its drawbacks, since the control is still held by the human [36]. In this regard, this article proposes to use the well-known potential field-based navigation method together with virtual reality devices to improve the current assisted teleoperation of mobile robots.

Virtual Reality-Based Interfaces

Technical advances in the development of virtual environments (VE) and virtual reality (VR) headsets and devices for the video games industry [46,47] or social media [48,49] have now made it possible to develop applications related to human–robot interaction. In particular, in mobile robot applications, some interesting works using VR can be found. For instance, the authors in [9] proposed an VR interface for training operators, who teleoperated the movement of a mobile robot with two arms for industrial pick-and-place tasks, and tested it with several users to determine the improvement obtained. Authors in [50] provided an approach to reduce the effects of time delays during the teleoperation based on VR and optimization data techniques. Authors in [51] developed a VR simulator that recreated a team of selective compliance assembly arms (SCARA) to include cloud resources to help users to improve the task performance. Authors in [52] presented an immersive SLAM-based VR system for the teleoperation of mobile manipulators in unknown environments. In this approach, the user totally guides the mobile robot, which is constrained into a limited area. A 3D real-time environment reconstruction map is shown in the VE, allowing the user to "see" the real environment.

The majority of the studies relating VR and the teleoperation of mobile robots are focused on improving the task performance (i.e., reducing the time needed to complete the operation, and incorporating real elements in the VE). However, to the best of the authors' knowledge, few of them are focused on human–robot interaction aspects: interface ergonomics, quality of the interface, ease of interaction with virtual elements, interference of the virtual elements with the task target, etc. Note that the improvement of all these features, which is the main goal of this work, can be decisive for the success of the developed interface.

1.3. Proposal

This paper proposes a new virtual reality-based interface for the teleoperation of mobile robots in unknown scenarios. The proposed interface is designed to be natural and immersive to the user, reducing the learning process of the interface. The proposed interface is fully described in the article, and its efficacy is experimentally demonstrated using the mobile robot Turtlebot3 Burger. In addition, a complete study with users of different ages and backgrounds is detailed to determine the quality and usability of the proposed interface.

Concretely, this work presents several contributions as highlighted below:

- Unlike the works mentioned above, this work presents an intuitive interface designed to teleoperate mobile robots in totally unknown environments. To do this, the user is able to guide the robot through the environment in order to benefit from the intelligence and adaptability of the human, whereas the robot is able to automatically avoid collisions with the objects in the environment in order to benefit from its fast response.
- Contrary to the aforementioned works, the proposed interface does not seek the realism of the virtual environment but provides all the minimum necessary elements that allow the user to carry out the teleoperation task in a more natural and intuitive way. Hence, the proposed interface establishes different virtual elements (e.g., mobile robot, user reference, 2D map of the environment, information related to the robot or task, and the 3D position of the objects detected in real-time, among others) that allow the user to quickly interact with the interface and successfully perform the robot teleoperation task.
- In contrast to the works about virtual reality interfaces mentioned above, where virtual reality controllers are used for interacting with the virtual environment, this work proposes the use of gamepads to carry out this interaction. Thus, this work aims to improve the ergonomics of the user, allowing them to teleoperate the robots in a natural way for long periods of time.
- This work is focused on improving the interaction between human users and interfaces for the teleoperation of mobile robots. In this sense, in addition to conventional studies, similar to those carried out in the abovementioned works to establish the viability and efficiency of the proposed interface, this work also carries out a study of the experience lived by users of different ages, gender and backgrounds when using the proposed interface in order to establish its degree of naturalness and intuition.

1.4. Content of the Article

The content of the article is as follows. Section 2 describes the VR-based interface developed in this work. Subsequently, the interface functionalities, performance and effectiveness of the proposed VR-based interface are shown in Section 3 through experimental results. Moreover, the usability of the interface as well as other aspects are also studied in Section 3 through several questionnaires and tests conducted with users of different ages and backgrounds. Finally, some conclusions are outlined in Section 4.

2. Proposed Application

2.1. Overview

The application developed in this work consists of two workspaces: the local workspace in which the VR headset is used and the remote workspace in which the robotic system operates, as shown in Figure 1.

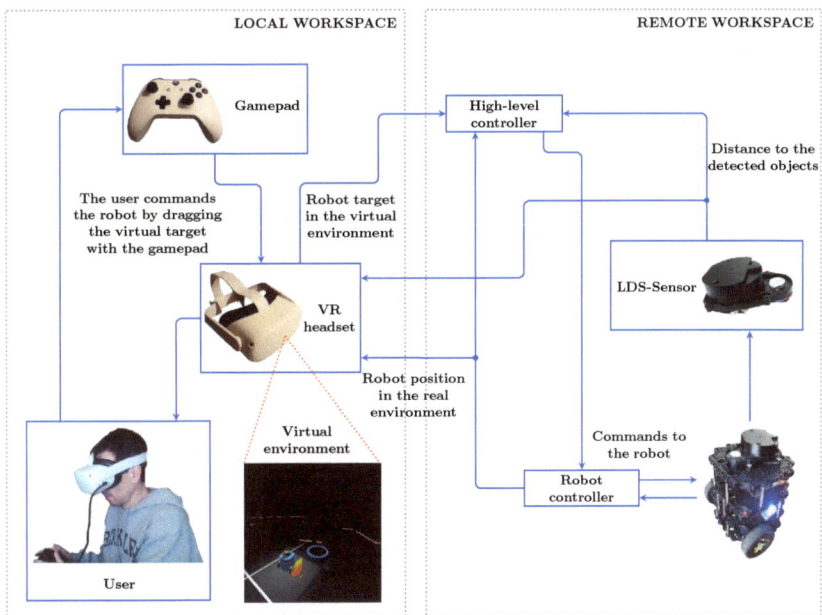

Figure 1. Remote human–robot interaction using VR with data from LDS sensor and the robot odometry.

In the *local workspace*, the user is able to visualize the robot and its environment by wearing the VR headset. Without loss of generality, this work uses the Oculus Quest 2 VR headset [53], with a LCD screen with a resolution of 1832 × 1920 pixels per eye and refresh frequency of up to 90 Hz, 6 GB of RAM, and a Quadcomm Snapdragon XR2 processor. In addition, this device allows standalone applications.

In this work, the *Unity Real-Time Development Platform* [54] is used to develop the virtual environment. Hence, the real robot is modeled and included in the virtual world. The location of the detected obstacles in the virtual world is updated according to that of the corresponding real-world objects, which is obtained online from sensor measurements. In particular, in the proposed application, the robot configuration is obtained reading the pose (i.e., position and orientation) values from the robot controller, whereas the accurate location of the detected objects is obtained using a 360° laser distance sensor (LDS) mounted on top of the robot.

In addition, a gamepad device is used to allow the user to drag the reference through the virtual workspace, thus resulting in the movement of both real and virtual robots. A Bluetooth communication is established between the gamepad and the VR headset. In this work, the Xbox wireless controller (gamepad) [55] is used. Note that virtual reality headsets use a different set of controllers [53], one per hand, to allow free movement to the user in order to achieve a better virtual reality experience. However, the ergonomics of these controllers is not developed for applications such as the one presented in this work, which is more related to conventional games. Hence, this paper proposed the use of gamepads, which is more intuitive, known by users and ergonomic for robot teleoperation applications.

In the *remote workspace*, the high level controller of the robot receives the position command from the VR application, which corresponds to the reference position in the virtual workspace that is given by the movement performed by user with the gamepad. The controller also receives from the LDS mentioned above the distance between the detected objects and the mobile robot boundary. Thus, according to these values, the high-level controller computes a proper robot velocity and commands the corresponding wheel speed values to the robot controller. In particular, the high-level controller used in this work is based on the well-known potential field method: on the one hand, the distance to the obstacles measured by the LDS sensor is used to compute a "repulsive" force in order to avoid collisions with the obstacles in the environment; on the other hand, the reference position provided by the user at every time instant is used to compute an "attractive" force. Therefore, this type of controller is purely *reactive* to the user teleoperation commands and to the obstacles surrounding the mobile robot. Thus, there is no kind of high-level planning and, hence, there is no a priori path to be followed. More details about the mentioned high-level controller for the robotic system are given in Section 2.3.

Without loss of generality, this work uses a commercial mobile robot, the Turtlebot3 Burger [56], which is equipped with two servos Dynamixel XL430-W250-T for the wheels, an OpenCR (32-bit ARM Cortex-M7) embedded controller (Robot controller), a Raspberry Pi-3 (High-level controller) and a 360° LiDAR sensor (LDS), see [56] for further details. The electronic and mechanical behavior of this mobile robot, as well as the low-level frequency control and time delays of the embedded controller developed by the robot manufacturer, are sufficient to carry out the validation of the approach proposed in this work. However, custom low-level controllers could be developed in order to improve its behavior.

2.2. Virtual Environment

The virtual environment consists of an "infinite" floor divided by a grid of 1m side squares. The user can modify the height of this floor to accommodate it to his/her point of view. The rest of the elements are put over this floor. In order to help the user to have a quick idea of the distance between objects, each square of the grid is divided into four small squares of 0.5 m of the side, depicting a mosaic of gray colors that allows to easily distinguish one from the others. In addition, a dark theme to the sky is chosen to facilitate the user visibility of the relevant elements present in the VE; see Figure 2. Next, a description of each element and the functionality of the proposed VE are detailed.

Figure 2 shows the main elements of the proposed VE. As commented before, the Turtlebot3 Burger mobile robot for the experimental sections is used in this work; see Section 3 for further details. The 3D model, representing the robot in the virtual space, consists of the main structure (body, in blue), the LDS sensor attached to the body, and the wheels of the mobile robot (in gray). It is worth mentioning that, in the virtual environment, the wheels rotate independently of each other to simulate the real movement of the robot. Note that in the proposed approach, the user does not directly move the mobile robot; rather, the user indicates the reference position that the robot has to track. If this reference position can be reached by the robot, the robot will move to the indicated location. Otherwise, the robot will hold on as close as possible to the indicated reference position, avoiding collisions with the obstacles in its environment. As shown in Figure 2a, the reference position provided by the user, which has to be tracked by the mobile robot, is represented as a blue circle, whereas the detected obstacles are represented by a set of quads getting into virtual brown "walls"; see Figure 2b,d. The transparency, color and height of these "walls" are chosen to indicate the presence of obstacles without disturbing the visibility of the user during the teleoperation task.

In addition, a 2D map is also developed to allow the user to have an orthogonal view of the 3D environment; see Figure 2a,b. The 2D map can be activated and deactivated by the user at any moment by pressing and releasing, respectively, a stick of the gamepad. Moreover, when the 2D map is activated, the user can still command the robot and simultaneously modify the map view, i.e., zoom in/out or move around the map. The user can see the following information in the 2D map: the detected objects (in yellow); the robot position (blue circumference); the reference position (green circumference); and a 1 m side square grid to easily locate the different elements in the map. Once the teleoperation task is finished, the user can save the 2D resulting map generated.

Furthermore, the user can activate a panel showing relevant task information, such as robot speed or the remaining distance to the target. This information automatically disappears after 3 s to reduce the number of command buttons.

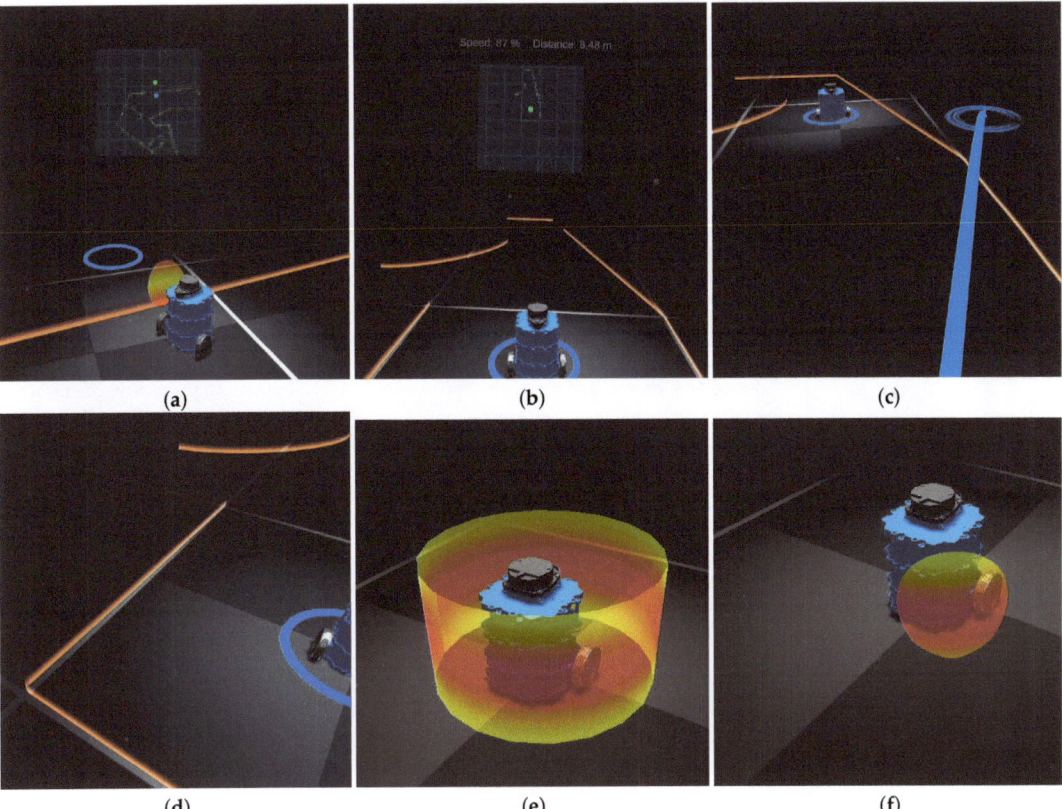

Figure 2. VE overview. (**a**) The 2D map view and 3D view. (**b**) Requested information data. (**c**) Teleporting (blue arrowed circle). (**d**) Detected objects (elements in brown). (**e**) Mobile robot boundary (full view). (**f**) Mobile robot boundary (local view). 2D map: robot (blue circumference in (**a**)); reference (green circumference in (**a**)); detected objects (yellow points in (**a**,**b**)). 3D environment: reference (blue circle in (**a**)); system information (i.e., robot velocity and distance to the target) in (**b**); teleporting (blue arrowed circle in (**c**)); detected objects (brown walls in all figures); mobile robot boundary as a circle (2D) or cylinder (3D) (red–yellow elements in (**e**,**f**)).

Note that, if the proposed element for the mobile robot boundary (i.e., the circle in 2D or cylinder in 3D; see Figure 2e) was shown at any moment, the user view of the robot and the other virtual objects would be difficult and may affect the user task performance. In order to overcome this, a new shader was developed [57] to measure the minimum distance between the detected obstacles and the mobile robot boundary. In this way, only the affected part of the boundary element is displayed. In addition, as the closest obstacle approaches to the mobile robot boundary, the corresponding part of the boundary element is gradually displayed; see Figure 2f.

Moreover, the user is allowed to move through the VE in two ways:

- *Physically:* the VR headset position and orientation is tracked at any moment and, hence, the user is able to move through the environment as if they were in the real workspace (In general, this movement is limited by a security region free of obstacles established a priori. To avoid this problem, one possibility could be the use of VR omnidirectional treadmills [58]).
- *Teleporting:* the user can "jump" from their current position to another position in the environment using the gamepad. Figure 2c shows the designed teleporting element, which consists of an animated blue arrowed circle. This element is designed according to the standard representation of teleporting in most current VR applications. Note that, when the teleporting option is activated, the user cannot simultaneously move the reference position of the robot for security reasons.

Finally, two types of sounds are developed to increase the feeling of reality in the VE:

- The movement of the robot produces a characteristic sound due to the robot servos, whose treble variation depends on the speed of the robot. To give it more realism, this sound is recorded directly from the actual sound of the robot moving at low speeds. The treble change of this base sound is carried out proportionally to the speed of the wheels, producing a real sensation of movement of the robot in the VE. This sound effect cannot be disabled by the user. In addition, this is a 3D sound that changes depending on the distance from the user to the robot position, providing the user with a more realistic level of immersion in the task.
- An alarm sound is also included to warn the user of collisions between the robot boundary and the obstacles in its environment. As in the previous case, this is also a 3D sound. However, contrary to the later, the user is allowed to deactivate this warning sound, since the nature of the proposed assisted teleoperation approach can lead to situations where the user, for instance, takes the robot to areas where collisions occur, or takes the robot to very tight zones where collisions cannot be avoided. In either case, the user's attention would be on the robot, so the visual effect of the boundary alone would suffice. Note also that this warning sound for long periods could become annoying.

2.3. High Level Controller: Mobile Robot Navigation with the Potential Field-Based Method

The well-known conventional potential field-based method [59] is typically used for mobile robot navigation with collision avoidance. In particular, this approach consists of using virtual forces, i.e., attractive and repulsive forces, to determine the robot movement, as detailed below.

The commonly used attractive and repulsive forces have the following form [60]:

$$\mathbf{F}_{att} = K_{att}\left(\mathbf{p}_{ref} - \mathbf{p}\right) \tag{1}$$

$$\mathbf{F}_{rep} = \begin{cases} K_{rep}\left(\rho^{-1} - \rho_0^{-1}\right)\rho^{-2}\nabla\rho & \text{if } \rho < \rho_0 \\ 0 & \text{otherwise,} \end{cases} \tag{2}$$

where vector $\mathbf{F}_{att}$ is the *attractive force* to the reference; vector $\mathbf{F}_{rep}$ is the *repulsive force* from the obstacles; the positive constants K_{att} and K_{rep} represent the gains of the attractive and repulsive forces, respectively; vectors $\mathbf{p}_{ref}$ and $\mathbf{p}$ are the reference position and the actual robot position, respectively; ρ is the minimum distance from the obstacles to the mobile robot boundary; vector $\nabla\rho$ represents the gradient of the mentioned minimum distance, i.e., a vector pointing from the closest obstacle to the mobile robot boundary; and ρ_0 is a positive constant denoting the distance of influence of the obstacles for the repulsive force.

Thus, the sum of all "forces" determines the magnitude and direction of the robot motion as follows:

$$\dot{\mathbf{p}}_{t,c} = \mathbf{F}_{att} + \mathbf{F}_{rep}, \tag{3}$$

where vector $\dot{\mathbf{p}}_{t,c}$ represents the commanded value for the velocity of the robot *tracking point*, i.e., the point of the mobile robot that tracks the reference signal.

Next, the specific mobile robot used in this work for the experimentation is taken into account to compute the minimum distance ρ between the detected obstacles and the mobile robot boundary, as well as the commands for the robot wheel velocities.

As mentioned before, due to the shape of the Turtlebot3 Burger, the 2D boundary for the mobile robot is simple modeled in this work as a circle (Without loss of generality, other 2D boundaries could also be considered for other specific mobile robots, e.g., a square or an ellipse, details omitted for brevity). Therefore, the minimum distance ρ between the detected obstacles and the mobile robot boundary is given by

$$\rho_i = R^{-2}\left(P_{x,i}^2 + P_{y,i}^2 - R^2\right)$$
$$\rho = \min\{\rho_i\}, \tag{4}$$

where R is the radius of the circle used to model the mobile robot boundary, $\mathbf{P}_i = [P_{x,i} \ P_{y,i}]^T$ is the 2D position of the i-th detected point of the obstacles relative to the center of the boundary circle, and ρ_i is the normalized distance from point $\mathbf{P}_i$ to the boundary circle. Note that this normalized distance has no units.

Since the Turtlebot3 Burger is a differential-drive mobile robot [61], the tracking point considered in this work is located on the longitudinal symmetry axis of the mobile robot and at a distance M from the rotation axle of the fixed wheels [62]. Hence, the commanded value for the mobile robot motion is given by [63]

$$\begin{bmatrix} v_c \\ \omega_c \end{bmatrix} = \begin{bmatrix} \cos(\theta) & \sin(\theta) \\ -\sin(\theta)/M & \cos(\theta)/M \end{bmatrix} \dot{\mathbf{p}}_{t,c} \tag{5}$$

$$\begin{bmatrix} \dot{\varphi}_{r,c} \\ \dot{\varphi}_{l,c} \end{bmatrix} = r^{-1} \begin{bmatrix} 1 & L/2 \\ 1 & -L/2 \end{bmatrix} \begin{bmatrix} v_c \\ \omega_c \end{bmatrix}, \tag{6}$$

where θ is the orientation angle of the mobile robot relative to the X-axis; r is the radius of the fixed wheels of the robot; L is the distance between the robot wheels; v_c and ω_c are the commanded value for the forward and angular velocities, respectively, of the mobile robot; and $\dot{\varphi}_{r,c}$ and $\dot{\varphi}_{l,c}$ are the commanded value for the angular velocity of the right and left wheels, respectively.

3. Results

With respect to the remote workspace hardware, Figure 3 shows the two different platforms that were used to demonstrate the suitability and effectiveness of the proposed approach. Figure 3a shows the simulator setup using Gazebo [64,65], whilst Figure 3b shows the real platform. In both cases, the robot used was the Turtlebot3 Burger, a differential-drive mobile robot equipped with two servos Dynamixel XL430-W250-T for the wheels, an OpenCR (32-bit ARM Cortex-M7) embedded controller (Robot controller), a RaspBerry Pi-3 (High-level controller), and an LDS, see [56] for further details. Obstacles with different shapes such as cylinders, ellipsoids (rounded corners) or boxes (sharp corners) were used in both platforms. Remark that the correct measurement of the distance from the mobile robot to the obstacles in the environment directly depends on the sensors used and the typology of the obstacle to be detected. In this work, an LDS sensor is sufficient to properly detect the obstacles used in the real experimentation. However, for objects with different characteristics (e.g., reflective materials and irregular shapes) other appropriate sensors (e.g., vision system, infrared sensors and ultrasonic sensors) could be required to obtain a proper obstacle detection so that these sensors could complement or replace the one used in this work.

With respect to the local workspace hardware, the Oculus Quest 2 VR headset [53] and the Xbox Wireless Controller (gamepad) [55] were used.

The communication protocol between the robot high-level controller and the VR headset was via Wi-Fi Ethernet TCP/UDP. The LSD data were updated at 1 Hz, and the robot pose (i.e., position and orientation) and user commands were updated at 20 Hz. The communication protocol between the VR headset and the Xbox wireless controller was via Bluetooth.

Figure 3. Experimental setup: remote environment. (**a**) Simulation setup. (**b**) Real setup.

The parameter values used for the high level controller of the robot are as follows: potential field-based method $\{\rho_0 = 0.35, K_{att} = 0.75, K_{rep} = 1\}$; robot kinematics $\{L = 0.16$ m, $M = 0.052$ m, $r = 0.033$ m$\}$; and boundary circle with radius $R = 0.18$ m and center located at the mobile robot tracking point.

3.1. Case Study 1: Virtual Application Functionalities and Behavior

A first experiment was conducted to show the proposed VE and its functionalities, which can be played in [66]. In this case, the Turtlebot3 Burger model using the Gazebo simulator was used, and the environment consisted of a cylinder obstacle and four rectangles defining the allowed square region; see Figure 3a. In particular, Figure 4 shows several frames of this experiment, whilst Figure 5 shows the trajectory and control performance of the overall experiment. The user can activate the 2D map option to see an orthogonal representation of the environment with the "discovered objects", and the location of the robot and the reference; see Figure 4a. The user is able to activate the task information data, e.g., robot velocity or target distance, at any moment; see Figure 4b. Note that these data depend on the application, and it would be easy to add the required information into the panel. Figure 4c shows the teleporting functionality. We remark that when this option is activated, the user cannot move the robot reference for security reasons. The obstacle avoidance capability can be seen from Figure 4c–f. Note that even though the user guides the reference through the cylinder obstacle, the robot successfully avoids this obstacle and reaches the reference when possible. This behavior can be better seen in Figure 5a,b. The repulsive force of the potential field-based navigation method becomes active around time instant 57 s when the distance ρ between the detected obstacles and the mobile robot boundary becomes lower than threshold ρ_0, see Figure 5a and Equation (2), causing the robot deviation from the trajectory marked by the reference (see Figure 5b). Note also that when the mentioned repulsive force is deactivated, i.e., when the distance ρ between the detected obstacles and the mobile robot boundary becomes larger than threshold ρ_0 (see Equation (2)), the robot returns to the path of the reference. Note that a so-called "trap situation" arises around time instant 115 s, i.e., the forward and angular velocities of the mobile robot are approximately zero; see Figure 5a. This is due to the fact that the robot has reached a corner; see position $X = Y = 2.5$ m in Figure 5b. Remark that these trap situations are typically present in potential field-based control schemes, and could be overcome if the user "helps" the robot in guiding the reference to an area reachable by the robot.

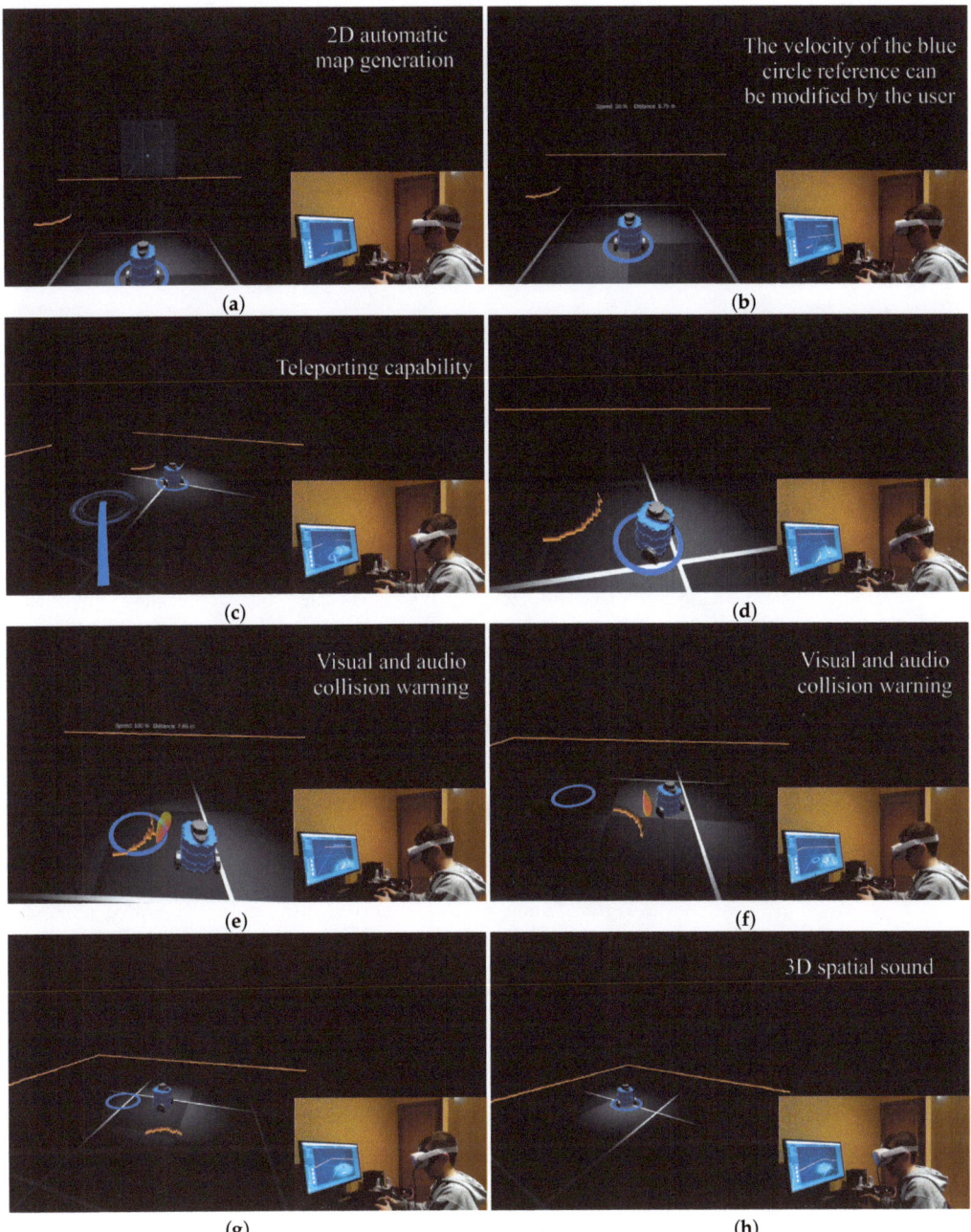

Figure 4. Case study 1: Frames of the video showing the functionalities of the proposed VR-based interface. See the video in [66]. (**a**) video: 0 min 16 s. (**b**) video: 0 min 21 s. (**c**) video: 0 min 39 s. (**d**) video: 0 min 43 s. (**e**) video: 0 min 49 s. (**f**) video: 0 min 57 s. (**g**) video: 1 min 00 s. (**h**) video: 1 min 05 s.

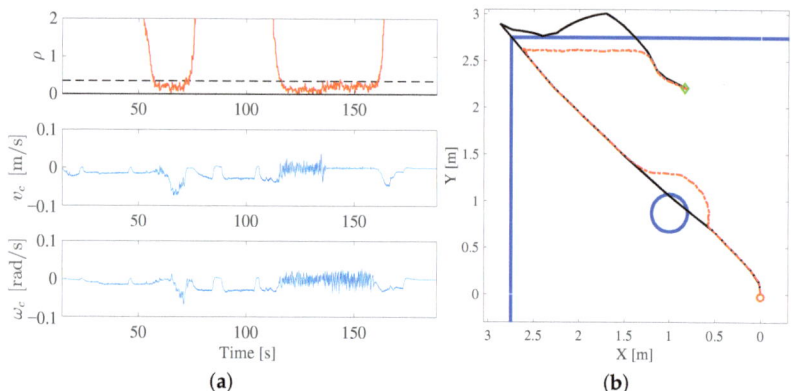

Figure 5. Case study 1: robot control performance. (**a**) Top graph: normalized distance ρ between the detected obstacles and the mobile robot boundary (the dashed line represents the distance threshold ρ_0 for the activation of the repulsive force). Middle and bottom graphs: linear and angular velocity commands for the mobile robot. (**b**) 2D robot trajectory: starting robot position (small orange circle); ending robot position (small green diamond); robot trajectory (red dashed line); user reference trajectory (solid black line); and obstacles (solid-thick blue lines).

In the video recording, the 3D sound effect can also be appreciate, i.e., both servo sounds and warning sounds are local to the robot, and the user perceives these sounds differently depending on the distance between the robot and the user.

3.2. Case Study 2: Real Robot Behavior

A second experiment was conducted to demonstrate the feasibility and suitability of the proposed virtual reality interface to control a real mobile robot. Figure 3b shows the remote environment used for this case study, which includes several obstacles located strategically to cause challenging situations, such as the avoidance of obstacles with round and sharp corners and trap situations. The video of this experiment can be played in [67].

For this second experiment, Figure 6 shows the normalized distance ρ between the detected obstacles and the mobile robot boundary together with the control velocity commands.

Moreover, Figure 7 shows several frames of this experiment related to the obstacle avoidance capability of the robot and how this is depicted in the VE. In particular, Figure 7a,c show the robot performance when avoiding an obstacle with rounded shape; see the time interval 45–74 s in the graphs of Figure 6a. Note that the robot deviates from the reference trajectory when the repulsive force of the potential field-based navigation method becomes active (i.e., $\rho < \rho_0$) (see the top graph in Figure 6a), and tries to go back to the reference once the mentioned repulsive force is deactivated, i.e., when $\rho > \rho_0$. In addition, Figure 7d–f show the robot performance when avoiding an obstacle with sharp corners; see time interval 85–97 s in the graphs of Figure 6a. As in the previous case, the activation of the repulsive force during this time span allows the mobile robot to successfully avoid this kind of obstacle (Figure 6b).

In addition, Figure 8 depicts several frames of this experiment to show how the robot deals with a trap situation, which occurs around time interval 137–175 s, see Figure 6a. As commented above, this behavior is typically present in potential field-based approaches and, in this case, the user successfully assists the robot to escape from this trap situation by guiding the reference trajectory to an area reachable by the robot.

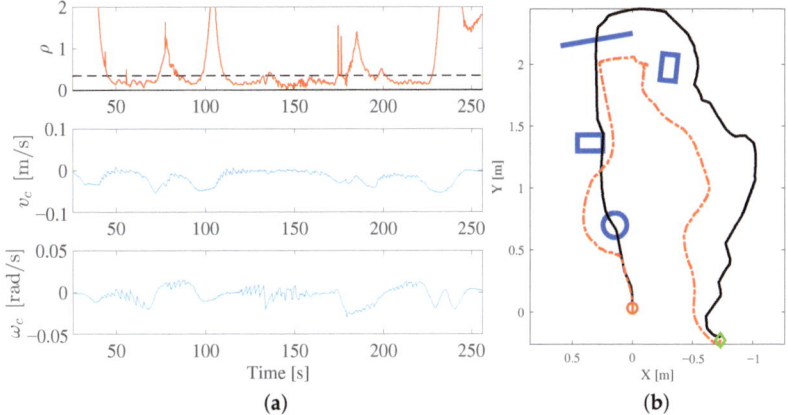

Figure 6. Case study 2: robot control performance. (**a**) Top graph: normalized distance ρ between the detected obstacles and the mobile robot boundary (the dashed line represents the distance threshold ρ_0 for the activation of the repulsive force). Middle and bottom graphs: linear and angular velocity commands for the mobile robot. (**b**) The 2D robot trajectory: starting robot position (small orange circle); ending robot position (small green diamond); robot trajectory (red dashed line); user reference trajectory (solid black line); and approximate location of the real obstacles (solid-thick blue lines).

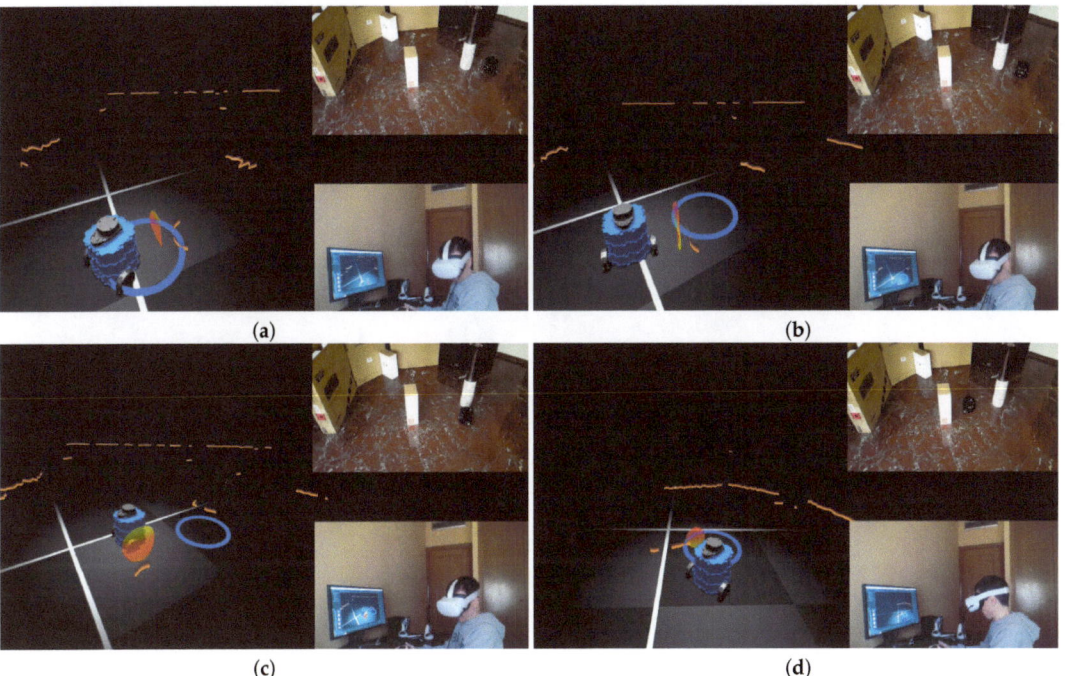

Figure 7. Cont.

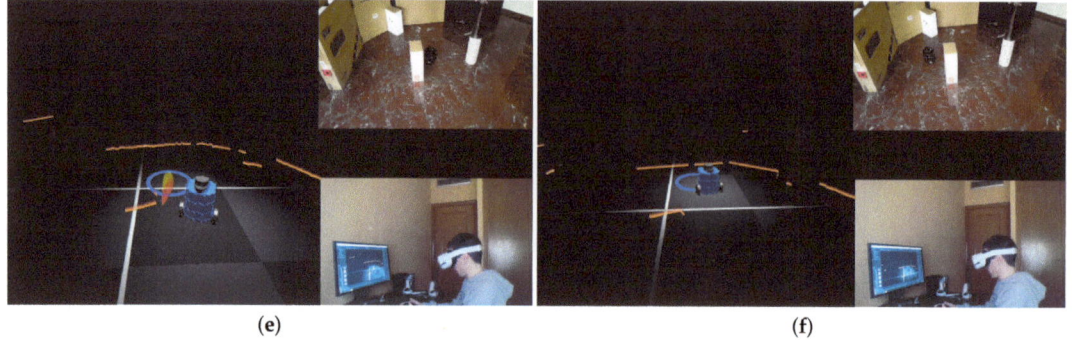

Figure 7. Case study 2: frames of the video showing obstacle avoidance situations. (**a**) video: 0 min 45 s. (**b**) video: 0 min 56 s. (**c**) video: 1 min 8 s. (**d**) video: 1 min 19 s. (**e**) video: 1 min 28 s. (**f**) video: 1 min 38 s.

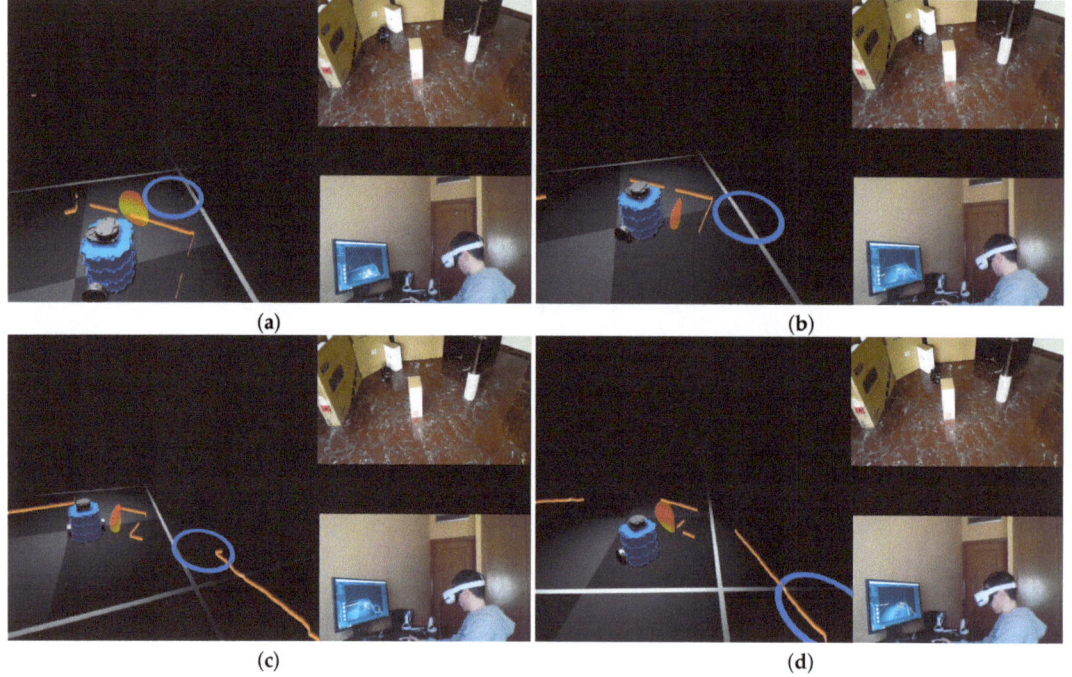

Figure 8. Case study 2: frames of the video showing a trap situation. (**a**) video: 2 min 20 s. (**b**) video: 2 min 32 s. (**c**) video: 2 min 42 s. (**d**) video: 2 min 55 s.

3.3. Usability Analysis Results

Similar to [68–70], several methods, such as the usability tests of applications, which are traditionally used to validate hardware and software, together with users' interviews, were conducted to show the advantages of the proposed approach.

Remark that most of the works proposing a new virtual reality interface for robot applications show its performance for just one user. However, there are few researchers that conduct some kind of usability test to prove its performance with several participants. For instance, in [7], a virtual reality application for the teleoperation of military mobile robotic systems was presented, and 15 participants were considered to prove its performance.

In [71], 10 participants were considered to validate a human–robot collaborative control in a virtual reality-based telepresence system. Finally, in [9], 11 participants were used to validate the mixed reality interface developed for robot teleoperation.

Note that the mentioned works considered a similar number of participants, ranging from 10 to 15 participants, and with an average value of 12. Therefore, 11 participants were selected in this work for the usability and presence questionnaires.

It is important to remark that considering a specific sample size gives rise to a certain margin of error [72]. In particular, for a sample of 11 participants and considering a confidence level of 95% and unlimited population size, the margin error is only 29.55%, which means that there is a 95% chance that the real value is within $\pm 29.55\%$ of the value obtained with the selected sample, which is fairly reasonable.

Furthermore, in order to have a representative sample, the 11 participants selected for the comparison experiment had different backgrounds. The main information about these participants is the following: 54.55% of the participants were female, whilst the remaining 45.45% were male; it was pretended to cover the maximum age range such that 18.18% of the participants were under 18 years old, 18.18% of them were between 18 and 40 years old, 18.18% of them were between 40 and 55 years old, 27.27% of them were between 55 and 70 years old, and 18.18% of the participants were older than 70 years old. With respect to their level of studies, 72.73% of the participants indicated basics studies, 18.18% of them indicated bachelor studies, and 9.09% of the participants indicated post-grade studies. In addition, 81.82% of the participants indicated that they had never used virtual reality headsets, whilst the remaining 18.18% of them indicated to have some experience with virtual reality applications and devices. Moreover, 63.64% of the participants indicated not having experience with video games and/or gamepad devices, whilst 36.36% of the participants indicated being video game players.

The procedure followed to conduct the tests was as follows. Firstly, a brief description of the virtual reality devices and robotic applications was given to each participant. Note that the task to be performed was to guide the mobile robot to a certain location to perform a rescue operation in the shortest possible time in an unknown environment. Hence, in second place, training was performed by each participant to become used to the VE and the control device (i.e., gamepad controls). In this case, the same scenario shown in Section 3.1 (see Figure 3a) with the Gazebo-based robot model was used. The training took around 15 min per participant.

After the training, the participant performed the required "rescue operation". In this case, a complete different scenario was used (see Figure 9) which was modeled using Blender 2.93 [73]. A demonstrative video can be played in [74]. All participants successfully performed the task, and the average time to complete it was 5 min 7 s, with a standard deviation of 17 s.

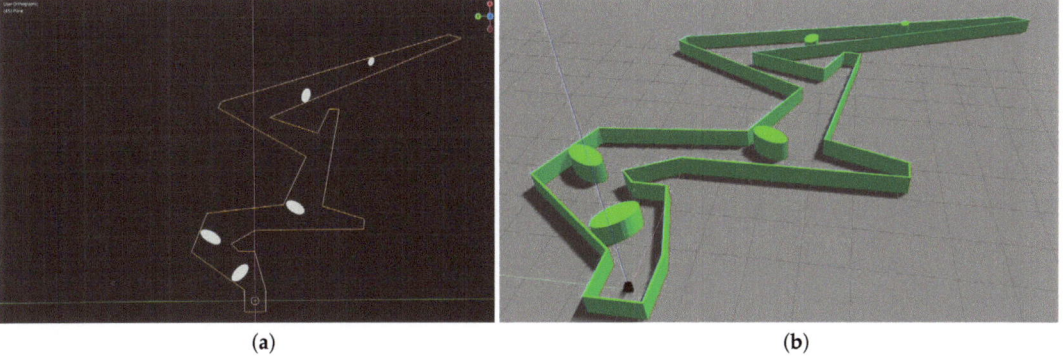

Figure 9. Circuit used in the usability and presence tests. (**a**) Blender-made circuit. (**b**) Gazebo environment.

After the test, the participants were asked to complete three standard questionnaires: the presence questionnaire (PQ) [75,76], the Igroup Presence Questionnaire (IPQ) [77–79], and the system usability scale (SUS) [80]. The PQ and IPQ questionnaires were chosen because they are widely used to evaluate the sense of presence in VEs, the realism, the interface and chosen devices quality, among other factors. The SUS questionnaire was used to test the usability of the proposed interface because it is short, concise and widely used.

The PQ was conducted in order to evaluate the user experience in the VE [75]. Twenty four of the twenty nine total questions of the third version of the PQ questionnaire were selected according to the nature of the proposed application; see Table 1. The PQ uses a seven-point Likert-type scale and has four subscales: *involvement*, *sensor fidelity*, *immersion* and *interface quality*.

Table 1. Questions of the PQ questionnaire [75,76].

PQ1	How much were you able to control events?
PQ2	How responsive was the environment to actions that you initiated (or performed)?
PQ3	How natural did your interactions with the environment seem?
PQ4	How much did the visual aspects of the environment involve you?
PQ5	How natural was the mechanism which controlled movement through the environment?
PQ6	How compelling was your sense of objects moving through space?
PQ7	How much did your experiences in the virtual environment seem consistent with your real world experiences?
PQ8	How compelling was your sense of moving around inside the virtual environment?
PQ9	How completely were you able to actively survey or search the environment using vision?
PQ11	How well could you move or manipulate objects in the virtual environment?
PQ12	How closely were you able to examine objects?
PQ13	How well could you examine objects from multiple viewpoints?
PQ14	How much did the auditory aspects of the environment involve you?
PQ15	How well could you identify sounds?
PQ16	How well could you localize sounds?
PQ17	Were you able to anticipate what would happen next in response to the actions that you performed?
PQ18	How quickly did you adjust to the virtual environment experience?
PQ19	How proficient in moving and interacting with the virtual environment did you feel at the end of the experience?
PQ20	How well could you concentrate on the assigned tasks or required activities rather than on the mechanisms used to perform those tasks or activities?
PQ21	How much delay did you experience between your actions and expected outcomes?
PQ22	How much did the visual display quality interfere or distract you from performing assigned tasks or required activities?
PQ23	How much did the control devices interfere with the performance of assigned tasks or with other activities
PQ24	How much did the control devices interfere with the performance of assigned tasks or with other activities

Figure 10 shows the results of the PQ. Concretely, Figure 10a shows the mean and standard deviation for each question of the PQ, whilst Figure 10b shows the mean, standard deviation and total percentage for each PQ subscale. In particular, the *Involvement* score was 95.19% with a standard deviation of 6.61, which means that the users paid close attention to the virtual reality environment and actively participated in all aspects present. The *sensor fidelity* score was 99.13% with a standard deviation of 2.26, which means that the users could observe from multiple views and interact with all objects present in the VE easily and without problems. The *immersion* score was 94.48% with a standard deviation of 6.05, which means that users could adapt themselves quickly and easily to the VE, and could perform the task without distractions. Finally, the *interface quality* score was 97.40% with a standard deviation of 3.92, which means that users did not perceive failures or malfunctions in the virtual reality interface during the tasks.

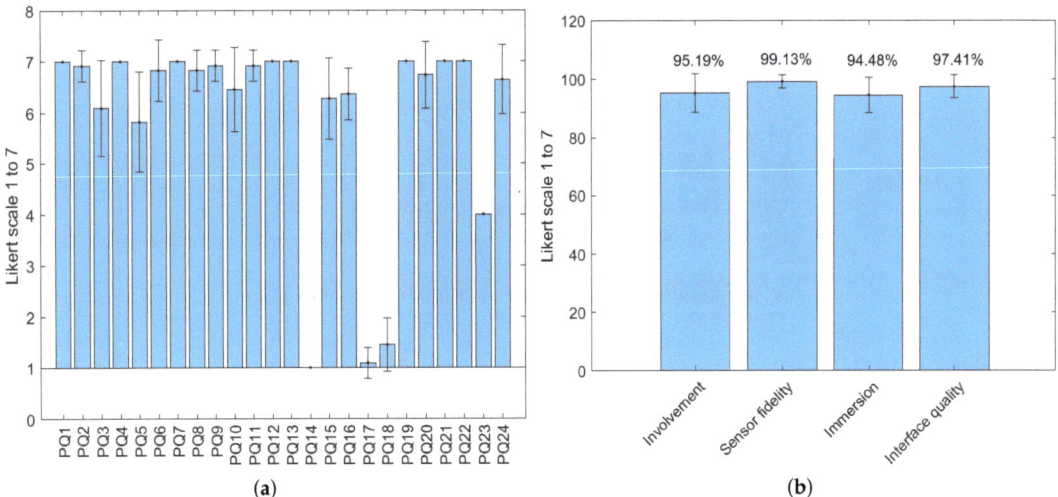

Figure 10. Results of the presence questionnaire. (**a**) Mean and standard deviation per question. (**b**) Subscale results (mean and standard deviation).

On the other hand, the IPQ was conducted in order to measure the sense of presence experienced by users in the proposed VE [77]. The IPQ is composed of 14 questions used to evaluate three subscales: *spatial presence*, i.e., the sense of being physically present in the VE; *involvement*, i.e., measuring the attention devoted to the VE and the involvement experience; and *experienced realism*, i.e., measuring the subjective experience of realism in the VE. In addition to this, the IPQ has an additional general item that assesses the general "sense of being there", and has high loadings on all three factors, especially on spatial presence. The IPQ questions are shown in Table 2.

Figure 11 shows the results of the IPQ. Concretely, Figure 11a shows the mean, and standard deviation for each question of the IPQ, whilst Figure 11b shows the mean, standard deviation and total percentage for each PQ subscale. In particular, the *general presence* score was 94.81% with a standard deviation of 6.87, which indicates that users felt like they were inside the VE. The *spacial presence* score was 99.74% with a standard deviation of 0.58, which means that users felt like they were physically present in the VE. The *involvement* score was 92.86% with a standard deviation of 9.51, which is very similar to that of the PQ, corroborating that users actively participated and focused on all aspects of the VE. Finally, the *experienced realism* score was 35.71% with a standard deviation of 42.86, which means that users felt in any moment that they were in a VE, with no realistic objects present in there. This coincides with the goal of the proposed approach, which was not to design a "realistic" scenario but a natural and user-friendly VE to be used in most of the current commercial VR headsets. Note that increasing realism implies more computational cost and the use of specialized hardware, i.e., graphic cards.

Table 2. Questions of the IPQ questionnaire [77–79].

IPQ1	In the computer generated world I had a sense of "being there"
IPQ2	Somehow I felt that the virtual world surrounded me
IPQ3	I felt like I was just perceiving pictures
IPQ4	I did not feel present in the virtual space
IPQ5	I had a sense of acting in the virtual space, rather than operating something from outside
IPQ6	I felt present in the virtual space
IPQ7	How aware were you of the real world surrounding while navigating in the virtual world? (i.e., sounds, room temperature, and other people)?
IPQ8	I was not aware of my real environment
IPQ9	I still paid attention to the real environment
IPQ11	I was completely captivated by the virtual world
IPQ12	How real did the virtual world seem to you?
IPQ13	How much did your experience in the virtual environment seem consistent with your real world experience?
IPQ14	The virtual world seemed more realistic than the real world

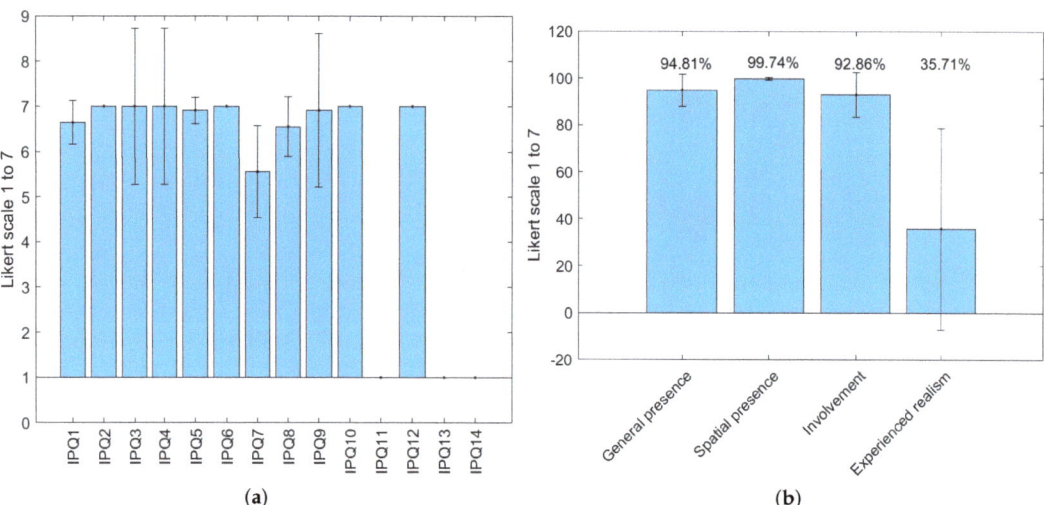

Figure 11. Results of the Igroup presence questionnaire. (**a**) Mean and standard deviation per question. (**b**) Subscales results (mean and standard deviation).

Regarding the SUS questionnaire, the overall perceived usability was 90.91 out of 100 (min 77.5; max 100; SD 7.18), which means that the proposed VR-based interface reached a high level of usability. In addition, Figure 12 shows the results obtained for each question of the SUS questionnaire, which are detailed in Table 3. Note that most of the participants would use this interface frequently and found the interface easy to use. The participants also indicated that all the interface functionalities were well integrated and that the proposed interface was consistent. Moreover, the participants felt confident with the interface.

Table 3. Questions of the SUS questionnaire [80].

SUS1	I think that I would like to use this system frequently
SUS2	I found the system unnecessarily complex
SUS3	I thought the system was easy to use
SUS4	I think that I would need the support of a technical person to be able to use this system
SUS5	I found the various functions in this system were well integrated
SUS6	I thought there was too much inconsistency in this system
SUS7	I would imagine that most people would learn to use this system very quickly
SUS8	I found the system very cumbersome to use
SUS9	I felt very confident using the system
SUS10	I needed to learn a lot of things before I could get going with this system

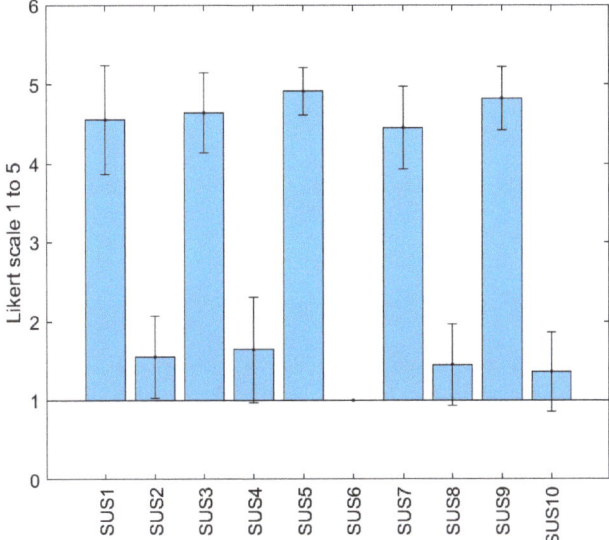

Figure 12. Results of the SUS questionnaire (mean and standard deviation).

4. Conclusions

A virtual reality-based interface for advanced assisted teleoperation of mobile robots was developed in this work to assist human operators to conduct operations, such as human rescue, bomb deactivation, etc. For this purpose, virtual reality and sensor feedback were used to provide the user an immersive virtual experience when remotely teleoperating the robot system in order to properly perform the task.

The main advantages of the proposal are twofold. Firstly, the proposed virtual environment is useful to provide a more natural manner to teleoperate these kind of robots, which improves the task performance. Secondly, the synergistic effect between the human, who provides flexibility to adapt to complex situations, and the robot, which is able to automatically avoid the obstacles in its environment, makes the proposed approach user friendly and allows the robot to deal with challenging situations, e.g., to escape from trap situations.

Furthermore, the feasibility and effectiveness of the proposed virtual reality interface for advanced assisted teleoperation of mobile robots were shown through experimental results, using a differential-drive mobile robot, the Turtlebot3 Burger, equipped with a 360°

LiDAR sensor. Although in this work, only the robot odometry and LiDAR sensor were used, the information provided from other sensors, such as vision systems, could be easily added in order to include in the local environment (virtual world) more information from the remote environment (real world).

In addition, several usability and presence questionnaires were carried out with users of different ages and backgrounds. The results showed that the proposed virtual reality based interface is intuitive, ergonomic and easy to use.

This work assumed that the robot goes through a totally unknown environment. If there is previous knowledge of the environment, one possibility would be to improve the teleporting option by showing the "allowed" areas in a blue circle (such as the one shown in this work) and the "not allowed" areas with a red circle, thus constraining the user movements within the virtual world.

Moreover, if the environment is totally or partially known, it would be interesting to introduce a trajectory planner, which in combination with the manual teleoperation carried out by the human, would lead to a semi-automatic teleoperation mode. In this mode, the planner would indicate the optimal trajectory to the human operator, who would be free to follow it or not depending on the situation.

In this work, the well-known potential field-based navigation method was used for the high-level controller of the mobile robot. However, other controllers could be considered to improve the performance of the mobile robot navigation in different ways, e.g., sliding mode control approaches [81] or intelligent model-free control approaches [82] could be used.

Author Contributions: Conceptualization, J.E.S. and A.M.; Funding acquisition, L.G. and J.T.; Investigation, J.E.S., A.M. and L.G.; Methodology, J.E.S.; Resources, L.G. and J.T.; Software, A.M.; Supervision, L.G. and J.T.; Validation, J.E.S.; Writing—original draft, J.E.S.; Writing—review & editing, L.G. All authors have read and agreed to the published version of the manuscript.

Funding: This research was funded by the Spanish Government (Grant PID2020-117421RB-C21 funded by MCIN/AEI/10.13039/501100011033) and by the Generalitat Valenciana (Grant GV/2021/181).

Conflicts of Interest: The authors declare no conflict of interest.

References

1. Saputra, R.P.; Rakicevic, N.; Kuder, I.; Bilsdorfer, J.; Gough, A.; Dakin, A.; de Cocker, E.; Rock, S.; Harpin, R.; Kormushev, P. ResQbot 2.0: An Improved Design of a Mobile Rescue Robot with an Inflatable Neck Securing Device for Safe Casualty Extraction. *Appl. Sci.* **2021**, *11*, 5414. [CrossRef]
2. Habibian, S.; Dadvar, M.; Peykari, B.; Hosseini, A.; Salehzadeh, M.H.; Hosseini, A.H.M.; Najafi, F. Design and implementation of a maxi-sized mobile robot (Karo) for rescue missions. *ROBOMECH J.* **2021**, *8*, 1. [CrossRef]
3. Sun, Z.; Yang, H.; Ma, Y.; Wang, X.; Mo, Y.; Li, H.; Jiang, Z. BIT-DMR: A Humanoid Dual-Arm Mobile Robot for Complex Rescue Operations. *IEEE Robot. Autom. Lett.* **2022**, *7*, 802–809. [CrossRef]
4. Schuster, M.J.; Müller, M.G.; Brunner, S.G.; Lehner, H.; Lehner, P.; Sakagami, R.; Dömel, A.; Meyer, L.; Vodermayer, B.; Giubilato, R.; et al. The ARCHES Space-Analogue Demonstration Mission: Towards Heterogeneous Teams of Autonomous Robots for Collaborative Scientific Sampling in Planetary Exploration. *IEEE Robot. Autom. Lett.* **2020**, *5*, 5315–5322. [CrossRef]
5. Jia, X.; Sun, C.; Fu, J. Mobile Augmented Reality Centred Ietm System for Shipping Applications. *Int. J. Robot. Autom.* **2022**, *37*, 147–162. [CrossRef]
6. Yin, K.; Sun, Q.; Gao, F.; Zhou, S. Lunar surface soft-landing analysis of a novel six-legged mobile lander with repetitive landing capacity. *Proc. Inst. Mech. Eng. Part C J. Mech. Eng. Sci.* **2022**, *236*, 1214–1233. [CrossRef]
7. Kot, T.; Novák, P. Application of virtual reality in teleoperation of the military mobile robotic system TAROS. *Int. J. Adv. Robot. Syst.* **2018**, *15*, 1–6. [CrossRef]
8. Kavitha, S.; SadishKumar, S.T.; Menaga, T.; Gomathi, E.; Sanjay, M.; Abarna, V.S. Military Based Voice Controlled Spy Bot with Weapon Detector. *Biosci. Biotechnol. Res. Commun.* **2020**, *13*, 142–146.
9. Grabowski, A.; Jankowski, J.; Wodzyński, M. Teleoperated mobile robot with two arms: The influence of a human-machine interface, VR training and operator age. *Int. J. Hum.-Comput. Stud.* **2021**, *156*, 102707. [CrossRef]
10. Li, C.; Li, B.; Wang, R.; Zhang, X. A survey on visual servoing for wheeled mobile robots. *Int. J. Intell. Robot. Appl.* **2021**, *5*, 203–218. [CrossRef]
11. Szrek, J.; Jakubiak, J.; Zimroz, R. A Mobile Robot-Based System for Automatic Inspection of Belt Conveyors in Mining Industry. *Energies* **2022**, *15*, 327. [CrossRef]

12. Khalaji, A.K.; Zahedifar, R. Lyapunov-Based Formation Control of Underwater Robots. *Robotica* **2020**, *38*, 1105–1122. [CrossRef]
13. Mahmud, M.S.A.; Abidin, M.S.Z.; Buyamin, S.; Emmanuel, A.A.; Hasan, H.S. Multi-objective Route Planning for Underwater Cleaning Robot in Water Reservoir Tank. *J. Intell. Robot. Syst.* **2021**, *101*, 9. [CrossRef]
14. Doss, A.S.A.; Venkatesh, D.; Ovinis, M. Simulation and experimental studies of a mobile robot for underwater applications. *Int. J. Robot. Autom.* **2021**, *36*, 10–17. [CrossRef]
15. Guzman Ortiz, E.; Andres, B.; Fraile, F.; Poler, R.; Ortiz Bas, A. Fleet Management System for Mobile Robots in Healthcare Environments. *J. Ind. Eng. Manag.-Jiem* **2021**, *14*, 55–71. [CrossRef]
16. Law, M.; Ahn, H.S.; Broadbent, E.; Peri, K.; Kerse, N.; Topou, E.; Gasteiger, N.; MacDonald, B. Case studies on the usability, acceptability and functionality of autonomous mobile delivery robots in real-world healthcare settings. *Intell. Serv. Robot.* **2021**, *14*, 387–398. [CrossRef]
17. Lim, H.; Kim, S.W.; Song, J.B.; Cha, Y. Thin Piezoelectric Mobile Robot Using Curved Tail Oscillation. *IEEE Access* **2021**, *9*, 145477–145485. [CrossRef]
18. Cardoso, J.C.S. Comparison of Gesture, Gamepad, and Gaze-Based Locomotion for VR Worlds. In Proceedings of the 22nd ACM Conference on Virtual Reality Software and Technology, Munich, Germany, 2–4 November 2016; pp. 319–320.
19. Kitson, A.; Hashemian, A.M.; Stepanova, E.R.; Kruijff, E.; Riecke, B.E. Comparing leaning-based motion cueing interfaces for virtual reality locomotion. In Proceedings of the 2017 IEEE Symposium on 3D User Interfaces (3DUI), Los Angeles, CA, USA, 18–19 March 2017; pp. 73–82.
20. Zhao, J.; Allison, R.S. Comparing head gesture, hand gesture and gamepad interfaces for answering Yes/No questions in virtual environments. *Virtual Real.* **2019**, *24*, 515–524. [CrossRef]
21. Solanes, J.E.; Muñoz, A.; Gracia, L.; Martí, A.; Girbés-Juan, V.; Tornero, J. Teleoperation of industrial robot manipulators based on augmented reality. *Int. J. Adv. Manuf. Technol.* **2020**, *111*, 1077–1097. [CrossRef]
22. Niemeyer, G.; Preusche, C.; Stramigioli, S.; Lee, D. Telerobotics. In *Springer Handbook of Robotics*; Siciliano, B., Khatib, O., Eds.; Springer International Publishing: Cham, Switzerland, 2016; pp. 1085–1108.
23. Bandala, M.; West, C.; Monk, S.; Montazeri, A.; Taylor, C.J. Vision-Based Assisted Tele-Operation of a Dual-Arm Hydraulically Actuated Robot for Pipe Cutting and Grasping in Nuclear Environments. *Robotics* **2019**, *8*, 42. [CrossRef]
24. Abi-Farraj, F.; Pacchierotti, C.; Arenz, O.; Neumann, G.; Giordano, P.R. A Haptic Shared-Control Architecture for Guided Multi-Target Robotic Grasping. *IEEE Trans. Haptics* **2020**, *13*, 270–285. [CrossRef] [PubMed]
25. Suarez, A.; Real, F.; Vega, V.M.; Heredia, G.; Rodriguez-Castaño, A.; Ollero, A. Compliant Bimanual Aerial Manipulation: Standard and Long Reach Configurations. *IEEE Access* **2020**, *8*, 88844–88865. [CrossRef]
26. Isop, W.A.; Gebhardt, C.; Nägeli, T.; Fraundorfer, F.; Hilliges, O.; Schmalstieg, D. High-Level Teleoperation System for Aerial Exploration of Indoor Environments. *Front. Robot. AI* **2019**, *6*, 95. [CrossRef] [PubMed]
27. Brantner, G.; Khatib, O. Controlling Ocean One: Human–robot collaboration for deep-sea manipulation. *J. Field Robot.* **2021**, *38*, 28–51. [CrossRef]
28. Sivčev, S.; Coleman, J.; Omerdić, E.; Dooly, G.; Toal, D. Underwater manipulators: A review. *Ocean Eng.* **2018**, *163*, 431–450. [CrossRef]
29. Chen, H.; Huang, P.; Liu, Z. Mode Switching-Based Symmetric Predictive Control Mechanism for Networked Teleoperation Space Robot System. *IEEE/ASME Trans. Mechatron.* **2019**, *24*, 2706–2717. [CrossRef]
30. Yoon, H.; Jeong, J.H.; Yi, B. Image-Guided Dual Master–Slave Robotic System for Maxillary Sinus Surgery. *IEEE Trans. Robot.* **2018**, *34*, 1098–1111. [CrossRef]
31. Saracino, A.; Oude-Vrielink, T.J.C.; Menciassi, A.; Sinibaldi, E.; Mylonas, G.P. Haptic Intracorporeal Palpation Using a Cable-Driven Parallel Robot: A User Study. *IEEE Trans. Biomed. Eng.* **2020**, *67*, 3452–3463. [CrossRef]
32. Chen, Y.; Zhang, S.; Wu, Z.; Yang, B.; Luo, Q.; Xu, K. Review of surgical robotic systems for keyhole and endoscopic procedures: State of the art and perspectives. *Front. Med.* **2020**, *14*, 382–403. [CrossRef]
33. Kapoor, A.; Li, M.; Taylor, R.H. Spatial Motion Constraints for Robot Assisted Suturing Using Virtual Fixtures. In Proceedings of the Medical Image Computing and Computer-Assisted Intervention—MICCAI 2005, Palm Springs, CA, USA, 26–29 October 2005; Duncan, J.S., Gerig, G., Eds.; Springer: Berlin/Heidelberg, Germany, 2005; pp. 89–96.
34. Kono, H.; Mori, T.; Ji, Y.; Fujii, H.; Suzuki, T. Development of Perilous Environment Estimation System Using a Teleoperated Rescue Robot with On-board LiDAR. In Proceedings of the 2019 IEEE/SICE International Symposium on System Integration (SII), Paris, France, 14–16 January 2019; pp. 7–10.
35. Johnson, M.; Vera, A. No AI Is an Island: The Case for Teaming Intelligence. *AI Mag.* **2019**, *40*, 16–28. [CrossRef]
36. Selvaggio, M.; Abi-Farraj, F.; Pacchierotti, C.; Giordano, P.R.; Siciliano, B. Haptic-Based Shared-Control Methods for a Dual-Arm System. *IEEE Robot. Autom. Lett.* **2018**, *3*, 4249–4256. [CrossRef]
37. Nicolis, D.; Palumbo, M.; Zanchettin, A.M.; Rocco, P. Occlusion-Free Visual Servoing for the Shared Autonomy Teleoperation of Dual-Arm Robots. *IEEE Robot. Autom. Lett.* **2018**, *3*, 796–803. [CrossRef]
38. Lu, Z.; Huang, P.; Liu, Z. Predictive Approach for Sensorless Bimanual Teleoperation Under Random Time Delays With Adaptive Fuzzy Control. *IEEE Trans. Ind. Electron.* **2018**, *65*, 2439–2448. [CrossRef]
39. Gorjup, G.; Dwivedi, A.; Elangovan, N.; Liarokapis, M. An Intuitive, Affordances Oriented Telemanipulation Framework for a Dual Robot Arm Hand System: On the Execution of Bimanual Tasks. In Proceedings of the 2019 IEEE/RSJ International Conference on Intelligent Robots and Systems (IROS), Macau, China, 3–8 November 2019; pp. 3611–3616.

40. Clark, J.P.; Lentini, G.; Barontini, F.; Catalano, M.G.; Bianchi, M.; O'Malley, M.K. On the role of wearable haptics for force feedback in teleimpedance control for dual-arm robotic teleoperation. In Proceedings of the 2019 International Conference on Robotics and Automation (ICRA), Montreal, QC, Canada, 20–24 May 2019; pp. 5187–5193.
41. Girbés-Juan, V.; Schettino, V.; Gracia, L.; Solanes, J.E.; Demeris, Y.; Tornero, J. Combining haptics and inertial motion capture to enhance remote control of a dual-arm robot. *J. Multimodal User Interfaces* **2022**, *16*, 219–238. [CrossRef]
42. García, A.; Solanes, J.E.; Gracia, L.; Muñoz-Benavent, P.; Girbés-Juan, V.; Tornero, J. Bimanual robot control for surface treatment tasks. *Int. J. Syst. Sci.* **2022**, *53*, 74–107. [CrossRef]
43. Selvaggio, M.; Ghalamzan, A.; Moccia, R.; Ficuciello, F.; Siciliano, B. Haptic-guided shared control for needle grasping optimization in minimally invasive robotic surgery. In Proceedings of the IEEE/RSJ International Conference on Intelligent Robots and Systems, Macau, China, 3–8 November 2019.
44. Girbés-Juan, V.; Schettino, V.; Demiris, Y.; Tornero, J. Haptic and Visual Feedback Assistance for Dual-Arm Robot Teleoperation in Surface Conditioning Tasks. *IEEE Trans. Haptics* **2021**, *14*, 44–56. [CrossRef]
45. Laghi, M.; Ajoudani, A.; Catalano, M.G.; Bicchi, A. Unifying bilateral teleoperation and tele-impedance for enhanced user experience. *Int. J. Robot. Res.* **2020**, *39*, 514–539. [CrossRef]
46. Navarro, R.; Vega, V.; Martinez, S.; Jose Espinosa, M.; Hidalgo, D.; Benavente, B. Designing Experiences: A Virtual Reality Video Game to Enhance Immersion. In Proceedings of the 10th International Conference on Applied Human Factors and Ergonomics/AHFE International Conference on Human Factors and Wearable Technologies/AHFE International Conference on Game Design and Virtual Environments, Washington, DC, USA, 24–28 July 2019. [CrossRef]
47. Tao, G.; Garrett, B.; Taverner, T.; Cordingley, E.; Sun, C. Immersive virtual reality health games: A narrative review of game design. *J. Neuroeng. Rehabil.* **2021**, *18*, 31. [CrossRef]
48. Shafer, D.M. The Effects of Interaction Fidelity on Game Experience in Virtual Reality. *Psychol. Pop. Media* **2021**, *10*, 457–466. [CrossRef]
49. Ho, J.C.F.; Ng, R. Perspective-Taking of Non-Player Characters in Prosocial Virtual Reality Games: Effects on Closeness, Empathy, and Game Immersion. *Behav. Inf. Technol.* **2020**, *41*, 1185–1198. [CrossRef]
50. Wang, J.; Yuan, X.Q. Route Planning of Teleoperation Mobile Robot based on the Virtual Reality Technology. *J. Robotics Netw. Artif. Life* **2020**, *7*, 125–128. [CrossRef]
51. Urrea, C.; Matteoda, R. Development of a virtual reality simulator for a strategy for coordinating cooperative manipulator robots using cloud computing. *Robot. Auton. Syst.* **2020**, *126*, 103447. [CrossRef]
52. Kuo, C.Y.; Huang, C.C.; Tsai, C.H.; Shi, Y.S.; Smith, S. Development of an immersive SLAM-based VR system for teleoperation of a mobile manipulator in an unknown environment. *Comput. Ind.* **2021**, *132*, 103502. [CrossRef]
53. Meta, Facebook Reality Labs (Redmond, DC, USA). Oculus Quest 2 Hardware Details. Available online: https://www.oculus.com/quest-2/ (accessed on 4 March 2022).
54. Unity (San Francisco, CA, USA). Unity Real-Time Development Platform. Available online: https://unity.com/ (accessed on 5 May 2022).
55. Microsoft (Redmond, DC, USA). Xbox Wireless Controller Hardware Details. Available online: https://www.xbox.com/en-US/accessories/controllers/xbox-wireless-controller (accessed on 4 March 2022).
56. Robotis (Lake Forest, CA, USA). Turtlebot3 Hardware Details. Available online: https://www.robotis.us/turtlebot-3/ (accessed on 4 March 2022).
57. Unity (San Francisco, CA, USA). Shaders Core Concepts. Available online: https://docs.unity3d.com/Manual/Shaders.html (accessed on 4 March 2022).
58. Virtuix (Austin, TX, USA). OmniOne Hardware Details. Available online: https://omni.virtuix.com/ (accessed on 4 March 2022).
59. Latombe, J.C. *Robot Motion Planning*; Kluwer: Boston, MA, USA, 1991.
60. Khatib, O. Real-time obstacle avoidance for manipulators and mobile robots. *Int. J. Robot. Res.* **1986**, *5*, 90–98. [CrossRef]
61. Gracia, L.; Tornero, J. Kinematic models and isotropy analysis of wheeled mobile robots. *Robotica* **2008**, *26*, 587–599. [CrossRef]
62. Gracia, L.; Tornero, J. Characterization of zero tracking error references in the kinematic control of wheeled mobile robots. *Robot. Auton. Syst.* **2009**, *57*, 565–577. [CrossRef]
63. Gracia, L.; Tornero, J. Kinematic control system for car-like vehicles. In Proceedings of the Ibero-American Conference on Artificial Intelligence, Seville, Spain, 12–15 November 2002; Springer: Berlin/Heidelberg, Germany, 2002; pp. 882–892.
64. Koenig, N.; Howard, A. Design and Use Paradigms for Gazebo, An Open-Source Multi-Robot Simulator. In Proceedings of the IEEE/RSJ International Conference on Intelligent Robots and Systems, Sendai, Japan, 28 September–2 October 2004; pp. 2149–2154.
65. Aguero, C.; Koenig, N.; Chen, I.; Boyer, H.; Peters, S.; Hsu, J.; Gerkey, B.; Paepcke, S.; Rivero, J.; Manzo, J.; et al. Inside the Virtual Robotics Challenge: Simulating Real-Time Robotic Disaster Response. *IEEE Trans. Autom. Sci. Eng.* **2015**, *12*, 494–506. [CrossRef]
66. Video of Experiment 1. 2022. Available online: https://media.upv.es/player/?id=7fac10d0-8ccd-11ec-ad20-231602f2b702 (accessed on 12 June 2022).
67. Video of Experiment 2. 2022. Available online: https://media.upv.es/player/?id=31aac3c0-8cca-11ec-a6b9-39f61182889c (accessed on 12 June 2022).

68. Blattgerste, J.; Strenge, B.; Renner, P.; Pfeiffer, T.; Essig, K. Comparing Conventional and Augmented Reality Instructions for Manual Assembly Tasks. In Proceedings of the 10th International Conference on PErvasive Technologies Related to Assistive Environments, Island of Rhodes, Greece, 21–23 June 2017; pp. 75–82. [CrossRef]
69. Attig, C.; Wessel, D.; Franke, T. Assessing Personality Differences in Human-Technology Interaction: An Overview of Key Self-report Scales to Predict Successful Interaction. In Proceedings of the HCI International 2017—Posters' Extended Abstracts, Vancouver, BC, Canada, 9–14 July 2017; Stephanidis, C., Ed.; Springer International Publishing: Cham, Switzerland, 2017; pp. 19–29.
70. Franke, T.; Attig, C.; Wessel, D. A Personal Resource for Technology Interaction: Development and Validation of the Affinity for Technology Interaction (ATI) Scale. *Int. J. -Hum.-Comput. Interact.* **2018**, *35*, 456–467. [CrossRef]
71. Du, J.; Do, H.M.; Sheng, W. Human-Robot Collaborative Control in a Virtual-Reality-Based Telepresence System. *Int. J. Soc. Robot.* **2021**, *13*, 1295–1306. [CrossRef]
72. Uboe, J. *Introductory Statistics for Business and Economics: Theory, Exercises and Solutions*; Springer International Publishing AG: Cham, Switzerland, 2017; ISBN 9783319709369.
73. Hess, R. *Blender Foundations: The Essential Guide to Learning Blender 2.6*; Focal Press: Waltham, MA, USA, 2010. Available online: https://www.sciencedirect.com/book/9780240814308/blender-foundations (accessed on 12 June 2022).
74. Video of Experiment 3. 2022. Available online: https://media.upv.es/player/?id=f45e38d0-8cce-11ec-ad20-231602f2b702 (accessed on 12 June 2022).
75. Witmer, B.G.; Singer, M.J. Measuring Presence in Virtual Environments: A Presence Questionnaire. *Presence Teleoperators Virtual Environ.* **1998**, *7*, 225–240. [CrossRef]
76. Witmer, B.G.; Jerome, C.J.; Singer, M.J. The Factor Structure of the Presence Questionnaire. *Presence Teleoperators Virtual Environ.* **2005**, *14*, 298–312. [CrossRef]
77. Schubert, T.; Friedmann, F.; Regenbrecht, H. The Experience of Presence: Factor Analytic Insights. *Presence Teleoperators Virtual Environ.* **2001**, *10*, 266–281. [CrossRef]
78. Regenbrecht, H.; Schubert, T. Real and Illusory Interactions Enhance Presence in Virtual Environments. *Presence Teleoperators Virtual Environ.* **2002**, *11*, 425–434. [CrossRef]
79. Schubert, T. The sense of presence in virtual environments: A three-component scale measuring spatial presence, involvement, and realness. *Z. für Medien.* **2003**, *15*, 69–71. [CrossRef]
80. Brooke, J. "SUS-A Quick and Dirty Usability Scale." *Usability Evaluation in Industry*; CRC Press: Boca Raton, FL, USA, 1996; ISBN 9780748404605.
81. Gracia, L.; Garelli, F.; Sala, A. Reactive Sliding-Mode Algorithm for Collision Avoidance in Robotic Systems. *IEEE Trans. Control. Syst. Technol.* **2013**, *21*, 2391–2399. [CrossRef]
82. Tutsoy, O.; Barkana, D.E.; Balikci, K. A Novel Exploration-Exploitation-Based Adaptive Law for Intelligent Model-Free Control Approaches. *IEEE Trans. Cybern.* **2021**, 1–9. in press. [CrossRef]

Article
Implementation of Autonomous Mobile Robot in SmartFactory

Radim Hercik *,†, Radek Byrtus †, Rene Jaros † and Jiri Koziorek

Department of Cybernetics and Biomedical Engineering, VSB–Technical University of Ostrava, 17. Listopadu 15, 708 33 Ostrava, Czech Republic
* Correspondence: radim.hercik@vsb.cz
† These authors contributed equally to this work.

Abstract: This study deals with the technology of autonomous mobile robots (AMR) and their implementation on the SmartFactory production line at the Technical University of Ostrava. The task of the mobile robot is to cooperate with the production line, take over the manufactured products, and then deliver them. The content also includes a description of the individual steps that were necessary to make the mobile robot operational, such as loading a virtual map of the space, creating a network for communication with the mobile robot, and programming it. The main part of the experiment deals with testing the accuracy of moving the mobile robot to each position and establishing communication between the production line and the mobile robot. A high accuracy is a necessity in this process. The result of the study is the configuration of the autonomous mobile robot. The repetitive precision of the approach of the autonomous mobile robot to a position is ±3 mm.

Keywords: AMR; autonomous; cooperation; MiR robot; SmartFactory

Citation: Hercik, R.; Byrtus, R.; Jaros, R.; Koziorek, J. Implementation of Autonomous Mobile Robot in SmartFactory. *Appl. Sci.* **2022**, *12*, 8912. https://doi.org/10.3390/app12178912

Academic Editors: Luis Gracia and J. Ernesto Solanes

Received: 5 August 2022
Accepted: 2 September 2022
Published: 5 September 2022

Publisher's Note: MDPI stays neutral with regard to jurisdictional claims in published maps and institutional affiliations.

Copyright: © 2022 by the authors. Licensee MDPI, Basel, Switzerland. This article is an open access article distributed under the terms and conditions of the Creative Commons Attribution (CC BY) license (https://creativecommons.org/licenses/by/4.0/).

1. Introduction

In general, robots for industry purposes were introduced in 1961 to achieve increasing elaborate tasks. They occur in tedious and repetitive tasks such as welding, painting, moving, or cutting with incredible precision [1–4]. These classic commercial robots suffer from a fundamental disadvantage, a lack of mobility. In contrast, mobile robots were introduced to be able to travel throughout the manufacturing plant to help flexibly with manufacturing processes. Fixed robots or robotic manipulators commonly operate in zones where humans cannot go. Rather, mobile robots share space with humans in human environments and act like cobots. These robots are not developed for mobility reasons, but due to their autonomy, their ability to maintain a sense of position and navigate without human intervention is paramount [2,5].

This work is focused on the application of autonomous industrial mobile robots (AMR). It is still a relatively new technology that is gradually finding use in industry, but also in other sectors [2,6,7]. The biggest advantages of autonomous robots include their independence and ability to orient themselves in space, without the need for external guidelines or other elements in the environment. Autonomous mobile robots orient themselves with the help of advanced sensors [8,9] and a virtual space map. They can be used in the fields of storage, transport, and production [1,10–12]. Panigrahi and their colleague presented in their review paper [13] the results of many research papers focused on precise robot navigation. This problem is not solved yet and it depends on many factors. Most problems occur due to processing time or position and direction estimation. Furthermore, research on planning algorithms [14,15] is still in progress and many researchers have also been testing different types of modern sensors for sensing the map and the actual position of the robot in the space in combination with the simulation [16,17].

In this paper, we demonstrate a real cooperation between an AMR and SmartFactory [18]. The study was carried out using a commercial AMR from Mobile Industrial Robots (MiR), a centralized control station for MiR robots (MiR FLEET), and an I/O module for MiR robots (MiR WISE) to create communication between them. Virtual maps and software (tasks) were created to enable us to experiment. The problem was the narrow space and the need for a precise approach of the robot to the SmartFactory premises. Several types of precise markers were used in the experiment. The result was different accuracies of the entrances. The autonomous mobile robots were then suitably complemented by the actual implementation of the camera surveillance system. This allowed the operator to always have an overview of the actual conditions around the robot.

The MiR autonomous mobile robots were chosen for the application. These mobile robotic platforms are ready for the industrial environment and are equipped with a combination of laser sensors, ultrasonic sensors, and cameras. Together, they allow robots to move safely around the environment and be able to respond to most types of obstacles [19]. It was also necessary to analyze the functions and behavior of the SmartFactory production line and then design suitable implementations of an autonomous mobile robot. The line produced a pair of products, each of them having a different target location, and, for this reason, a pair of mobile robot implementations, the so-called tasks, was designed. The MiR100 mobile robot was used to operate the production line.

The main objective of this paper was to provide an analysis of the accuracy of the position findings of autonomous mobile robots using marker labeling. This was demonstrated through an example of an application that links an autonomous mobile robot to SmartFactory. The novelty of the paper is the experiment with different types of markers to get the most accurate position of the robot in the production line and its statistical evaluation.

Contribution

- This work presents a method of communication of the production line with an autonomous mobile robot MiR100, which is performed wirelessly using an input/output card.
- The autonomous mobile robot MiR100 navigates to the final position using precise object markers. The maximum repeated accuracy of approaching the position is ±3 mm.
- The work brings a comparison of different types of precise marker objects in relation to the repeated accuracy of the approach of an autonomous mobile robot in position. It turns out that not all types of marker objects show the same results.
- The work also describes basic information about industrial mobile robots, its applications and current research.

2. Autonomous Mobile Robots

This section describes the chosen autonomous mobile robot and its parameters. The selected mobile robots are developed by the MiR company; specifically, a MiR100 model was found for the demonstration tasks. This mobile robot is designed for transportation purposes and to automate logistics. Its designation is based on the weight it can transfer (100 kg). The model is equipped with advanced sensors, which means that the robot moves autonomously in the environment and responds to surrounding obstacles. Table 1 provides basic information about the model [19].

The selected model is the smallest one and, thanks to its dimensions, it is possible to navigate this robot into the production line. The top of the robot is also supplemented by a superstructure, on which the products from the production line are placed. Figure 1 shows a photo of the mentioned mobile robot.

Table 1. Specifications of the MiR100 mobile robot [20].

Property	Unit	Value
Model	—	MiR100
Length	mm	890
Width	mm	580
Height	mm	352
Weight	kg	70
Max. load capacity	kg	100
Max. forward speed	m/s	2
Max. backward speed	m/s	1.5
Turning radius	mm	520
Positioning accuracy	mm	±50
Operating time	hours	10
Ambient temp. range	°C	10–40
I/O connectors	—	USB, Ethernet
Safety I/O connectors	—	—
Wi-Fi	—	Dual-band; ac/g/n/b
Bluetooth	—	4.0 Low Energy
SICK microScan3	—	2x S300 (360°)
3D Camera	—	2x Intel RealSense™

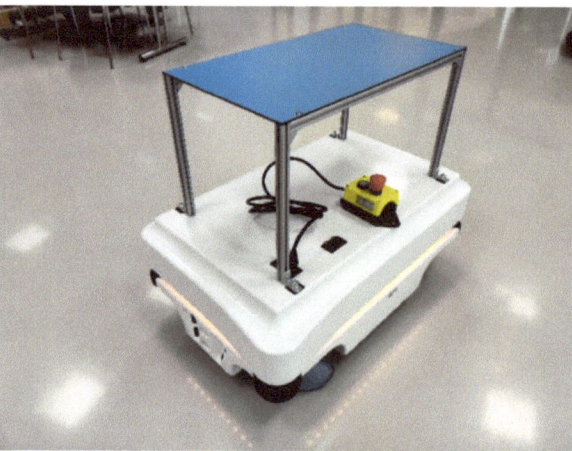

Figure 1. Mobile robot MiR100.

All configurations and settings of the mobile robot (MiR, MiR FLEET, WISE digital input, and output cards) are performed via a Web interface. Each web interface is different according to the needs of a particular device but is very similar in style [10]. The navigation system is the core of the autonomous mobile robot. Its goal is to plan the route from starting point A to destination point B. These points are determined by the user, but the journey is already planned completely, autonomously, and automatically. An advanced navigation system, which consists of several parts, is responsible for determining the correct route and navigating the robot to the destination. Figure 2 shows the principle of system operation. For clarification, it should be noted that IMU is inertial measurement unit.

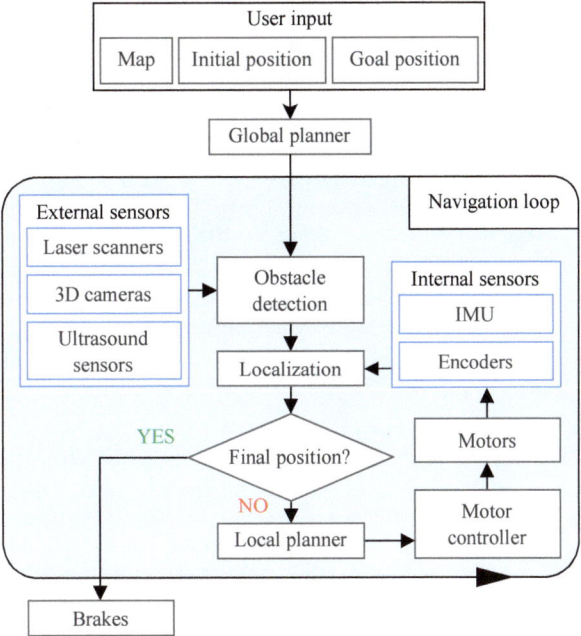

Figure 2. Navigation principle of mobile robots [20].

2.1. Navigation System

For the navigation system to be able to find the route, it needs initialization data according to which it will plan the route. The user enters the information about where the robot should arrive. However, to plan a route, the mobile robot must also know the space in which it moves and its current position. For orientation in space, a virtual map is used, which is stored in the robot's memory and contains data about all walls and obstacles. This map must be created before it is possible to use the mobile robot. Once the virtual map is created, points can be inserted into it through which the robot moves. However, it is possible to edit the map using zones, landmarks, and special planning rules.

After obtaining all the data for the start of route planning, the route is planned by the robot itself, which is in charge of the global planning system. This is an algorithm that generates a route to the desired point. However, it is important that the global planning system generates the path to the destination only once and follows only the fixed obstacles that are recorded on the virtual space map. This means that if a new obstacle arises in the environment of the robot that is not recorded on its virtual map, the global planning system does not know about this obstacle and plans a journey despite this obstacle. The planned route is shown on the map or on the dashboard using dots. If the robot cannot complete the move, planning is terminated with an error message, and the whole mission is suspended.

The local planning system, unlike the global planning system, runs in a continuous cycle throughout the robot's operation. Its task is to respond to obstacles in the immediate vicinity of the robot that are detected by sensors and not recorded on a virtual map. In the case of detecting an obstacle on a route, the local planning task is to determine the route through which the mobile robot can bypass the obstacle. If an obstacle is out of range or out of the sensor's field of view, the system does not take this obstacle into account. In a route that is created using global planning, the robot dodges the obstacle only to embrace the obstacle and then returns to the generated original route. The mobile robot route can be blocked so that the system cannot find a detour route. In this case, the mobile robot has a set count of attempts, that is, how many times the robot tries to find a new route. The route can be blocked, for example, by a person who just walks through and then clears the way.

If the mobile robot does not find its way in any of the set attempts, it pauses the active mission and waits for further instructions.

2.2. Obstacle Detection

The obstacle detection system is constantly active, and its main purpose is to detect obstacles around the robot. Information about the current location of surrounding obstacles is also used to determine the current position of the mobile robot on the map or when placing the mobile robot on the map. Three types of sensors are used to detect obstacles. These are laser sensors, ultrasonic sensors, and 3D cameras.

- Laser sensors: The MiR100 mobile robot is equipped with a pair of SICK S300 laser sensors. Each sensor has a viewing angle of 270° and is placed in opposite corners of the mobile robot to cover all 360° around the robot (Figure 3a). However, these sensors have several limitations. They can only detect obstacles at a height of 200 mm from the floor and cannot detect transparent obstacles (glass). For some reflective surfaces, the data may be inaccurate. False obstructions may be detected when the sensor is exposed to direct light.
- Three-dimensional cameras: Another way to detect obstacles is with a pair of Intel RealSense^{TM} cameras on the front; see Figure 3b. The cameras are intended for indoor navigation only, not as obstacle detection safety sensors. An important feature is the ability to detect the height of individual obstacles in the environment. According to this, the mobile robot can determine whether it will fit under the obstacle or not. The height of the mobile robot is set manually in the web interface. The pair of cameras occupy a space from 180 to 1950 mm in front of the robot with a viewing angle of 118° and a height of 1800 mm. Three-dimensional cameras also have several limitations. Unlike 360° laser sensors, they can only detect objects in front of a mobile robot. They cannot detect transparent or reflective objects or steps that descend. Distance determination may be inaccurate when detecting objects with repeating patterns. False obstructions can be detected when exposed to direct light.
- Ultrasonic sensors: The robot is equipped with four ultrasonic sensors; see Figure 3c. Two sensors are located in the back of the mobile robot and two are located in the front wheels of the mobile robot. Ultrasonic sensors are used to detect obstacles that could not be detected with a laser sensor or 3D cameras. The front sensors can detect obstacles of 10 to 200 mm, while the rear sensors detect obstacles at distances of 10 to 350 mm.

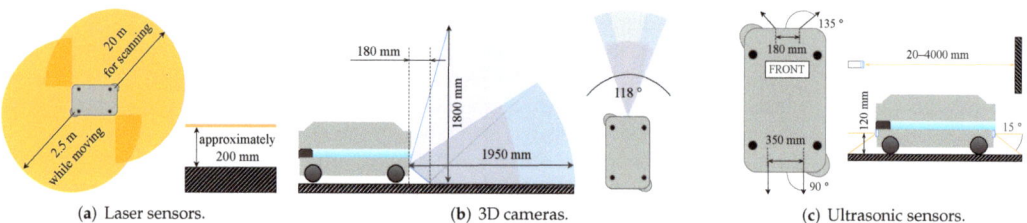

Figure 3. Obstacle detection system [20].

The information from all mentioned sensors has a fundamental effect on the speed of the robot's movement in the given space, see Figure 4, Tables 2 and 3. When a mobile robot travels at low speed, it primarily guards the space and obstacles in its immediate vicinity. However, if the mobile robot is traveling at a higher speed, it has much more space to be able to brake if an obstacle occurs. The robot's speed automatically changes according to the conditions of the environment in which the mobile robot moves. When the robot moves forward, it is also taking care of the situation behind him. The maximum speed of the robot can be limited using commands during mission creation.

In Zone 1 in Table 2, you can see a negative speed for the forward direction. It should be noted that in this zone, the robot performs 3 consecutive actions: reversing, stopping, and slowly moving forward. Zone 5 then shows the maximum forward speed of the robot. Then, in Zone 1 in Table 2, you can see the positive speed for the backward direction. It should be noted that in that zone, the robot performs 3 consecutive actions: forward, standstill, and slowly backward. Zone 5 then shows the maximum backward speed of the robot.

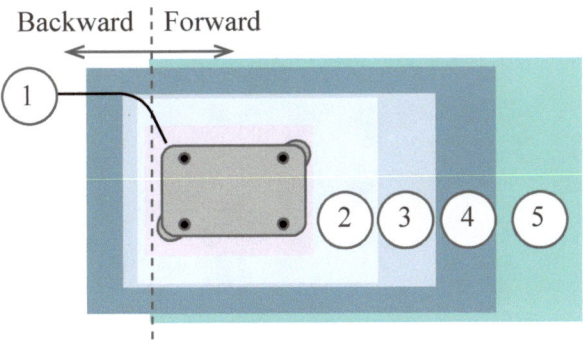

Figure 4. Mobile robot speed zones scheme [19].

Table 2. Robot speed zones (forward) [20].

Zone	Speed (m/s)	Guarded Space (mm)
1	−1.4 to 0.2	0 to 20
2	0.21 to 0.4	0 to 120
3	0.41 to 0.8	0 to 290
4	0.81 to 1.1	0 to 430
5	1.11 to 2.0	0 to 720

Table 3. Robot speed zones (backward) [20].

Zone	Speed (m/s)	Guarded Space (mm)
1	−0.14 to 1.8	0 to 20
2	−0.20 to −0.15	0 to 120
3	−0.40 to −0.21	0 to 290
4	−1.5 to −0.41	0 to 430

3. Analysis of the Use of Mobile Robots in SmartFactory

SmartFactory is a classroom, within a new CPIT TL3 building, specialized in Industry 4.0 technologies such as modern manufacturing processes, robotics, and automation, and a fully automated production line is also located there. This production line contains a digitized production process with Industry 4.0 elements such as product variability, predictive maintenance, augmented reality, or digital twins. The 3D model of the SmartFactory production line can be seen in Figure 5. Here, two types of products are manufactured in a fully automated process. The line enables product assembly using a fully automated process, product testing, product inspection, and product layout.

The products can be manufactured using individual components available in the warehouse; in addition, they must be placed on a platform. The platform is used for transfers between individual workplaces. A total of four robotic arms are installed on the production line. The first is used to operate the warehouse (component removal, product disassembly, product export from the line, and more). For this purpose, it is equipped with two tools that are automatically changed as needed. The other two arms are part of two fully automated production areas for the assembly of products. The third is used for automated product disassembly; the components are then stored back in the warehouse. The last robotic arm is part of the manual workplace for cooperation with staff or students. There are also two workplaces for fully manual staffing. There is also a test station for the final inspection of products. Electrical and visual inspections can be performed.

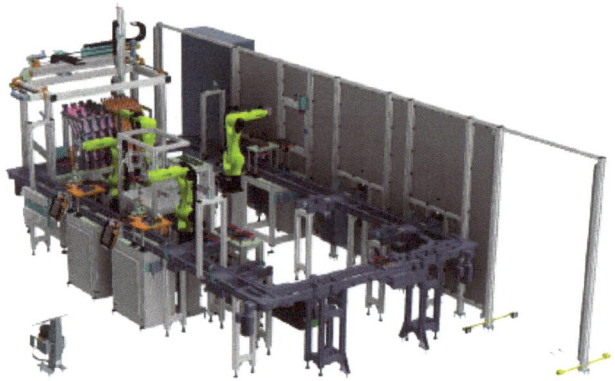

Figure 5. Three-dimensional model of the SmartFactory production line.

The request to start the production of products is entered through visualization from the control workplace. When ordering a product, it is possible to choose the type of product and the electronics that the product will contain. In the case of a second product, you can choose the color of the individual plastic cubes that will be placed on the product. The product may include electronics for the function of a pedometer, thermometer, or heart rate monitor.

3.1. Products

The first type of product consists of electronics and plastic parts printed using a 3D printer. It is called product design. There are three types of electronic devices: a pedometer, a thermometer, and a heart rate monitor. Each electronic piece belongs to a slightly modified plastic case. This product cannot be dismounted, it is fully functional, and it is intended as a customer product.

The second product consists of individual plastic parts and offers more options for individualization by the customer. As with the first product, it is possible to choose the type of electronics (pedometer, thermometer, heart rate monitor) and also the color of each of the eight plastic cubes. After the cubes are mounted on the base plate, the electronics are inserted into the resulting frame. The finished product is presented using a mobile robot on the premises of SmartFactory and is then returned to the line, where the product is automatically disassembled into individual components, and then stored in the warehouse.

3.2. Use of an Industrial Mobile Robot

The autonomous mobile robot in combination with an automated production line also offers the possibility of a fully automated production process and subsequent delivery of the product. The mobile robot is able to take the finished product from the line space and deliver it to the required location. It takes over the product directly on the premises of the line, where it arrives automatically. The KUKA [21] robotic arm, located in the middle of the production line, is used to move the product from the belt of the production line to the mobile robot. Unlike other robotic arms, it is equipped with a carriage, thanks to which it can move around the entire space of the production line.

The robot loading position is located in relatively narrow spaces below the conveyor belt. The mobile robot has to approach this position autonomously with high accuracy. After receiving the product, the mobile robot moves according to the specific implementation.

4. Experimental Setup

In this section, experimental delivery routes and the integration of a mobile robot into the SmartFactory production line are presented. As mentioned above, the production line produces two types of products. The production line does not contain any collection point for the final product and is surrounded by security features that prevent the possibility of entering the line. For this reason, the MiR100 mobile robot took care of the product's journey from the line to the customer. Since the production line produced two types of products, two possible implementations were proposed.

For navigation in a selected space, the robot used a virtual map. It was necessary to create this map before the robot started moving. The virtual map contained information on obstacles, zones, robot positions, markers, and other elements needed to control the robot. The virtual map could be created directly on the Web interface of the mobile robot. Since the robot oriented itself on the map using fixed, unchanging obstacles, it was recommended to have at least 60% of them on the map. The environment had to stay the same over time as much as possible. If the conditions changed rapidly, a new virtual map had to be created. Once the virtual map was created, it was possible to create missions.

4.1. Delivery and Presentation of the Product

The purpose of the first implementation of the mobile robot was to ensure the delivery of the finished product design from the line to the customer. Figure 6 shows the route of presentation and delivery of the product design. In the starting position, the robot was in front of the charging station or was charging. The customer used visualization to order a product, which the line then produced and passed the information to the mobile robot that the product was ready. The mobile robot reached the position on the production line where the product was handed over with the help of a robotic arm. The product was then removed from the line area, where the customer could take it over from the mobile robot. As soon as the customer removed the product, the mobile robot moved to a position in front of the charging station, where it waited for the next call from the line.

The second implementation of the mobile robot ensured the presentation of the assembled product produced in the SmartFactory line. The task of the implementation was to take the finished product, drive it along the route, and then return the product back to the line. The robot was in a starting position in front of or near the charging station, waiting for a signal that the product was assembled. When the signal was received, the mobile robot arrived at the charging position on the line and took the product back. It walked around the SmartFactory window with the product, then exited the line area so that any followers could view the product, and then returned to its position in the line. In this position, the product was unloaded from the mobile robot and returned to the production line where it was again disassembled. In this implementation, it was necessary for the mobile robot to approach the position with great precision when returning the product.

4.2. Cooperation with SmartFactory

There was a local network within 192.168.0.x/24, which was used for the control systems, robotic arms, sensors, and other devices on the line. Additionally, a Wi-Fi router was used to connect mobile robots, laptops, or smartphones. Although the Wi-Fi router was part of the production line network, it was powered independently, so the mobile robot network worked even when the production line was off. See Figure 7 for more detailed information.

Two other devices were also connected to this network, which communicated directly with the mobile robots. The first device was the MiR FLEET, which took care of the cooperation of several mobile robots. MiR FLEET is a web-based supervision application, that enables centralized control of multiple AMRs. The second device was the WISE module, which provided external communication with the mobile robot via digital inputs and outputs. It enabled communication between an AMR and the production line or some other device.

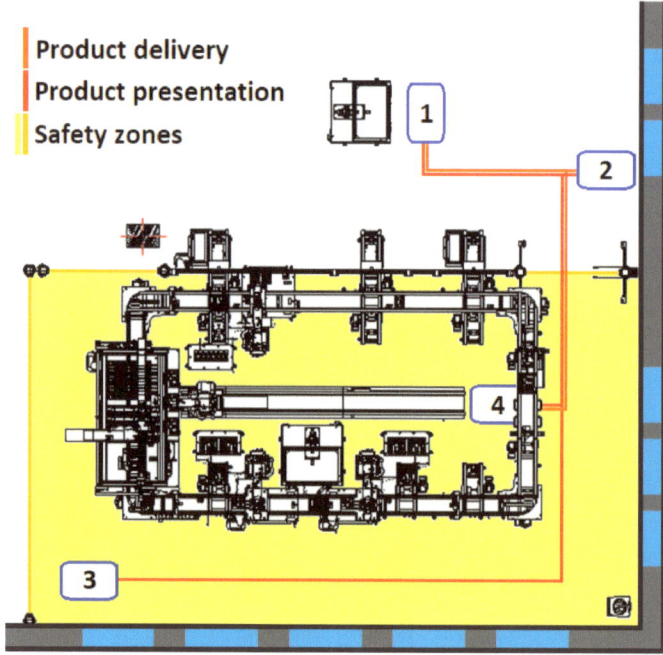

Figure 6. Delivery and presentation route of the product design. The block 1 represents the product delivery position, 2 represents the starting position, 3 represents the presentation position and in front of the windows, and 4 represents the product pickup position.

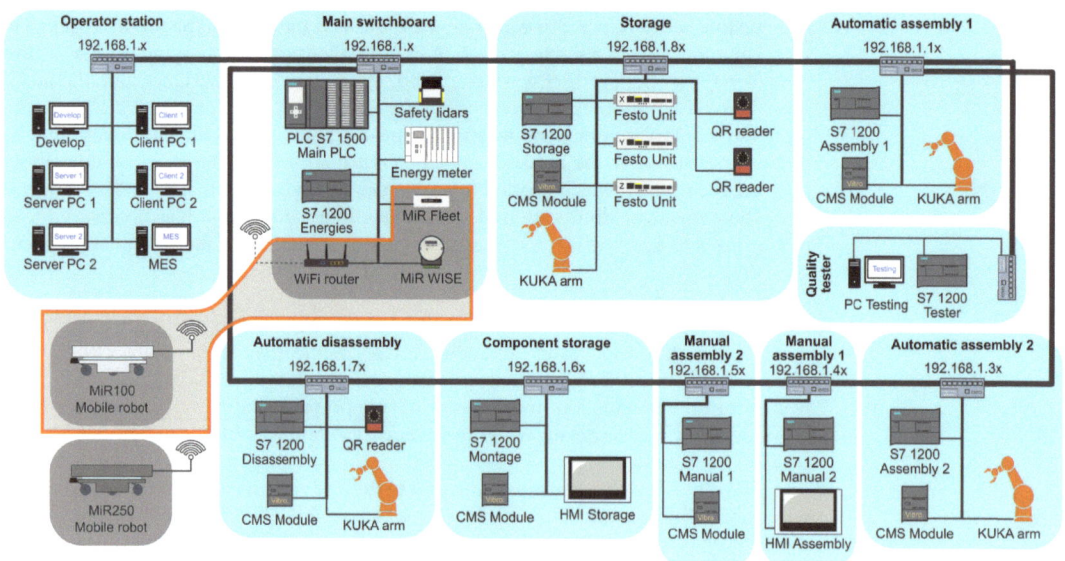

Figure 7. SmartFactory network diagram. The highlighted gray part is the solution presented.

4.2.1. Communication

The task of the mobile robot was to automatically take over the products from the production line and transport them to the designated place. For this functionality, it was necessary to ensure communication between the line and the mobile robot. Communication was provided by the WISE-4050/LAN module. It is equipped with 4 digital inputs and 4 digital outputs. The module is connected to the line switchboard and communicates directly with the C system, which controls the production line using inputs and outputs. To pair a mobile robot with a WISE module, it is necessary to place them on the same network. After pairing, instructions to read the digital input or change the digital output can be entered into robot missions. Since 8 digital signals were used for communication between the mobile robot and the production line, it was necessary that both the mobile robot side and the line side, and the programmable logic controller (PLC) knew the exact purpose of the signal. Communication was also necessary for the need of shutting down the safety barriers and gates, as the robot would otherwise activate them and set up a disruptive process. For this reason, individual signals were assigned a specific meaning. All signals required for communication are listed below.

- DO0: The mobile robot sends a signal that it is ready on the line to pick up the product;
- DO1: The mobile robot sends a signal that it is ready on the product collection line (LEGO);
- DO2: The mobile robot sends a signal that it is ready to call from the line;
- DI0: The mobile robot receives a signal to arrive at the line;
- DI1: The mobile robot receives a signal that it is loaded/unloaded;
- DI2: The mobile robot receives a signal that it has finished.

4.2.2. Implementation

The program for MiR mobile robots was created using individual commands, such as logic functions, move functions, docking functions, and more. These functions were then grouped into so-called "missions". The robot's mission was therefore a grouping of commands that determined what the robot should do in a particular mission. Within the mission, the individual commands were executed sequentially and if the robot had already fulfilled all commands, the mission was terminated. Missions were launched to the robot via a web interface, and it was possible to add more missions to the queue for the robot to complete. If the mobile robot had no mission in the queue, nor did it perform any active mission, it stood still and waited for the mission to be assigned.

- Movement and positioning
    - Move: The mobile robot moves to a position on map;
    - Docking: The mobile robot moves to a marker or charging station;
    - Rel. move: The mobile robot moves to a relative position.
- Logic functions
    - Charging: The mobile robot starts charging;
    - If: Conditioning decision function;
    - Loop: Cycle repeated execution of commands.
- WISE I/O module control
    - Set output: Switch on/off the output on a WISE module;
    - Read input: Read the actual value on the digital input of a WISE module;
    - Wait for input: Detection of the input on a WISE module.
- Other functions
    - Mission call: Perform a mission in another mission;
    - Light: Sets the style and color of the robot lights;
    - Sound: The ability for the mobile robot to play a sound.

The mobile robot MiR100 had the task of communicating with the production line in SmartFactory and taking the manufactured products. According to the proposed implementation, the mobile robot took a pair of products from the line. Each pair of products had a different final delivery position, and the mobile robot had to recognize which product was currently being delivered. It received this information from the line. The mobile robot also monitored the level of the battery so that it could operate continuously and was always ready to take the product. The entire programming code was divided into five missions, where the first was the main mission, and the rest were submissions for specific actions; see Figure 8.

A: Main mission
B: Waiting for product
C: Delivery A—LEGO product delivery mission
D: Delivery B—product design delivery mission
E: Charging mission

4.2.3. Precise Robot Positioning

In order to always be able to place the product in the same place on the robot superstructure, it was necessary for the mobile robot to approach the line in the loading position with great accuracy. If the mobile robot took the design of the product and then passed it on to the customer, this accuracy was not very necessary. However, if the mobile robot returned with a LEGO product and requested that the product be removed back to the line, an accuracy of a few millimeters was required. The mobile robot product loaded and unloaded the KUKA robotic arm, which always moved to the same position. This meant that when LEGO loaded a product onto a mobile robot, it expected the product to be in the same place when it was unloaded. The MiR100 mobile robot did not always move to the exact same position, and it was possible that when returning to the line, it was shifted by a few millimeters or even centimeters. The arm expected that the product would be in a completely different position. From this, three options were considered to achieve this.

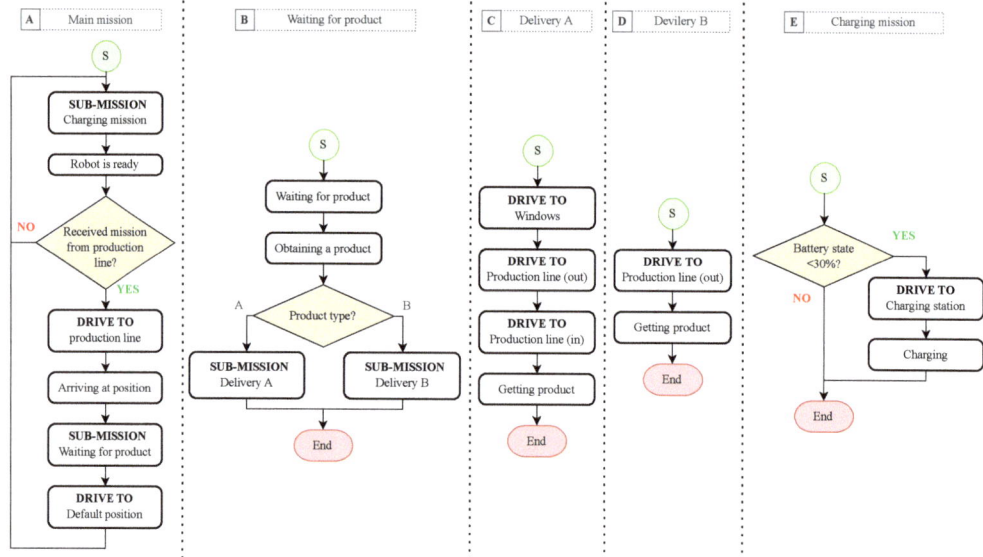

Figure 8. Program functionality diagram.

Camera

The first and at the same time the most technologically demanding possible solution was the use of a camera. The camera would be placed on a robotic arm and recognize the position of the product by recognizing the shapes of objects. The robotic arm would tilt over the mobile robot and use a camera to determine the exact location of the product on the mobile robot. The camera would pass this location to the robotic arm, who would know exactly where the product is located and how to grasp the product. The camera solution has one major advantage, but also disadvantages. When using the camera, the robot could enter the line differently each time, and its accuracy would not be necessary. A big advantage would be the ability to move the product on the platform of a mobile robot. The camera would always detect the position of the product, even if it was moved or rotated in a different direction from the original position. This would allow the customer to view the product and then place it back on the mobile robot. The disadvantage of the solution is the price and the high technical complexity. To enable image recognition, it would be necessary to connect the camera to the line control system and create a program that recognizes products.

Distance Sensors

Distance sensors were another possible solution to make missions and paths more precise. In the first case, the sensors would be placed on the body of the mobile robot and would sense the exact distance from the selected obstacles. After approaching the line, the mobile robot would use sensors to check whether it was in the exact position and, if necessary, adjust its position. However, this solution encounters a problem in communication with the mobile robot. Communication with the MiR100 mobile robot using the WISE module only allows control of digital inputs and outputs. For the purpose of this solution, it would be necessary to transfer the analog value from the sensors to the robot. A second variant was the placement of sensors on the production line. Instead of detecting the position of the mobile robot, the sensors would sense the position of the product on the robot. When using two laser sensors, one would sense the position of the product on the X-axis, and the other would sense the sensor in the position on the Y-axis.

Markers

The last solution considered was to enter the line using markers. Markers are a direct solution for a mobile robot to ensure that it approaches positions with a certain accuracy. Several types of markers can be used to navigate the mobile robot. These are V, L, VL, and bar-markers. Each marker has a specific shape and dimension that must be strictly adhered to during production. The marker should be placed directly in front of the mobile robot in the position where the robot will approach. This solution is the most accurate and accuracy also depends on the marker type used.

The planning algorithm used input parameters from the configuration interface of the robot. It meant that it was possible to configure which type of marker was currently in use. Each time the robot was approaching the final position, it was scanning the area for a marker specified using a configuration interface.

5. Results

Several tests were performed to verify exactly how the mobile robot could approach positions. The tests included moving the mobile robot to a position on the map, but also to different types of markers. The manufacturer states that each type of marker provides a different accuracy, and of all types of markers, the VL-marker is listed as the most accurate.

During the testing, we checked three distances. Distance between the mobile robot and the line profile on the left and right sides. The third distance checked was the distance between the robot's front and the rail to move the robotic arm. As part of the testing of each type of marker, a total of 100 robot entrances were performed on the lines. At each attempt, the mobile robot always drove out of the line area and then back to the position in the line, possibly using a marker. The data thus obtained were represented by a box plot and basic statistical indicators. The results demonstrated the accuracy with which the mobile robot approached a given location. The distance was read using three laser range finders.

5.1. Positioning without Marker

First, the accuracy of the position was tested in the absence of a marker. The mobile robot approached the position created on the virtual map. Since the robot guarded its surroundings and the line space was too narrow for the robot, it was necessary to place the position slightly in front of the line space. After approaching the position, a command was sent to the robot to use the command Relative move to move a certain distance forward into the line space. The command partially allowed the robot to drive into narrow spaces without the mobile robot detecting them as obstacles. The command Relative move had no effect on the accuracy of approaching the position on the map and only moved the robot on the given axis, always by the same distance.

From the test, it could be observed that if the robot only approached the position in the virtual map, it achieved a considerable inaccuracy. The variance of the measured values reached up to 25 mm in the case of the distance from the edge of the robot arm path. Thus, for AMR navigation, it was necessary to use the right type of marker to get the best results.

5.2. Using a VL-Marker

A VL-marker was used to specify the approach of the mobile robot to the position on the line. From the data from the manufacturer and distributor of robots, this is the most accurate marker, owing to which the mobile robot should achieve the highest accuracy.

Ideally, the marker should be placed in front of the robot. Due to the limited space in the line, the marker was placed slightly on the right side. During the initial creation of the marker, the robot approached directly opposite the marker. However, the markers allowed one to set the offset, and it was a matter of shifting or adjusting the final position of the robot on the marker. The offset could be set for the X-axis, the Y-axis, and the rotation.

5.3. Using an L-Marker

Another type of marker tested was the L-marker. Like other markers, it had exactly the given dimensions, which had to be observed with an accuracy of ±1 mm. For the use of the L-marker, no degree of accuracy was given with which the mobile robot could guide the marker.

5.4. Using a V-Marker

This marker was also used for AMR positioning. In shape, it contained the same "V" shape cutout as the VL-marker, but no longer contained another area to the right of the cutout, as the VL-marker did. It was therefore a smaller and lighter version of the VL-marker, which did not achieve greater accuracy than an L-marker.

5.5. Using a Bar-Marker

The bar-marker is a very simple type of marker. The bar-marker consists of two parts, which are built at a given distance from each other and between which the AMR moves. With this marker, we achieved the second worst results.

From the measured results, it can be observed that the L-marker further refined the approach of the robot to the exact position. The result of this test showed that thanks to the L-marker, the AMR could repeatedly approach the position with greater accuracy than with the VL-marker. The test, therefore, refuted the distributor's claim that the VL-marker was the most accurate. For detailed information, see Figure 9 and Table 4.

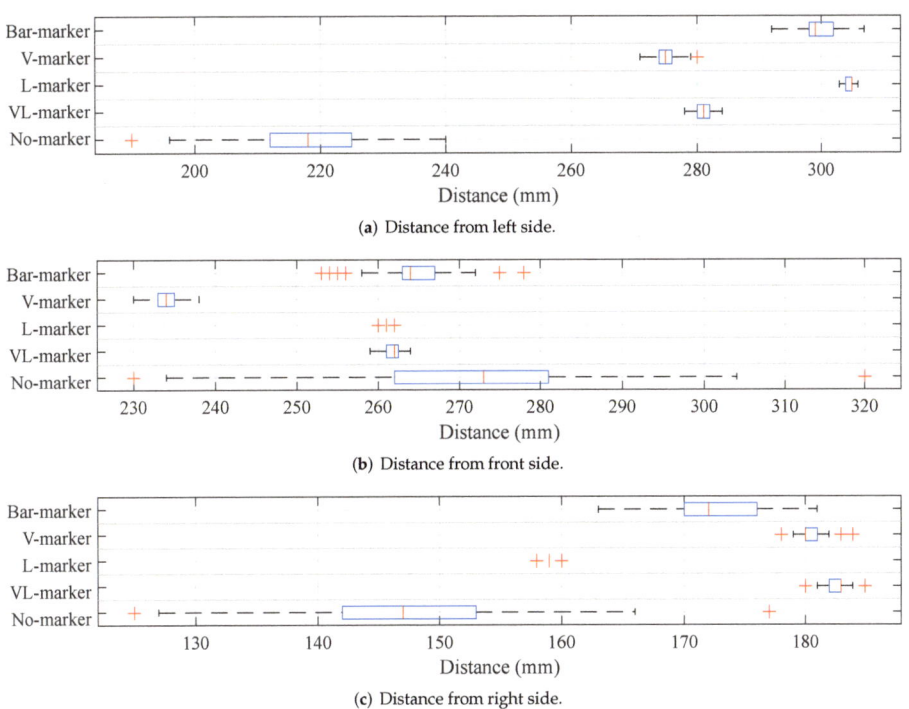

Figure 9. Box plots that compare the accuracy of individual markers on different sides.

Table 4. Accuracy test results.

Meas. #	L-Marker			VL-Marker			Bar-Marker			V-Marker			No Marker		
	Left (mm)	Front (mm)	Right (mm)	Left (mm)	Front (mm)	Right (mm)	Left (mm)	Front (mm)	Right (mm)	Left (mm)	Front (mm)	Right (mm)	Left (mm)	Front (mm)	Right (mm)
1	304	261	159	282	259	184	294	264	179	282	259	184	203	270	131
2	304	261	159	281	262	182	297	268	170	281	262	182	218	285	146
3	304	262	159	281	262	181	297	262	181	281	262	181	216	254	140
4	304	261	160	280	261	183	298	265	178	280	261	183	227	249	166
5	304	261	159	283	261	181	300	253	176	283	263	181	217	264	147
6	305	261	159	280	262	183	299	271	163	280	261	183	228	266	150
7	305	260	159	283	261	181	304	258	169	283	262	181	222	270	150
8	303	261	159	281	261	182	302	263	166	283	262	182	230	270	146
9	304	261	159	281	262	184	303	266	172	283	262	180	215	243	132
⋮	⋮	⋮	⋮	⋮	⋮	⋮	⋮	⋮	⋮	⋮	⋮	⋮	⋮	⋮	⋮
100	305	261	160	282	262	182	300	265	163	281	262	180	217	268	164
Mean	304.4	261.1	159.2	281.3	261.5	182.2	298.7	265.0	171.4	281.3	261.5	182.2	213.9	262.5	145.7
StD	0.599	0.408	0.545	1.266	1.168	1.156	2.841	5.716	4.052	2.038	1.966	1.0815	9.233	14.357	7.630

During testing, the mobile robot encountered an error when it could not reach the L-marker in (b). The L-marker was placed as in (a) so that the mobile robot did not have a problem in position. The problem occurred only during the final shooting of the robot in parallel with the marker. Instead of turning, the robot got stuck in the shooting phase and moved back and forth about 5°. After checking the robot's status through the web interface, the robot still performed the docking process and did not show any errors. Even after a certain time, the robot did not exit this cycle and it was necessary to end the program that was executed. The problem was solved by moving the marker to another location and reading the marker onto the map. After that, the problem did not manifest itself.

Figure 10 describes the positioning of the different markers during the test according to the manufacturer's recommendations.

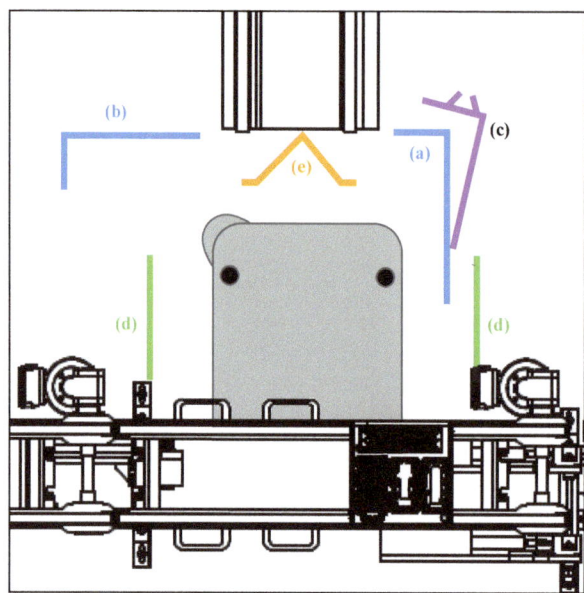

Figure 10. (**a**) L-marker, good position; (**b**) L-marker, problematic position; (**c**) VL-marker; (**d**) bar-markers; (**e**) V-marker.

Another complication occurred when adding a marker to a virtual map. If the mobile robot was chosen to detect the position of the marker in the environment, it could not determine the position of the marker. Instead of the real L-marker, the mobile robot detected the corner of the production line as the L-marker. This was despite the completely inconsistent dimensions, which differed significantly from the given dimensions for the L-marker. Therefore, when the L-marker was loaded, an obstacle was placed in this corner so that it would no longer be detected as a marker.

6. Conclusions and Future Work

This paper described the implementation of an industrial autonomous mobile robot MiR100 in SmartFactory. The production line produced a pair of products that were not distributed outside the premises of the line, and therefore it was not possible to take possession of the produced product. For this reason, the mobile robot was used to distribute the finished products around the SmartFactory premises. The line produced design products and customizable LEGO products. The design product was intended for the target customer, to whom the product was delivered by the mobile robot. The LEGO product was not intended for customers and was only used to demonstrate what the line was capable of. The mobile robot drove the LEGO product through the SmartFactory premises and then returned the LEGO product back to the line, which then disassembled it into its individual components.

In the first step of the implementation, it was necessary to create a virtual map of the SmartFactory, according to which the mobile robot had to orient itself in space. Individual obstacles, forbidden zones, positions, and markers necessary for the implementation were inserted into the map. The SmartFactory contained its own wireless fidelity (Wi-Fi) network, to which all the devices needed to operate the robot and communicate with the production line were connected. Communication with the line was provided by the WISE module, which contained four digital inputs and four digital outputs. Each digital signal had a clear meaning and was sufficient for communication between the mobile robot and the production line. The program for operating the production line was divided into individual missions. In order to start the operation of the production line, the main mission had to be started on the mobile robot, which was already calling the next sub-mission. The manufactured products were transferred to the mobile robot by a robotic arm. When loading products onto the robot, the positioning accuracy of the mobile robot was not important. When unloading the LEGO product that the robotic arm returned to the line, a high precision was required to position the robotic arm correctly. This accuracy was not achieved by the mobile robot, so we came up with three suggestions to improve the accuracy. Using a camera to determine the exact position of the product, using external sensors to accurately position the mobile robot, and using markers to increase the positioning accuracy. After consulting and considering the complexity of the solution, we decided to use markers. Since the mobile robot supported multiple types of markers, we tested their accuracy. The L-marker came out best in the tests.

The result was a fully automated process for operating the production line. The MiR100 mobile robot could respond to a call from the line, then arrive to collect the product, take it over and make its presentation or delivery to the desired location. The operation also included battery monitoring and automatic recharging if necessary.

We see the potential for improving the way we communicate in future developments. The communication used by the WISE module is limited to data types and a small number of inputs and outputs. During further development, communication via a representational state transfer API (REST API) supported by a mobile robot is planned. In addition, the robotic arm will be retrofitted with a camera. If the robotic arm was equipped with a camera, the capabilities of the mobile robot would be expanded. Without the camera, the LEGO product must remain in the same position as the robotic arm. Using the camera, the LEGO product could be removed from the mobile robot and then returned. The viewer would then be able to view the LEGO product themselves. The camera would then identify the position of the LEGO product and relay this information to the robotic arm.

The main contribution and the results obtained were that a statistical analysis of the mobile robot's run-up on different types of markers was performed to determine the repeated run-up accuracy. Here, it was found that the most suitable marker type was the L type, where the mobile robot had a repetitive error of $\pm$ 3mm. This output is essential for applications where the industrial arm is transferring products to the mobile robot, but also for the reverse, where products are removed from the mobile robot. Repeated pick-up accuracy is therefore crucial. Despite the fact that MiR offered a ready-made solution, it was necessary to verify the behavior of the robot in real conditions, where its navigation was hampered, in particular by the narrow space in the production line area, the conveyor belt which was in a position partially above the mobile robot at the moment of the robot's run-up, and the number of structural elements in close proximity to the robot. All these elements can affect the accuracy of the robot's sensors and scanners. In such a confined space, the robot is constrained by its own safety zone settings, which eliminate the possibility of robot movement and may limit the final positioning accuracy compared to the accuracy declared in the manufacturing documentation.

Author Contributions: Conceptualization, R.H., R.B. and R.J.; methodology, R.H. and R.B.; software, R.H. and R.B.; validation, R.H., R.B. and R.J.; formal analysis, R.J.; investigation, R.H. and R.B.; resources, J.K.; data curation, R.H. and R.B.; writing—original draft preparation, R.H., R.B. and R.J.; writing—review and editing, R.H., R.B. and R.J.; visualization, R.H. and J.K.; supervision, J.K.; project administration, J.K.; funding acquisition, J.K. All authors have read and agreed to the published version of the manuscript.

Funding: This work was supported by the European Regional Development Fund in Research Platform focused on Industry 4.0 and Robotics in Ostrava project CZ.02.1.01/0.0/0.0/17_049/0008425 within the Operational Program Research, Development and Education. This work was also supported by the Virtual Instrumentation for test and measurement systems SP2022/88.

Institutional Review Board Statement: Not applicable.

Informed Consent Statement: Not applicable.

Data Availability Statement: Not applicable.

Conflicts of Interest: The authors declare no conflict of interest.

Abbreviations

The following abbreviations are used in this manuscript:

AMR	Autonomous mobile robot
API	Application programming interface
CPIT TL3	Building in VSB campus with sophisticated management system
IMU	Inertial measurement unit
KUKA	Robotic arm from KUKA company
MiR	Mobile Industrial Robots
MiR100	Autonomous mobile robot from the MiR Company
MiR FLEET	Centralized control station for MiR robots
MiR WISE	I/O module for MiR robots
PLC	Programmable logic controller
SICK S300	Type of laser sensor
REST API	Representational state transfer API
Wi-Fi	Wireless fidelity

References

1. Chen, X.Q.; Chen, Y.Q.; Chase, J.G. Mobiles Robots—Past Present and Future. In *Mobile Robots-State of the Art in Land, Sea, Air, and Collaborative Missions*; IntechOpen: Vienna, Austria, 2009. [CrossRef]
2. Siegwart, R.; Nourbakhsh, I.R.; Scaramuzza, D. *Introduction to Autonomous Mobile Robots*, 2nd ed.; MIT Press: Cambridge, MA, USA, 2011.
3. McMorris, B. *A History Timeline of Industrial Robotics*; Futura Automation: Bengaluru, India, 2019.
4. Alatise, M.B.; Hancke, G.P. A Review on Challenges of Autonomous Mobile Robot and Sensor Fusion Methods. *IEEE Access* **2020**, *8*, 39830–39846. [CrossRef]
5. Marques, F.; Gonçalves, D.; Barata, J.; Santana, P. Human-Aware Navigation for Autonomous Mobile Robots for Intra-factory Logistics. In Proceedings of the 6th International Workshop, Symbiotic 2017, Eindhoven, The Netherlands, 18–19 December 2017; Ham, J., Spagnolli, A., Blankertz, B., Gamberini, L., Jacucci, G., Eds.; Springer International Publishing: Cham, Switzerland, 2018; pp. 79–85. [CrossRef]
6. Majchrzak, M. AMR market expands rapidly: The market for autonomous mobile robots (AMRs) is growing fast, and there is a lot of demand globally for them in traditional automation, in non-automotive sectors. *Control. Eng.* **2020**, *67*, M11.
7. Fragapane, G.; Hvolby, H.H.; Sgarbossa, F.; Strandhagen, J.O. Autonomous Mobile Robots in Hospital Logistics. In *Proceedings of the Advances in Production Management Systems. The Path to Digital Transformation and Innovation of Production Management Systems*; Lalic, B., Majstorovic, V., Marjanovic, U., von Cieminski, G., Romero, D., Eds.; IFIP Advances in Information and Communication Technology; Springer International Publishing: New York, NY, USA, 2020; pp. 672–679. [CrossRef]
8. Surmann, H.; Nüchter, A.; Hertzberg, J. An autonomous mobile robot with a 3D laser range finder for 3D exploration and digitalization of indoor environments. *Robot. Auton. Syst.* **2003**, *45*, 181–198. [CrossRef]
9. Kramer, J.; Scheutz, M. Development environments for autonomous mobile robots: A survey. *Auton. Robot.* **2007**, *22*, 101–132. [CrossRef]
10. Chen, H.; Cheng, H.; Zhang, B.; Wang, J.; Fuhlbrigge, T.; Liu, J. Semiautonomous industrial mobile manipulation for industrial applications. In Proceedings of the 2013 IEEE International Conference on Cyber Technology in Automation, Control and Intelligent Systems, Nanjing, China, 26–29 May 2013; pp. 361–366. [CrossRef]
11. Unger, H.; Markert, T.; Müller, E. Evaluation of use cases of autonomous mobile robots in factory environments. *Procedia Manuf.* **2018**, *17*, 254–261. [CrossRef]
12. *Autonomous Mobile Robot (AMRs) Types and Uses*; Conveyco: Bristol, UK, 2020.
13. Panigrahi, P.K.; Bisoy, S.K. Localization strategies for autonomous mobile robots: A review. *J. King Saud Univ.-Comput. Inf. Sci.* **2021**, *34*, 6019–6039. [CrossRef]
14. Fragapane, G.; De Koster, R.; Sgarbossa, F.; Strandhagen, J.O. Planning and control of autonomous mobile robots for intralogistics: Literature review and research agenda. *Eur. J. Oper. Res.* **2021**, *294*, 405–426. [CrossRef]
15. Tzafestas, S.G. Mobile Robot Control and Navigation: A Global Overview. *J. Intell. Robot. Syst.* **2018**, *91*, 35–58. [CrossRef]
16. Iqbal, J.; Xu, R.; Sun, S.; Li, C. Simulation of an Autonomous Mobile Robot for LiDAR-Based In-Field Phenotyping and Navigation. *Robotics* **2020**, *9*, 46. [CrossRef]

17. Gatesichapakorn, S.; Takamatsu, J.; Ruchanurucks, M. ROS based Autonomous Mobile Robot Navigation using 2D LiDAR and RGB-D Camera. In Proceedings of the 2019 First International Symposium on Instrumentation, Control, Artificial Intelligence, and Robotics (ICA-SYMP), Bangkok, Thailand, 16–18 January 2019; pp. 151–154. [CrossRef]
18. CPIT TL3—Smart Factory. Available online: http://smartfactory.vsb.cz/index.html (accessed on 20 July 2022).
19. Mobile Robot from Mobile Industrial Robots–MiR100. Available online: https://www.mobile-industrial-robots.com/solutions/robots/mir100/ (accessed on 20 July 2022).
20. User Guide for MiR100 Autonomous Mobile Robots. 2021. Available online: https://gibas.nl/wp-content/uploads/2021/01/mir100-user-guide_31_en.pdf (accessed on 20 July 2022).
21. KUKA—Industrial Intelligence 4.0: Beyond Automation. Available online: https://www.kuka.com/ (accessed on 20 July 2022).

Article

Occupancy Reward-Driven Exploration with Deep Reinforcement Learning for Mobile Robot System

Albina Kamalova *, Suk Gyu Lee and Soon Hak Kwon

Department of Electrical Engineering, Yeungnam University, Gyeongsan 38541, Korea
* Correspondence: dyupleks@gmail.com; Tel.: +82-10-9921-6172

Abstract: This paper investigates the solution to a mobile-robot exploration problem following autonomous driving principles. The exploration task is formulated in this study as a process of building a map while a robot moves in an indoor environment beginning from full uncertainties. The sequence of robot decisions of how to move defines the strategy of the exploration that this paper aims to investigate, applying one of the Deep Reinforcement Learning methods, known as the Deep Deterministic Policy Gradient (DDPG) algorithm. A custom environment is created representing the mapping process with a map visualization, a robot model, and a reward function. The actor-critic network receives and sends input and output data, respectively, to the custom environment. The input is the data from the laser sensor, which is equipped on the robot. The output is the continuous actions of the robot in terms of linear and angular velocities. The training results of this study show the strengths and weaknesses of the DDPG algorithm for the robotic mapping problem. The implementation was developed in MATLAB platform using its corresponding toolboxes. A comparison with another exploration algorithm is also provided.

Keywords: mobile-robot system; reinforcement learning; deep neural network; mapping; exploration; navigation

Citation: Kamalova, A.; Lee, S.G.; Kwon, S.H. Occupancy Reward-Driven Exploration with Deep Reinforcement Learning for Mobile Robot System. *Appl. Sci.* **2022**, *12*, 9249. https://doi.org/10.3390/app12189249

Academic Editors: Luis Gracia and J. Ernesto Solanes

Received: 24 July 2022
Accepted: 11 September 2022
Published: 15 September 2022

Publisher's Note: MDPI stays neutral with regard to jurisdictional claims in published maps and institutional affiliations.

Copyright: © 2022 by the authors. Licensee MDPI, Basel, Switzerland. This article is an open access article distributed under the terms and conditions of the Creative Commons Attribution (CC BY) license (https://creativecommons.org/licenses/by/4.0/).

1. Introduction

In the past two decades, an enormous number of works on the mobile-robot exploration domain or the so-called mapping or map coverage have been published [1,2]. Generally, every novel exploration technique aims to solve three basic challenges. The first is to explore fully a given space using an onboard robot-vision system. The second is to not encounter any obstacles while driving through. The next is to optimize the driving course in the exploration, saving time and energy costs. This represents a bigger picture of mapping, addressing only problematics.

Delving deeper into the field, various characteristics of an exploration can be discovered. For instance, for environment types, the exploration can be conducted indoors, outdoors [3], on cluttered rough terrain [4,5], in a post-disaster extreme environment [6], in the ocean [7], or on a planetary surface [8]. The exploration can have requirements based on the map type (grid map [9], octomap [10], point cloud map [11], semantic map [12]) or the approach (deterministic [13,14], stochastic [15], artificial intelligence [16,17], SLAM-(Simultaneous Localization and Mapping) type [18,19]). In addition, the exploration can be processed by different robot systems [20]: a mobile-robot system or multi-robot system. These various characteristics are the reasons why mapping the field is an important topic in robotics and why it remains relevant today.

In mobile-robot exploration, a robot is launched into a space with entirely unknown information about the indoor environment. A robot can have vision using a sensor or camera that senses at a certain sensing distance or image resolution, respectively. During mapping, the robot drives towards and perceives more knowledge about the environment. It can have a task or an action command while it moves in the environment. The task can be a point in the environment, which is called a local point or a waypoint [21]. The computation of the waypoints in the mapping is conducted by a computational algorithm, which many scholars have attempted to either modify in combination with other techniques or create new ones. In this study, the exploration does not use the waypoint concept. Instead, the robot moves by following the action command being transmitted to the robot motors.

The final result of the robotic exploration is a finite map. The map is a data model of the robot's surroundings. The robot needs the map on a regular basis to have knowledge of its position for further missions. Object recognition, object segmentation, planning movement, and many other typical human activities in indoor space are required for an existing known map, which is true for a robot as well.

Artificial intelligence (AI) is a significant topic in science nowadays [22]. It is believed that AI is a general term, which describes how computers or hardware systems can think and behave like a human. A subfield of AI is machine learning [23]. It is mainly focused on learning from data training. Over decades, machine learning evolved into deep learning, which could transform the data into multiple-layer representations due to feature detection or pattern classification [24]. The considerable success of some applications, such as image recognition, speech recognition, email spam filtering, and the winning of AlphaGo in the board game Go, motivated developers around the world to apply machine learning or deep learning techniques in various fields.

The process of the learning divides machine learning, deep or otherwise, into three subfields: supervised learning, unsupervised learning, and reinforcement learning [25]. In the first two types of learning, only neural networks are considered, which are trained with and without labeled input data, respectively. The third type, reinforcement learning (RL), differs from the first two such that a neural network in RL can be employed as a nonlinear approximator function; this is why the term Deep Reinforcement Learning (deep-RL) is used. The deep-RL can be understood with the concept of an agent, environment, action, observation, and reward, all of which will be discussed in detail. RL is classified into two types: model-based and model-free. The model-based RL has the model of an environment and a planning of agent dynamics, whereas an agent of the model-free RL learns only by values, without explicitly knowing an environment model. Most applications, like this study, are based on model-free RL. In the model-free category, there are three approaches of algorithms for an agent's learning: value-based, policy-based, and actor-critic. The value-based algorithms are when an agent uses the value function to evaluate the goodness or badness of states. In turn, the policy-based algorithms follow a policy of an agent's behavior, which is a map from state to action. The actor-critic approach is a mix of value-based and policy-based algorithms; this approach is applied in this paper. Figure 1 shows the summary of machine learning classification from artificial intelligence to RL algorithms.

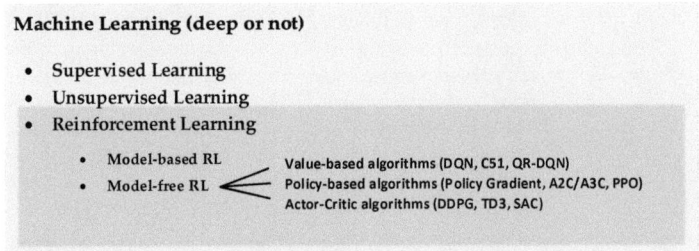

Figure 1. The family of machine learning techniques.

In this study, the model-free actor-critic RL approach aims to solve the mobile robot exploration problem in indoor environments. There are several algorithms that can be listed under the actor-critic category: Deep Deterministic Policy Gradient (DDPG), Twin Delayed Deep Deterministic Policy Gradients (TD3), Proximal Policy Optimization (PPO), Soft Actor Critic (SAC), and Asynchronous Advantage Actor Critic (A3C). In this study, the off-policy DDPG algorithm is selected for the mapping problem. The DDPG algorithm is useful for robotics applications because it allows the control of electric motors due to continuous output data. The remaining algorithms mentioned above are able to provide continuous actions as well. However, the DDPG learns directly from the observation data, which corresponds to the mapping problem using a laser sensor. In addition, the DDPG algorithm is not often applied to mobile-robot exploration problems, which is a motivation for the authors to study it in practical application.

The contribution of this study is as follows. A custom environment was created especially for exploration using the occupancy map and the robot movement. The environment evaluates the robot's motion for learning the unknown space using a reward function. In the same way, it denounces the robot for the negative occasions, such as obstacle collisions. Another contribution is the creation of the DDPG agent and training process for the custom environment. At the end of the paper, the positive and negative results of using the DDPG algorithm are presented for the mapping problem. The comparison of the DDPG algorithm and the nature-inspired exploration algorithm shows the advantages and disadvantages of each approach.

It is important to clarify the terminology in this section, as the names for the mobile-robotics and deep-RL fields intersect. The word "environment" is used in both topics, but the meanings are not the same. The environment in mapping means a physical or simulated space with walls and furniture, for example, a room- or an office-like environment. In deep-RL, the environment is the description of the input/output data reactions, model visualization, and reward function. In the proceeding sections, the RL environment will be used to denote this, and the absence of RL means the terms are related to the mobile-robot system.

This paper is structured as follows. Section 2 discusses the related works of the deep-RL algorithms in the mobile-robot field. In Section 3, the theory of deep-RL and DDPG algorithms are explained in detail. In Section 4, the occupancy reward-driven exploration based on the DDPG agent is proposed. The reward parameters and training options are discussed in Section 5. Finally, the simulation results and the comparison are presented in Section 6, which prove the proposed concept in practice.

2. Related Works

With the development of machine learning algorithms, the robotics field obtained novel and alternative resolutions in its domain along with existing classical methods [26]. Although AI and its concept are not a new trend in computer science [27,28], in robotics, a significant number of applications based on machine learning and its deep learning subdomain have been launched recently, with modern AI appearing with the combination of "big data" and neural network architectures [24,29].

In terms of the applications of deep learning in robotic mapping, two major groups of approaches can be highlighted. The first one is deep learning with widely used convolutional neural network (CNN) architecture. It can be said that CNN was inspired by human vision in the manner of how a human is able to perceive objects and use this knowledge for a multitude of tasks. The major function of CNN is to extract features out of images and then to classify them as an object. Thus, it follows that the robot motion based on CNN can be realized in a case when a robot is equipped with a visual sensor that is a camera. An example is the research [30] on mobile-robot exploration using a hierarchical structure that fuses CNN layers with decision-making process. It obtains RGB-D information from the camera as the input and generates the moving direction as the output for the Turtlebot robot. In the same vein, CNN is applied for exploration in another study [31]. In spite of the fact that it is trained on the basis of input images of the floor plans, the output result returns images containing the labels of exit locations in the building. It is assumed that the search of exit locations in the building refers also to the robotic exploration problem and can be called a semantic or visual exploration. More segmentation is processed in another study [32], capturing the labels (books, ceiling, a chair, floor, a table, etc.) from RGB-D video. CNN and dense Simultaneous Localization and Mapping (SLAM) are applied together in order to add the semantic predictions to a map from multiple viewpoints. The human walk trajectories were predicted by CNN in Ref. [33]. The output results help the robot use this information for avoiding obstacles and planning further tasks. Concluding the discussion on the CNN-related approach, it can be emphasized that there are still limitations in training. It is assumed that CNN learns offline, whereas the mobile-robot exploration usually works online. This is why CNN-based mapping is sometimes considered an impractical solution [34].

The second branch of the robot exploration based on deep learning pertains to deep-RL. Neural networks are also employed in this approach with several numbers of layers, hence, the term "deep-RL". However, NNs are considered function approximators or the so-called policies that can efficiently operate large numbers of actions and states during training. Based on the field of application, a designer can select an appropriate neural network type among built-in RL approximators and well-known approximators, like CNN and RNN.

Table 1 presents related works on mobile-robot exploration. The authors analyzed and sorted out the literature based on the main classifications of the RL framework: algorithm, environment, and map representation. In the study of Kollar et al. [35], it can be seen that the support vector machine algorithm, which is related to supervised machine learning, was applied instead of a deep neural network. The exploration is formulated into a model of partially observable Markov decision process (POMDP). The output result in this work is the optimization of the trajectory in the mapping process. In their study [36], Lei Tai et al., proposed to build a map of the corridor environment using depth sensor information. The CNN model extracts the features from the environment, and the value-based Deep Q-network (DQN) executes the obstacle avoidance for the Turtlebot robot. However, its reward strategy does not stimulate the robot to further and faster explore the uncertainties involved. The static values of 1 and −50 can be referred to as the navigation strategy rather than the mapping. The research of Zhelo et al. [37] investigated the reward function known as an intrinsic reward. The robot navigation is trained using targets by the asynchronous advantage actor-critic algorithm (A3C) with external and intrinsic rewards. Apart from the reward, the novel term "mapless navigation" is proposed for the exploration, which is used in other studies, but only for the navigation problem [38–40]. Mapless navigation is when the robot drives without any knowledge of the environment (such as obstacle position and the frontier line between explored and unknown areas) to the targets whose positions are visible due to visible light or Wi-Fi signal localization. This kind of navigation for the exploration problem does not have the ability to build any finite map acquisitions.

End-to-end navigation in an unknown environment based on DDPG with long short-term memory (LSTM) is presented in the study of Z. Lu et al. [41]. Its reward function impels the robot to avoid dynamic obstacles and to choose a smooth trajectory. Chen et al. [42] offered the idea to explore uncertainties via exploration graphs in conjunction with graph neural networks and RL. The deep Q-network agent predicts the robot's optimal sensing action in belief space. The graph abstraction optimizes and generalizes data for the learning process. This combination of the approaches showed efficient mapping results in the comparison with other policy categories of graph neural networks and RL agents. The study of H. Li et al. [43] proposed a new decision approach based on deep-RL. The approach is a Fully Convolution Q-network (FCQN) with an auxiliary task that receives the grid map of the partial environment as input and returns the control policy as output. Shurmann et al. [44] presented and demonstrated real-time exploration using the Turtlebot robot mounted with an RGB-D camera and Hokuyo laser sensor. To conclude the discussion on the deep-RL-related exploration group, Ref. [45], focusing on the search for uncertainties in an occupancy map, can be presented. Refs. [43,45], which use the occupancy-driven reward function, are shown in Table 1. The strategy of keeping the robot moving towards new areas during the process is a key function in mobile-robot exploration. In the same way, the reward function is a significant component in the deep-RL framework. This is the reason for the authors' interest in the reward strategy applied in the related works and their proposed contribution in this work.

Table 1. Related works on the mobile-robot exploration using deep-RL.

	RL Algorithm		RL Environment			Map Representation
	Approximator	Agent	Input	Output	Reward	
T. Kollar et al. [35]	Support Vector Machine Policy Learning	Policy Search Dynamic Programming	Laser sensor	Discrete action	Squared error reward function	Occupancy map
L. Tai et al. [36]	CNN	Deep Q-network	RGB-D camera	Discrete actions of 3 moving directions	Keep moving is value 1, collision or stop are -50	Corridor environment, Turtlebot, Gazebo
O. Zhelo et al. [37]	Actor-critic network	A3C agent	Laser sensor	Continuous actions	Intrinsic reward	Simulated environment, 3 maps with different floor plans
Z. Lu et al. [41]	Actor-critic network with LTSM module	DDPG agent	Laser sensor, target points	Continuous actions: linear and angular velocities	Novel reward function for avoiding collision	Gazebo
F. Chen et al. [42]	Graph neural networks	Deep Q-network agent	Laser sensor	Sensing action	Raw reward	Occupancy map
H. Li et al. [43]	FCQN with auxiliary task	Deep Q-network agent	Partial map	Discrete action	Heuristic reward function	Occupancy map, ROS
H. Surmann et al. [44]	Actor-critic network	Fast Hybrid CPU/GPU version of A3C agent	Laser sensor, RGB-D camera	Continuous actions: linear and angular velocities	Goal reached is value 20, collision is value of -20	Simulated and real environment, ROS
J. Zhang et al. [45]	Actor-critic network and Neural-SLAM	A3C with generalized advantage estimator	Laser sensor	Discrete action	-0.04 values for each step, -0.96 for collision, $\frac{1}{3\times 5}$ for new grid	Occupancy map, Gazebo

There are many other studies that focus on solving other problems encountered in mobile-robot systems. In particular, deep-RL is frequently applied in navigation [46–52], path planning [53,54], and collision avoidance [55–58].

3. Background

This section discusses the theory concept of Reinforcement Learning and its continuous control method—deep deterministic policy gradient (DDPG) [59].

3.1. Reinforcement Learning

Reinforcement Learning (RL) is a goal-oriented approach that extracts successful actions in an area of concern during its training. This method allows a robot to make correct decisions for a task without human intervention. The RL consists of two main parts: an agent and the RL environment (Figure 2).

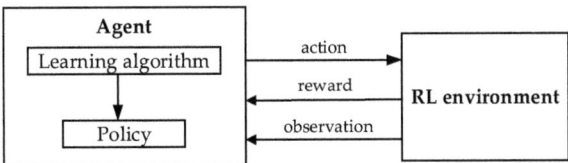

Figure 2. RL system.

The process of RL starts with the environment sending its initial observation (or so-called state) to the agent. According to its computation, the agent makes the action in response to this observation. By this, the action changes the environment, which can be good or bad. Then, the environment sends a new observation and a reward for the last action to the agent. It receives and updates its knowledge and then takes the next action based on the computational analysis. The process repeats in this manner until the environment gives the signal of the end of an episode.

The agent can be seen as a computational controller. It contains a policy and a learning algorithm. The policy is a function approximator (deep neural network), which selects appropriate actions with regards to the observations from the RL environment. The learning algorithm component is to search an optimal policy by maximizing the cumulative reward. It continuously updates the policy parameters based on reward, actions, and observations.

In this study, we applied the actor-critic agent belonging to the class of RL algorithms. There are several known varieties of actor-critic agents, which use either a deterministic actor or stochastic actor, with Q-value critic or a value critic. The difference among them is in the manner of how the data of an actor and critic are updated in the process.

3.2. Actor-Critic Deep Deterministic Policy Gradient Algorithm

The DDPG algorithm is a model-free, online, off-policy RL method. The DDPG agent uses a deterministic actor and Q-value critic. The DDPG agent searches for an optimal policy that maximizes the expected cumulative long-term reward. It can be applied only for an RL environment with continuous action spaces [59].

In the DDPG algorithm, the actor-critic architecture applies four function approximations: deterministic actor network, target actor network, critic network, and target critic network. Considering each separately, Figure 3a represents the actor architecture, in which the actor $\mu(O, \theta^\mu)$ directly maps the observations O_i to corresponding actions a_i, which maximizes the long-term reward R. In Figure 3b, the critic $Q(O, A, \theta^Q)$ takes actions and observations and returns the corresponding expectation Q of long-term reward. The parameters θ^μ and θ^Q are network weights. The general actor-critic architecture is represented in Figure 3c, in which the RL environment passes the observation to the actor and critic. The actor determines the action and sends it to the critic. That is, the critic estimates the value of how much reward the agent will obtain from this situation. Combining the value with the reward R gives the estimated value of receiving the current observation and making the current action.

Figure 3. Cont.

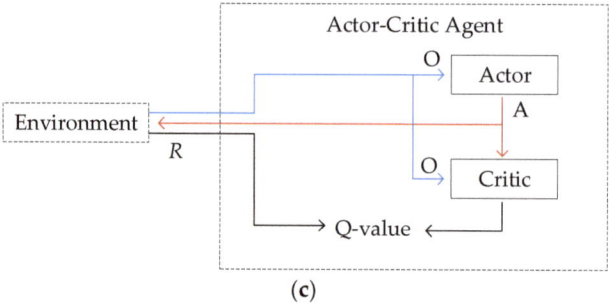

Figure 3. Architectures: (**a**) actor, (**b**) critic, (**c**) actor-critic.

The actor target network $\mu'\left(O, \theta^{\mu'}\right)$ and critic target network $Q'\left(O, A, \theta^{Q'}\right)$ are time−delayed copies of their original networks that slowly track the actor and critic networks. The main role of the target networks is to improve the stability in the learning by periodically saving the actor and critic parameters. The weight parameters $\theta^{\mu'}$ and $\theta^{Q'}$ of the actor and critic target networks are updated by the equations below for $\tau \ll 1$:

$$\theta^{Q'} \leftarrow \tau\theta^Q + (1-\tau)\theta^{Q'} \qquad (1)$$

$$\theta^{\mu'} \leftarrow \tau\theta^\mu + (1-\tau)\theta^{\mu'} \qquad (2)$$

The critic side of the DDPG algorithm updates the critic by minimizing the loss between target y and the original Q value of the critic network through the following equation:

$$L = \frac{1}{M}\sum_i \left(y_i - Q\left(O_i, a_i, \theta^Q\right)\right)^2 \qquad (3)$$

The target y is calculated using the Bellman equation:

$$y_i = r_i + \gamma Q'\left(O_{i+1}, \mu'\left(O_{i+1}, \theta^{\mu'}\right), \theta^{Q'}\right) \qquad (4)$$

where Q' is the next Q value obtained from target networks, γ is the discount factor, and r is the reward at time i.

The actor side of the DDPG algorithm updates the actor parameters using the sampled policy gradient using the following equation:

$$\nabla_{\theta^\mu} J \approx \frac{1}{M}\sum_i \nabla_a Q\left(O_i, A, \theta^Q\right)\Big|_{A=\mu(O_i, \theta^\mu)} \cdot \nabla_{\theta^\mu}\mu(O_i, \theta^\mu) \qquad (5)$$

Here, $\nabla_a Q\left(O_i, A, \theta^Q\right)$ is the gradient of the critic output with respect to the action computed by the actor network. The gradient of the actor output is $\nabla_{\theta^\mu}\mu(O_i, \theta^\mu)$ with respect to the actor parameters [60].

In the discussion of the DDPG algorithm, which incorporates DQN [61], two trick techniques with data, the replay buffer and the minibatch, cannot be excluded. The replay buffer is like a data stack with 'last in—first out' principal operation. The experience tuples (O_i, a_i, r_i, O_{i+1}) from the RL environment are added to the end of the buffer so that the oldest experience is pushed out. The replay buffer can have a large size, and the large size should be set. The large collection of experiences allows the data not to fall into convergence and divergence issues. The minibatch is a randomly sampled experience taking from the replay buffer. In Equations (3) and (5), the notation M is the minibatch size or the number of sampled experiences. In each time step, the Q-value and policy of critic and actor networks are updated by sampling a minibatch using the batch normalization technique.

For the continuous action spaces of the DDGP algorithm, the exploration is done by adding noise to the current policy using the following equation:

$$a_i = \mu(O_t|\theta^\mu) + N_i \tag{6}$$

where N_i is stochastic noise.

4. The Proposed Occupancy-Reward-Driven Exploration

This section presents the mobile-robot exploration approach using the model-free deep-RL technique, which is DDPG. In the beginning, the issues of the mapping process are discussed. Then, the model of Markov Decision Process (MDP) for the robotic exploration system is presented. The actions, states, and rewards as elements of MDP were introduced in Section 3 in the discussion of the RL framework and DDPG algorithm. Here, we present the MDP model specially designed for the mobile-robot mapping process while noting that the MDP is a model that allows the description of the RL environment only.

Afterwards, the section introduces the main components of the custom RL environment, with its occupancy reward function created for the mobile-robot exploration. Then, the agent of the actor-critic networks is demonstrated at the end of this section.

4.1. The Robotic Exploration Problem Formalization

Robotic mapping is a process where a real environment is converted into a digital model by a robot or a group of robots. If we decompose this process into entities, we assume that we obtain two main objects: a robot and an occupancy map. The robot object has a sensor, a position, and velocity parameters. The occupancy map object is massive, with a certain number of cells and their probabilistic values being modified at each time step (Figure 4). The robot begins to run from the initial position. Operating the simulation, this position can be any x-, y-coordinates of the free space on the map. In the real-world experiment, the initial position has zero values on the map, no matter where the robot is currently in a room [21].

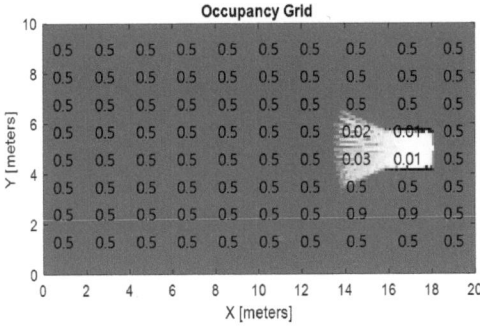

Figure 4. The occupancy map visualization with occupancy probability values of uncertainties (0.5) and explored values (varying from 0.0010 to 0.5). The map size is defined as 20 by 10. It is only for representing the figure window of the simulation and is not used in the algorithm computation.

As the robot moves in the environment, the occupancy map is updated from every robot position, expanding the terrain acquisition. Step by step, the laser sensor touches new areas or seen areas, which return different probabilities values from the occupancy map. The values from the occupancy map at time t are known as explored segments in this study.

With the aim of continuous and safe driving, some others aspects should be analyzed and planned for the correct sequential decisions. One of these is obstacle avoidance. The decision of turning left or right can be made based on the available visibility for the robot as detected by the laser sensor. The maximum sensing range is a known parameter, depending on the sensor model. Based on the maximum range value, the minimum threshold for the reaction to an obstacle can be defined through test runs. The other parameters for continuous driving are the linear and angular velocities. Their values govern and characterize the robot's behavior. The linear velocity is responsible for forward and backward motions. When the robot turns, the angular velocity deals with the turning motions.

These metrics, such as the explored segments at each time step, the minimum distance threshold for the obstacle avoidance, and the linear velocity and angular velocity, are synchronized and adjusted in the reward function below.

4.2. MDP Model for the Robotic Exploration

In this paper, the MDP model for robot exploration is formalized as follows. At each iteration t, the laser sensor emits and inserts the rays on the occupancy map. If the rays return any numeric data, it means that they hit an obstacle that is located nearby. Otherwise, data of NaN format (Not a Number) denote the absence of obstacles and the presence of free space. Both these types of data are the observations, O_t, that are sent to the DDPG agent from the RL environment. For the sake of clarity, the occupancy map is a form of visualization in the RL environment. Furthermore, the function approximator inside of the agent generates and passes actions a_t, which are the robot velocities. The RL environment receives the actions, upgrades the occupancy map, and computes a scalar reward r_t according to the changes. Figure 5 illustrates the MDP model based on the robot exploration process.

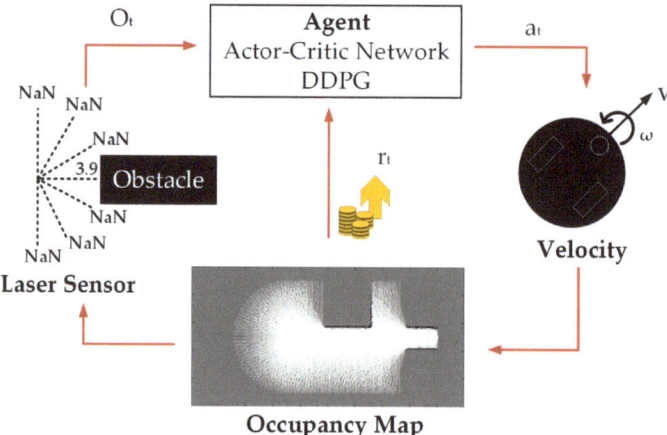

Figure 5. The MDP model of the mobile-robot exploration task.

The reward is a key parameter that motivates the system in making the appropriate decisions. This means that the reward has a strong effect on the motion of the robot. In this paper, the reward is computed according to the explored segments of the occupancy map in each time step t. Since the reward is calculated on the RL environment side, the RL environment for the mobile-robot exploration is presented first below. Then, the reward function is introduced in detail in Section 4.4.

4.3. Reinforcement Learning Environment of the Mobile-Robot Exploration

The proposed RL environment, which is presented in Algorithm 1, has a class structure with property values and several certain functions [62]. It is presented in Algorithm 1. The constructor function is the main one, in which the action and observation specifications are defined with their maximum and minimum value ranges. The reset function is called every time the exploration is launched and when the episode is finished during training. In our custom RL environment, in lines 8–15, the reset function sets the map visualization to the initial uncertainties, sets the robot's initial position, resets the observation values, and activates the ROS interface for the laser scan data and velocity commands.

Algorithm 1: The RL environment for the mobile-robot exploration

1:	**classdef** ExplorationRLEnv
2:	**properties** maxRange = 4.095
3:	**methods**
4:	**function** constructor
5:	define observation O with lower and upper limit values
6:	define action a with lower and upper limit values
7:	**end**
8:	**function** reset
9:	initialize robotPose, observation
10:	map = occupancyMap
11:	enableROSInterface
12:	isDone = false
13:	isBumpedObs = false
14:	reward = 0;
15:	**end**
16:	**function** [observation, reward, isDone] = step (constructor, action)
17:	scanMsg = receive(scanSub)
18:	scan = lidarScan(scanMsg)
19:	observation = scan.Ranges
20:	insertRay(map, robotPose, scan, maxRange)
21:	velMsg.Linear.X = action(1)
22:	velMsg.Angular.Z = action(2)
23:	send (velPub, velMsg)
24:	**if** the last 3 robotPose values are the same
25:	isBumpedObs = true
26:	**end**
27:	**if** isMapExplored = true || isBumpedObs = true
28:	isDone = true
29:	resetSimulation
30:	clear('node')
31:	**else**
32:	isDone = false
33:	**end**
34:	**if** t is equal 1
35:	exp = totalMapValues
36:	**else**
37:	exp = previousReward–totalMapValues
38:	previousReward = totalMapValues
39:	**end**
40:	reward at time t
41:	**end**
42:	**end**
43:	**end**

Another required function for the RL environment is the step function. The whole process of an episode is carried out in the step function. The action as the input parameter of the step function is taken from the actor-critic neural network of the DDPG agent at each iteration and passed to the robot as the commands of the linear and angular velocities by the ROS publisher node (lines 21–23). The observation as the output parameter receives the sensing laser ranges from the sensor and inserts the rays into the occupancy map in lines 17–20.

Lines 24–26 show the robot's collision with obstacles in the mapping. The logic of these lines is such that if the values of the robot position are not changed in the last three iterations, the robot has hit an obstacle and cannot avoid it. In essence, the robot does not try to avoid the obstacle as usually occurs using classical algorithms. It only detects the collisions as a bad event that should not be repeated in the next episodes. As the simulation results will show in the next section, this straightforward logic satisfies and can operate correctly for the mobile-robot motion. If the experiment runs in real-world conditions, then a bumper sensor can be used on the robot to detect the collision with an obstacle.

In lines 27–33, the *isDone* as the output parameter is applied, which is a flag of the episode states. When the flag has true value, the current episode must be finished, and the exploration process should be aborted. This happens in two cases: a map is fully explored or the robot hits an obstacle.

The reward function of lines 34–40 is discussed next in detail.

4.4. Occupancy-Reward-Driven Exploration

The occupancy reward is a function that encourages the robot to seek in unexplored areas to collect knowledge about the indoor environment. The information is gathered from the map with occupancy probability values. In this study, the reward is computed based on the occupancy map $M(n, m)$ of size $n \times m$. For each time step of an episode, the sum of all map values is summed up and stored in M variable using the following equation:

$$M_t = \sum_{i=0, j=0}^{n, m} m(i, j) \tag{7}$$

In order to observe the amount of explored segment discovered in each time step, the M of the current time must be deducted from those of the previous time:

$$E_t = M_t - M_{t-1} \tag{8}$$

The function approximator with the reward that is computed only by the explored segments can satisfy the continuous robot driving. However, it was seen during the training process that the robot trajectory is not optimal and not power-efficient. The robot spins constantly.

In view of this undesirable motion, the reward function is proposed as follows:

$$r_t = k \times v_t + q \times w_t^2 + d \times s + f \times E_t \tag{9}$$

where v_t and w_t are linear and angular velocities at time t received from the actor-critic network. The variable s denotes the range of the sensor rays. When the sensor does not meet with the obstacle, the reward obtains the most significant value; in contrast, when the obstacle comes near, the s decreases the reward function. $k, q, f,$ and d are coefficients for the normalization of the reward range.

The reward function should have a range or threshold that can vary. Thus, the actor-critic network during the training process should distinguish between reward values for providing appropriate actions in the RL environment. As equation 9 shows, r_t consists of four factors: linear velocity, angular velocity, sensing ranges, and quantity of the explored segment discovered in one time step. Each has its own priority of how much this factor affects the reward function. The order of priorities in the reward function will be presented in the next section.

Finally, all the rewards are summed as G at the end of the episode after a predefined competing number of time steps, as shown in Equation (10):

$$G = r_t + r_{t+1} + \ldots + r_{t+1} \tag{10}$$

Speaking about the reward, it is necessary to consider the penalty as well. In lines 24–26 of Algorithm 1, the code catches the occasion of obstacle collision. When this happens, the current episode should stop, and the neural network should learn about the unfavorable event. In this case, the reward is assigned a negative number as punishment.

4.5. Deep Deterministic Policy Gradient Agent for the Mobile-Robot Exploration

The RL environment has been constructed. Next, the DDPG agent is presented for the mobile-robot exploration task in Algorithm 2. In general, it can be seen that the agent consists of two main parts: actor-critic network and training.

In lines 1–3, the information about input and output parameters is obtained. These parameters allow the agent to communicate with the RL environment, receiving data and sending computed data.

Algorithm 2: The DDPG agent for the mobile-robot exploration environment

1:   env = ExplorationRLEnv
2:   action = env.getActionInfo
3:   observation = env.getObservationInfo
4:   critic = **rlQValueFunction**(criticNetwork, observation, action, criticOpts)
5:   actor = **rlContinuousDeterministicActor**(actorNetwork, observation, action, actorOpts)
6:   agent = **rlDDPGAgent**(actor, critic, agentOpts)
7:   trainStats = **train**(agent, env, trainOpts)

In line 4, the Q-value critic is created using the MATLAB (R2021b release) built-in function, *rlQValueFunction*. Inside the function, four parameters are listed. The main one is a critic network. The remaining ones are the input and output parameters, and setting options of the critic network. Figure 6 shows the architecture of the critic network. It can be seen that the critic network has two paths that later merge into one. The first path starts from the observation data formed in the feature input layer. The observation path contains the fully connected and the relu layers. The second path begins from the action data with 2-D inputs and also contains the fully connected layer. These two paths merge into the addition layer. The output of the critic network is a Q-value, which is a single neuron.

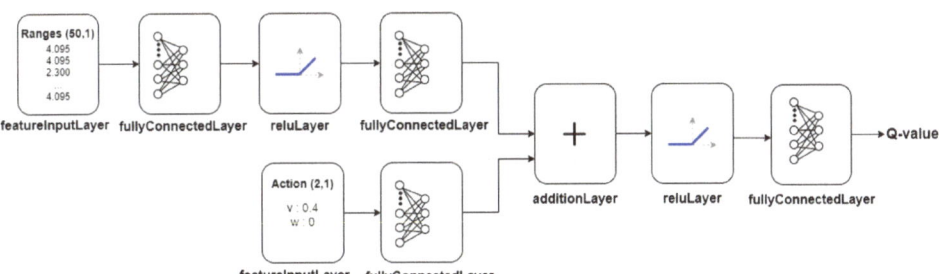

Figure 6. Critic network with 50-D input of observation path and 2-D input of action path. The network ends with the single-neuron output of the Q-value.

Next, the deterministic actor is created in line 5 using the built-in function, *rlContinious DeterministicActor*. The actor network is presented in Figure 7. It has one sequence of layers, and it provides direct mapping from the observation to continuous action within tanh scaling. It should be noted that the actor transmits the output data to the critic as illustrated in Figure 3c in Section 3.

Furthermore, in line 6, the DDPG agent is composed, applying the critic and actor in the *rlDDPGAgent* function. It is important to note here that the setting options, such as *agentOpts*, affect the agent learning. They can be tuned according to the results. In Section 5, values of the setting options are presented for the exploration simulation.

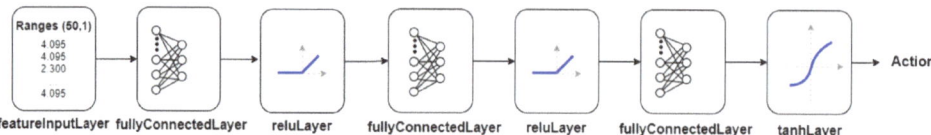

Figure 7. Actor network with 50-D input and 2-D output.

In line 7, the training is launched using the agent and the RL environment. The results are discussed in Section 5.

5. Reward Estimation and Training Options

In this section, the reward function is discussed. The limits and parameter priorities are presented in values. Then, in Section 5.2, the training options of the DDPG agent are performed with their values as well.

5.1. The Reward Estimation

In Section 4.4, we proposed the reward function r_t in Equation (9) for the mobile-robot exploration. The value limit or range for the reward function, which is important to set when using the deep-RL technique, was also discussed. The point is that the RL agent defines the good and bad actions according to the reward function. If the value fluctuates in a chaotic way, then the actor-critic network cannot determine the positive and negative decisions. This is the main reason the value limits for the reward function are defined. When estimating the value, know the upper and lower limits for the parameters in the reward function must be known, which are the linear velocity, the angular velocity, the sensing range distance, and the explored segment.

In Table 2, the value limits for the reward parameters are presented. It can be seen that the upper limit for the observation is 4.095, which is the maximum sensor range in the simulation. The lower limit is zero. The continuous actions are linear v and angular w velocities, with 0.4 as upper limits and 0 and -0.4 as lower limits, respectively. The maximum explored segment E is 239, which the sensor of the robot can occupy in the probability occupancy map at time t visiting completely new and free areas. The parameters are normalized in the upper and lower thresholds of the reward function, -0.2 and 0.8, respectively.

Table 2. The value limits for the reward parameters.

	O	v	w	E
Upper limit	$[4.095 \ldots 4.095]'$	0.4	0.4	239
Lower limit	$[0 \ldots 0]'$	0	-0.4	0

To adjust the parameters, the coefficients k, q, d, f are introduced in Equation (9). However, the priorities of the four parameters in the reward function are included in the coefficient as well, which affects the robot motion in the exploration process. Thus, the priorities can be described as follows: 30% for linear velocity, -20% for angular velocity, 20% for sensing ranges, and 30% for the explored segment. Converting the percentage to numbers, the coefficients are as follows: $k = 0.75$, $q = -1.25$, $d = 0.07$, and $f = 0.0013$. In real-world applications, the proposed coefficients can be used without changes when the robot is Turtlebot2 and the laser sensor is Hokuyo (model no. urg-04lx-ug01). For other cases, the values of the coefficients should be calculated individually according to robot kinematics and sensor specifications.

Figure 8 illustrates the above discussion on parameters affecting the reward function to a greater and lesser extent and the adjustment in their values in one common range. The lower and upper limits are -0.2 and 0.8, respectively.

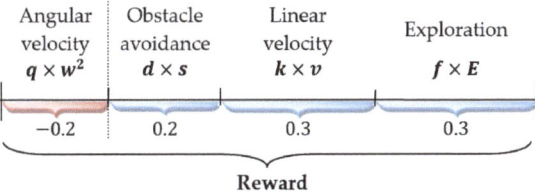

Figure 8. The reward function normalization.

It is appropriate to clarify the reason why angular velocity (w) has a negative value in the reward function. When the robot drives straight in an obstacle-free area, w equals 0. Driving straight is the most optimal motion according to the mapping and the power energy cost. This is why any other values of the angular velocity, $w < 0$ for turning to the right side and $w > 0$ to the left side, are negative for the reward function.

5.2. Training Agent

The training is the process of learning and storing the experience for the actor-critic agent. The training options affect the DDPG agent. Consequently, it changes the RL environment.

In Algorithm 2, the DDPG agent for the mobile-robot exploration is presented. In this section, *criticOpts*, *actorOpts*, *agentOpts*, and *trainOpts* options are given in more detail. Table 3 shows the training option values of the actor-critic neural network. The learning rate option is used to specify the training time needed to reach the optimal result. The L_2 regularization factor is used to avoid the overfitting of the training. To speed up the training, GPU can be activated by the "use device" option. We used the local GPU device embedded in the PC, the GeForce GTX 1050 Ti model (compute capability 6.1).

Table 3. The options for the actor and critic.

Critic and Actor Options	
Learn rate	10^3
L_2 Regularization factor	10^4
Gradient threshold	1
Use device	gpu

The agent and training options are presented in Table 4. The sample time option is the time interval of output data returned from the simulation. During training, the DDPG agent stores the simulation data using the experience buffer. In turn, the mini-batch selects the data from the buffer randomly and upgrades the actor and critic. The agent noise option is the stochastic noise model that is added at each time step to the agent.

Table 4. The options for the agent and training.

Agent Option		Training Option	
Sample time	0.1	Max episodes	500
Experience buffer length	10^6	Max steps per episode	150
Discount Factor	0.995	Score averaging window length	50
Mini batch size	100	Stop training criteria	average reward
Target Smooth Factor	0.001	Stop training value	100
Agent noise options	10^{-5}	Verbose	true
		Plots	training process

In the training option, the simulation parameters were selected. The simulation runs five hundred times (max episodes). The training can finish under one of these two conditions: (1) 500 episodes have been completed or (2) the average total rewards have reached one hundred values for the last 50 simulations.

In MATLAB, it is worth noting that the simulation results can be saved as a file, which can be loaded again to continue the training process using *save* and *load* commands.

6. Simulation Results and Comparison

In practice, the deep-RL method is about two program files that interact with each other. One of them is the RL environment with reward function and map visualization; another consists of the DDPG agent with the actor-critic network and training option settings. They communicate jointly by input data, output data, and reward.

In this section, the simulation results are presented. The comparison with other algorithms is demonstrated at the end of the section.

6.1. Simulation Results

The training DDPG agent and the exploration are carried out online. It means that the robot drives in one episode until time runs out, up 150 steps. Figure 9 shows the environments in which the robot tries to build the maps for two experiments. The first environment is a simple one without obstacles inside the room. The environment of Figure 9b is a more sophisticated version of the first one with obstacles. During the training, the robot drives in one of the environments of Figure 9. Step by step, as it moves during the mapping, it upgrades the occupancy map of Figure 10. It should be noted that the location coordinates of walls and obstacles are not used in the computation. The environments in Figure 9 can be treated as the simulated rooms, which can be easily substituted by real-world environments.

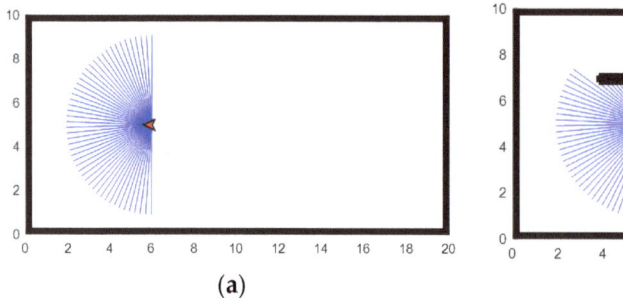
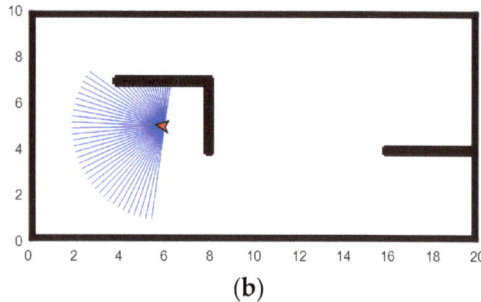

Figure 9. The environments of 20 × 15 m size for the two experiments: (**a**) simple environment, (**b**) environment with obstacles.

Figure 10 demonstrates the exploration results of training the DDPG agent. Two results from each experiment are presented in (a) map coverage percentage and (b) total reward value. The results were captured during the training according to the greatest values.

Here, it is important to explain the reason for presenting two map results for one experiment. The results of map (a) and map (b) are different because creating a reward function based on only one goal, mapping, does not return a positive result. Several robot behaviors were found to be inappropriate, such as collisions with obstacles, being stuck in one place without any motion, and turning to one side episode after episode. These occurred because the linear velocity, angular velocity, and sensing ranges should be considered in the reward function as they are in the proposed occupancy reward function. This is why the greatest result of the map coverage is not equal to the greatest result of the reward function.

Experiment 1 in the simple environment

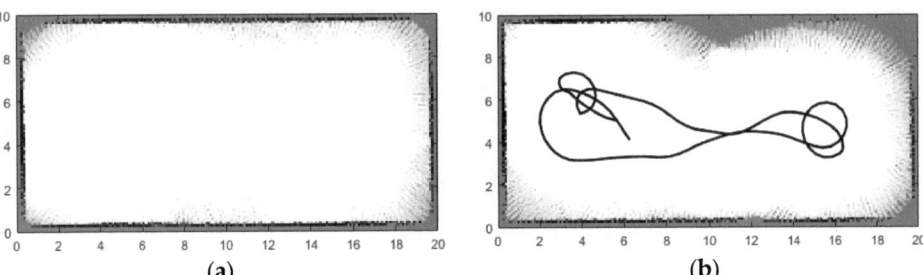

Experiment 2 in the environment with obstacles

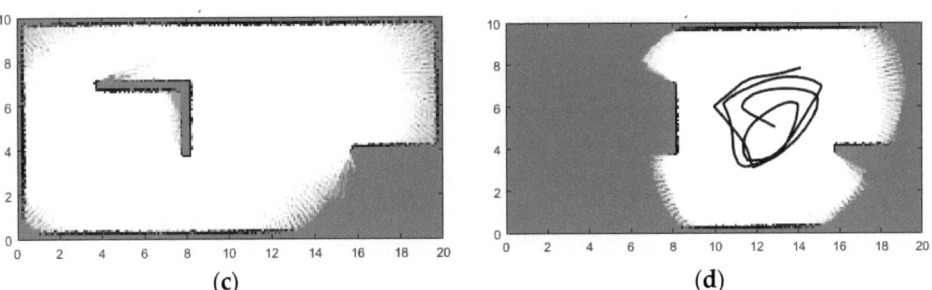

Figure 10. The mapping results of the DDPG agent in the custom environments. (**a**) Map coverage: 99%, Initial positions: x = 6, y = 4. (**b**) Total reward (G): 90, Initial positions: x = 6, y = 4. The black line is the robot trajectory. (**c**) Map coverage: 86%, Initial positions: x = 13, y = 5. (**d**) Total reward (G): 67, Initial positions: x = 13, y = 5. The black line is the robot trajectory.

Nonetheless, a full map coverage was obtained. This proves that the DDPG agent is able to provide 99% of the exploration in the simple map (Figure 10a). The greatest reward value ($G = 90$) returns a positive result of the exploration in Figure 10b.

In Experiment 2, the training of the DDPG agent was carried out in the environment with obstacles (Figure 10c,d). Two results with the greatest values were taken for the map coverage and reward function categories. It can be seen that the results are worse compared to the results of Experiment 1. Only 86% of the map was explored. The reward function value is 67, which is less than 90.

Based on our practice with the DDPG agent in the mobile-robot exploration, several conclusions can be drawn:

- The agent can solve the mapping problem, especially in a simple environment.
- The reward function can be described as the single objective function. The navigation and exploration of new areas using the reward function of DDPG agent are insufficient for the exploration.
- The mapping performance deteriorates when the number of obstacles in the environment is increased.
- Increasing the training time did not improve the mapping results. As Figure 11 shows, the overfitting of the neural network occurs in the training after 500 episodes.
- The mapping is a real-time procedure, and the training of the DDPG agent works online as well. The two together used as one system can be considered a time-consuming process.

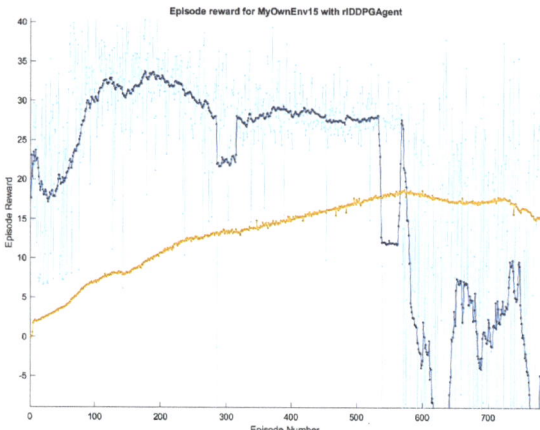

Figure 11. The episode reward graph during the training. The light blue line is the reward function. The dark blue line is the average of the reward function. The orange line is the trained critic data. It can be seen that the overfitting of the actor-critic occurred after 500 episodes.

The experimental results of the proposed occupancy reward-driven exploration using the DDPG agent are recorded and demonstrated in video [63].

6.2. Comparison

In this subsection, the deep-RL and the nature-inspired algorithms are compared. In the authors' previous studies [21], the GWO algorithm for mobile-robot exploration showed the best result compared with the other nature-inspired optimization techniques. As a consequence, the GWO exploration algorithm is selected for the comparison analysis.

Table 5 presents the comparison between the proposed occupancy reward-driven exploration and the nature-inspired exploration. The GWO exploration algorithm works with waypoints. To enable the robot to move somewhere, it needs to provide the robot a point to go to and check that the robot reaches the point in each time step. The continuous action is a more nature-driven action for the robot.

Table 5. Comparison analysis of the GWO exploration and the DDPG agent exploration. The advantages are highlighted in bold.

	Robot Motion	Development	Processing Result	Map Coverage
GWO exploration	Waypoints	Waypoint computation, algorithm logic	Waiting for the best result	91.21%, average result of 10 simulation runs
DDPG exploration	**Continuous actions**	**Two files of RL environment and RL agent**	Long training of the agent	99% for simple environment, 86% for complex environment

Considering the development criteria, the GWO exploration algorithm requires more work in implementation than the DDPG one. A waypoint should be calculated based on some known parameters (frontier points, robot position) and algorithm logic, which should be considered in the programming. In this case, the DDPG agent is the more intelligent and straightforward developing tool. It should describe the RL environment and denote a reward function. The training process and a neural network find appropriate decisions for the RL environment.

The processing result criteria is about obtaining the best performance of the algorithm. The GWO exploration is a stochastic algorithm that returns different results every simulation run. The best result is unpredictable. It can appear in the first 10 simulation runs or 100 runs. It needs to test and wait for the best result using the GWO exploration algorithm. For the DDPG exploration, the training takes a long time, for instance, 57 h (around 3 days) for the one-experiment result presented in Figure 10.

Considering the map coverage criteria, the DDPG exploration has the greatest percentage result. However, it is only for the free-obstacle environment. Thus, the two approaches are not universal algorithms for the mapping problem. This is a disadvantage.

6.3. Developing Tools

In this study, the DDPG agent was implemented in the MATLAB platform. Several libraries were involved in the exploration simulation: Reinforcement Learning Toolbox, ROS Toolbox, GPU Coder Toolbox, Robotics System Toolbox, Parallel Computing Toolbox, Navigation Toolbox, and Mapping Toolbox.

The exploration with the single robot in the binary occupancy environment and the occupancy map was implemented using *ExampleHelperRobotSimulator* class.

7. Conclusions

In this paper, the Deep Deterministic Policy Gradient algorithm of deep Reinforcement Learning was deployed in the robotic mapping domain. The custom environment with a reward function was created considering the robot motion principles and the occupancy map visualization. The actor-critic neural network received the sensor data and sent the continuous actions for the robot. The actions in the custom environment were evaluated by the proposed occupancy reward function. The training shows that the DDPG agent can solve the mapping problem in the simple free space with wall obstacles. However, its reward strategy does not stimulate the robot enough for it to explore faster and more efficiently. The reward function is only able to evaluate a single parameter, which is a single action.

Author Contributions: A.K. conceived and designed the algorithm. A.K., S.G.L. and S.H.K. designed and performed the experiments. A.K., S.G.L. and S.H.K. wrote the paper. A.K., S.G.L. and S.H.K. formulated the mathematical model. A.K. supervised and finalized the manuscript for submission. All authors have read and agreed to the published version of the manuscript.

Funding: This research received no external funding.

Conflicts of Interest: The authors declare no conflict of interest.

References

1. Lluvia, I.; Lazkano, E.; Ansuategi, A. Active mapping and robot exploration: A survey. *Sensors* **2021**, *21*, 2445. [CrossRef] [PubMed]
2. Lin, H.Y.; Huang, Y.C. Collaborative complete coverage and path planning for multi-robot exploration. *Sensors* **2021**, *21*, 3709. [CrossRef] [PubMed]
3. Shin, F.A.J.; Jang, S.B.H. Development of Autonomous Navigation Performance Criteria and Related Test Methods for Autonomous Mobile Robot in the Outdoor Environment. In Proceedings of the 2021 21st International Conference on Control, Automation and Systems (ICCAS), Jeju, Korea, 12–15 October 2021; IEEE: Piscataway, NJ, USA, 2021; pp. 1653–1656.
4. Hu, H.; Zhang, K.; Tan, A.H.; Ruan, M.; Agia, C.; Nejat, G. A sim-to-real pipeline for deep reinforcement learning for autonomous robot navigation in cluttered rough terrain. *IEEE Robot. Autom. Lett.* **2021**, *6*, 6569–6576. [CrossRef]
5. Niroui, F.; Zhang, K.; Kashino, Z.; Nejat, G. Deep reinforcement learning robot for search and rescue applications: Exploration in unknown cluttered environments. *IEEE Robot. Autom. Lett.* **2019**, *4*, 610–617. [CrossRef]
6. Delmerico, J.; Mintchev, S.; Giusti, A.; Gromov, B.; Melo, K.; Horvat, T.; Cadena, C.; Hutter, M.; Ijspeert, A.; Floreano, D.; et al. The current state and future outlook of rescue robotics. *J. Field Robot.* **2019**, *36*, 1171–1191. [CrossRef]
7. Ludvigsen, M.; Sørensen, A.J. Towards integrated autonomous underwater operations for ocean mapping and monitoring. *Annu. Rev. Control* **2016**, *42*, 145–157. [CrossRef]
8. Hong, S.; Shyam, P.; Bangunharcana, A.; Shin, H. Robotic Mapping Approach under Illumination-Variant Environments at Planetary Construction Sites. *Remote Sens.* **2022**, *14*, 1027. [CrossRef]

9. Sun, Z.; Wu, B.; Xu, C.Z.; Sarma, S.E.; Yang, J.; Kong, H. Frontier detection and reachability analysis for efficient 2D graph-slam based active exploration. In Proceedings of the 2020 IEEE/RSJ International Conference on Intelligent Robots and Systems (IROS), Las Vegas, NV, USA, 24 October 2020–24 January 2021; IEEE: Piscataway, NJ, USA, 2020; pp. 2051–2058.
10. Sun, L.; Yan, Z.; Zaganidis, A.; Zhao, C.; Duckett, T. Recurrent-octomap: Learning state-based map refinement for long-term semantic mapping with 3-d-lidar data. *IEEE Robot. Autom. Lett.* **2018**, *3*, 3749–3756. [CrossRef]
11. Lin, J.; Zhang, F. A fast, complete, point cloud based loop closure for lidar odometry and mapping. *arXiv* **2019**, arXiv:1909.11811.
12. Chaplot, D.S.; Gandhi, D.P.; Gupta, A.; Salakhutdinov, R.R. Object goal navigation using goal-oriented semantic exploration. *Adv. Neural Inf. Process. Syst.* **2020**, *33*, 4247–4258.
13. Wurm, K.M.; Stachniss, C.; Burgard, W. Coordinated multi-robot exploration using a segmentation of the environment. In Proceedings of the 2008 IEEE/RSJ International Conference on Intelligent Robots and Systems, Nice, France, 22–26 September 2008; IEEE: Piscataway, NJ, USA, 2008; pp. 1160–1165.
14. Burgard, W.; Moors, M.; Stachniss, C.; Schneider, F.E. Coordinated Multi-Robot Exploration. *IEEE Trans. Robot.* **2005**, *21*, 376–386. [CrossRef]
15. Albina, K.; Lee, S.G. Hybrid Stochastic Exploration Using Grey Wolf Optimizer and Coordinated Multi-Robot Exploration Algorithms. *IEEE Access* **2019**, *7*, 14246–14255. [CrossRef]
16. Tai, L.; Liu, M. Mobile robots exploration through cnn-based reinforcement learning. *Robot. Biomim.* **2016**, *3*, 24. [CrossRef] [PubMed]
17. Tai, L.; Liu, M. Towards cognitive exploration through deep reinforcement learning for mobile robots. *arXiv* **2016**, arXiv:1610.01733.
18. Xu, X.; Zhang, L.; Yang, J.; Cao, C.; Wang, W.; Ran, Y.; Tan, Z.; Luo, M. A Review of Multi-Sensor Fusion SLAM Systems Based on 3D LIDAR. *Remote Sens.* **2022**, *14*, 2835. [CrossRef]
19. Mur-Artal, R.; Tardós, J.D. Orb-slam2: An open-source slam system for monocular, stereo, and rgb-d cameras. *IEEE Trans. Robot.* **2017**, *33*, 1255–1262. [CrossRef]
20. Gautam, A.; Mohan, S. A review of research in multi-robot systems. In Proceedings of the 2012 IEEE 7th international conference on industrial and information systems (ICIIS), Chennai, India, 6–9 August 2012; IEEE: Piscataway, NJ, USA, 2012; pp. 1–5.
21. Kamalova, A.; Kim, K.D.; Lee, S.G. Waypoint Mobile Robot Exploration Based on Biologically Inspired Algorithms. *IEEE Access* **2020**, *8*, 190342–190355. [CrossRef]
22. Webster, C.; Ivanov, S. Robotics, artificial intelligence, and the evolving nature of work. In *Digital Transformation in Business and Society*; Palgrave Macmillan: Cham, Switzerland, 2020; pp. 127–143.
23. Mahesh, B. Machine learning algorithms-a review. *Int. J. Sci. Res.* **2020**, *9*, 381–386.
24. LeCun, Y.; Bengio, Y.; Hinton, G. Deep learning. *Nature* **2015**, *521*, 436–444. [CrossRef]
25. Mnih, V.; Kavukcuoglu, K.; Silver, D.; Rusu, A.A.; Veness, J.; Bellemare, M.G.; Graves, A.; Riedmiller, M.; Fidjeland, A.K.; Ostrovski, G.; et al. Human-level control through deep reinforcement learning. *Nature* **2015**, *518*, 529–533. [CrossRef]
26. Thrun, S.; Burgard, W.; Fox, D. Probalistic robotics. *Kybernetes* **2006**, *35*, 1299–1300. [CrossRef]
27. Alexandre, F.; Dominey, P.F.; Gaussier, P.; Girard, B.; Khamassi, M.; Rougier, N.P. When Artificial Intelligence and Computational Neuroscience meet. In *A Guided Tour of Artificial Intelligence Research*; Springer: Cham, Switzerland, 2020; pp. 303–335.
28. Haenlein, M.; Kaplan, A. A brief history of artificial intelligence: On the past, present, and future of artificial intelligence. *Calif. Manag. Rev.* **2019**, *61*, 5–14. [CrossRef]
29. Tai, L.; Liu, M. Deep-learning in mobile robotics-from perception to control systems: A survey on why and why not. *arXiv* **2016**, arXiv:1612.07139.
30. Tai, L.; Li, S.; Liu, M. Autonomous exploration of mobile robots through deep neural networks. *Int. J. Adv. Robot. Syst.* **2017**, *14*, 1729881417703571. [CrossRef]
31. Caley, J.A.; Lawrance, N.R.; Hollinger, G.A. Deep learning of structured environments for robot search. *Auton. Robot.* **2019**, *43*, 1695–1714. [CrossRef]
32. McCormac, J.; Handa, A.; Davison, A.; Leutenegger, S. Semanticfusion: Dense 3d semantic mapping with convolutional neural networks. In Proceedings of the 2017 IEEE International Conference on Robotics and automation (ICRA), Singapore, 29 May–3 June 2017; IEEE: Piscataway, NJ, USA, 2017; pp. 4628–4635.
33. Doellinger, J.; Spies, M.; Burgard, W. Predicting occupancy distributions of walking humans with convolutional neural networks. *IEEE Robot. Autom. Lett.* **2018**, *3*, 1522–1528. [CrossRef]
34. Sünderhauf, N.; Brock, O.; Scheirer, W.; Hadsell, R.; Fox, D.; Leitner, J.; Upcroft, B.; Abbeel, P.; Burgard, W.; Milford, M.; et al. The limits and potentials of deep learning for robotics. *Int. J. Robot. Res.* **2018**, *37*, 405–420. [CrossRef]
35. Kollar, T.; Roy, N. Trajectory optimization using reinforcement learning for map exploration. *Int. J. Robot. Res.* **2008**, *27*, 175–196. [CrossRef]
36. Tai, L.; Liu, M. A robot exploration strategy based on q-learning network. In Proceedings of the 2016 IEEE International Conference on Real-Time Computing and Robotics (RCAR), Angkor Wat, Cambodia, 6–10 June 2016; IEEE: Piscataway, NJ, USA, 2016; pp. 57–62.
37. Zhelo, O.; Zhang, J.; Tai, L.; Liu, M.; Burgard, W. Curiosity-driven exploration for mapless navigation with deep reinforcement learning. *arXiv* **2018**, arXiv:1804.00456.

38. Tai, L.; Paolo, G.; Liu, M. Virtual-to-real deep reinforcement learning: Continuous control of mobile robots for mapless navigation. In Proceedings of the 2017 IEEE/RSJ International Conference on Intelligent Robots and Systems (IROS), Vancouver, BC, Canada, 24–28 September 2017; IEEE: Piscataway, NJ, USA, 2017; pp. 31–36.
39. Jin, J.; Nguyen, N.M.; Sakib, N.; Graves, D.; Yao, H.; Jagersand, M. Mapless navigation among dynamics with social-safety-awareness: A reinforcement learning approach from 2d laser scans. In Proceedings of the 2020 IEEE International Conference on Robotics and Automation (ICRA), Paris, France, 31 May–31 August 2020; IEEE: Piscataway, NJ, USA, 2020; pp. 6979–6985.
40. Shi, H.; Shi, L.; Xu, M.; Hwang, K.S. End-to-end navigation strategy with deep reinforcement learning for mobile robots. *IEEE Trans. Ind. Inform.* **2019**, *16*, 2393–2402. [CrossRef]
41. Lu, Z.; Huang, R. Autonomous mobile robot navigation in uncertain dynamic environments based on deep reinforcement learning. In Proceedings of the 2021 IEEE International Conference on Real-time Computing and Robotics (RCAR), Xining, China, 15–19 July 2021; IEEE: Piscataway, NJ, USA, 2021; pp. 423–428.
42. Chen, F.; Martin, J.D.; Huang, Y.; Wang, J.; Englot, B. Autonomous exploration under uncertainty via deep reinforcement learning on graphs. In Proceedings of the 2020 IEEE/RSJ International Conference on Intelligent Robots and Systems (IROS), Las Vegas, NV, USA, 24 October 2020–24 January 2021; IEEE: Piscataway, NJ, USA, 2020; pp. 6140–6147.
43. Li, H.; Zhang, Q.; Zhao, D. Deep reinforcement learning-based automatic exploration for navigation in unknown environment. *IEEE Trans. Neural Netw. Learn. Syst.* **2019**, *31*, 2064–2076. [CrossRef] [PubMed]
44. Surmann, H.; Jestel, C.; Marchel, R.; Musberg, F.; Elhadj, H.; Ardani, M. Deep reinforcement learning for real autonomous mobile robot navigation in indoor environments. *arXiv* **2020**, arXiv:2005.13857.
45. Zhang, J.; Tai, L.; Liu, M.; Boedecker, J.; Burgard, W. Neural slam: Learning to explore with external memory. *arXiv* **2017**, arXiv:1706.09520.
46. Xiang, J.; Li, Q.; Dong, X.; Ren, Z. Continuous control with deep reinforcement learning for mobile robot navigation. In Proceedings of the 2019 Chinese Automation Congress (CAC), Hangzhou, China, 22–24 November 2019; IEEE: Piscataway, NJ, USA, 2019; pp. 1501–1506.
47. Wang, J.; Elfwing, S.; Uchibe, E. Modular deep reinforcement learning from reward and punishment for robot navigation. *Neural Netw.* **2021**, *135*, 115–126. [CrossRef]
48. Zhang, J.; Springenberg, J.T.; Boedecker, J.; Burgard, W. Deep reinforcement learning with successor features for navigation across similar environments. In Proceedings of the 2017 IEEE/RSJ International Conference on Intelligent Robots and Systems (IROS), Vancouver, BC, Canada, 24–28 September 2017; IEEE: Piscataway, NJ, USA, 2017; pp. 2371–2378.
49. Quan, H.; Li, Y.; Zhang, Y. A novel mobile robot navigation method based on deep reinforcement learning. *Int. J. Adv. Robot. Syst.* **2020**, *17*, 1729881420921672. [CrossRef]
50. Zhu, K.; Zhang, T. Deep reinforcement learning based mobile robot navigation: A review. *Tsinghua Sci. Technol.* **2021**, *26*, 674–691. [CrossRef]
51. Kollmitz, M.; Koller, T.; Boedecker, J.; Burgard, W. Learning human-aware robot navigation from physical interaction via inverse reinforcement learning. In Proceedings of the 2020 IEEE/RSJ International Conference on Intelligent Robots and Systems (IROS), Las Vegas, NV, USA, 24 October 2020–24 January 2021; IEEE: Piscataway, NJ, USA, 2020; pp. 11025–11031.
52. Zhu, Y.; Mottaghi, R.; Kolve, E.; Lim, J.J.; Gupta, A.; Fei-Fei, L.; Farhadi, A. Target-driven visual navigation in indoor scenes using deep reinforcement learning. In Proceedings of the 2017 IEEE International Conference on Robotics and Automation (ICRA), Singapore, 29 May–3 June 2017; IEEE: Piscataway, NJ, USA, 2017; pp. 3357–3364.
53. Xin, J.; Zhao, H.; Liu, D.; Li, M. Application of deep reinforcement learning in mobile robot path planning. In Proceedings of the 2017 Chinese Automation Congress (CAC), Jinan, China, 20–22 October 2017; IEEE: Piscataway, NJ, USA, 2017; pp. 7112–7116.
54. He, Z.; Wang, J.; Song, C. A review of mobile robot motion planning methods: From classical motion planning workflows to reinforcement learning-based architectures. *arXiv* **2021**, arXiv:2108.13619.
55. Niu, H.; Ji, Z.; Arvin, F.; Lennox, B.; Yin, H.; Carrasco, J. Accelerated sim-to-real deep reinforcement learning: Learning collision avoidance from human player. In Proceedings of the 2021 IEEE/SICE International Symposium on System Integration (SII), Iwaki, Japan, 11–14 January 2021; IEEE: Piscataway, NJ, USA, 2021; pp. 144–149.
56. Song, H.; Li, A.; Wang, T.; Wang, M. Multimodal Deep Reinforcement Learning with Auxiliary Task for Obstacle Avoidance of Indoor Mobile Robot. *Sensors* **2021**, *21*, 1363. [CrossRef] [PubMed]
57. Feng, S.; Sebastian, B.; Ben-Tzvi, P. A collision avoidance method based on deep reinforcement learning. *Robotics* **2021**, *10*, 73. [CrossRef]
58. Xiao, W.; Yuan, L.; He, L.; Ran, T.; Zhang, J.; Cui, J. Multi-goal Visual Navigation with Collision Avoidance via Deep Reinforcement Learning. *IEEE Trans. Instrum. Meas.* **2022**, *71*, 2505809. [CrossRef]
59. Lillicrap, T.P.; Hunt, J.J.; Pritzel, A.; Heess, N.; Erez, T.; Tassa, Y.; Silver, D.; Wierstra, D. Continuous control with deep reinforcement learning. *arXiv* **2015**, arXiv:1509.02971.
60. Available online: https://www.mathworks.com/help/reinforcement-learning/ug/ddpg-agents.html (accessed on 18 May 2022).
61. Mnih, V.; Kavukcuoglu, K.; Silver, D.; Graves, A.; Antonoglou, I.; Wierstra, D.; Riedmiller, M. Playing atari with deep reinforcement learning. *arXiv* **2013**, arXiv:1312.5602.
62. Available online: https://www.mathworks.com/help/reinforcement-learning/ug/create-custom-matlab-environment-from-template.html (accessed on 18 May 2022).
63. YouTube Video. Available online: https://youtu.be/SS1h7hn9ZBE (accessed on 23 July 2022).

Article

A Comparative Study of Control Methods for X3D Quadrotor Feedback Trajectory Control

Tanzeela Shakeel [1,†], Jehangir Arshad [2,*,†], Mujtaba Hussain Jaffery [2], Ateeq Ur Rehman [3], Elsayed Tag Eldin [4,*], Nivin A. Ghamry [5] and Muhammad Shafiq [6,*]

1. Department of Computer Science, University of Management and Technology, Lahore 54000, Pakistan
2. Department of Electrical & Computer Engineering, COMSATS University Islamabad Lahore Campus, Lahore 54000, Pakistan
3. Department of Electrical Engineering, Government College University, Lahore 54000, Pakistan
4. Faculty of Engineering and Technology, Future University in Egypt, New Cairo 11835, Egypt
5. Faculty of Computers and Artificial intelligence, Cairo University, Giza 3750010, Egypt
6. Department of Information and Communication Engineering, Yeungnam University, Gyeongsan 38541, Korea
* Correspondence: jehangirarshad@cuilahore.edu.pk (J.A.); elsayed.tageldin@fue.edu.eg (E.T.E.); shafiq@ynu.ac.kr (M.S.)
† These authors contributed equally to this work.

Abstract: Unmanned aerial vehicles (UAVs), particularly quadrotor, have seen steady growth in use over the last several decades. The quadrotor is an under-actuated nonlinear system with few actuators in comparison to the degree of freedom (DOF); hence, stabilizing its attitude and positions is a significant challenge. Furthermore, the inclusion of nonlinear dynamic factors and uncertainties makes controlling its maneuverability more challenging. The purpose of this research is to design, implement, and evaluate the effectiveness of linear and nonlinear control methods for controlling an X3D quadrotor's intended translation position and rotation angles while hovering. The dynamics of the X3D quadrotor model were implemented in Simulink. Two linear controllers, linear quadratic regulator (LQR) and proportional integral derivate (PID), and two nonlinear controllers, fuzzy controller (FC) and model reference adaptive PID Controller (MRAPC) employing the MIT rule, were devised and implemented for the response analysis. In the MATLAB Simulink Environment, the transient performance of nonlinear and linear controllers for an X3D quadrotor is examined in terms of settling time, rising time, peak time, delay time, and overshoot. Simulation results suggest that the LQR control approach is better because of its robustness and comparatively superior performance characteristics to other controllers, particularly nonlinear controllers, listed at the same operating point, as overshoot is 0.0% and other factors are minimal for the x3D quadrotor. In addition, the LQR controller is intuitive and simple to implement. In this research, all control approaches were verified to provide adequate feedback for quadrotor stability.

Keywords: X3D quadrotor; closed-loop system; PID; LQR; fuzzy control; model reference adaptive PID

1. Introduction

Unmanned aerial vehicles (UAVs) have recently acquired a great deal of interest for military and civil research applications when a human operator is too risky and time-consuming. Quadrotors have attracted the interest of scientists in the fields of robotics, automation, and aviation. A quadrotor is a rotorcraft with a simple nonlinear construction for vertical take-off and landing (VTOL). It is a system with four actuator inputs that are under actuated [1]. It features six degrees of freedom, with three translation positions: longitudinal (x-axis), lateral (y-axis), and height (z-axis), as well as three rotational states (roll ϕ, pitch θ and yaw ψ). The thrust of the four rotors controls these output states. The thrust of the four rotors regulates these output states. Due to its fundamental dynamic

nature, it offers a great maneuverability advantage. It has a good hovering ability and a quick response for tracking [2]. It is widely used in both outdoor and indoor situations for research and monitoring. High-performance quadrotor control in intense and maneuverable flight is a challenging problem due to the complex nature of the dynamic model, severe coupling, and nonlinear characteristics. Scientists may use the control of quadrotors for testing and evaluating novel concepts in a range of disciplines, including flight control theory, navigation, and real-time systems.

Many researchers from all around the globe have detailed various methods for operating quadrotor UAVs, to the extent of developing an effective stabilizing and navigation system based on the standard control input. A PID controller is extensively used in many industrial applications because of its simplicity and ease of implementation, on the other hand, the LQR controller provides better performance concerning certain measures of performance; fuzzy controller and adaptive PID controller are also extensively implemented for nonlinear systems. Many investigations have been performed on the application of PID, LQR, fuzzy, state feedback, and other control methods to quadrotor UAVs as a plant, but there has been relatively little study on the comparison of linear and nonlinear control methods. The study in [3] proposed a method for simulating and establishing parameters for a quadcopter to analyze and improve the performance of this system and its stability. The system was mounted on a structure that could be freely moved along a vertical axis. The computer received real-time data from sensors and measuring devices. The paper [4] proposed a comparison of nonlinear and linear control methods for quadrotor systems. In this paper [5], a comparison of PID and LQR control techniques is provided. Both controllers provide appropriate feedback for quadrotor stability, according to this study. For the quadrotor's flip operation, Byung-Yoon Lee compares the performance of three distinct types of attitude control systems [6]; PID, sliding mode and open-loop controllers are all used in his article to develop quadrotor attitude controllers. PID control is one of the most often used control strategies [1], [7] along with back-stepping [8,9], nonlinear H∞ control [10], Kalman filter [11], and so on. Other control methodologies, such as fuzzy control systems, are also investigated and applied to a quadrotor, as discussed in [12,13]. In the research in [14,15], the implementation, testation, validation, authentication, and comparison of LQR, PID, and state feedback controllers have been performed on an X3D Quadrotor in NI LabVIEW simulation. The application of sub-super-stochastic matrices to bipartite tracking control in sign networks is presented in [16]. The research [17] represented an innovative decentralized control strategy for the Cucker–Smale model to analyze the leader–follower flocking behavior on networks that encompass both cooperative and rival relationships between agents.

The research [18] addressed the PID and LQR controller implementation for the Qball X4 trajectory tracking. Simulations and experiments were conducted to compare the performance of the developed control strategies. A mathematical model was developed in the research paper [18] to simulate the behavior of a quadrotor with four motors driven by PID using a simple approach. In the study [19], feedback linearization and the LQR controller were proposed to stabilize the quadrotor attitude in the trajectory. A gain-scheduling fuzzy controller for quadrotor position and height control was proposed in the research [19]. The study [20] compared and implemented three controllers into an actual quadrotor in real-time, including PID, LQR, and backstepping. The research [21] offered three robust procedures for controlling a quadrotor in a predetermined trajectory based on the MIT rule and sliding-mode methods. A variety of commonly used quadrotor controllers were described in the previous study. With their algorithms, many control techniques have their strengths and limitations. As a result, the quadrotor's applications and performance determine the appropriate controller. The strengths and limitations of several controllers for controlling quadrotor systems are presented in Table 1.

Table 1. Strengths and Limitations of Quadrotor Control Techniques.

Controllers	Strengths	Limitation
PID	Gain selection is simple; steady-state error can be avoided.	Cannot deal with disturbance or noise, and cannot handle multiple configurations simultaneously.
LQR	It can handle many inputs and outputs.	Not able to overcome steady-state errors.
Backstepping	The model must be systematic and recursive; a precise model is not essential. It can control system nonlinearities, overcome inadequate disturbances, and guarantee stability.	Over-parameterization; selecting appropriate parameters is difficult.
Fuzzy Logic	It provides a viable solution to a complex and uncertain model and does not demand a precise model.	Control rules and system analysis are difficult to develop. It takes a long time to adjust the parameters.
H∞	When the system is multivariable and the channels are cross-coupled, it performs well.	A well-designed model is required.
Sliding Mode Controller (SMC)	The performance of high nonlinearity is excellent. Less sensitivity to perturbations and uncertainty in the model.	The chattering problem can lead to system instability.
Model Predictive Control (MPC)	Predicts future state behaviors; works with multiple input and output simultaneously; can manage input and output constraints; and noise and disruptions are not a challenge.	Tracking is slow.
Adaptive Controller	When parameters are uncertain, the dynamic and disturbance model are always changing; engineering effectiveness is comparably acceptable.	It takes time to adapt to the new parameters.

The primary motivation of this research is to show the experimental results of well-known and recently developed theoretical studies in the field of modern control system design and analysis for the quadrotor system. One of the most significant properties of control systems analysis is stability. Control systems must meet specified criteria for the system under investigation to operate as desired in both transient and steady-state response values that are as close to the desired value as possible. Therefore, the research presents the development and comparison of the quadrotor control system. The quadrotor plant is initially linearized for hover flight before the linear control approaches are implemented. This research compares the performance of linear and nonlinear control techniques, taking into consideration the restricted onboard computer resources. Because of the constraints imposed by nonlinearity factors and external disturbances, the primary goal is to maintain the translation position's stability, attitude, and altitude of an x3D quadrotor. The key contribution of the proposed research is to develop control systems for x3D quadrotors that will allow them to control the translation position (x, y, z) while stabilizing its attitude angles ($roll\ \phi$, $pitch\ \theta\ and\ yaw\ \psi$) by forcing the position (x, y, z) and yaw (ψ) to track their respect to reference inputs while keeping the roll (ϕ) and pitch (θ) angles negligible [21]. The desired parameters, such as rise time, settling time, peak time, and maximum percent overshoot, and steady-state errors are analyzed in the MATLAB Simulink environment for the x3D quadrotor. As a result, the suggested solutions are more practical and feasible. The significant contributions of this research are as follows:

- SIMULINK simulation of nonlinear X3D quadrotor model to validate control approaches.
- Two linear control systems are implemented: the conventional PID and the LQR control system.
- Two nonlinear control systems are implemented: fuzzy control and model reference adaptive PID controller (MRAPC) using MIT rules.

- Performance comparison of all controllers for quadrotor trajectory tracking based on transient response. The proposed controllers' performance is anticipated to be better in the presence of parameter uncertainty and external disturbances.

The following is the format of this paper: The mathematical model of an X3D quadrotor is presented in Section 2. The quadrotor's control methods are discussed in Section 3. The study and comparison of the aforementioned control strategies for an X3D quadrotor are presented in Section 4. The conclusion is found in Section 5.

2. Mathematical Modeling of X3d Quadrotor

Kinematics and dynamics are the two parts of the X3D model system and are described using the Newton–Euler theorem rules as: (1) A quadrotor has a symmetrical and rigid frame, (2) the quadrotor's center of gravity is the same as the body's fixed frame origin, (3) the propellers have a rigid design, (4) the square of the propeller's speed determines thrust and drag. The X3D quadrotor parameter list is mentioned in Table 2. The complexity of the re-evaluated X3D model, as illustrated in Figure 1, has been significantly decreased. Equation (1) gives the onboard controller's input vector.

$$U = [U_\phi, U_\theta, U_\psi, U_{thrust}] \tag{1}$$

Table 2. X3D Quadrotor parameter list.

Parameters	Symbol	Value
Quadrotor Mass	m	0.54 kg
Gravity Acceleration	g	9.807 m/s^2
Arm length of Quadrotor	L	0.225 m
Inertia Moment	I_{xx}	0.022 kg.m^2
	I_{yy}	0.022 kg.m^2
	I_{zz}	0.0018 kg.m^2

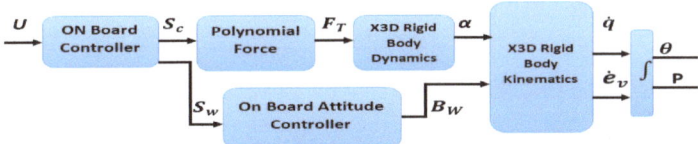

Figure 1. X3D Quadrotor re-evaluation model.

The angular velocity (S_ω) and collective thrust (S_c) outputs of the onboard controller are delivered from the kinematics of the reference body X3D, which results in the system's final output in terms of translation position (**P**) and orientation (**Θ**). The Newton–Euler formulation provides a comprehensive mathematical account of quadrotor dynamics [14]. Position, Euler angle, linear velocity, and angular velocity are among the 12-degree-of-freedom output states described by Equation (2).

$$12 - DOF = [x, y, z, \phi, \theta, \psi, \dot{x}, \dot{y}, \dot{z}, \dot{\phi}, \dot{\theta}, \dot{\psi}] \tag{2}$$

The right-handed system is the inertial (Earth) frame of reference $E = [O_e, X_e, Y_e, Z_e]$ and denotes the origin, which is the center of the earth. Its purpose is to determine the quadrotor's location. Right-handedness is reflected in the bodily frame of reference as $B = [O_B, X_B, Y_B, Z_B]$ and denotes the origin, which is located at the quadrotor's center of gravity. It is used to figure out the quadrotor's orientation with the earth frame.

In the body frame, the torque, the force F_B, angular velocity ω_B, and linear velocity v_B are all computed. The body and the earth reference frames are shown in Figure 2. The coordinates of the quadrotor (body frame) can be aligned with the earth frame in the following sequence: Z_e on the earth, the frame is aligned to the yaw angle on the body frame Z_B (positive ψ), Y_e is aligned to the pitch angle on Y_B (positive θ), and X_e is aligned to the roll angle on X_B (positive φ). Rotation matrices ($xφD, yθD, zψD$) about the three axes (roll, pitch, and yaw) are described in Equation (3).

$$xφD = [1\ 0\ 0\ 0\ cos\ cos\ φ\ \ sin\ sin\ φ\ \ 0\ -sin\ sin\ φ\ \ cos\ cos\ φ\ ]yθD \\ = [cos\ cos\ θ\ \ 0\ -sin\ sin\ θ\ \ 0\ 1\ 0\ sin\ sin\ θ\ \ 0\ cos\ cos\ θ\ ]zψD \\ = [cos\ cos\ ψ\ \ -sin\ sin\ ψ\ \ 0\ sin\ sin\ ψ\ \ cos\ cos\ ψ\ \ 0\ 0\ 0\ 1] \quad (3)$$

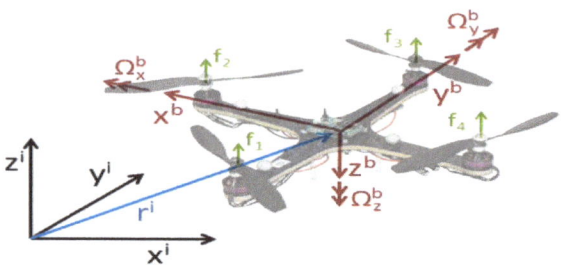

Figure 2. Body and Earth Reference Frame Illustration.

By multiplying a frame with a direction cosine matrix (DCM), a reference frame may be converted from earth to body and vice versa (DCM) [1] as in Equation (4).

$$DCM = EBD(Θ) = (xφD).(yθD).(zψD) \quad (4)$$

Equation (5) gives an orthogonal rotation matrix from the body frame to the inertia (earth) frame.

$$EBD(Θ) = [cos\ cos\ θ\ cos\ cos\ ψ\ \ cos\ θ\ sin\ sin\ ψ\ \ -sin\ sin\ θ\ \ sin\ sin\ φ sin\ sin\ θ\ sin\ sin\ ψ\ -cos\ cos\ φ\ sin\ sin\ ψ \\ sin\ sin\ φ\ sin\ sin\ θ\ sin\ sin\ ψ\ +cos\ cos\ φ\ cos\ cos\ ψ\ \ sin\ sin\ φ cos\ sin\ θ\ cos\ φ\ sin\ sin\ θ\ cos\ cos\ ψ \\ +sin\ sin\ φ\ sin\ sin\ ψ\ \ sin\ sin\ φ\ cos\ cos\ θ\ \ cos\ φ\ cos\ cos\ θ\ ] \quad (5)$$

In Equation (6), the translational velocity V_E of the X3D is given about the earth frame.

$$V_E = \dot{P} = BED(Θ).V_B \quad (6)$$

Equations (7) and (8) can be used to convert angular velocities in the body frame to angular velocities in the earth frame.

$$(\dot{Θ}) = BEH(Θ).B_ω \quad (7)$$

$$[\dot{φ}\ \dot{θ}\ \dot{ψ}] = \begin{bmatrix} 1\ 0\ φ\ \ θ\ φ\ \ 0\ φ\ -φ\ 0\ \dfrac{φ}{θ}\ \dfrac{φ}{θ} \end{bmatrix}[p\ q\ r] \quad (8)$$

Equation (9) can be used to compute the angular velocity in the body frame.

$$B_ω = S_ω . K_ω \quad (9)$$

Equation (10) can be used to determine the angular velocity in the earth frame.

$$E_ω = \dot{Θ} = BEH(Θ).B_ω \quad (10)$$

All external forces are added together to provide the overall force operating on the X3D quadrotor. As seen in Equation (11).

$$TotBF = RotorBF + gBF \quad (11)$$

where $RotorBF = 1BF + 2BF + 3BF + 4BF$.

The upward forces created by the X3D rotors are $1BF$ to $4BF$, and F_g is the force impacting the body. The angular velocity of rotors affects the $RotorBF$.

The nonlinear Simulink model of the x3D quadrotor is presented in Figure 3. The nonlinear dynamic equations of the x3D quadrotor are linearized using a first-order Taylor approximation to implement the linear controller. The X3D near the hover position's aggregate linearized equations may be expressed as Equation (14):

$$\dot{x} = V_x, \; \dot{y} = V_y, \; \dot{z} = V_z$$
$$\dot{\phi} = p, \; \dot{\theta} = q, \; \dot{\psi} = r \quad (12)$$
$$\dot{V}_x = -\phi g \; \dot{V}_y = \theta g \; \dot{V}_z = \frac{F_z + I_f \cdot V_z}{m}$$

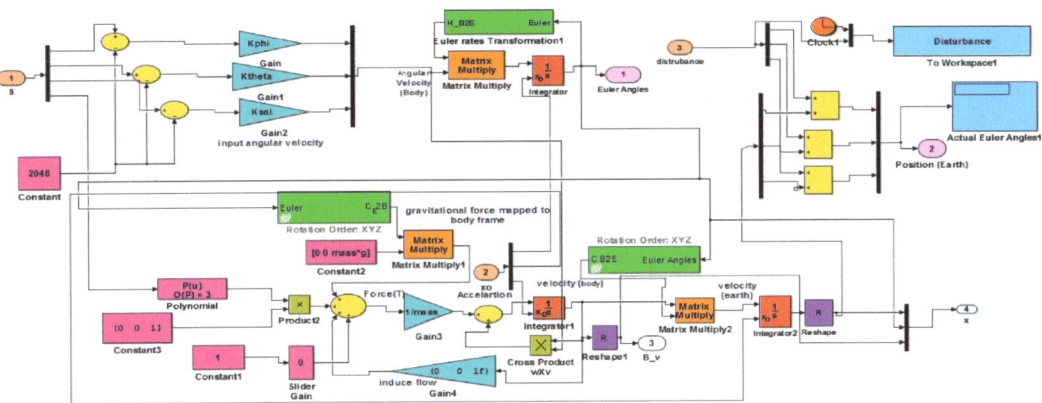

Figure 3. X3D Quadrotor Nonlinear Simulink model.

3. X3D Quadrotor Controller Design

For an X3D quadrotor control system, two control loops are suggested, as shown in Figure 4. The position controller in the outer control loop controls the system's slower dynamics (longitudinal and lateral translations), while the attitude/altitude controller in the inner control loop controls the system's quicker dynamics (attitude and altitude).

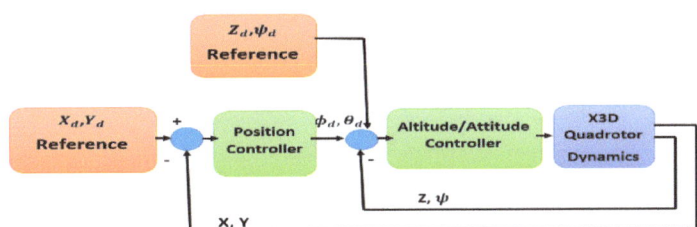

Figure 4. Closed-loop Control System for X3D Quadrotor.

The quadrotor's intended rotor speed is output by the attitude/altitude controller. The PID controller, LQR controller, fuzzy logic controller, and model reference adaptive PID using MIT rule controller were used in this research to stabilize the translation position and attitude/altitude of an X3D quadrotor.

3.1. PID Control System

PID controllers are the most fundamental feedback controllers that are frequently utilized in many industrial applications [22]. A PID controller calculates an error value that distinguishes between the desired set point and the measured process value. By changing the process control inputs, the controller tries to decrease the error. To use the PID controller for achieving ideal values for a better control system, a complete mathematical model of the plant is required to determine the three parameters (proportional gain K_P, integral gain K_I, and derivative gain K_D) [23]. Six PID controllers for attitude/altitude stabilization and translation trajectories are presented in this research. The attitude angles are controlled by three PID controllers (ϕ, θ and ψ). The altitude (z-axis) of the X3D quadrotor is controlled by one PID controller, while the longitudinal and lateral positions (x-axis and y-axis) are controlled by two PID controllers. Hence, the attitude is determined by the positions. The Euler angles' preliminary conditions are set to (0, 0, and 0) to begin the experiment. The angular velocity and thrust for the X3D quadrotor are then generated by combining all PID controllers with the combinational control. Figure 5 depicts the PID controller feedback loops for an X3D quadrotor [24]. Equation (13) illustrates the discrete-time transfer function for each PID controller.

$$PID = \left(K_P + Z^{-1}K_D + \frac{1}{Z^{-1}}K_I\right) \tag{13}$$

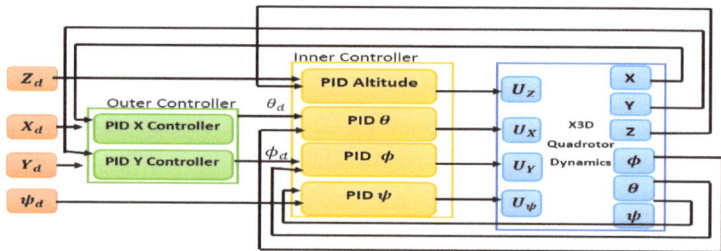

Figure 5. X3D Quadrotor PID Controllers.

In Equations (14) and (15), the equations for PID attitude control are provided.

$$e_{attitude} = \Theta_{refreance} - \Theta_{measured} \cdot EBD(\Theta) \tag{14}$$

$$\Theta_{desire} = e_{attitude}.PID \tag{15}$$

Similar to PID for attitude control, PID for height control $(z-axis)$ and PID for translation position control $(x-axis\ and\ y-axis)$ are calculated. The height $(z-axis)$ and intended angular velocity are used as inputs in the combination control step, and following saturation, thrust and the actual angular velocity are transmitted to the X3D quadrotor's nonlinear model, as shown in Equations (16)–(18). The classical discrete PID is implemented in all the controller blocks, and the parametric gain values are listed in Table 3.

$$\omega_{desire} = (\Theta_{desire} - \Theta_{measured}).EBH(\Theta) \tag{16}$$

$$U_{[X,\ Y,\psi]} = sat\{\omega_{desire}\} \tag{17}$$

$$U_Z = sat\{Z_{desire}\} \tag{18}$$

Table 3. Parametric Gain values of each PID Controllers.

Parametric Gain	Controllers		
	PID Altitude (Z)	PID (X, Y)	PID (Φ, θ, ψ)
K_P	1.5	2	1
K_I	0	0	0
K_D	0.5	1	0.1

3.2. LQR Control System

The linear quadratic regulator (LQR) controller has been widely used in engineering applications such as voltage source inverters and wheeled inverted pendulum vehicles [25]. There is comparably little research on using the LQR control technique to track and stabilize the quadrotor. The LQR control system is designed to give optimum control while being cost-effective [26]. Owing to the significant uncertainties and nonlinearities in quadrotor dynamics, as well as model unreliability due to parameter fluctuations and linearity approximation, implementing the LQR control system on the quadrotor is a difficult undertaking. As a result, the quadrotor system dynamics are described by a linear state–space equation, with a quadratic cost function as the least appropriate cost function [27]. Equations (19) and (20) depicts the form of the continuous state–space model:

$$\dot{x}_s(t) = Ax_s(t) + Bu(t) \qquad (19)$$

$$y(t) = Cx_s(t) + Du(t) \qquad (20)$$

To develop the continuous state–space model, the X3D's linearized state–space Equation (21) and (22) is employed. The A matrix is shown below, with $C = I_{9X9}$ and $D = 0_{9x4}$ as the C and D matrices, respectively.

$$\dot{x}_s(t) = A\ x_s(t) \qquad (21)$$

$$\begin{bmatrix} \dot{x}\ \dot{y}\ \dot{z}\ \dot{\phi}\ \dot{\theta}\ \dot{\psi}\ \dot{V}_x\ \dot{V}_y\ \dot{V}_z \end{bmatrix} = [0\,0\,0\,0\,0\,0\,0\,0\,0\ \ \ 0\,0\,0\ \ \ 0\,0\,0\ \ \ 0\,0\,0\ \ \ 1\,0\,0\,0\,1\,0\,0\,0\,1\ \ \ 0\,0\,0\,0\,0\,0\,0\,0\,0\,0\,0\,0\,0\,0\,0\ \ \ 0\,0\,0\,0\,0\,0\,0\,0\,0\ \ \ 0\,0\,0\,0\,0\,g\,0\,0\,0 \\ -g\,0\,0\ \ \ 0\,0\,0\ \ \ 0\,0\,0\ \ \ 0\,0\,0\,0\,0\,0\,0\,0\,\tfrac{l_f}{m}] [x\ y\ z\ \phi\ \theta\ \psi\ V_x\ V_y\ V_z] \qquad (22)$$

Equation (23) derives the discrete case quadratic cost function.

$$J = \sum_{k=0}^{\infty} \left| x_k^T Q x_k + u_k^T R u_k \right. \qquad (23)$$

The weighted matrices of the state vector and input vector, respectively, are Q and R. The Q and R gain matrices for simulation were determined using Bryson's method. Equation (24) yields the Q and R gain matrices for the X3D quadrotor.

$$\begin{aligned} Q &= [10\ 0\ 0\ 0\ 10\ 0\ 0\ 20\ \ \ 0\,0\,0\,0\,0\,0\,0\,0\,0\ \ \ 0\,0\,0\,0\,0\,0\,0\,0\,0\ \ \ 0\,0\,0\,0\,0\,0\,0\,0\,0\ \ \ 5\,0\,0\,0\,5\,0\,0\,0\,10\ \ \ 0\,0\,0\,0\,0\,0\,0\,0\,0\ \ \ 0\,0\,0\,0\,0\,0\,0\,0\,0\ \ \ 0\,0\,0\,0\,0\,0\,0\,0\,0\ \ \ 1\,0\,0\,0\,1\,0\,0\,0\,1] \\ &= [10\ 0\ 0\ 10\ \ \ 0\,0\,0\,0\ \ \ 0\,0\,0\,0\ \ \ 10\ 0\ 0\ 10\ \ ] \end{aligned} \qquad (24)$$

The parameters k, P, and e for the LQR system may be retrieved using the MATLAB lqr function, as indicated in Equation (25).

$$[k, P, e] = lqr(A, B, Q, R) \qquad (25)$$

3.3. Fuzzy Logic Control System

The correlation between the input data and the output action is described using human language descriptions in fuzzy logic. It is a mathematical system that takes analog input values and compares them to variables that need values between 0 and 1 [28]. The proper process input is determined by a fuzzy controller's fuzzy membership function and inference rule. The quadrotor's translation position must be controlled while its attitude (roll, pitch, and yaw angle) must be stabilized [29]. In this article, an X3D quadrotor is controlled using Mamdani's fuzzy inference approach. The quadrotor's attitude (desired angles of roll, pitch, and yaw) is controlled by three fuzzy controllers, denoted as FC (ϕ), FC (θ) and FC (ψ), respectively (desired angles of roll ϕ, pitch θ, and yaw ψ) [30]. FC (Z) determines the altitude of the quadrotor. The quadrotor's translation position is controlled by two additional fuzzy controllers, FC (X) and FC (Y). The states φ and θ are used to control the X and Y positions, respectively. All six fuzzy logical controllers use the same two identical inputs as described below.

- Error (e) denotes the difference between the desired and measured signals.
- Derivative error (de) is the error rate.

Figure 6 depicts the implementation of a fuzzy system for quadrotor control. Error is stabilized between $[-1, +1]$ and $[-3, +3]$, whereas the error rate is stabilized between $[-3, +3]$.

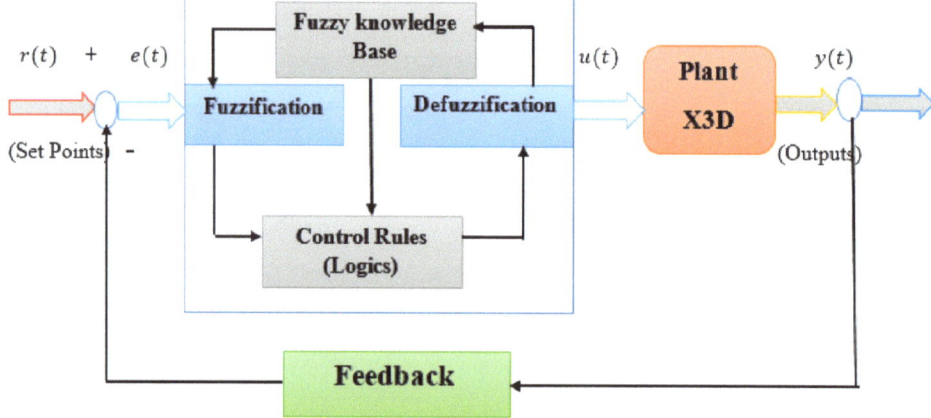

Figure 6. X3D Quadrotor Control using a Fuzzy Controller.

The output with three fuzzy logic values (N, Z, and P) is used for the input variables e and de, as indicated in Table 4; N stands for negative, Z for zero, and P for positive. Table 1 explains the rules: If the error (e) is negative and the rate of error (de) is negative, then the output will be negative. Figure 7 depicts all of the FCs' controller inputs as well as membership functions.

Table 4. X3D Quadrotor's Fuzzy Rules.

		Error (e)		
		$FC\ (X), FC(Y), FC\ (\phi), FC(\theta)$		
		P	Z	N
	P	P	P	Z
	Z	P	Z	N
Rate of Error (de)	N	Z	N	N
		$FC\ (Z), FC(\psi)$		
		P	Z	N
	P	Z	Z	N
	Z	Z	N	P
	N	N	P	P

The surface view of all Fuzzy controllers is shown in Figures 8 and 9.

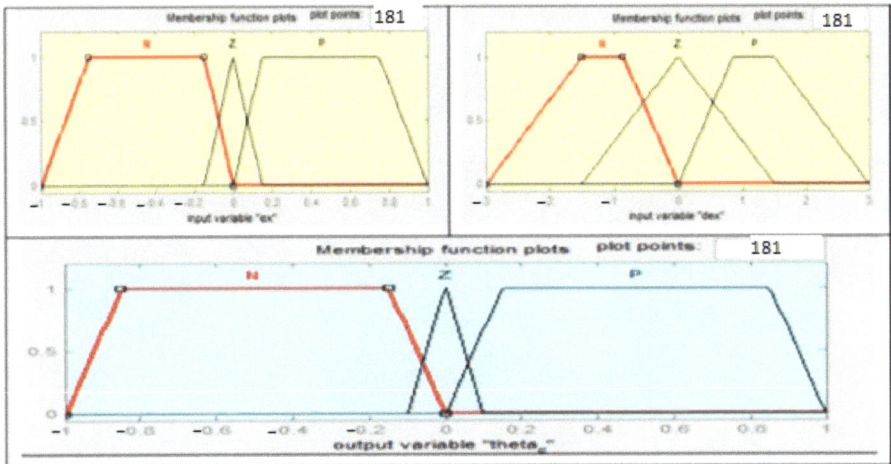

Figure 7. Error, Rate of Error, and Output Membership Functions.

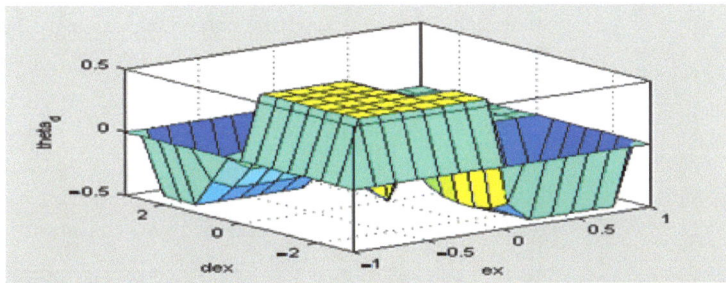

Figure 8. Surface view of FC (Z), FC (ψ).

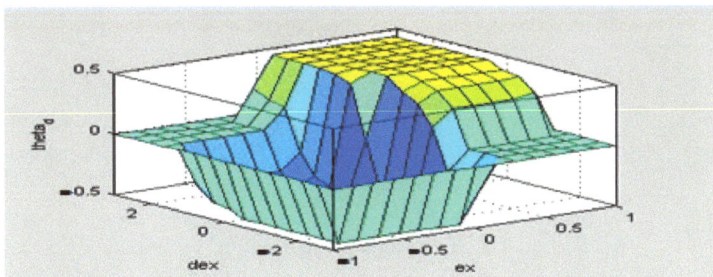

Figure 9. Surface view of FC (X), FC(Y), FC (ϕ), FC (θ).

3.4. Model Reference Adaptive PID Control System Based on MIT Rule

Numerous controllers, including PI, PD, PID, and feedback, can be adapted utilizing particular adaptation methods to improve system performance. In this research, the model reference adaptive PID controller based on MIT rule was used to investigate the fast-tracking and stability control of quadrotor [31]. The Massachusetts Institute of Technology (MIT) developed the MRAC-based MIT rule in 1960 [32]. It employs the model reference adaptation control technique to ensure that the actual plant output follows the output of the reference model when the reference inputs are the same for any practical system with undetermined and unpredictable characteristics that can be adjusted by control settings [33] as illustrated in Figure 10. This section presents the MIT-rule-based design parameter adaption rules for a PID controller. The following are the steps to creating an MRAC using the MIT rule. Obtain the MRAC system reference model that yields the desired trajectory y_m.

$$G_m(s) = \frac{y_m(s)}{u_c(s)} = \frac{\alpha s + \omega_n^2}{s^2 + 2s\zeta\omega_n + \omega_n^2} \qquad (26)$$

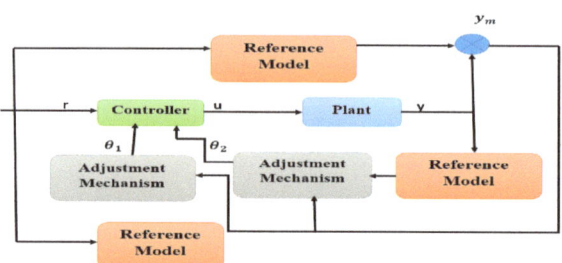

Figure 10. MRAC System with MIT Rules.

Closed-loop characteristics such as settling time t_S and overshoot (OS) are used to estimate the damping ratio ζ and natural frequency ω_n. Table 5 lists the specifications of the reference model for the X3D quadrotor.

Table 5. X3D Quadrotor reference model specifications.

Parameters	Values
Settling time	20s
Damping ratio	0.707
Steady-state error	0%

The transfer function of the reference model is changed as follows:

$$G_m(s) = \frac{y_m(s)}{u_c(s)} = \frac{0.1058}{s^2 + 0.1496 + 0.1058} \qquad (27)$$

1. State the adaptive law of MRAC system for PID controller as

$$u(t) = K_P e(t) + K_I \int_0^t e(t)dt - K_D \frac{dy_p}{dt} \qquad (28)$$

where $e(t) = u_c - y_p$

The PID controller's transfer function in Laplace domain is described in Equation (29)

$$U(s) = K_P E + \frac{K_I}{s} E - K_D s y_p \qquad (29)$$

2. State the tracking error e for the system as

$$e = r - y_p \qquad (30)$$

where r is the system reference input.

$$\frac{de}{dt} = -\frac{dy_p}{dt} \qquad (31)$$

3. As stated in Equation (34), estimate the adaption error ε.

$$\varepsilon = y_p - y_m \tag{32}$$

where y_p denotes the plant output and y_m denotes the reference model output.

4. As follows, describe the MIT rule, which is described as the temporal rate Φ of change proportional to the cost function's (J) negative gradient.

$$\frac{d\Phi}{dt} = -\gamma \frac{\partial J}{\partial \Phi} = -\gamma e \frac{\partial e}{\partial \Phi} \tag{33}$$

For calculating the value of PID controller parameters ($\dot{K}_P$, $\dot{K}_D$, $\dot{K}_I$), use the MIT Rule (gradient method). The following are the estimated adjustment parameters.

$$\begin{aligned}
\frac{dK_p}{dt} &= -\gamma_p \varepsilon \left(\frac{s}{s^2 + 2s\zeta\omega_n + \omega_n^2} \right) e \\
\frac{dK_I}{dt} &= -(\gamma_I) \varepsilon \left(\frac{1}{s^2 + 2s\zeta\omega_n + \omega_n^2} \right) e \\
\frac{dK_D}{dt} &= \gamma_D \varepsilon \left(\frac{s^2}{s^2 + 2s\zeta\omega_n + \omega_n^2} \right) y_p
\end{aligned} \tag{34}$$

For the approximate parameters K_P, K_I and K_D of adaptation, the law is as (35).

$$\begin{aligned}
\theta_1 = K_p &= -\left(\frac{\gamma_p}{s}\right) \varepsilon \left(\frac{s}{s^2 + 2s\zeta\omega_n + \omega_n^2} \right) e \\
\theta_2 = K_I &= -\left(\frac{\gamma_I}{s}\right) \varepsilon \left(\frac{1}{s^2 + 2s\zeta\omega_n + \omega_n^2} \right) e \\
\theta_3 = K_D &= \left(\frac{\gamma_p}{s}\right) \varepsilon \left(\frac{s^2}{s^2 + 2s\zeta\omega_n + \omega_n^2} \right) y_p
\end{aligned} \tag{35}$$

The value of the adaptation gain (γ) has a direct relationship with the convergence rate.

The simulation results show that it is correct for small values (γ) but impulsive for high values, indicating that the right selection of (γ) is critical. The quadrotor's attitude (roll ϕ, pitch θ, and yaw ψ) is controlled by three MARC adaptive PID controllers, indicated by MARC ϕ, MARC θ and MARC ψ, respectively. MARC Z oversees controlling the quadrotor's height, while MARC X and MARC Y are in charge of controlling the quadrotor's position. The architecture of the MARC adaptive PID controller with MIT rule including all six degrees of freedom (DOF) quadrotor output is shown in Figure 11. Three PID controller parameters (K_P, K_I, and K_d) can be modified using the MARC system and the MIT rule to make the nonlinear X3D Quadrotor stable and track to the appropriate reference input.

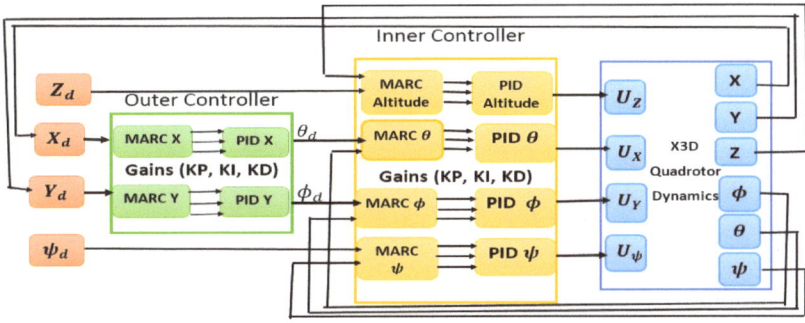

Figure 11. MRAC Adaptive PID Controller with MIT for an X3D Quadrotor.

4. Simulation Results

All linear and nonlinear controllers can provide system stability and optimum performance under their nominal conditions. It is indeed challenging to obtain equivalent results from both the simulation and the real-time experiment due to highly precise parameter adjustment and nonlinear parameters and dynamics. Researchers generally use modelled linear controllers because of their simplicity of design and implementation, as well as their ability to produce high-quality experimental data. On the other hand, robustness, noise and disturbance elimination, limitation control at the endpoints, and more precise trajectory tracking are all advantages of nonlinear controllers [34–36]. Therefore, theoretical studies reveal that linear controllers such as LQR and PID are good at maintaining stability under nominal conditions but not so good at ensuring robustness. The fuzzy controller, on the other hand, cannot guarantee nominal stability but can offer adequate and excellent maneuvering performance. Furthermore, hybrid and adaptive controllers are created as units in which many controllers can work together to provide the finest balance of robustness, nominal stability, flexibility, optimality, simplicity, tracking ability, rapid response, and disturbance rejection to a system, among other features. High computation, a large amount of training data, estimation error, and the existence of uncertainty are the issues that these controllers must confront to achieve satisfying performance, even though they are capable of ensuring remarkable outcomes when the system is disturbed by uncertainty. For example, LQR becomes LQG when the Kalman filter is used to generate a state observer and eliminate signal noise. Secondly, to achieve excellent maneuvering performance, a model reference adaptive controller is used to update the PID controller gain. Figure 12 shows the proposed control structure, which includes a control unit, an X3D Quadrotor, an inertial measurement unit (IMU), and a Kalman filter. The reference input will be received first by the quadrotor system. It measures the translational position and rotational position, velocities, and accelerations of the X3D Quadrotor at a specified time. The output of the quadrotor is then sent to the IMU sensor, which includes a three-axis accelerometer and a gyroscope. The Kalman filter is used to rectify and filter the output of an IMU sensor before it is fed back to the control unit. The control unit then generates an output that is equivalent to the thrust that all motors must provide in order to maintain the well-defined requirements of the X3D quadrotor. The proposed control structure mentioned above is implemented in the MATLAB Simulink environment. To evaluate the performance of all control systems for the specified reference position, unit step tests are performed in all the three axes, x, y, and z. Desired references for step input at the xyz positions are set to 1. The simulation period of an X3D Quadrotor system is defined as 30, 50, and 400 s, correspondingly, for positional testing (x, y, and z) among suggested controllers.

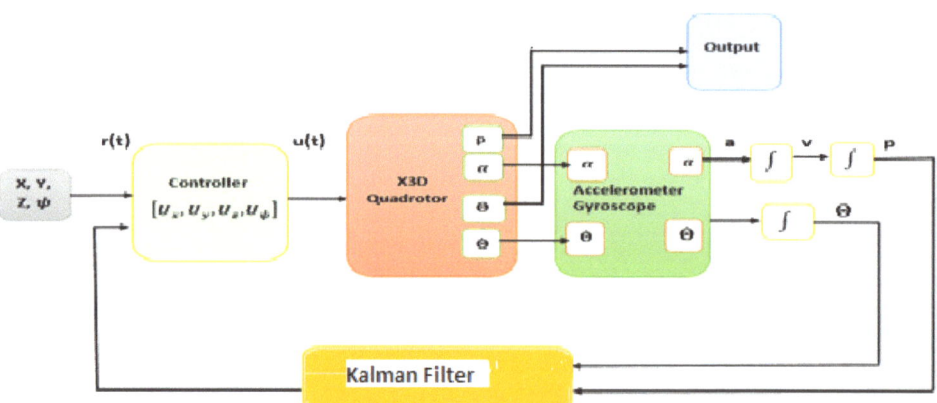

Figure 12. Quadrotor closed-loop control system.

Figures 13–18 illustrate the output response of the closed-loop control system for the longitudinal position (x-axis), lateral position (y-axis), altitude (z-axis), and attitude (roll, pitch, and yaw angle) for each of the four controllers. All controllers work well in keeping the quadrotor in the proper reference position, as can be seen in these figures. Tables 6–8 provides the comparison of step test results in terms of rising time, settling time, peak time, and overshoot for all three dimensions (x, y, and z). Figures 13 and 14 show the X and Y position responses, whereas Figure 15 shows the height (z-axis) response.

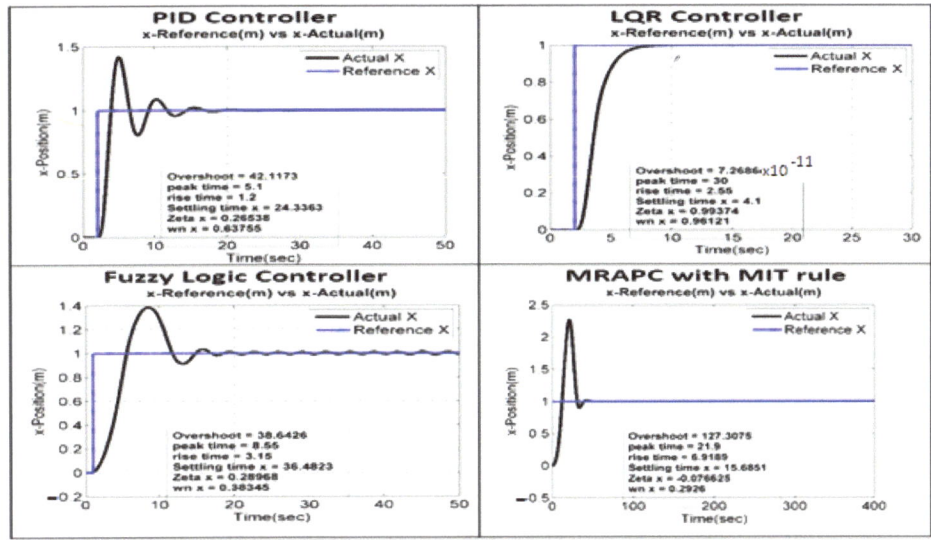

Figure 13. Step response result of all control systems along the x-axis.

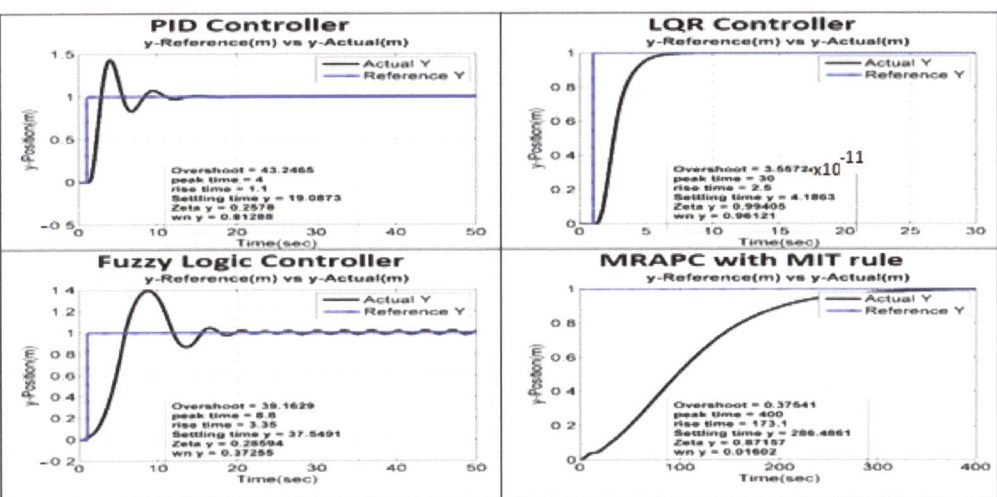

Figure 14. Step response result of all control systems along the y-axis

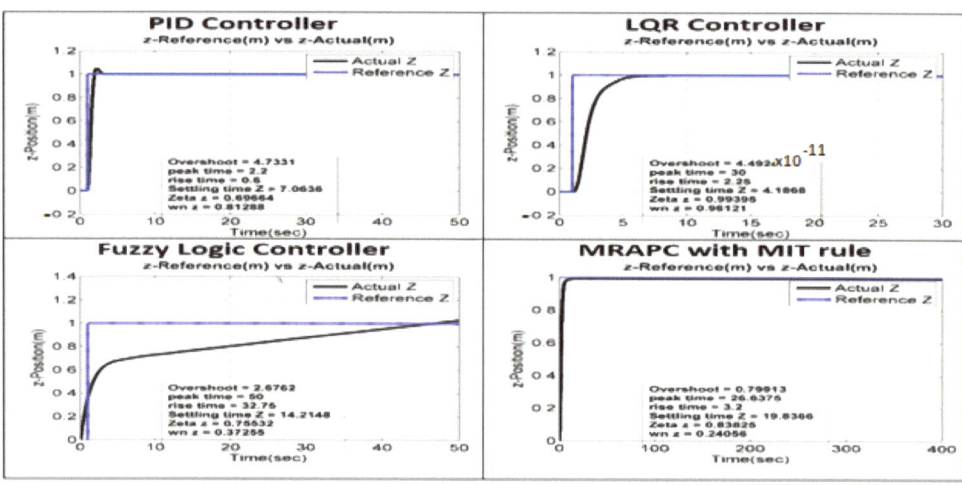

Figure 15. Step response result of all control systems along the z-axis

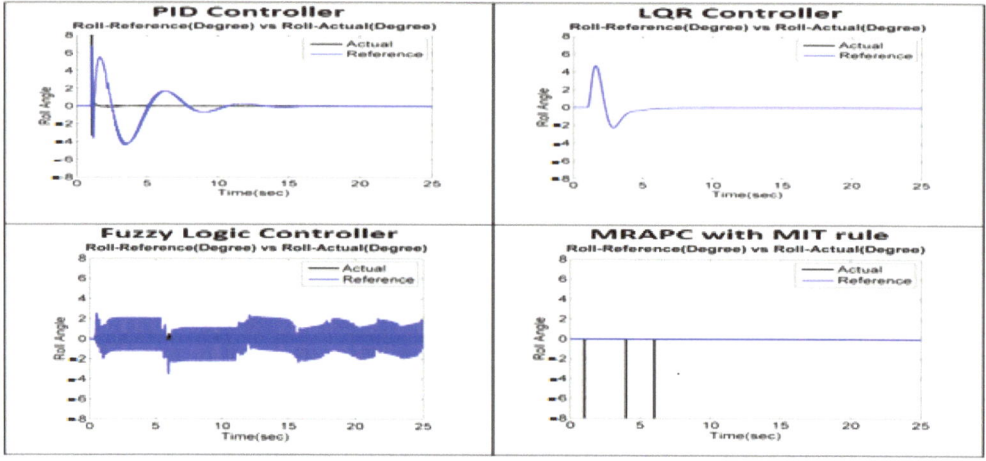

Figure 16. Roll (φ) Control result depending on step input for all control systems.

The aggregate performance of the PID controller, LQR controller, fuzzy controller, and MRAPC with MIT rule controller appears to be satisfactory, as demonstrated in Figure 13 and Table 6, where the root mean square error (RMSE) and normalized root mean square error (NRMSE) for simulations are less than 1 m along the x-axis. Although, the LQR controller is superior to others because it reduces overshoot, rising time, and settling time along the x-axis. Nevertheless, the performance of PID, LQR, fuzzy, and MRAPC with MIT rule appears to be good, as demonstrated in Figure 14 and Table 7, where the root mean square error (RMSE) and normalized root mean square error (RMSE) for simulations are below 1 m along the y-axis.

In terms of overshoot, rising time, and settling time along the y-axis, the LQR controller performs better.

According to Figure 15 and Table 8, the LQR controller achieves superior results along the z-axis than other control approaches because there is no overshoot, the rising time is shorter, and the settling time is shorter. In Figure 16, the LQR controller stabilizes the roll angle in 4 s, which is a much quicker period than the findings of other controllers.

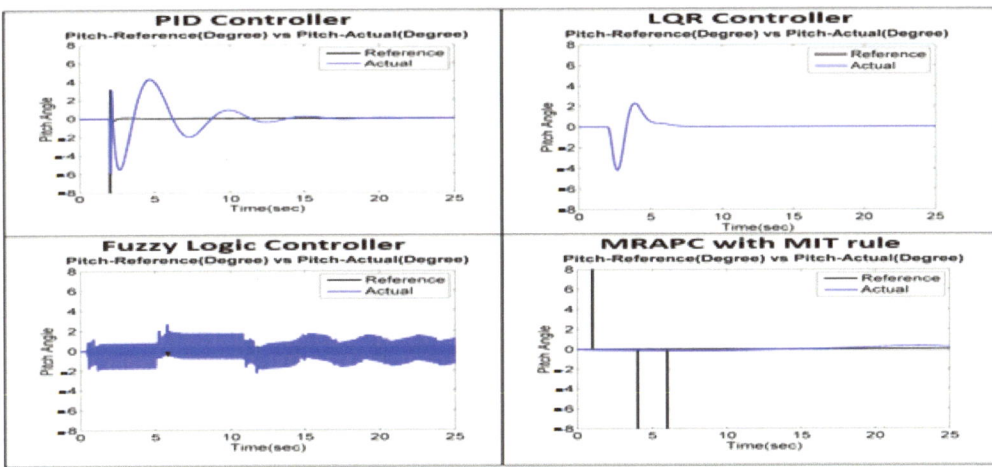

Figure 17. Pitch (θ) Control result depending on step input for all control systems.

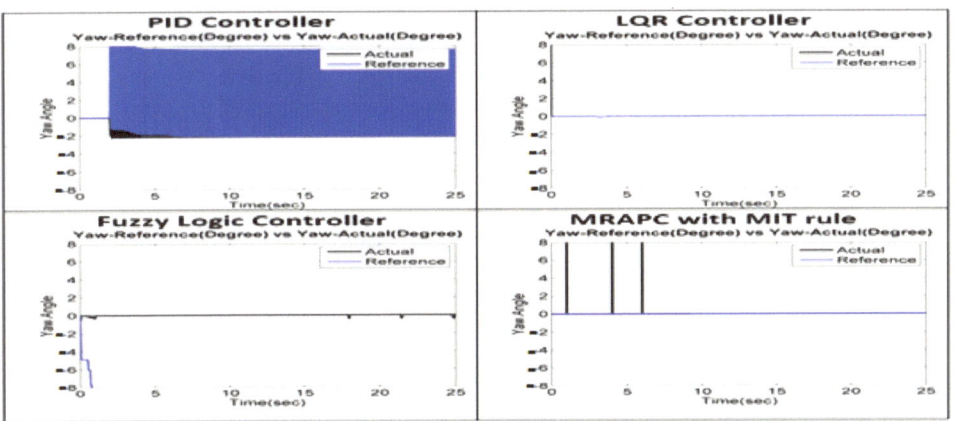

Figure 18. Yaw (ψ) Control result depending on step input for all control systems.

Table 6. Performance comparison of all controllers for the longitudinal position (*x*-axis).

Controllers	Performance Index (*x*-axis)					
	Setting Time T_S	Rise Time T_r	Overshoot (%)	Peak Time T_p	RMS Error	NRMS Error
PID	24.3	1.2	4.2	5.1	0.16	0.11
LQR	4.18	2.55	0.0	30	0.21	0.21
Fuzzy Logic	36.48	3.15	38.64	8.8	0.23	0.17
MRAPC with MIT	17.24	7.1	119.58	22.5	0.22	0.10

The LQR controller, as shown in Figure 17, requires a shorter time to stabilize the pitch angle than other controllers.

Figure 18 demonstrates that the system has a negligible yaw angle in the case of the LQR controller structure.

Table 7. Performance comparison of all controllers for the lateral position (Y-axis).

Controllers	Performance Index (y-axis)					
	Setting Time T_S	Rise Time T_r	Overshoot (%)	Peak Time T_p	RMS Error	NRMS Error
PID	19.08	1.1	43.2	4	0.17	0.12
LQR	4.18	2.5	0.0	30	0.21	0.21
Fuzzy Logic	37.54	3.35	39.162	8.8	0.24	0.18
MRAPC with MIT	170.74	104.7	8.8	213.1	0.425	0.426

Table 8. Performance comparison of control techniques for Z-position.

Controllers	Performance Index (z-axis)					
	Setting Time T_S	Rise Time T_r	Overshoot (%)	Peak Time T_p	RMS Error	NRMS Error
PID	7.06	0.6	4.7	2.2	0.08	0.08
LQR	4.16	2.25	0.0	30	0.18	0.18
Fuzzy Logic	14.21	32.75	2.67	50	0.814	0.815
MRAPC with MIT	21.86	3.3	0.77	26.85	0.056	0.056

5. Conclusions

The system proposed in this manuscript is a quadrotor. Controlling and stabilizing the quadrotor is a substantial issue due to nonlinearity and under-actuated configurations, such as a lower number of control inputs than degrees of freedom (DOF). A comparison of four alternative control methods, such as the LQR controller, PID controller, fuzzy controller, and model reference adaptive PID controller using the MIT rule, has been provided in this article for an X3D quadrotor. These controllers demonstrate the stability, robustness, and control of a quadrotor during maneuvers and trajectory tracking in the presence of nonlinear dynamics. The results of simulations demonstrate that given the identical translation position, altitude, and attitude inputs, each control system responds differently. However, based on the features that are required for the quadrotor application, it is possible to select the most suited system. When compared to other controllers at almost the same operating conditions, the LQR controller yields the highest accuracy in x, y, and z-step performance. The LQR controller has a 0.0% overshoot and a 4.1% shorter settling time than other controllers, particularly nonlinear controllers. In terms of the highest settling time and overshoot, the model reference adaptive PID controller using the MIT rule performs the worst. It is worth mentioning that the linear controller methods are quite ubiquitous and easy to implement, and they may be used for a wide range of real-world control systems. For potential research directions, all the controllers will be deployed on the X3D quadrotor board, and the X3D quadrotor's real-time performance, validation, and authentication of all control systems will be monitored; in addition, other machine learning and deep learning algorithms will be implemented for autonomous operation.

Author Contributions: Conceptualization, T.S., J.A., M.H.J., A.U.R., E.T.E., N.A.G. and M.S.; methodology, T.S., J.A., M.H.J., A.U.R., E.T.E., N.A.G. and M.S.; software, T.S. and J.A.; validation, M.H.J. and A.U.R.; formal analysis, T.S., E.T.E., N.A.G. and M.S.; investigation, M.H.J. and M.S.; resources, E.T.E. and N.A.G.; data curation, T.S. and J.A.; writing—original draft preparation, T.S., J.A., M.H.J., A.U.R., E.T.E., N.A.G., M.S.; T.S., J.A., M.H.J., A.U.R., E.T.E., N.A.G. and M.S.; visualization, M.H.J.; supervision, M.H.J. and M.S.; project administration, E.T.E. and N.A.G.; funding acquisition, E.T.E. and N.A.G. All authors have read and agreed to the published version of the manuscript.

Funding: This research was supported by Future University Researchers Supporting Project Number FUESP-2020/48 at Future University in Egypt, New Cairo 11845, Egypt.

Institutional Review Board Statement: Not applicable.

Informed Consent Statement: Not applicable.

Data Availability Statement: Not applicable.

Conflicts of Interest: The authors declare that they have no conflicts of interest to report regarding the present study.

References

1. Shakeel, T. *Simulated Closed Loop Trajectory Control System of X3D Quadrotor in Ubiquitous Gesture Controlled Environment*; COMSATS Institute of Information Technology: Lahore, Pakistan, 2016.
2. Shehzad, M.F.; Bilal, A.; Ahmad, H. Position & attitude control of an aerial robot (quadrotor) with intelligent pid and state feedback lqr controller: A comparative approach. In Proceedings of the 16th International Bhurban Conference on Applied Sciences and Technology (IBCAST), Islamabad, Pakistan, 8–12 January 2019; pp. 340–346.
3. Sain, D.; Mohan, B. Modeling, simulation and experimental realization of a new nonlinear fuzzy PID controller using Center of Gravity defuzzification. *ISA Trans.* **2021**, *110*, 319–327. [CrossRef] [PubMed]
4. Zulu, A.; John, S. A review of control algorithms for autonomous quadrotors. *Open J. Appl. Sci.* **2014**, *4*, 547–556. [CrossRef]
5. Al-Younes, Y.M.; Al-Jarrah, M.A.; Jhemi, A.A. Linear vs. nonlinear control techniques for a quadrotor vehicle. In Proceedings of the 7th International Symposium on Mechatronics and Its Applications, Sharjah, United Arab Emirates, 20–22 April 2010; pp. 1–10.
6. Argentim, L.M.; Rezende, W.C.; Santos, P.E.; Aguiar, R.A. PID, LQR and LQR-PID on a quadcopter platform. In Proceedings of the 2013 International Conference on Informatics, Electronics and Vision (ICIEV), Dhaka, Bangladesh, 17–18 May 2013; pp. 1–6.
7. Wang, H.; Gelbal, S.Y.; Guvenc, L. Multi-Objective Digital PID Controller Design in Parameter Space and Its Application to Automated Path Following. *IEEE Access* **2021**, *9*, 46874–46885. [CrossRef]
8. Jiang, J.; Qi, J.; Song, D.; Han, J. Control platform design and experiment of a quadrotor. In Proceedings of the 32nd Chinese Control Conference, Xi'an, China, 26–28 July 2013; pp. 2974–2979.
9. Khan, A.; Jaffery, M.H.; Javed, Y.; Arshad, J.; Rehman, A.U.; Khan, R.; Bajaj, M.; Kaabar, M.K. Hardware-in-the-Loop Implementation and Performance Evaluation of Three-Phase Hybrid Shunt Active Power Filter for Power Quality Improvement. *Math. Probl. Eng.* **2021**, *2021*, 8032793. [CrossRef]
10. Raffo, G.V.; Ortega, M.G.; Rubio, F.R. An integral predictive/nonlinear $H\infty$ control structure for a quadrotor helicopter. *Automatica* **2010**, *46*, 29–39. [CrossRef]
11. Sarwar, S.; Javed, M.Y.; Jaffery, M.H.; Arshad, J.; Ur Rehman, A.; Shafiq, M.; Choi, J.-G. A novel hybrid MPPT technique to maximize power harvesting from pv system under partial and complex partial shading. *Appl. Sci.* **2022**, *12*, 587. [CrossRef]
12. Menhaj, M.B.; Fakurian, R.S.F. Fuzzy controller design for quadrotor UAVs using minimal control input. *Indian J. Sci. Res.* **2014**, *1*, 157–164.
13. Camboim, M.M.; Villanueva, J.M.M.; de Souza, C.P. Fuzzy Controller Applied to a Remote Energy Harvesting Emulation Platform. *Sensors* **2020**, *20*, 5874. [CrossRef]
14. Ang, K.H.; Chong, G.; Li, Y. PID control system analysis, design, and technology. *IEEE Trans. Control. Syst. Technol.* **2005**, *13*, 559–576.
15. Liu, C.; Pan, J.; Chang, Y. PID and LQR trajectory tracking control for an unmanned quadrotor helicopter: Experimental studies. In Proceedings of the 2016 35th Chinese Control Conference (CCC), Chengdu, China, 27–29 July 2016; pp. 10845–10850.
16. Shi, L.; Zheng, W.X.; Shao, J.; Cheng, Y. Sub-super-stochastic matrix with applications to bipartite tracking control over signed networks. *SIAM J. Control. Optim.* **2021**, *59*, 4563–4589. [CrossRef]
17. Shi, L.; Cheng, Y.; Shao, J.; Sheng, H.; Liu, Q. Cucker-Smale flocking over cooperation-competition networks. *Automatica* **2022**, *135*, 109988. [CrossRef]
18. Zouaoui, S.; Mohamed, E.; Kouider, B. Easy tracking of UAV using PID controller. *Period. Polytech. Transp. Eng.* **2019**, *47*, 171–177. [CrossRef]
19. Kuantama, E.; Tarca, I.; Tarca, R. Feedback linearization LQR control for quadcopter position tracking. In Proceedings of the 2018 5th International Conference on Control, Decision and Information Technologies (CoDIT), Thessaloniki, Greece, 10–13 April 2018; pp. 204–209.
20. Chovancová, A.; Fico, T.; Duchoň, F.; Dekan, M.; Chovanec, Ľ.; Dekanova, M. Control methods comparison for the real quadrotor on an innovative test stand. *Appl. Sci.* **2020**, *10*, 2064. [CrossRef]
21. Mahmoud, O.E.; Roman, M.R.; Nasry, J.F. Linear and nonlinear stabilizing control of quadrotor UAV. In Proceedings of the 2014 International Conference on Engineering and Technology (ICET), Cairo, Egypt, 19–20 April 2014; pp. 1–8.
22. Canbek, K.O.; Oniz, Y. Trajectory Tracking of a Quadcopter Using Fuzzy-PD Controller. In Proceedings of the 2021 13th International Conference on Electrical and Electronics Engineering (ELECO), Bursa, Turkey, 25–27 November 2021; pp. 109–113.
23. Salih, A.L.; Moghavvemi, M.; Mohamed, H.A.; Gaeid, K.S. Flight PID controller design for a UAV quadrotor. *Sci. Res. Essays* **2010**, *5*, 3660–3667.
24. Aboelhassan, A.; Abdelgeliel, M.; Zakzouk, E.E.; Galea, M. Design and Implementation of Model Predictive Control Based PID Controller for Industrial Applications. *Energies* **2020**, *13*, 6594. [CrossRef]
25. Ali, A.T.; Tayeb, E.B.M. Adaptive PID controller for DC motor speed control. *Int. J. Eng. Invent.* **2012**, *1*, 26–30.

26. Bouabdallah, S. *Design and Control of Quadrotors with Application to Autonomous Flying*; Epfl: Lausanne, Switzerland, 2007.
27. Espinoza-Fraire, T.; Saenz, A.; Salas, F.; Juarez, R.; Giernacki, W. Trajectory Tracking with Adaptive Robust Control for Quadrotor. *Appl. Sci.* **2021**, *11*, 8571. [CrossRef]
28. Jaffery, M.H. *Precision Landing and Testing of Aerospace Vehicles*; University of Surrey: Guildford, UK, 2012.
29. Yue, M.; An, C.; Sun, J. Zero dynamics stabilisation and adaptive trajectory tracking for WIP vehicles through feedback linearisation and LQR technique. *Int. J. Control.* **2016**, *89*, 2533–2542. [CrossRef]
30. Choudhury, S.; Acharya, S.K.; Khadanga, R.K.; Mohanty, S.; Arshad, J.; Ur Rehman, A.; Shafiq, M.; Choi, J.-G. Harmonic Profile Enhancement of Grid Connected Fuel Cell through Cascaded H-Bridge Multi-Level Inverter and Improved Squirrel Search Optimization Technique. *Energies* **2021**, *14*, 7947. [CrossRef]
31. Sampath, B.; Perera, K.; Wijesuriya, W.; Dassanayake, V. Fuzzy based stabilizer control system for quad-rotor. *Int. J. Mech. Aerosp. Ind. Mechatron. Eng.* **2014**, *8*, 455–461.
32. Bhatkhande, P.; Havens, T.C. Real time fuzzy controller for quadrotor stability control. In Proceedings of the 2014 IEEE International Conference on Fuzzy Systems (FUZZ-IEEE), Beijing, China, 6–11 July 2014; pp. 913–919.
33. Ghamri, R. Design of an Adaptive Controller for Magnetic Levitation System Based Bacteria Foraging Optimization Algorithm. Master's Thesis, Islamic University, Islamabad, Pakistan, 2014.
34. Pankaj, S.; Kumar, J.S.; Nema, R. Comparative analysis of MIT rule and Lyapunov rule in model reference adaptive control scheme. *Innov. Syst. Des. Eng.* **2011**, *2*, 154–162.
35. Korul, H.; Tosun, D.C.; Isik, Y. A Model Reference Adaptive Controller Performance of an Aircraft Roll Altitude Control System. In *Recent Advances on Systems, Signals, Control, Communications and Computers*; WSEAS: Attica, Greece, 2015; pp. 971–978.
36. Roy, R.; Islam, M.; Sadman, N.; Mahmud, M.; Gupta, K.D.; Ahsan, M.M. A Review on Comparative Remarks, Performance Evaluation and Improvement Strategies of Quadrotor Controllers. *Technologies* **2021**, *9*, 37. [CrossRef]

Article

Real-Time Stereo Visual Odometry Based on an Improved KLT Method

Guangzhi Guo [1,2], Zuoxiao Dai [1,*] and Yuanfeng Dai [1,2]

[1] Shanghai Institute of Technical Physics, Chinese Academy of Sciences, Shanghai 200083, China
[2] University of Chinese Academy of Sciences, Beijing 100049, China
* Correspondence: daizx@mail.sitp.ac.cn

Abstract: Real-time stereo visual odometry (SVO) localization is a challenging problem, especially for a mobile platform without parallel computing capability. A possible solution is to reduce the computational complexity of SVO using a Kanade–Lucas–Tomasi (KLT) feature tracker. However, the standard KLT is susceptible to scale distortion and affine transformation. Therefore, this work presents a novel SVO algorithm yielding robust and real-time localization based on an improved KLT method. First, in order to improve real-time performance, feature inheritance is applied to avoid time-consuming feature detection and matching processes as much as possible. Furthermore, a joint adaptive function with respect to the average disparity, translation velocity, and yaw angle is proposed to determine a suitable window size for the adaptive KLT tracker. Then, combining the standard KLT method with an epipolar constraint, a simplified KLT matcher is introduced to substitute feature-based stereo matching. Additionally, an effective veer chain matching scheme is employed to reduce the drift error. Comparative experiments on the KITTI odometry benchmark show that the proposed method achieves significant improvement in terms of time performance than the state-of-the-art single-thread approaches and strikes a better trade-off between efficiency and accuracy than the parallel SVO or multi-threaded SLAM.

Keywords: stereo visual odometry; feature inheritance; adaptive KLT tracker; veer chain matching

1. Introduction

As an essential simultaneous localization and mapping (SLAM) front end, visual odometry (VO) has been developed over the past decades [1]. The VO fundamental is incrementally estimating the rotational and translational changes of consecutive image frames [2]. Since monocular VO cannot determine the scale information of motion, stereo VO (SVO) with an extra camera means that depth information is available through triangulation of a well-calibrated stereo rig. Although existing methods can provide very accurate and robust trajectory estimates with a relative position error better than 2% [3], their practical usage is limited because of the computational burden. For instance, SOFT2 [4] accomplished the optimal performance on the KITTI leaderboard in terms of rotational and translational accuracy thus far, while the processing speed was only 10 Hz on a 2.5 GHz CPU with four cores.

Currently, this challenging problem has been extensively studied in VO work. Most SVO methods typically consist of feature detection, stereo matching, feature tracking, and motion estimation [5]. In general, improvements in time performance can be divided into three groups. First, since one of the main reasons for the aforementioned problem is that the feature detector and robust motion estimator tend to take most of the SVO time, as reported in [6], real-time SVO can be achieved by employing a more compact feature detector or motion estimator. With a much simpler Sobel filter as the feature detector, the work in [7] developed a real-time SVO at a minimum computational complexity using the KITTI odometry dataset. Although their system is able to run at 0.05 s per frame on a single CPU core @ 2.5 GHz, the simplified detector and matcher are susceptible to scale distortion or affine transformation. Second, given prior knowledge of ego-motion from other systems, such as an inertial measurement unit and wheel encoder-based odometry [8–10], the range of searching for features and matching can be greatly reduced. However, this method is prone to a large error accumulation, especially for vehicles losing traction on large rocks and steep slopes [9,10]. Another common solution is parallelization through multithread programming [11], FPGA, or GPU acceleration [12,13]. The four-thread architecture of OV^{2}SLAM [14] can run at 200 Hz on a 3.0 GHz CPU with eight cores. A real-time SVO that relies on heavy parallelism can limit its applications in mobile vehicles [7]. Therefore, the main purpose of this work was to develop a single-thread SVO without any prior knowledge of the motion to produce real-time and robust localization on a standard CPU.

According to the publicly available KITTI leaderboard, the fast and robust visual odometry (FRVO) in [6] exceeds all other validated methods in real-time performance. In their implementation, a pruning corner detector and an improved Kanade–Lucas–Tomasi (KLT) tracker are able to reduce the computational complexity of SVO. The speed of FRVO is 0.03 s per frame on a 3.5 GHz CPU, with an average translation error of 1.26% and a rotation error of 0.0038 deg/m. However, to determine a suitable window size for the KLT tracker, FRVO requires a dense disparity map to be provided beforehand and the abovementioned time performance does not include the time for a dense disparity computation, which is usually a time-consuming process. In this paper, the proposed approach achieves better real-time performance on a lower-speed processor with similar localization accuracy. Instead of the three improvements mentioned above, a new approach is proposed to reduce computational complexity through both feature inheritance (FI) and an improved KLT method. The KLT improvements include an adaptive KLT tracker (AKT) and a simplified KLT matcher (SKM). The proposed approach is most similar to the SVO in [15]. A KLT tracker [16] is also used in a similar way to avoid both feature detection and matching in a new frame, but with several important distinctions that are summarized in the following steps:

1. By analyzing the relationship between the motion experienced by the feature, the average disparity, the translation velocity, the yaw angle, and the adaptive window size for the AKT must by necessity be jointly determined, which can significantly improve the tracking accuracy in the presence of scale distortion and affine transformation.
2. The AKT tracks the inherited features between only the left images of two consecutive frames, and the SKM is performed in a new stereo frame, which can avoid computationally expensive feature detection and feature-based stereo matching processes as much as possible.
3. To limit the drift error, an effective veer chain matching (VCM) scheme is introduced.
4. A systematic evaluation using the KITTI dataset [17] was performed. The experimental results show that the proposed SVO can achieve better real-time performance in comparison to the other state-of-the-art approaches without deteriorating the localization accuracy.

The rest of the paper is organized as follows. Section 2 concisely outlines the proposed SVO, which is explained in detail in Section 3. Section 4 outlines several comparative experiments that were conducted to demonstrate the effectiveness of the proposed approach, and the conclusions are made in Section 5.

2. Method Overview

Figure 1 depicts the workflow of the proposed SVO which can be outlined in the following steps:

1. Searching for a series of SURF key points in the first stereo frame and computing their normalized descriptors with 64 dimensions.
2. With the epipolar constraint, stereo matching is performed using the Euclidean distance between the SURF descriptors.
3. A subset of the matched features is selected by means of bucketing to ensure the features are uniformly distributed over the image plane.

4. The three-dimensional (3-D) coordinates of the selected features are computed using triangulation.
5. The two-dimensional (2-D) features are tracked between the left images in frames $k-1$ and k using the AKT.
6. The SKM is performed by combining the standard KLT method [16] with the epipolar constraint. Then, the 3-D coordinates of the matched features are computed through triangulation.
7. The perspective-3-point (P3P) algorithm [18] is carried out in a random sample consensus (RANSAC) framework [19] to estimate the ego-motion from the 3-D-to-2-D correspondences.
8. The maximum likelihood estimator (MLE) [9,10] is applied to produce a robust ego-motion estimation.
9. The features inherited from Step 5 between the left images in frames k and $k+1$ are continuously tracked. If the number of new tracked features is smaller than a predefined threshold N, repeat from Step 1. Otherwise, the features are inherited successfully and repeat from Step 6. The threshold is set to 30 to ensure both computational accuracy and efficiency. This process is called FI.
10. After Step 8, for a turning maneuver, the drift error is reduced via a VCM scheme. This scheme consists of a veer frame detection process and a veer frame matching process. If this is the first time through the corner or the intersection, a veer frame update will collect the current frame as the unique keyframe of this corner. If not, the motion between the current veer frame and the first veer frame of this corner is estimated and the drift error is corrected. This novel scheme will be described in Section 3.

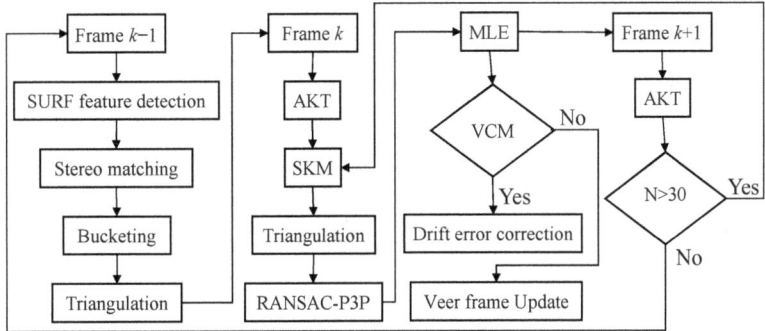

Figure 1. Flowchart of the proposed approach.

3. Detailed Description of the Method

A detailed description of the steps required in the proposed SVO algorithm is provided in this section.

3.1. Feature Detection and Stereo Matching

Many feature detectors have appeared in SVO research, such as Harris [20], Shi-Tomasi [16], FAST [21], SIFT [22], and SURF [23]. These detectors have their own advantages and disadvantages. Note that both SIFT and SURF have been proven to be invariant to certain changes in perspective. The latter builds upon the former but uses box filters to border on the Gaussian, contributing to a faster computation [3]. Therefore, in this work, a SURF detector was employed to search for interest points in a first stereo frame and compute the SURF descriptors, where the stereo frame represents the left and right images taken at the same time.

After feature detection, stereo matching was performed on the basis of the similarity of the SURF descriptors, and an epipolar constraint was imposed. Specifically, with respect to the similarity measurement, the Euclidean distance between each descriptor in the left image and all the descriptors in the right image was calculated. Two feature points are considered to have correspondence only if their descriptors satisfy both conditions. First, the distance between two candidate points is less than a predefined threshold. In this case, for the normalized SURF descriptor, the distance threshold was set to 0.35. In addition, the distance from all other candidate points is larger than a certain threshold. This is implemented by checking whether the ratio between the closest and the second closest match is small enough. Typically, the ratio threshold for determining whether the correspondence is still live is set to 0.6. In addition, the epipolar constraint means that, for a well-calibrated stereo rig, the row coordinates of the correspondence feature points are approximately equal to the noise tolerance of one pixel.

3.2. Bucketing and Triangulation

Some studies have found that not all detected feature points are suitable for accurate tracking [16]. The work presented in [24] confirmed that feature selection can significantly reduce the number of iterations in the RANSAC scheme. This means that a subset of carefully selected features can not only prevent estimation bias, but also improve the real-time performance of SVO. Thus, it is generally required that the feature points should be uniformly distributed over the image plane, which can be implemented through bucketing technique [25]. In this case, each image is split into 50 × 50 pixel-sized blocks, i.e., buckets. In every bucket, only the strongest feature is kept, and the others are discarded.

Afterward, the 3-D coordinates of the selected features are calculated using intersecting rays projected through the stereo observation models, i.e., triangulation, as shown in Figure 2. In the absence of error, the rays of the same feature points in the stereo frame ($\mathbf{q}_l$ and $\mathbf{q}_r$) intersect at point $\mathbf{P}$ in the 3-D spatial space. However, due to image noise, camera model uncertainty, and matching error, they do not always intersect. The shorter the distance between the two rays is, the more accurate the results that stereo matching can obtain. In the implementation, the feature correspondences which intersection distance is greater than 0.1 m is eliminated.

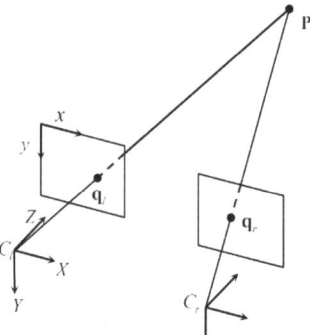

Figure 2. Stereo observation model.

3.3. Adaptive KLT Tracker and Simplified KLT Matcher

In successive stereo frame $k-1$, the AKT tracks the selected features to acquire their pixel coordinates in frame k. First, the optical flow corresponding to the feature point is solved in two consecutive left images I_{k-1}^L and I_k^L. In the notation, the superscripts L and

R index the "left" and "right" images, respectively, and the subscript k indexes the frame. The AKT minimizes Equation (1) using the Newton–Raphson method:

$$\mathbf{d} = \underset{\mathbf{d}}{\operatorname{argmin}} \iint_{W_{k-1}} \left[I_k^L(\mathbf{x}+\mathbf{d}) - I_{k-1}^L(\mathbf{x}) \right]^2 \omega(\mathbf{x})d\mathbf{x} \qquad (1)$$

where $\mathbf{x} = (u,v)$ is a feature point; $\mathbf{d} = (\Delta u, \Delta v)$ is the translation of the feature window's center; W_{k-1} is the adaptive window; and $\omega(\mathbf{x})$ is a Gaussian weighting function. The correct optical flow computation of feature correspondences in frame $k-1$ generates the tracked features in the left image in frame k.

Because the standard KLT tracker assumes that the feature patch undergoes only translation motion, a fixed-window KLT is susceptible to scale distortion and affine transformation [26]. A small feature window is sensitive to noise, whereas a large feature window may not exhibit a clear or sharp response. In the following paragraphs, we indicate that it would be better to determine an adaptive window size for the KLT using the average disparity, the translation velocity, and the yaw angle. From the FRVO discussion in [6], a larger window size should be used for features with large motion, while a smaller window size should be used for a feature with small motion. FRVO uses disparity information to represent the motion experienced by the features, as shown in Figure 3; thus, an adaptive window size for the KLT is employed based on the disparity field. On a large scale, this must be true. However, for a specific feature, a large disparity does not mean that a large window is necessarily suitable. Especially for a feature near the road, a large motion is often accompanied by a large affine transformation. The experimental results demonstrate that a small window allows for a better tracking accuracy. Therefore, the proposed method does not pursue the optimal tracking accuracy for every feature, but for better overall performance. Instead of a dense disparity map, the average disparity is used as an indicator for the adaptive window size, which also reduces the computational complexity. On the other hand, disparity alone is not sufficient to characterize the motion of features. For example, when the translation velocity of the camera is slow, the local optical flow vector of each feature is small. Alternatively, for a turning maneuver, Figure 4 shows that the feature with a small disparity still has a larger optical flow vector. At this point, the tracking error tends to increase rapidly if the AKT relies on disparity information. Therefore, in addition to the average disparity in the current frame, the translation velocity of the camera and the yaw angle in the previous frame should be used to guide the adaptive window strategy. This makes it possible to use a small window for the AKT even when the disparity of features is large. Based on the discussion above, a joint adaptive function (JAF) is built as follows:

$$W_k = c_d(d_k - d_0) + c_v(v_{k-1} - v_0) + c_\alpha(\alpha_{k-1} - \alpha_0) + b \qquad (2)$$

where W_k is the adaptive window size for the AKT in frame k; d_k, v_{k-1}, and α_{k-1} are the average disparity in frame k, the translation velocity of the camera, and the yaw angle in frame $k-1$, respectively; d_0, v_0, and α_0 are the constant offsets; c_d, d_v, and c_α are the disparity, the velocity, and the yaw angle weighting coefficients, respectively; and b is the base window size. The parameters (d_0, v_0, α_0, c_d, c_v, c_α, and b) are empirically set to be (20 pixels, 1.0 m/frame, 0.02 rad, 1, 10, -100, and 17), respectively. Meanwhile, the window size B_k has the lower and upper bounds of 5 and 49, respectively. Note that the adaptive window size is determined using the first-order approximation. An interesting future direction would be to explore a nonlinear model for the JAF and obtain the above parameters in a learning framework.

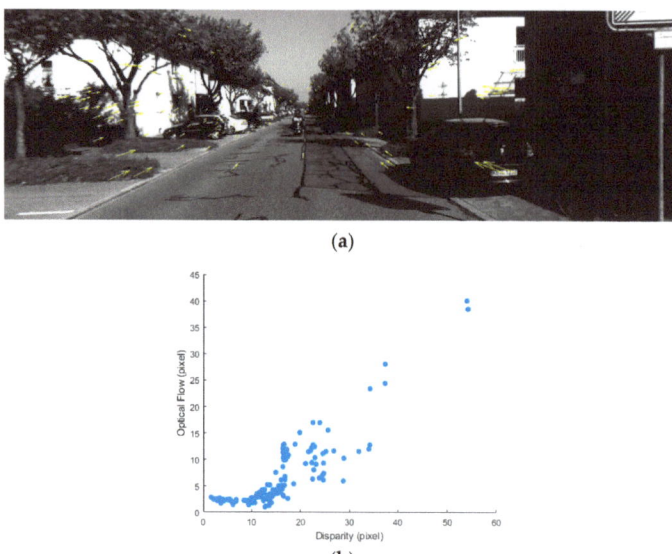

Figure 3. (**a**): Feature point tracking results in frame 0 on sequence 00 of the KITTI odometry dataset. The yellow arrow indicates the optical flow vector of the feature point. (**b**): Relationship between the disparity and the optical flow when the translation velocity is fast and the yaw angle is small; features with a large disparity are prone to large motion and features with a small disparity are prone to small motion. Each blue dot corresponds to a feature point in (**a**).

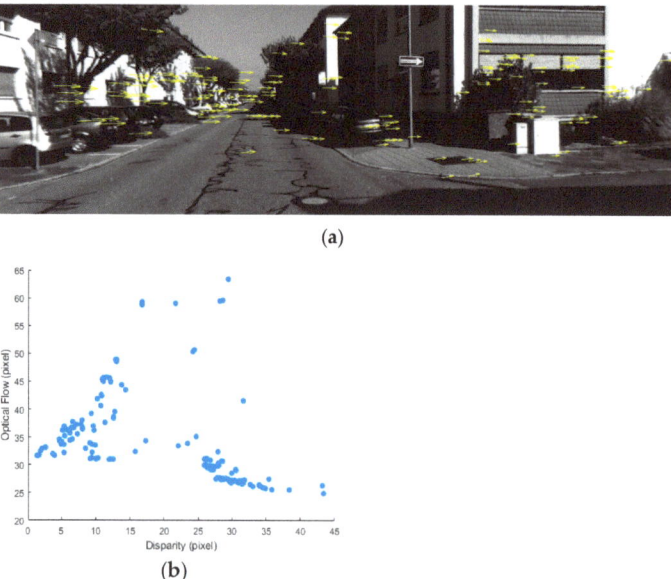

Figure 4. (**a**): Feature point tracking results in frame 99 on sequence 00 of the KITTI odometry dataset. The yellow arrow indicates the optical flow vector of the feature point. (**b**): Relationship between the disparity and the optical flow for a turning maneuver; regardless of the size of the disparity, all features have large motion. Each blue dot corresponds to a feature point in (**a**).

After the tracking step, for a rectified stereo frame, stereo matching can be conducted strictly along the epipolar line. Combining the KLT method with the epipolar constraint, the component of the displacement **d** in the row direction is approximately equal to zero. This means that the SKM looks for feature correspondences only in the column direction. Thus, the SKM between the left and right images I_k^L and I_k^R in frame k can be represented as follows:

$$d = \operatorname*{argmin}_{d} \iint_W \left[I_k^L(u, v+d) - I_k^R(u,v) \right]^2 \omega(u,v) du dv \qquad (3)$$

where d is the disparity. The resulting set is also projected to 3-D space via triangulation.

Afterward, when estimating the camera pose in frame $k+1$, the input to the new AKT is no longer the output of the SURF detector but the output of the SKM, i.e., the FI. This means that the new SURF feature detection will be taken into account only if the number of new tracked features is lower than a predefined threshold. Due to the FI, the AKT, and the SKM, the approach presented here can avoid both feature detection and feature-based stereo matching as much as possible. Consequently, the computational time is considerably reduced.

3.4. RANSAC-P3P and Maximum Likelihood Estimator

Almost all robust SVO methods employ the RANSAC scheme for motion estimation when there are noise and outliers with the feature detector, matcher, and tracker. In this paper, ego-motion is estimated through the RANSAC-P3P reported by Fischler and Bolles in [19], where a set of closed-form hypotheses on the minimum number of data needed to obtain a solution is solved, and the hypothesis that shows the highest consensus with the other data is selected as an initial solution. Then, the MLE [9,10] is applied to produce a final, corrected ego-motion estimation between the two consecutive frames.

3.5. Veer Chain Matching

As there is scale distortion and affine transformation due to rotation, the KLT tracking error tends to increase rapidly for a turning maneuver. To limit the drift error, an easy and effective VCM scheme is proposed, which draws inspiration from the loop closing of the ORB-SLAM2 [11]. However, this VCM scheme employs a veer frame detector and matcher, avoiding the time-consuming loop closure detection and achieving high accuracy, especially for an urban environment with more corner loops.

Generally, in order to form a closed loop in a trajectory, one of the following conditions should be met: (1) there is a large veer in the trajectory, or (2) there is a long-term cumulative turn in the same yaw direction. Inspired by this, a vehicle would only be possible to revisit a site through a corner or after a turning maneuver. Figure 5 shows the path reconstructed from our SVO method compared to the ground truth data on sequence 00 of the KITTI odometry dataset. The vehicle leaves corner A on frames 123 and 1271. The VCM scheme can correct the drift error on the next visit.

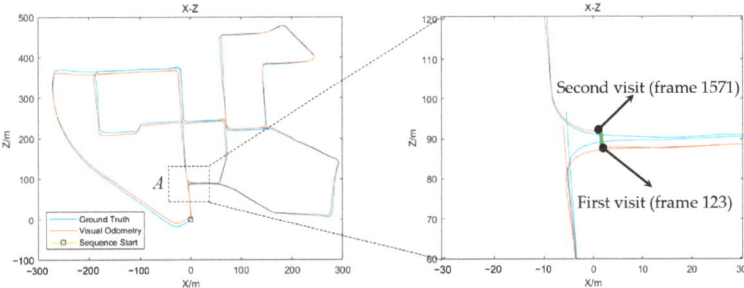

Figure 5. VCM on sequence 00. The green line indicates the drift error correction of frame 1571 where the vehicle revisits corner A.

The basic idea of VCM is to detect veer frames using the yaw angle of the current frame relative to the previous frame. As shown in Figure 6, when there is a large angle of veer in the trajectory, there must be a large peak in the yaw angle diagram. Thus, if the yaw angle is larger than some threshold, this demonstrates that a turning maneuver is underway, and the corresponding stereo frame is regarded as a veer frame. Once a key veer frame is obtained, the VCM scheme is triggered to reduce the drift error. The key to the above approach is to determine the yaw angle threshold. A large threshold angle is likely to lead to missing detection, while a small threshold angle reduces the time efficiency of the VCM. It can be observed that the size of the yaw angle peak is proportional to the velocity and the veer angle. Therefore, in this case, 50% of the yaw angle peak is taken as the threshold when passing through a right-angle corner at a slower speed, which is 0.03 rad. If this is the first time through the corner or the intersection, the last veer frame will be regarded as the unique keyframe of the corner. These keyframes and their locations are collected into a set V. The reason for this is that the drift error can always be corrected when the vehicle leaves the corner. When a key veer frame is detected, this information is used to reduce the drift in the vehicle path. If the SVO revisits these locations, veer frame matching is performed between the current veer frame and all the keyframes in the set V. Here, the ZNCC method [25] is used. If the number of matched features is larger than some threshold, the motion estimator between the corresponding veer frame pair can correct the drift error. In the implementation, the threshold is set to 45. Otherwise, a veer frame update will regard the current veer frame as the unique keyframe of this corner. Although the veer frame matcher is not triggered the next time the vehicle goes straight through the corner, due to the introduction of the veer frame detector, the match still has a very high precision and recall rate, especially in an urban environment with more corner loops. Moreover, the VCM scheme is obviously much faster than loop closure detection.

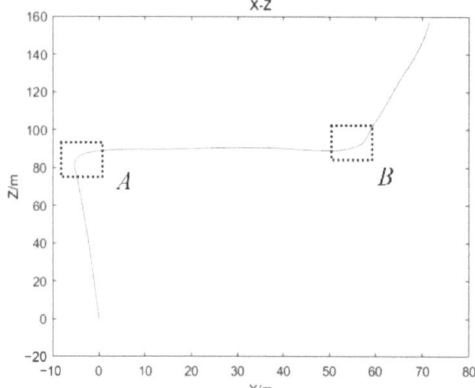
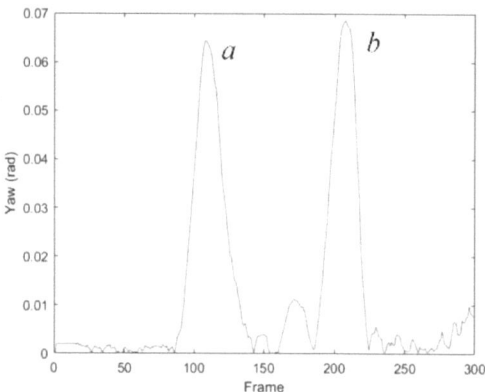

Figure 6. The veers A and B in the trajectory (**left**) correspond to the peaks a and b in the yaw angle diagram (**right**), respectively.

4. Experimental Results

In this section, the proposed approach was evaluated using the publicly available KITTI odometry dataset, which is composed of captured videos along with an accurate ground truth. The rectified stereo images with a size of 1241×376 are recorded at a frequency of 10 Hz. In the following experiments, for each training sequence of the KITTI dataset except sequence 01, thirty trials were conducted, and the average translational error e_t, the average rotational error e_r relative to the ground truth, and the runtime per frame were employed as the performance metrics. For sequence 01, a highway scenario with largely distant image areas driving at high speed does not apply to the KLT tracker. Therefore, the performance of this method was evaluated on the other 10 training sequences, which included urban and rural scenarios. All of the experiments were performed using a PC with an Intel Core i5 9500 3.0 GHz processor and a 16 GB RAM using a single thread. In order to prove that the improved algorithm could greatly reduce the computational complexity without notably compromising the localization accuracy, MATLAB was used to conduct the simulation experiments on the prototype of the algorithm (there is no code optimization). Even so, the system could run at 15 Hz.

Considering the trajectory, Figure 7 shows the path reconstructed from our SVO compared to the ground truth data on several sequences of the KITTI dataset. They have the same shapes. Table 1 shows the average translation error and rotation error on the 10 training sequences. Although sequences 01 and 05 with corner loops have 3723 m and 2204 m of traveling, respectively, the proposed SVO with the JAF and the VCM can obtain an average translation error of 0.9496% and 0.5957%, and a rotation error of 0.0008 deg/m and 0.0016 deg/m, respectively. Meanwhile, sequences 03 and 07 without corner loops have a shorter path (561 m and 695 m, respectively); hence, the proposed approach also has a high localization accuracy, with an average translation error of 1.0257% and 0.6460%, and a rotation error of 0.0005 deg/m and 0.0055 deg/m, respectively. The results in Figure 7e,f have been obtained without the VCM scheme for a long path, which leads to a slightly worse error. However, there is no difference in runtime. This means that the proposed VCM can greatly improve the localization accuracy while not sacrificing time performance. Furthermore, the proposed method was compared to a version that determines the AKT window size using only disparity information, as shown in Table 1. One can observe that both the JAF and the VCM help to significantly improve the localization accuracy. On average, the translation and rotation errors on the 10 train sequences are (1.1361%, 0.0021 deg/m) and (1.6254%, 0.0023 deg/m), respectively. Therefore, the AKT using the JAF performs 30% better than the AKT using only disparity information, while the JAF does not require extra runtime.

Table 1. Comparison of the proposed method to a version that determines the AKT window size using only disparity information on the KITTI dataset. (deg/m stands for degrees per meter).

Sequence	SVO + FI + AKT + SKM + VCM + JAF			SVO + FI AKT + SKM + VCM + Disparity		
	Runtime (s)	e_t (%)	e_r (deg/m)	Runtime (s)	e_t (%)	e_r (deg/m)
00	0.0729	0.9496	0.0008	0.0703	1.3844	0.0012
02	0.0734	1.2011	0.0013	0.0650	1.2042	0.0009
03	0.0358	1.0257	0.0005	0.0397	1.7008	0.0010
04	0.0546	0.5361	0.0001	0.0600	1.6663	0.0001
05	0.0597	0.5957	0.0016	0.0599	1.0291	0.0015
06	0.0978	1.1253	0.0006	0.0922	1.7430	0.0011
07	0.0585	0.6460	0.0055	0.0612	0.8742	0.0068
08	0.0635	2.1540	0.0004	0.0674	2.9020	0.0011
09	0.0670	1.3569	0.0015	0.0711	1.9772	0.0015
10	0.0744	1.7708	0.0091	0.0752	1.7731	0.0075
avg	0.0658	1.1361	0.0021	0.0662	1.6254	0.0023

To further evaluate the improvement in time performance, Table 1 shows the average runtime per frame of the 10 training sequences. Thanks to the FI, the AKT, and the SKM, the proposed SVO thread runs at 0.0658 s per frame with a standard deviation of 0.0161 s. This means that the proposed SVO can run in real time at 15 Hz on the KITTI odometry dataset. The deviation is mainly caused by the differences in the number of scenario features and corner loops. Because the data in Table 1 are normally distributed, a Mann–Whitney U nonparametric test was used to further analyze the differences in runtime, e_t and e_r, between the two versions. The test was performed with the help of an SPSS v24 computer program using a 95% confidence level. The hypotheses of this test are as follows:

- $H^a_{runtime}$, H^a_{et}, and H^a_{er} represent no significant difference in runtime, e_t and e_r, between the two versions, respectively.

- $H^b_{runtime}$, H^b_{et}, and H^b_{er} represent a significant difference in runtime, e_t and e_r, between the two versions, respectively.

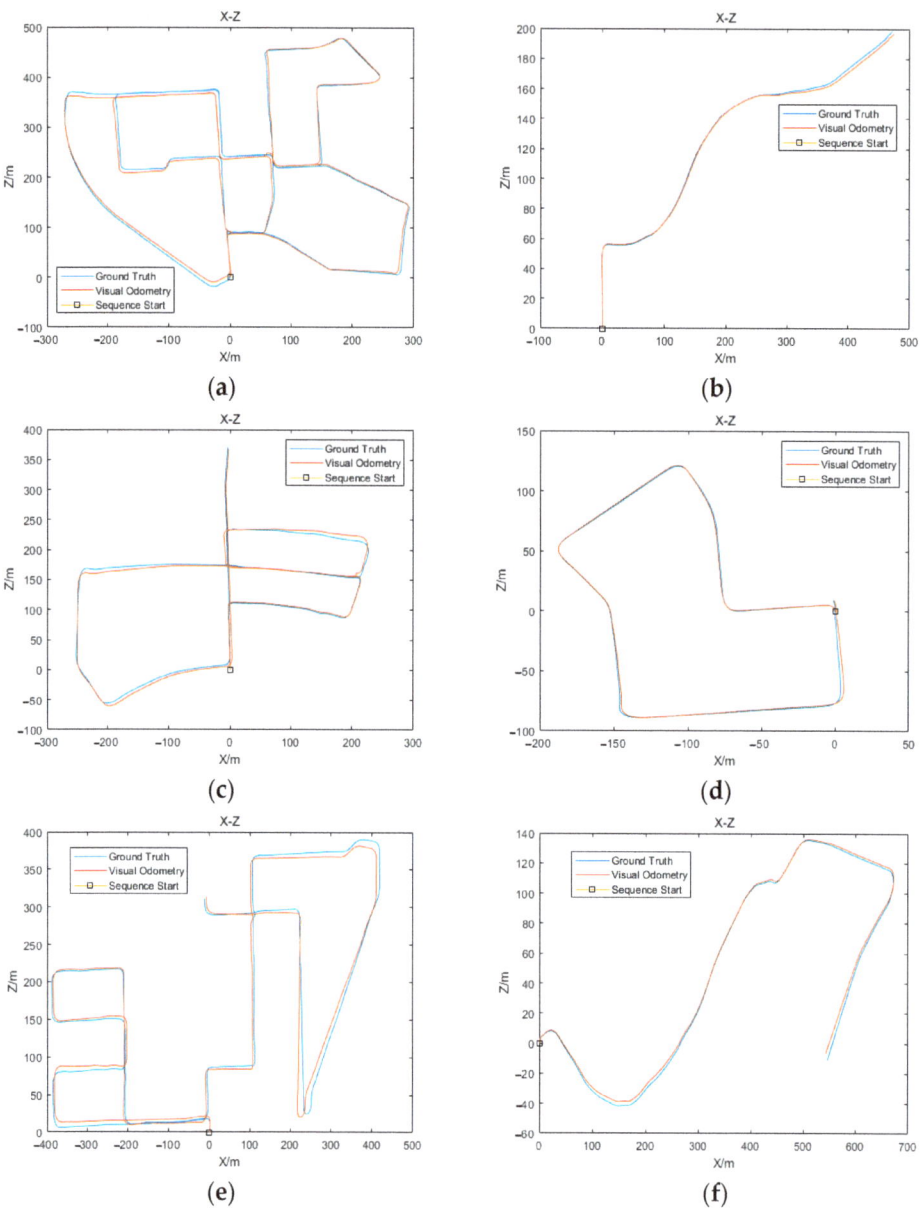

Figure 7. Reconstructed path for (**a**) sequence 00; (**b**) sequence 03; (**c**) sequence 05; (**d**) sequence 07; (**e**) sequence 08; and (**f**) sequence 10.

As shown in Table 2, the Mann–Whitney U test results demonstrate that $H^a_{runtime}$, H^b_{et} and H^a_{er} are acceptable ($P_{runtime} = 0.7624 > 0.05$, $P_{et} = 0.0059 < 0.05$, and $P_{er} = 0.6224 > 0.05$), which means that the JAF can significantly improve the robustness and accuracy without increasing the runtime. This beneficial behavior is mainly because the translation velocity and the yaw angle in the JAF have already been computed in the previous frame.

Table 2. Hypothesis Testing.

Test Data	Runtime	e_t	e_r
Mann–Whitney U	46.0000	25.0000	43.5000
Wilcoxon W	101.0000	80.0000	99.5000
Z	−0.3024	−1.8898	−0.4925
Asymp. Sig. (2-tailed)	0.7624	0.0059	0.6224

Moreover, on sequences 05 (with corner loops) and 07 (without corner loops), the comparison of the average processing times at every stage between our method and a version without the FI and VCM that performs SURF detection, feature-based stereo matching, AKT, and SKM at each frame is shown in Table 3. It can observe that the proposed method helps reduce runtime significantly, and the times spent on feature detection, stereo matching, and motion estimation are reduced by approximately 3 times. In conclusion, the total processing times are reduced by more than 40%.

Table 3. Processing time in milliseconds of each stage for sequences 05 and 07 in the KITTI dataset.

Stage	Our Method		SVO (Without FI and VCM)	
	Seq. 05	Seq. 07	Seq. 05	Seq. 07
Feature detection	20.4340	19.8128	61.0502	62.4008
Stereo matching	1.8556	1.8549	5.6062	6.3031
AKT	4.1532	3.6080	2.6890	2.8666
SKM	2.5029	2.5025	2.5195	2.5339
VCM	18.1453	17.9953	\	\
Motion estimation	4.1176	5.0820	22.3288	16.9736
Total	59.7044	59.4217	103.0680	100.0306

For completeness, several real-time systems were compared in the subsequent experiments in order to evaluate the performance of the proposed algorithm. They included the SOFT2 [4], the most accurate SVO; the ORB-SLAM2 [11], a complete SLAM system that has four parallel threads; the FRVO [7], the fastest single-thread SVO on the KITTI leaderboard until now; the SVO-FPGA [12], a multiple master-slave FPGA architecture for a SIFT-based SVO; and the VOLDOR [13], a dense indirect VO based on GPU. Table 4 shows the runtime, the average translation error, and the average rotation error of the proposed method compared to other methods, using always the results published by the original authors. Although the proposed approach is slightly less accurate than SOFT2, the ORB-SLAM2, and the FRVO, all can provide very accurate estimations. In particular, the proposed method outperforms in terms of runtime. The proposed approach is 34% better than the SOFT2 and is similar to the ORB-SLAM2. However, the ORB-SLAM2 splits SLAM into four parallel threads and is more costly, while the proposed SVO is a single-thread system. For the FRVO, the runtime of 0.03 s does not include the time for the dense disparity map computation, which is usually a time-consuming process and requires at least an extra 0.03 s. The proposed approach jointly determines the suitable KLT window size using the average disparity, the translation velocity, and the yaw angle; thus, no time-consuming computation of a dense disparity map is needed. Although the accuracy of the proposed method is slightly inferior in terms of relative translation errors, with an error of 1.14% against the 0.98% of the FRVO, its main advantage is the real-time performance even on a lower-speed processor. Moreover, Table 4 compares the performance of our method and two state-of-the-art SVO methods that are implemented in parallel with the FPGA and the GPU, namely the SVO-FPGA and the VOLDOR. It can be observed that the proposed method can strike a good trade-off between efficiency and accuracy and can greatly improve the computational efficiency, while not needing to sacrifice accuracy. Furthermore, the results confirm that the proposed algorithm can run much faster in C/C++. This distinctly demonstrates that the three strategies, i.e., the FI, the AKT, and the SKM, in the proposed method contribute to a significant improvement in the SVO real-time performance.

Table 4. Comparison of state-of-the-art methods on the KITTI dataset.

Method	Runtime (s)	e_t (%)	e_r (deg/m)	Environment
SOFT2	0.1	0.71	0.0024	2.5 GHz (C/C++)
ORB-SLAM2	0.06	0.73	0.0022	3.6 GHz (C/C++)
FRVO	0.03 (excluding the time for disparity map computation)	0.98	0.0056	3.5 GHz (C/C++)
SVO-FPGA	0.0301	2.7	\	4.2 GHz +FPGA
VOLDOR	0.1	1.32	0.0042	GPU
Proposed	0.0658	1.14	0.0021	3.0 GHz (MATLAB)

5. Conclusions

This paper presents a novel algorithm for stereo visual odometry that avoids time-consuming feature detection and matching processes as much as possible based on feature inheritance, an adaptive KLT tracker, and a simplified KLT matcher, which can greatly reduce computational complexity without notably compromising the localization accuracy. Based on the average disparity, the translation velocity, and the yaw angle, the proposed method can jointly determine a suitable window size for the KLT tracker, which effectively mitigates the effect of scale distortion and affine transformation. Furthermore, an effective veer chain matching scheme can be employed to limit the drift error. In the experiments, the method presented here was tested on the KITTI odometry dataset and compared with other methods. According to the experimental results, although the translation error of the proposed SVO is slightly less accurate than some state-of-the-art methods, with an error of 1.14% against an error of 0.71% for the SOFT2, an error of 73% for the ORB-SLAM2, and an error of 0.98% for the FRVO, the proposed method can strike a good trade-off between efficiency and accuracy. Efficiency is achieved in that the system is able to run at 15 Hz on a single-thread CPU @ 3.0 GHz, outperforming even the parallel or multi-threaded approaches in the balance between high accuracy and low computational complexity.

Author Contributions: Conceptualization, G.G. and Z.D.; methodology, G.G.; software, G.G.; validation, G.G., Z.D. and Y.D.; formal analysis, G.G.; investigation, G.G.; resources, G.G. and Y.D.; data curation, G.G. and Y.D.; writing—original draft preparation, G.G.; writing—review and editing, G.G.; visualization, G.G.; supervision, Z.D. All authors have read and agreed to the published version of the manuscript.

Funding: This research received no external funding.

Institutional Review Board Statement: Not applicable.

Informed Consent Statement: Not applicable.

Data Availability Statement: Not applicable.

Conflicts of Interest: The authors declare no conflict of interest.

References

1. Chen, Y.; Mei, Y.; Wan, S. Visual Odometry for Self-Driving with Multihypothesis and Network Prediction. *Math. Probl. Eng.* **2021**, *2021*, 1930881. [CrossRef]
2. He, M.; Zhu, C.; Huang, Q.; Ren, B.; Liu, J. A review of monocular visual odometry. *Vis. Comput.* **2020**, *36*, 1053–1065. [CrossRef]
3. Fraundorfer, F.; Scaramuzza, D. Visual odometry: Part II: Matching, robustness, optimization, and applications. *IEEE Robot. Autom. Mag.* **2012**, *19*, 78–90. [CrossRef]
4. Cvišić, I.; Marković, I.; Petrović, I. Recalibrating the KITTI Dataset Camera Setup for Improved Odometry Accuracy. In Proceedings of the 2021 European Conference on Mobile Robots (ECMR), Bonn, Germany, 31 August–3 September 2021; pp. 1–6.

5. Fraundorfer, F.; Scaramuzza, D. Visual odometry: Part I: The first 30 years and fundamentals. *IEEE Robot. Autom. Mag.* **2011**, *18*, 80–92.
6. Wu, M.; Lam, S.K.; Srikanthan, T. A Framework for Fast and Robust Visual Odometry. *IEEE T. Intell. Transp.* **2017**, *18*, 3433–3448. [CrossRef]
7. Geiger, A.; Ziegler, J.; Stiller, C. Stereoscan: Dense 3d reconstruction in real-time. In Proceedings of the IEEE Intelligent Vehicles Symposium (IV), Baden-Baden, Germany, 5–9 June 2011; pp. 963–968.
8. Wan, W.; Liu, Z.; Di, K.; Wang, B.; Zhou, J. A Cross-Site Visual Localization Method for Yutu Rover. In Proceedings of the International Archives of the Photogrammetry, Remote Sensing and Spatial Information Sciences (ISPRS), Suzhou, China, 14–16 May 2014; Volume XL-4.
9. Cheng, Y.; Maimone, M.; Matthies, L. Visual odometry on the Mars exploration rovers. In Proceedings of the 2005 IEEE International Conference on Systems, Man and Cybernetics, Waikoloa, HI, USA, 12 October 2005; pp. 903–910.
10. Maimone, M.; Cheng, Y.; Matthies, L. Two years of visual odometry on the mars exploration rovers. *J. Field Robot.* **2007**, *24*, 169–186. [CrossRef]
11. Mur-Artal, R.; Tardós, J.D. ORB-SLAM2: An Open-Source SLAM System for Monocular, Stereo, and RGB-D Cameras. *IEEE Trans. Robot.* **2017**, *33*, 1255–1262. [CrossRef]
12. Chien, C.H.; Hsu, C.C.J.; Chien, C.J. Multiple Master-Slave FPGA Architecture of a Stereo Visual Odometry. *IEEE Access* **2021**, *9*, 103266–103278. [CrossRef]
13. Min, Z.; Yang, Y.; Dunn, E. VOLDOR: Visual Odometry From Log-Logistic Dense Optical Flow Residuals. In Proceedings of the 2020 IEEE/CVF Conference on Computer Vision and Pattern Recognition (CVPR), Seattle, WA, USA, 13–19 June 2020; pp. 4898–4909.
14. Ferrera, M.; Eudes, A.; Moras, J.; Sanfourche, M.; Le Besnerais, G. OV^{2}SLAM: A Fully Online and Versatile Visual SLAM for Real-Time Applications. *IEEE Robot. Autom. Lett.* **2021**, *6*, 1399–1406. [CrossRef]
15. Moreno, F.A.; Blanco, J.L.; González, J. An efficient closed-form solution to probabilistic 6D visual odometry for a stereo camera. In Proceedings of the International Conference on Advanced Concepts for Intelligent Vision Systems (ACIVS), Delft, The Netherlands, 28–31 August 2007; Springer: Berlin/Heidelberg, Germany, 2007; Volume 4678, pp. 932–942.
16. Shi, J. Good features to track. In Proceedings of the IEEE Conference on Computer Vision and Pattern Recognition (CVPR), Seattle, WA, USA, 21–23 June 1994; pp. 593–600.
17. Geiger, A.; Lenz, P.; Stiller, C.; Urtasun, R. Vision meets robotics: The kitti dataset. *Ind. Robot.* **2013**, *32*, 1231–1237. [CrossRef]
18. Alismail, H.; Browning, B.; Dias, M.B. Evaluating pose estimation methods for stereo visual odometry on robots. In Proceedings of the 11th International Conference on Intelligent Autonomous Systems (IAS-11), Ottawa, ON, Canada, 30 August–1 September 2010; pp. 101–110.
19. Fischler, M.A.; Bolles, R.C. Random sample consensus: A paradigm for model fitting with applications to image analysis and automated cartography. *Commun. ACM* **1981**, *24*, 381–395. [CrossRef]
20. Harris, C.G.; Pike, J. 3D positional integration from image sequences. *Image Vision Comput.* **1988**, *6*, 87–90. [CrossRef]
21. Rosten, E.; Drummond, T. Machine learning for high-speed corner detection. In *European Conference on Computer Vision (ECCV)*; Springer: Berlin/Heidelberg, Germany, 2006; Volume 3951, pp. 430–443.
22. Lowe, D.G. Distinctive image features from scale-invariant keypoints. *Int. J. Comput. Vision* **2004**, *60*, 91–110. [CrossRef]
23. Bay, H.; Tuytelaars, T.; Van Gool, L. SURF: Speeded Up Robust Features. In *European Conference on Computer Vision (ECCV)*; Springer: Berlin/Heidelberg, Germany, 2006; Volume 3951, pp. 404–417.
24. Cvišić, I.; Petrović, I. Stereo odometry based on careful feature selection and tracking. In Proceedings of the 2015 European Conference on Mobile Robots (ECMR), Lincoln, UK, 2–4 September 2015; pp. 1–6.
25. Silva, H.; Bernardino, A.; Silva, E. Probabilistic egomotion for stereo visual odometry. *J. Intell. Robot. Syst.* **2015**, *77*, 265–280. [CrossRef]
26. Ramakrishnan, N.; Srikanthan, T.; Lam, S.K.; Tulsulkar, G.R. Adaptive Window Strategy for High-Speed and Robust KLT Feature Tracker. In *Image and Video Technology*; PSIVT 2015; Lecture Notes in Computer Science; Bräunl, T., McCane, B., Rivera, M., Yu, X., Eds.; Springer: Cham, Switzerland, 2015; Volume 9431, pp. 355–367.

Article

Point–Line-Aware Heterogeneous Graph Attention Network for Visual SLAM System

Yuanfeng Lian [1,2,*], Hao Sun [2] and Shaohua Dong [3]

1. Beijing Key Laboratory of Petroleum Data Mining, Beijing 102249, China
2. Department of Computer Science and Technology, China University of Petroleum, Beijing 102249, China
3. Pipeline Technology and Safety Research Center, China University of Petroleum, Beijing 102249, China
* Correspondence: lianyuanfeng@cup.edu.cn

Abstract: Simultaneous localization and mapping (SLAM), as an important research topic in robotics, is useful but challenging to estimate robot pose and reconstruct a 3-D map of the surrounding environment. Despite recent success of several deep neural networks for visual SLAM, those methods cannot achieve robust results in complex industrial scenarios for constructing accurate and real-time maps due to the weak texture and complex geometric structure. This paper presents a novel and efficient visual SLAM system based on point–line-aware heterogeneous graph attention network, which combines points and line segments to solve the problem of the insufficient number of reliable features in traditional approaches. Firstly, a simultaneous feature extraction network is constructed based on the geometric relationships between points and points and points and lines. To further improve the efficiency and accuracy of the geometric association features of key regions, we design the point–line-aware attention module to guide the network to pay attention to the trivial features of both points and lines in images. Moreover, the network model is optimized by a transfer-aware knowledge distillation strategy to further improve the system's real-time performance. Secondly, to improve the accuracy of the point–line matching, we design a point–line heterogeneous graph attention network, which combines an edge aggregation graph attention module and a cross-heterogeneous graph iteration module to conduct learning on the intragraph and intergraph. Finally, the point–line matching process is transformed into an optimal transport problem, and a near-iterative method based on a greedy strategy is presented to solve the optimization problem. The experiments on the KITTI dataset and a self-made dataset demonstrate the better effectiveness, accuracy, and adaptability of our method than those of the state of the art in visual SLAM.

Keywords: visual SLAM; point–line aware; knowledge distillation; heterogeneous graph attention network

1. Introduction

Simultaneous localization and map construction technology, as the key to autonomous movement of robots, is widely used in unmanned driving, virtual reality, mobile robots, and other fields [1–5]. Compared with laser SLAM, vision-based SLAM has a low power consumption, low cost, miniaturization, and other advantages, and its theoretical and application value is very prominent [6]. Visual SLAM constructs a map of the surrounding environment by obtaining the plane image information of the real world through a camera. The pose state of the camera is inferred by the extracted feature information or pixel grayscale. Visual SLAM methods can be classified into four categories: feature-point-based methods [6–8], feature-line-based methods [9–12], feature-plane-based methods [12,13], and the combination of the above methods [14–20], according to the kind of features used to estimate the trajectory. The existing empirical methods cannot deal effectively with complex industrial scenarios due to occlusion, illumination, and deformation issues. In recent years, research on visual SLAM based on deep learning has attracted widespread attention. Serra et al. [21] used deep convolution to extract a point description with the L2 norm as a similarity measure to enhance the robust matching between key points and their local image features. Since a single feature descriptor cannot generate an effective key-point detection, Shend et al. [22] proposed an end-to-end trainable matching network, RF-Net, based on a receptive field to achieve a more efficient key-point detection. In order to solve the problem of the low localization accuracy caused by the lack of key-point shape perception in the joint learning of feature detectors and descriptors, Luo et al. [23] applied a deformable convolutional network with a dense spatial transformation to enhance the dynamic receptive field and improve the ability to express local shapes. Sarlin et al. [24] proposed a graph neural network, SuperGlue, based on attention aggregation, which used the optimal transmission model for matching optimization and realized the pose estimation in both indoor and outdoor environments. Combining a convolutional network with a recurrent network, Tang et al. [25,26] proposed a geometric correspondence network (GCN), which used an end-to-end learning method to detect key points and generate descriptors for improving the accuracy of the pose estimation. Aimed at the problem of decreased localization accuracy caused by the partial occlusion of line segments, Pautrat et al. [27] used a self-supervised network for line detection and for extracting line-segment descriptors, which improved the robustness of line-segment matching. The above-mentioned feature detection algorithms based on deep learning fused multilevel features, which did not deeply explore the association and constraint relationship between point and line features.

In industrial production scenarios, there are many complex background objects such as various buildings, pipelines, production equipment, and safety signs that lack corner points or contain repeated textures. The point features in the image are not specific enough, which makes them unable to provide an accurate position estimation. In addition, the mismatch of line features greatly increases the time complexity of the computation. In general, although existing methods have achieved certain results in feature detection and matching tasks, due to the uneven light, single texture, and complex scene structure in industrial scenarios, the pose estimation is easily degraded. How to efficiently fuse point and line information to build a more stable visual SLAM system is still a difficult problem that needs further research. Our main contributions can be summarized as follows:

- To solve the problem of weak point–line extraction ability in complex scenes, a point–line synchronous geometric feature extraction network, PL-Net, is proposed. We use an optimized residual block-feature pyramid network (ORB-FPN) to extract the feature map of the input image. In the point extraction branch, based on the point-aware module, the multiscale context is aggregated to obtain features with rich receptive fields. Moreover, the edge information is used for the line extraction branch to improve the accuracy of the line-segment detection. In order to make the network lightweight, a transfer-aware knowledge distillation method is proposed to compress the model for generating the point–line feature in the extraction task.
- Targeting a high accuracy and efficiency, a heterogeneous attention graph neural network (HAGNN) is presented, which uses an edge-aggregated graph attention network (EAGAT) to iterate the vertices of the heterogeneous graph constructed from points and lines. To enhance the performance of the point–line matching, a cross-heterogeneous graph interaction (CHGI) is used for harmonizing heterogeneous information between graphs.
- By transforming the point–line matching process into an optimal transport problem, a greedy inexact proximal point method for optimal transport, GIPOT, is proposed, which calculates the optimal feature assignment matrix to find the global optimal solution for the point–line matching problem.

2. SLAM System Framework

The framework of the SLAM system proposed in this paper is shown in Figure 1. Firstly, a new image is input into the PL-Net network to detect key points and line segments, and the corresponding descriptors are obtained through the point–line-aware attention module to enhance the feature expressiveness for both points and lines in images. Then, the point and line features of the two images are transferred to the point–line heterogeneous graphs, which are constructed by using the point and line features as the vertices and connecting a vertex to its neighbors within a fixed radius. Secondly, the attention network HAGNN obtains the enhanced features and inputs them into the GIPOT to generate point-line matching results and calculate the pose of the current frame. Finally, by reprojecting the features in the local map to the current frame, the projection error is calculated for the backend processing of SLAM to complete the map.

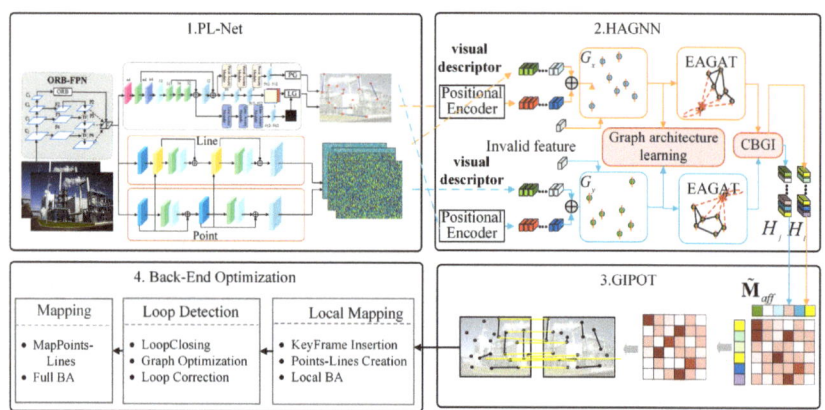

Figure 1. System overview. The system has four components: 1. The point–line feature extraction network (PL-Net) extracts key points, line segment and their descriptors (Section 3.1). 2. A heterogeneous graph attention network (HAGNN) is added with the positional encoding, which has N EAGAT and GBGI layers (Section 3.2). 3. A greedy near iterative matching (GIPOT) module is used to match the transformed features, which computes the affinity matrix $\tilde{M}_{aff}$ and the assignment matrix. (Section 3.3). 4. The backend optimization includes local mapping, loop detection, and mapping.

3. Methodology

3.1. Point–Line Feature Extraction Network

The point–line feature extraction network PL-Net is shown in Figure 2. Firstly, the ORB-FPN module was used to extract the features of each layer for the image, and the PG module completed the key-point extraction. Then, the center point map and displacement map were generated through the branch of the line-segment perception module. Finally, the point–line descriptor was generated through convolution and upsampling operations.

3.1.1. ORB-FPN Module

As shown in Figure 2, an optimized residual block (ORB) is designed based on the Nesterov acceleration gradient (NAG) algorithm to enhance the expressive ability of target features [26]. Then, we have:

$$y_{k+1} = x_k + \beta(x_k - x_{k-1}) \tag{1}$$

$$x_{k+1} = y_{k+1} - \alpha \nabla f(y_{k+1}) \tag{2}$$

where x_k and y_{k+1} denote the output and input of the first layer of the network, and α and β represent the learning rate and momentum parameters, respectively. $\nabla f(y_{k+1})$ is the gradient of the objective function f at y_{k+1}, and f is a smooth function satisfying the Lipschitz property. When the momentum parameter $\beta = 0$, the NAG algorithm is equivalent to the standard gradient descent algorithm. When $\beta > 0$, it optimizes the combination of α and β to accelerate convergence.

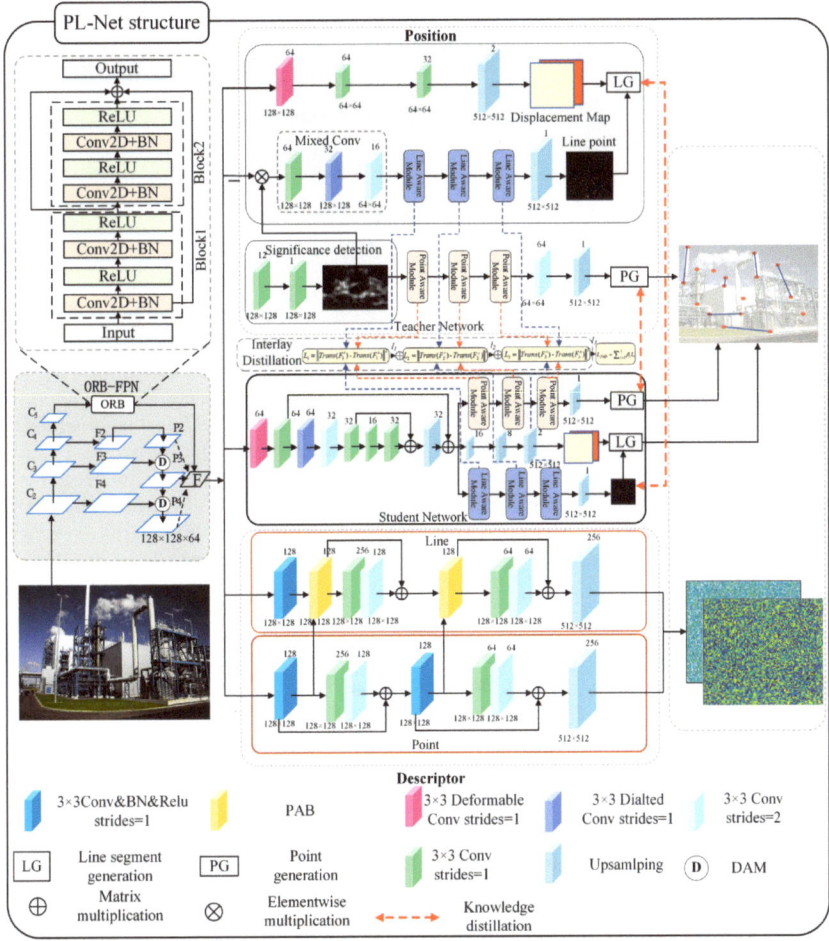

Figure 2. The framework of our proposed network PL-Net. We input two images of size 512 × 512 and then obtain key points, line segment, and their descriptors through the ORB-FPN, extraction module, and descriptor module. The gray box in the upper-right corner shows the structure of the ORB-FPN. The upper gray branch is responsible for extracting points and lines. The lower red branch is used to extract the point–line descriptor

In the neural network propagation process, the transmission of the signal from the first layer to the last layer is expressed as:

$$L_{i+1} = \sigma(U_i L_i) \quad (3)$$

where L_{i+1} is the features of the $i+1$th layer in the network, and σ represents the activation function. Suppose U is a symmetrical positive definite matrix; let $V = \sqrt{U}$ and $\mu = VL$; then, for the nonlinear activation function $\sigma(\mu)$, there is a function $g(\mu)$, when $g'(\mu) = \sigma(\mu)$. We have:

$$\nabla \sum_i g\left(V_j^T \mu\right) = U\sigma\left(U^T L\right) = U\sigma(UL) \quad (4)$$

The objective function $f(\mu)$ is defined as:

$$f(\mu) = \frac{\|\mu^2\|}{2} - \sum_i g\left(V_j^T \mu\right) \quad (5)$$

where V_i is the ith column of V. Then,

$$\nabla f(\mu_i) = \beta_i - V\sigma(V\mu_i) \qquad (6)$$

Equation (2) can be expressed by:

$$\mu_{i+1} = \mu_i + \beta(\mu_i - \mu_{i-1}) - \alpha((1+\beta)\nabla f(\mu_i) - \beta\nabla f(\mu_{i-1})) \qquad (7)$$

Recovering L by $L = V^{-1}\mu$ leads to:

$$L_{i+1} = ((1+\beta)(1-\alpha) - \alpha\beta)L_i + \beta(1-\alpha)L_{i-1} + \alpha(1+\beta)\sigma(UL_i) \qquad (8)$$

where $\sigma(UL_i)$ is the ith layer feed-forward network, and the ORB module structure is shown in Figure 2.

In order to aggregate the FPN multiscale feature information, a dual attention module (DAM) was designed to perform the feature aggregation. As shown in Figure 3, firstly, in order to obtain the position and channel information of the feature, the shallow feature map $x \in \mathbb{R}^{W \times H \times D_1}$ was passed through a global pooling operation and compression to generate the position vector $x_p \in \mathbb{R}^{W \times H \times 1}$ and the channel vector $x_c \in \mathbb{R}^{1 \times 1 \times D_1}$, respectively. Then, the position vector x_p computed the weight of each position with a sigmoid activation function and multiplied it with the feature map x_p to generate the spatial position feature map $F^p \in \mathbb{R}^{W \times H \times D_1}$, which was defined as:

$$F^p = \sigma(x) \otimes x \qquad (9)$$

where x is the shallow feature map, and σ is the sigmoid activation function. Similarly, the convolution of the ReLU activation function, defined as $f(x) = max(0,x)$, and the sigmoid activation function was performed on the channel vector x_c. The weight of each channel was calculated and multiplied by the feature map x to generate the feature map $F^c \in \mathbb{R}^{W \times H \times D_1}$, which was defined as follows:

$$F^c = \sigma(\delta(W_2(W_1(gp(x))))) \otimes x \qquad (10)$$

where δ is the ReLU activation function, and W_1 and W_2 are convolution operations with sizes $1 \times 1 \times D_1/16$ and $1 \times 1 \times D_1$, respectively. Finally, the final output feature map F was obtained by fusing the feature maps F^p, F^c, and x'. Then,

$$F = [(x \oplus F^p \oplus F^c), x'] \qquad (11)$$

where $\oplus$ represents the addition of the corresponding elements of two matrices.

The input image was passed through the ORB-FPN module, which denoted the output of the backbone as $\{C_2, C_3, C_4, C_5\}$ with strides of $\{4, 8, 16, 32\}$. $\{F_2, F_3, F_4\}$ were obtained after a 1×1 convolution with the same 128-dimensional channel features. Finally, the ORB module was added to enhance the acceptance domain of the output feature by using the backbone network on C_5 to separate the important context information. After interpolation and maximum pooling of the extracted context features and the generated three feature maps, an elementwise summation was performed to obtain features F.

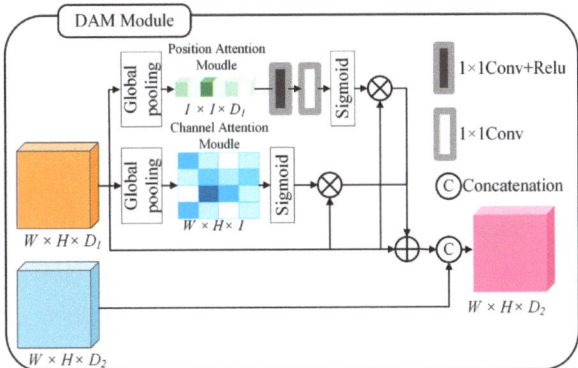

Figure 3. The dual attention module. The attention mechanism is adopted to adaptively aggregate different features, where the weights are normalized with the softmax function.

3.1.2. Key-point Detection Module

As shown in Figure 2, the key-point detection module consisted of three point perception modules and two 3 × 3 convolutions with a stride length of 1. A batch normalization layer and ReLU layers were added between each convolutional layer. The output vector was processed through a sigmoid activation function, so that the pixel values of the saliency map were between 0 and 1. Then, through the key-point perception module and convolution processing, the convolution operation was used to discriminate whether the 8 × 8 area prediction contained key points. Finally, the key points were detected by using the nonmaximum suppression (NMS) method in the key-point generation module (PG).

The point-aware module was used to capture the relationship between key points. As shown in Figure 4, the key-point extraction branch embedded a context enhancement module, which improved the feature expression ability. The output feature $y^p \in \mathbb{R}^{W \times H \times D}$ was obtained by fusing the convolutional features of different scales, which took $y^p \in {W \times H \times D}$ as input. The above process was defined as:

$$y^p = W_1[x^p, BN(W_1 x^p), BN(W_2 x^p), BN(W_3 W_1 x^p)] \tag{12}$$

where x^p is the input feature, W_1, W_2, and W_3 are convolution operations with sizes of 1 × 1, 2 × 2, and 3 × 3, respectively. BN is a normalization, and $[]$ is a splicing operation.

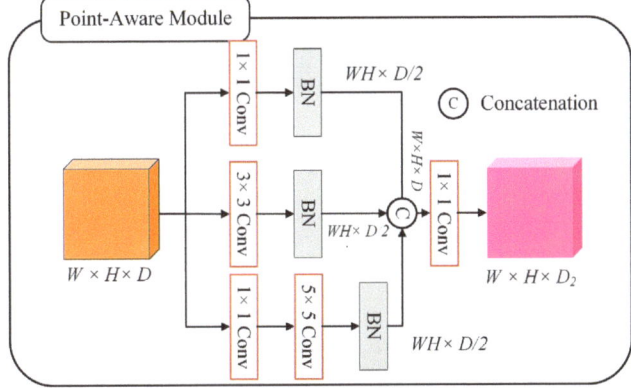

Figure 4. The point-aware module. BN means batch normalization.

3.1.3. Line-Segment Detection Module

The line-segment detection module extracted the features of the plane image through the ORB-FPN module and then input it to the line-segment extraction module to generate a midpoint with two symmetrical endpoints as the line-segment detection result. The extraction of the line segment's center point [28] used the classification model to judge whether the pixel was the center point of the line segment. Since the shape of the line segment was narrow and long, a large receptive field was required to classify the center of the line segment. Therefore, a hybrid convolution module was introduced by stacking three convolutional layers, a 3×3 deformable convolutional layer and two 3×3 dilated convolutional layers. The receptive field of the network was increased while reducing the parameters of the network. Then, three line-segment perception modules were used to enhance the feature representation ability. Finally, a deconvolution layer was used to restore the size of the output map to 512×512, which represented the center point of the line segment on the output feature map. The displacement regression task of the line-segment extraction branch was designed to predict the angle and length of the end point relative to the midpoint. It was composed of a 3×3 deformable convolution layer and two 3×3 convolutional layers with a stride of 1. The relevant displacement was indexed by the position through the output map. Finally, the CAL [29] was used for the line-segment generation, and the two endpoints of the line segment were defined as follows:

$$(x_{l_s}, y_{l_s}) = (x_{l_c}, y_{l_c}) + \frac{\alpha}{2}(\cos\theta, \sin\theta) \tag{13}$$

$$(x_{l_e}, y_{l_e}) = (x_{l_c}, y_{l_c}) - \frac{\alpha}{2}(\cos\theta, \sin\theta) \tag{14}$$

where (x_{l_c}, y_{l_c}) is the coordinates of the root node, α is the length of the line segment, and θ is the rotation angle.

In the line-segment detection, a line-aware module was introduced to effectively extract line shape features. As shown in Figure 5, the line-segment-aware module adopted the improved self-attention mechanism, which took the feature $x^L \in \mathbb{R}^{W \times H \times D}$ as input and fused the self-attention features to generate the final output feature $y^L \in \mathbb{R}^{W \times H \times D}$; the above process was defined as follows:

$$y^L = x^L \oplus W_1(\alpha(W_q x^L \times W_k x^L) \times W_v x^L) \tag{15}$$

where x^L is the input feature, W_1, W_q, W_k, and W_v are the learned weight matrices, which were implemented as 1×1 convolutions, and $\oplus$ means that the corresponding elements of the two matrices are added.

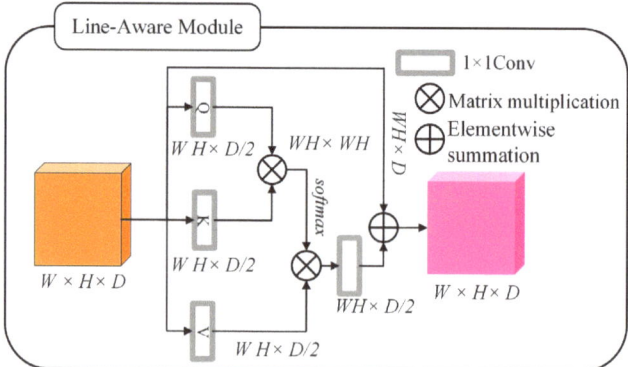

Figure 5. The line-aware module.

3.1.4. Parallel Attention Module

To efficiently merge the two branches of point descriptors and line descriptors, we designed a parallel attention module (PAB) based on self-attention and channel attention. As shown in Figure 6, the output features of the key-point description branch contained line-edge information with a strong correlation. In order to improve the accuracy of the line descriptor, a lightweight attention mechanism was used to assign more weights for the features of useful regions. The output feature map of the point description branch was expressed as $X_E \in \mathbb{R}^{C \times H \times W}$. A one-dimensional convolution of X_E was performed to obtain the spatial attention map $A_E \in \mathbb{R}^{C \times H \times W}$. The edge feature map $X_E^S \in \mathbb{R}^{C \times H \times W}$ was calculated as: $X_E^S = a(X_E \odot A_E) + X_E$, where a is a learnable parameter that was initialized to 0. The CAEU module was designed to calculate a channel attention map, which recalibrated the weight of the channel and obtained the fused feature map $X_F^S \in \mathbb{R}^{C \times H \times W}$ from $X_F^S = X_E^S \otimes \delta(Conv1 \times 1(Conv1 \times 1(GAP(X_E^S))))$. Finally, the final output $X_F^{SC} \in \mathbb{R}^{2C \times H \times W}$ of PAB was obtained by concatenating X_T^S and X_F^S together.

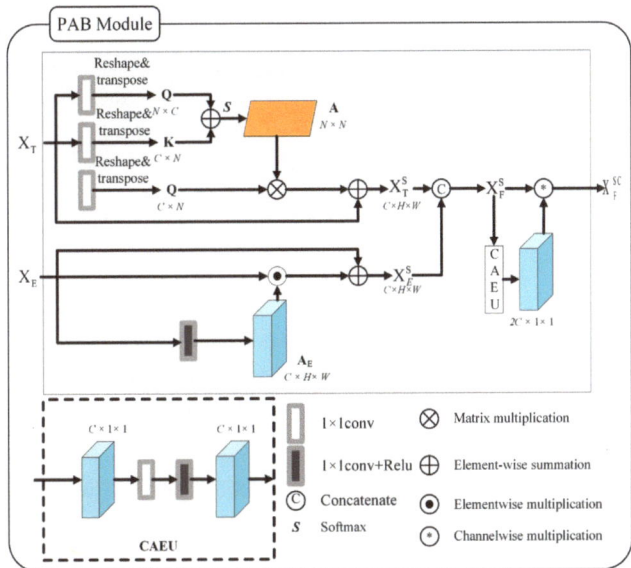

Figure 6. The parallel attention block (PAB). The PAB is designed to transfer important information to the line branch output (X_F^{SC}). The pink box in the lower-left corner shows the structure of the CAEU.

3.1.5. Network Output Distillation

In order to reduce the increasing computation cost caused by the introduction of the attention mechanism and the point–line perception module, we further compressed the point–line detection model PL-Net. A transfer-aware method is presented to transfer the information from the teacher model to the student network. The knowledge distillation strategy (KD) [30–32] was used to fine-tune the accuracy of the recovery model. As shown in Figure 2, the multiples tasks were combined with the teacher network and the student network to guide the training of the student feature extraction. In the training process, the adaptive weighted multitask distillation was realized, and X_{tea}, Y_{tea}, and Z_{tea} represented the key point of the teacher model, the center point of the line segment, and the output of the line-segment regression feature layer, respectively. The student model corresponded to the feature layers X_{stu}, Y_{stu}, and Z_{stu}. The mean squared error (MSE) function was applied to the multitask distillation. The loss function of the training distillation was:

$$\begin{cases} L_p^S = \|X_{tea} - X_{stu}\|^2 \\ L_{root}^S = \|Y_{tea} - Y_{stu}\|^2 \\ L_{dis}^S = \|Y_{tea} - Y_{stu}\|^2 \end{cases} \quad (16)$$

where L_p^S, L_{root}^S, and L_{dis}^S denote the key point, the line segment's center point, and the distillation loss of the line-segment regression task, respectively. Then, the weighted distillation loss was defined as:

$$L_{MSE}^s = \sum_l \omega_l L_l^s \quad (17)$$

where L_{MSE}^s is the multitask distillation loss, and ω_l represents the weight value of the verification loss.

3.1.6. Interlayer Knowledge Distillation

Different from the network output distillation, the student network was further enhanced by performing an interlayer knowledge distillation between the output of the teacher model and the student model. The aware modules of each student layer were associated with the relevant target-layer-aware modules for knowledge transfer. The layer's knowledge distillation loss was defined as:

$$L_{FMD} = \sum_{(s_l, t_l) \in C} Dist(Trans^t(F_{tl}^t), Trans^s(F_{sl}^s)) \quad (18)$$

Then, the overall loss was obtained as:

$$L_{total} = L_{MSE}^s + \beta L_{FMD} \quad (19)$$

where $Trans(\cdot)$ means to convert the feature map of the perception module into a specific manual representation through the attention map. C is the perception module, and F_{tl}^t and F_{sl}^s are the feature layers of the lth layer of the student model and the teacher model, respectively. The distance function $Dist(\cdot)$ was used for computing the distillation loss of the feature maps, and β was a hyperparameter.

3.2. Heterogeneous Graph Attention Network

As shown in Figure 7, consider two images I and I', and the number of two feature sets m and n belonging to them, respectively. Let $d \in \mathbb{R}^D$ be the feature descriptor, where D is the dimension of the descriptor. We utilized an attention graph neural network to integrate the contextual cues and enhance its feature expression ability.

Position encoders were used for the two input features, and the key points and lines positions were embedded into a high-dimensional vector by adding position encoding to $\widehat{F}_1$ and $\widehat{F}_2$; thus, we had:

$$f_i = d_i + \text{MLP}(P_i) \quad (20)$$

$$\text{MLP}(P_i) = W_a \sigma(W_b P_i) \quad (21)$$

where P_i is the position of the feature, d_i is the descriptor information, and $\sigma(\cdot)$ is the ReLU activation function.

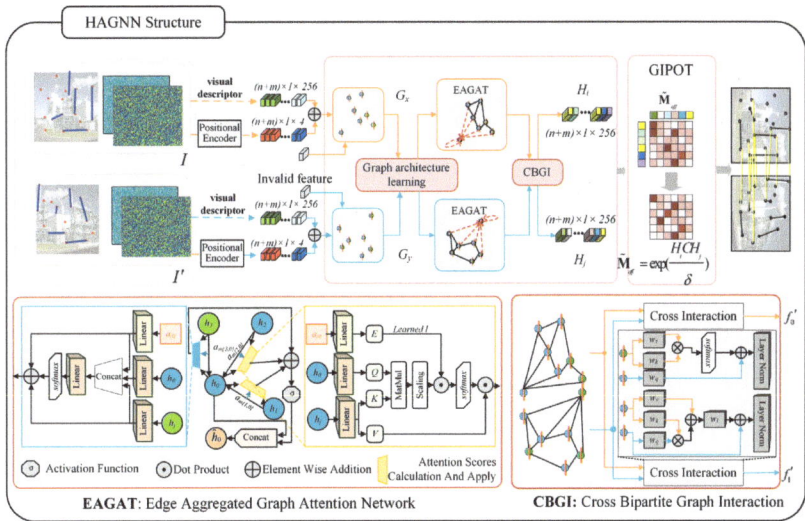

Figure 7. The overall structure of HAGNN. The first stage embeds the key points and line positions I and I' into a high-dimensional vector, which generates G_x and G_y. Graph architecture learning is used to construct the graph. The two graphs can generate discriminative features through EAGAT and CBGI. The second stage computes the affinity matrix and the assignment matrix between two sets H_i and H_j and uses the assignment matrix to find matches and filter nonmatches.

3.2.1. Edge-Clustering Graph Attention Module

We propose an edge-aggregated graph attention network (EAGAT) based on GAT [33], which uses edge information for feature enhancement during the aggregation process. In order to make full use of the information of edge features, these different types of links used different attention mechanisms. For features of the same nature (points and points, lines and lines), the self-attention mechanism was used for the aggregation. For features of different nature (points and lines), the cascade method was used for the aggregation. Let the feature of the vertex v'_i in the graph be f_i, defined as:

$$f'_i = \sigma(\sum_{j \in \mathcal{N}_s} softmax(\frac{W^a f_i W^\beta f_j}{\sqrt{d_k}} W^\gamma a_{ji}) W^\varepsilon f_j + \sum_{j \in \mathcal{N}_d} softmax([W^a f_i || W^\beta f_j || W^\gamma a_{ji}]) W^\varepsilon) || f_i \tag{22}$$

where W^a, W^β, W^γ, and $W^\varepsilon \in \mathbb{R}^{f'_\eta \times f_\eta}$ represent the weight parameters, $\mathcal{N}_s$ is the feature set of the same nature, $\mathcal{N}_d$ represents the feature set of different properties, and σ is the ReLU activation function.

3.2.2. Cross-Heterogeneous Graph Iteration Module

Due to the affinity learning problem of message passing between graphs in graph matching, a point–line heterogeneous graph message-passing method is proposed to enhance the node features through an interactive correlation. The edge features and node features were aggregated in two ways. For nodes of the same nature (points and points, lines and lines), we used linear attention for the aggregation, and for nodes of different properties (points and lines), we used the aggregation method of the self-attention mechanism. Then, $f'_{si} \in \mathbb{R}^{f'\eta}$ is expressed as:

$$f'_{si} = \text{LN}\{\sum_{j \in \mathcal{N}_{di}} (softmax[(W_v f_j)(W_k f_j)^T] + W_q f_{si})\}$$
$$+ \text{LN}\{\sum_{j \in \mathcal{N}_{si}} (W_l((W_q f_{si})(W_k f_j)^T + W_k f_j) + f_{si}\} \quad (23)$$

where $v_{l/r} \in \mathbb{R}^{f'\eta}$ is the feature node of the two graphs, $W_{(\cdot)}$ is the weight parameter, and LN represents a layer normalization (LN).

3.3. Greedy near Iterative Matching Module

The output H_i of the last layer in the graph neural network is the feature of graph I'. H_j is the feature of graph I', and the point–line distance matrix $G \in \mathbb{R}^{+N_1 \times N_2}$ can be expressed as:

$$G = f_{aff}(H_i, H'_j), i \in v_1, j \in v_2 \quad (24)$$

where f_{aff} is the weighted bilinear function, defined as:

$$f_{aff}(H_i, H'_j) = \exp(\frac{H_i^T K H_j^T}{\tau}) \quad (25)$$

where the feature is an n-dimensional vector, namely $\forall i \in v_1, j \in v_2$ and $H_i^T, H_j^T \in \mathbb{R}^{n \times n}$, $K \in \mathbb{R}^{n \times n}$ is the weight matrix of the affinity function, and τ is the regularization parameter. In the matching process, due to the inconsistency of point and line types, a direct fusion may cause a mismatch of point and line types. For this reason, we regarded the unit block diagonal matrix as the initial coupling matrix $\Gamma^{(1)}$ so that the relationship between point features and line features in the iterative process minimized the matching cost. Then, we had:

$$\Gamma^{(1)} \leftarrow \begin{bmatrix} 11_P & 0 \\ 0 & 11_L \end{bmatrix} \quad (26)$$

where P is the number of points after completion, and L is the number of lines after completion. Then, the point–line discrete distribution Sinkhorn distance [34,35] was defined as:

$$W_\in(u,v) = \min_{\Gamma \in \Sigma(u,v)} \langle C, \Gamma \rangle + \lambda h(\Gamma) \quad (27)$$

where u and v are probability vectors, $W_\in(u,v)$ is the distance between u and v, the matrix $C = [c_{ij}] \in \mathbb{R}^{+n \times n}$ is the cost matrix, and c_{ij} is the distance between u_i and v_j. The regularization term $h(\Gamma) = \sum_{i,j} \Gamma_{ij} \ln \Gamma_{ij}$. The proximal point iteration method [35] was used to solve Equation (25). According to the proximal point iteration method, it is defined as the Bregman divergence:

$$D_h(x,y) = \sum_{i=1}^{n} x_i \ln \frac{x_i}{y_i} - \sum_{i=1}^{n} x_i - \sum_{i=1}^{n} y_i \quad (28)$$

After introducing the near-end point iteration, Equation (27) can be rewritten as:

$$\Gamma^{(t+1)} = \underset{\Gamma \in \Sigma(u,v)}{\text{argmin}} \langle C, \Gamma \rangle + \beta^t D_h(\Gamma, \Gamma^{(t)}) \quad (29)$$

Substituting the Bregman divergence Equation (28) into Equation (29), it becomes

$$\Gamma^{(t+1)} = \underset{\Gamma \in \Sigma(u,v)}{\operatorname{argmin}} \langle C', \Gamma \rangle + \beta^t h(\Gamma) \tag{30}$$

where $C' = C - \beta^t \ln \Gamma^{(t)}$; we used the greedy strategy to update the best row or column and defined the distance matrix

$$\rho(x,y) = y - x + \log \frac{x}{y} \tag{31}$$

According to Equations (29) and (30), the affinity matrix was updated to find the best matching relationship, and the specific algorithm flow is shown in Algorithm 1.

Algorithm 1: GIPOT(μ, v, G).

Input: Point–line features of graph network output H_i and H_j
Output: $\Gamma^{(t+1)}$
initialize $\Gamma^{(1)} \leftarrow \begin{bmatrix} 11_p & 0 \\ 0 & 11_L \end{bmatrix}$, $G \leftarrow f_{aff}(H_i, H'_j)$
begin
    for $t = 1, 2, 3 \ldots$ **do**
        $Q \leftarrow G \odot \Gamma^{(t)}$
        $I \leftarrow \operatorname{argmax}_i \rho(u_i, u_i(Q))$
        $J \leftarrow \operatorname{argmax}_j \rho(u_j, u_j(Q))$
        $\Gamma^{(1)} \leftarrow diag(\exp(a)) Q diag(\exp(b))$
        if $\rho(u_I, u_I(Q)) > \rho(u_J, u_J(Q))$ **then**
            $a_I \leftarrow a_I + \log \frac{u_I}{u_I(Q)}$
        else
            $a_J \leftarrow a_J + \log \frac{u_J}{u_J(Q)}$
        end
        $\Gamma^{(1)} \leftarrow diag(\exp(a)) Q diag(\exp(b))$
    end
end

3.4. Loss Function

In order to realize the matching of points and lines, the point–line extraction loss, descriptor extraction loss, and point–line matching loss were used as the loss functions during model training.

3.4.1. Point–Line Extraction Loss

In the training stage of the point and line extraction branch, the output included the root node's confidence map, key-point map, and displacement map. The losses of these three tasks were combined into Equation (32), defined as follows:

$$L_{PLE} = L_{root} + L_p + L_{dis} \tag{32}$$

The ground truth of the root-point confidence map was constructed by marking the root-point positions on a zero map. A weighted binary cross-entropy loss L_{root} was used to supervise this task, which was defined as:

$$L_{root} = -\sum_i \widetilde{R}_i \log R_i + (1 - \widetilde{R}_i) \log(1 - R_i) \tag{33}$$

where $\widetilde{R}_i$ and R_i are the prediction and true label of the root node of the line segment, respectively. The true value of the key point was marked with the ORB feature. $L_p(X, Y)$ was defined as:

$$L_p(X, Y) = \frac{1}{H_c w_c} \sum l_p\left(T^{ij}, \widetilde{T^{ij}}\right) \tag{34}$$

$$l_p\left(T^{ij}, \widetilde{T^{ij}}\right) = -\log\left(\frac{\exp(T_k^{ij})}{\sum_1^{64} \exp(T_k^{ij})}\right) \tag{35}$$

The displacement part of the line segment relative to the root node was used to locate the length and angle of the line segment, which used the L1 loss and L1 smoothing loss, respectively defined as:

$$L_{dis} = \sum_{i=1}^{m} \begin{cases} |\theta^i - \hat{\theta}^i| + 0.5 * (\rho^i - \hat{\rho}^i)^2 & if |\rho^i - \hat{\rho}^i| < 1 \\ |\theta^i - \hat{\theta}^i| + |\rho^i - \hat{\rho}^i| - 0.5 & otherwise \end{cases} \tag{36}$$

where θ^i and ρ^i represent the actual line segment's length and angle, and $\hat{\theta}^i$ and $\hat{\rho}^i$ are the predicted line segment's length and angle, respectively.

3.4.2. Point–Line Descriptor Loss

Denote the original image as I, and apply the homography transformation for I to form a new image I'. Since the homography transformation is known, the corresponding relationship between key points and line segments on I and I' can be obtained. Therefore, the loss function can be defined as:

$$L_d(\theta, \{d_a^\theta, d_+^\theta, d_-^\theta\}) = [m + \|d_a^\theta - d_+^\theta\|^2 - \min_{d_-^\theta \in d_-^\theta} \|d_a^\theta - d_-^\theta\|^2]_+ \tag{37}$$

where the parameter m was set to 0.5, d_a^θ is the descriptor on I of the anchor point, d_+^θ is the matching descriptor on I' of the positive sample, and d_-^θ is the set of nonmatching descriptors on I' of the negative sample.

3.4.3. Matching Loss

For a matching network using the L2 loss, the loss function can be expressed as:

$$L_m = \frac{1}{|M_{gt}|} \sum_{(i,j) \in M_{gt}} \frac{1}{\sigma^2(i)} \|M(i,j) - M_{gt}(i,j)\|_2 \tag{38}$$

where $\sigma^2(i)$ is the confidence variance of feature i. $M(i,j)$ is the matching probability of feature i and feature j, and M_{gt} is the real-valued matrix obtained by the homography transformation.

3.4.4. Normalization

The total loss function was the sum of the above loss functions:

$$L_{sum} = \lambda_1 L_{PLE} + \lambda_2 L_d + \lambda_3 L_m \tag{39}$$

where λ_1, λ_2 and λ_3 represent the coefficients of each loss function, respectively. $\lambda_{1,2,3} = \{0.25, 0.25, 0.5\}$.

4. Experiments and Evaluation

4.1. Model Training Details

A wide range of experiments were performed on different datasets to demonstrate the efficacy of our method. Our approach was evaluated with several evaluation criteria by comparing to the typical SLAM methods on the KITTI dataset [36]. We used the training set of Wireframe [37] with the ground truth to train our models and the other compared methods. The training process used data enhancement techniques such as random Gaussian noise, motion blur, and brightness level changes to improve the network's robustness ability for changes in lighting and viewing angles. For end-to-end training of the point–line matching network, our network was implemented in Pytorch [38] using the Adam [39] optimizer to train the network with an initial learning rate of 1×10^{-5} and a decay of the learning rate by 20 at each epoch. We trained our model on a GeForce GTX2080Ti GPU.

4.2. KITTI Dataset Evaluation

We tested the proposed algorithm on the KITTI dataset [36]. The quantitative evaluations for the different SLAM systems were the absolute trajectory error (ATE) [40] and the relative pose error (RPE) [41] based on translations and rotations. Table 1 shows the performance of this system was better than ORB-SLAM2, especially in sequences with strong lighting, motion blur, and low texture areas, such as 06 and 09. It can be seen that the multifeature fusion not only improved the accuracy of the algorithm but also avoided the degradation problem that may occur in the pose solution algorithm when using a single feature.

Table 1. Comparison between ATE and RPE on different SLAM algorithms.

Seq	ORB-SLAM2			Our		
	ATE (m)	RPE_{trans} (%)	RPE_{rot} (deg/m)	ATE (m)	RPE_{trans} (%)	RPE_{rot} (deg/m)
00	1.266	52.5	0.363	1.233	2.9	0.122
01	4.296	3.4	0.420	2.616	4.8	0.044
02	12.790	4.3	0.107	12.721	3.6	0.077
03	0.403	0.8	0.072	0.385	2.0	0.055
04	0.466	2.2	0.055	0.192	2.1	0.040
05	0.348	2.3	0.144	0.402	1.7	0.056
06	1.184	3.9	0.089	0.572	1.8	0.042
07	0.439	1.3	0.076	0.436	1.6	0.046
08	3.122	12.1	0.076	2.874	3.9	0.054
09	3.319	15.0	0.104	1.537	2.2	0.054
10	0.927	2.6	0.090	0.989	2.1	0.060

Figure 8 shows the comparison results of ORB-SLAM2 and the method in this paper on KITTI's partial sequences. It can be seen that the algorithm of this paper was equivalent to ORB-SLAM2 as a whole. However, in sequences such as 00, 02, and 09, it showed that our method had the best results. On the other hand, the ORB-SLAM2 lost track easily and did not have a whole trajectory.

Figure 9 depicts the variation curve of the pose estimation error with the number of training iterations. When we used more than 80 iterations, the rotation and translation errors were relatively small while the performance improved, which showed that the algorithm in this paper had a good convergence.

Figure 10 visualizes the statistical error property between our system and ORB-SLAM2 on sequence 09 of KITTI. It shows that our model achieved obviously a better performance than ORB-SLAM2 in terms of the root-mean-square error (controlled within 2 m), extreme value error, and the sum of the squared errors. Figure 10b shows the columnar statistical comparison of postural errors; our model was better than ORB-SLAM2 in the APE distribution range of the algorithm.

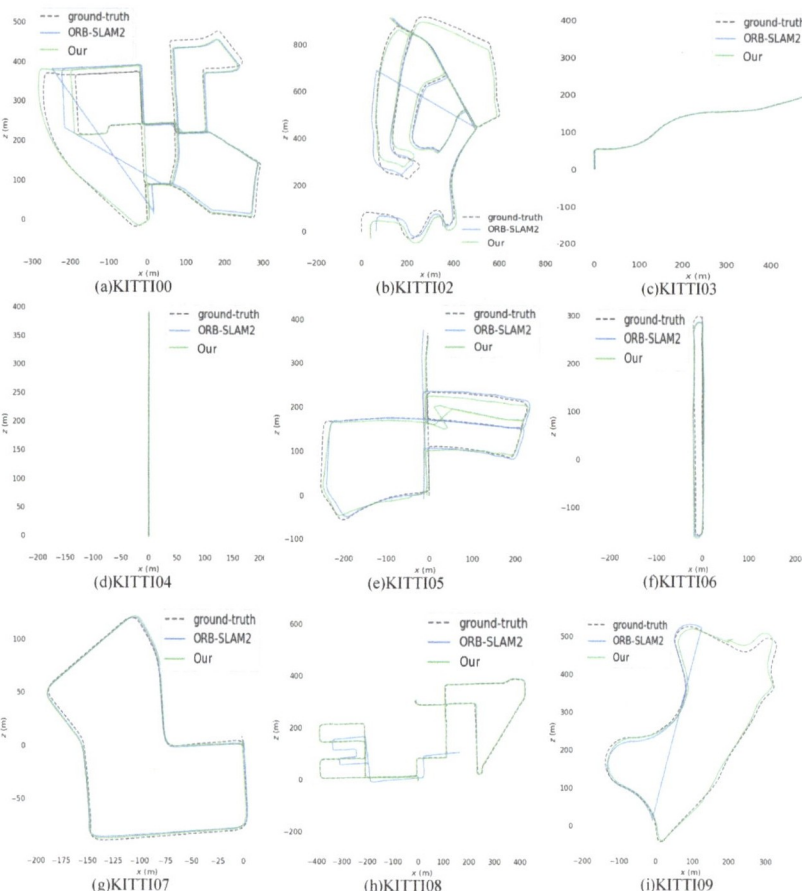

Figure 8. Comparison of trajectories estimated by our SLAM method, ORB-SLAM2, and the ground truth on the KITTI dataset.

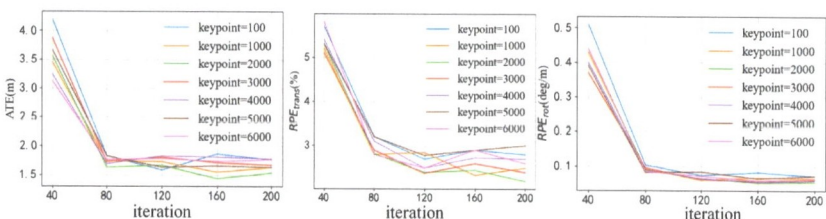

Figure 9. The variation curve of the pose estimation error with the number of training iterations on sequence 09 of KITTI. Each color represents a different number of sampling points.

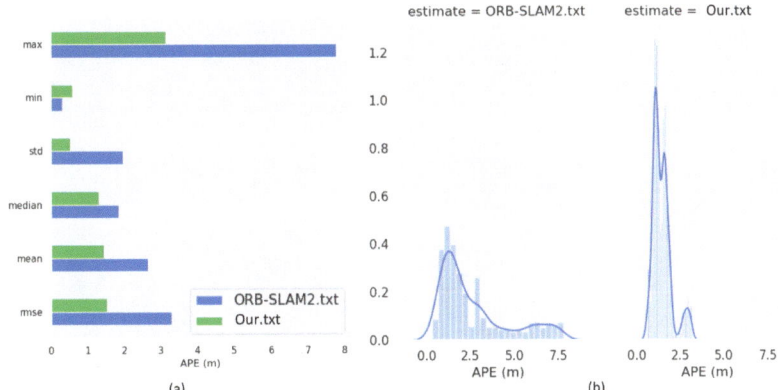

Figure 10. Comparison of the statistical error property between our system and ORB-SLAM2 on sequence 09 of KITTI. (**a**) Quantitative index chart of ATE. (**b**) Histogram of ATE.

4.3. Real Data Evaluation

As shown in Figure 11, the feasibility of the algorithm was verified on a physical and virtual oil and gas station, where the virtual simulation platform with a quadruped robot was built with Unity3D.

Figure 11. The experimental robot platform. (**a**) The physical experimental robot platform with robot hardware including a camera, depth camera, and IMU. An additional GPS/RTK was used for the ground-truth estimation. (**b**) The virtual simulation platform.

To show the effects of point and line features on the SLAM system, we intercepted two frames of images for extracting the features by PL-Net and matching by HAGNN. As shown in Figure 12, it can be seen that the combination of point and line could make the SLAM algorithm obtain richer and more diverse feature information.

The virtual simulation platform used a quadruped robot to inspect the oil field equipment. As shown in Figure 13, this trajectory was compared with the ground truth by using the evaluation package to obtain the RPE and APE. It can be seen that the area with a larger error was basically distributed at the corner of the trajectory. The RMSE was 17.5 m. Overall, the trajectory of our method was consistent with the ground truth with a high accuracy.

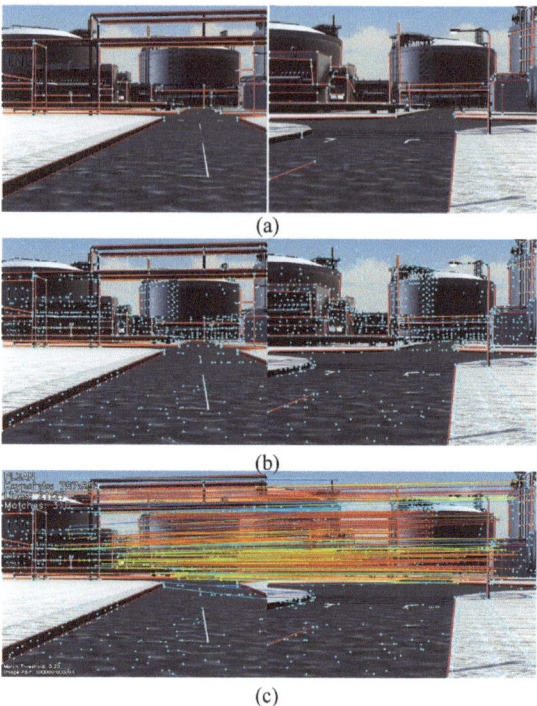

Figure 12. The effect of point–line feature tracking. (**a**) The line-segment extraction results. (**b**) The point and line-segment extraction results. (**c**) The point and line matching results. We visualized the matching results with RGB color.

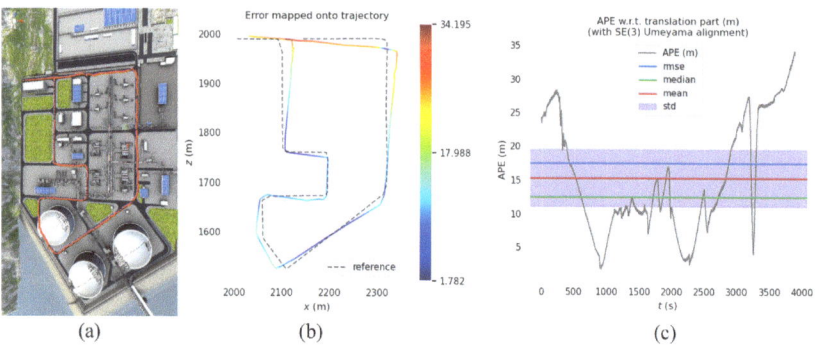

Figure 13. Simulation platform experiment. (**a**) The simulation platform. (**b**) The error mapped onto trajectory. (**c**) RMSE of ATE in meters after translation and scale alignment.

4.4. GIPOT Experiment

In order to illustrate the convergence of GIPOT with different β, the Wasserstein distance of two one-dimensional Gaussian distributions was measured as an evaluation index. As shown in Figure 14a, the blue equation was $0.5N(70, 8) + 0.5(35, 10)$, the red equation was $0.4N(80, 9) + 0.6N(40, 10)$, where $N(\mu, \sigma^2)$ is the probability density function of the one-dimensional Gaussian distribution, μ and σ^2 are the mean and variance, respectively. Figure 14b shows the convergence of GIPOT under different conditions. Compared with the Sinkhorn method, the convergence of the GIPOT iteration was quicker when β was large.

GIPOT could converge to the exact Wasserstein distance with a complexity comparable to that of Sinkhorn.

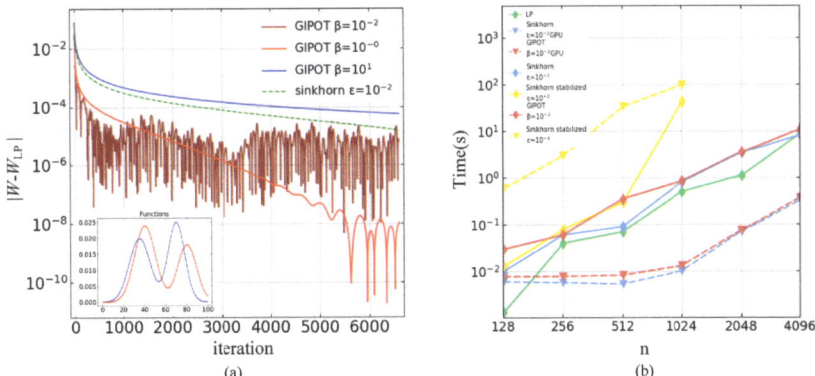

Figure 14. The difference graph of the Wasserstein distance. (**a**) GIPOT under different conditions and convergence trajectory graph. We also plotted the ones for the Sinkhorn method for comparison. (**b**) The average time of GIPOT and Sinkhorn iterations under different conditions.

4.5. Ablation Study

We used two datasets to demonstrate our proposed knowledge distillation. The result of the teacher network and the student network are shown in Figure 15. Compared with the true value, both models could identify key points and line segments with high precision. Although there were some small missing line segments and connection errors in the results of the student network, the expression of the line-segment structure in the environment was basically accurate. The quantitative comparison is shown in Table 2. Although the performance of the student network was slightly lower than that of the teacher network, the operation speed was increased by 73%.

Table 2. Quantitative evaluation of PL-Net point-line detection knowledge distillation method on Wireframe dataset and YorkUrban dataset.

Method	Wireframe dataset			YorkUrban dataset			FPS
	F^H	sAP	LAP	F^H	sAP	LAP	
Student	77.5	58.9	59.8	64.6	25.9	32.0	12.5
Teacher	80.6	57.6	61.3	67.2	27.6	34.3	7.2

To verify the role of the multifeature fusion in the SLAM system, the root-mean-square error (RMSE) of the ATE index under different feature combinations was calculated. The experimental results are given in Table 3, where the point–line feature combination method used in this paper significantly improved the accuracy of the pose estimation. To evaluate our design decisions, we evaluated four different variants with results. This ablation study, presented in Table 4, showed that all HAGNN blocks were useful and brought substantial performance gains. "No EAGAT" replaced all EAGAT layers with CHGI layers, and the matching accuracy decreased by 9.7%. "No CHGI" replaced all CHGI layers with EAGAT layer, and the precision of the resulting matching decreased by 22.6%, "No HAGNN" replaced the graph neural network with a single linear projection, and the precision of the resulting matching decreased by 26.1%.

Figure 15. Qualitative evaluation of PL-Net point–line detection knowledge distillation method on the Wireframe dataset and the YorkUrban dataset.

Table 3. Results of ablation experiment in term of the RMSE of ATE (Unit: m).

Seq	P-SLAM	L-SLAM	PL-SLAM	ORB-SLAM2	LSD-SLAM	PTAM
00	1.203	6.233	1.233	1.266	5.347	2.842
01	3.934	12.367	2.616	4.296	—	3.358
02	7.689	—	12.721	12.790	—	13.742
03	0.393	5.457	0.385	0.403	7.431	2.302
04	0.347	13.824	0.192	0.466	—	2.773
05	0.863	—	0.402	0.348	1.293	0.456
06	0.884	—	0.572	1.184	—	1.024
07	0.255	—	0.436	0.439	—	0.423
08	3.122	—	2.874	3.122	—	3.358
09	2.625	4.783	1.537	3.319	11.395	2.048
10	0.447	5.824	0.989	0.927	2.841	0.768

The proposed HAGNN was compared with two feature matching methods: the nearest neighbor (NN) method and SuperGlue. As show in Table 5, it can be seen clearly that HAGNN had a significantly higher pose estimation accuracy than all competitors, which showed a higher feature expression ability.

Table 4. Ablation of HAGNN.

	Known		Unknown	
	Match Precision	Matching Score	Match Precision	Matching Score
No EAGAT	79.6	29.5	55.3	15.6
No CHGI	66.7	25.3	48.2	18.5
No HAGNN	63.2	19.4	51.2	10.3
Full	89.3	34.2	78.3	23.8

Table 5. Experimental results of the pose estimation. Matching PL-Net features with HAGNN resulted in a significantly higher pose accuracy (AUC), precision (P), and matching score (MS) than with handcrafted or other learned methods.

Feature	Matcher	Pose Estimation AUC			P	MS
		@5°	@10°	@20°		
SIFT	NN	7.89	10.22	35.30	43.4	1.7
SIFT	SuperGlue	23.68	36.44	49.44	74.1	7.2
SuperPoint	NN	9.80	18.99	30.88	22.5	4.9
SuperPoint	SuperGlue	34.18	44.32	64.16	84.9	11.1
LSD + LBD	NN	5.43	7.83	28.54	32.5	1.3
SOLD^2	NN	18.34	13.22	23.51	63.6	6.2
SuperPoint + SOLD^2	Ours	35.86	44.73	64.43	85.3	12.3
Ours	Ours	36.67	44.26	64.73	86.6	12.7

5. Conclusions

In this paper, we proposed a point–line-aware heterogeneous graph attention network for a visual SLAM system. Combining the point- and line-aware attention modules based on an attention-driven mechanism, the geometric association features of key regions was further extracted, and the model was simplified by a transfer-aware knowledge distillation strategy. By improving the accuracy of image point–line matching, a point–line heterogeneous graph attention network was proposed, which realized the feature aggregation by conducting learning on the intragraph and intergraph. Based on the optimal transport theory, we proposed a greedy inexact proximal point method that could effectively solve the point–line matching problem. Experiments on a public dataset and a self-made dataset showed qualitatively and quantitatively that our model had stronger robustness and a better generalization ability. One limitation of our feature matching was that it was not easy to estimate the pose error due to the interference of dynamic objects. Thus, in a future study, we will introduce the cross-frame semantic information in the network for dynamic environments.

Author Contributions: Conceptualization, Y.L. and H.S.; methodology, Y.L.; software, H.S.; validation, S.D.; formal analysis, H.S.; investigation, Y.L.; resources, H.S.; data curation, Y.L.; writing—original draft preparation, H.S.; writing—review and editing, Y.L.; visualization, H.S.; supervision, Y.L.; project administration, Y.L.; funding acquisition, Y.L. All authors have read and agreed to the published version of the manuscript.

Funding: This research was funded by NSFC 61972353, NSF IIS-1816511, OAC-1910469 and Strategic Cooperation Technology Proiects of CNPC and CUPB: ZLZX2020-05.

Institutional Review Board Statement: Not applicable.

Informed Consent Statement: Not applicable.

Data Availability Statement: Not applicable.

Conflicts of Interest: The authors declare no conflict of interest.

References

1. Yousif, K.; Bab-Hadiashar, A.; Hoseinnezhad, R. An overview to visual odometry and visual SLAM: Applications to mobile robotics. *Intell. Ind. Syst.* **2015**, *1*, 289–311. [CrossRef]
2. Demim, F.; Nemra, A.; Boucheloukh, A.; Louadj, K.; Hamerlain, M.; Bazoula, A. Robust SVSF-SLAM algorithm for unmanned vehicle in dynamic environment. In Proceedings of the 2018 International Conference on Signal, Image, Vision and Their Applications (SIVA), Guelma, Algeria, 26–27 November 2018; pp. 1–5.
3. Demim, F.; Nemra, A.; Boucheloukh, A.; Kobzili, E.; Hamerlain, M.; Bazoula, A. SLAM based on adaptive SVSF for cooperative unmanned vehicles in dynamic environment. *IFAC-PapersOnLine* **2019**, *52*, 73–80. [CrossRef]
4. Kuo, X.Y.; Liu, C.; Lin, K.C.; Lee, C.Y. Dynamic attention-based visual odometry. In Proceedings of the IEEE/CVF Conference on Computer Vision and Pattern Recognition Workshops, Seattle, WA, USA, 14–19 June 2020; pp. 36–37.

5. Teixeira, B.; Silva, H.; Matos, A.; Silva, E. Deep learning for underwater visual odometry estimation. *IEEE Access* **2020**, *8*, 44687–44701. [CrossRef]
6. Lee, T.; Kim, C.-H.; Cho, D.-i.D. A monocular vision sensor-based efficient SLAM method for indoor service robots. *IEEE Trans. Ind. Electron.* **2018**, *66*, 318–328. [CrossRef]
7. Zhang, L.; Koch, R. An efficient and robust line segment matching approach based on LBD descriptor and pairwise geometric consistency. *J. Vis. Commun. Image Represent.* **2013**, *24*, 794–805. [CrossRef]
8. Cho, H.; Kim, E.K.; Kim, S. Indoor SLAM application using geometric and ICP matching methods based on line features. *Robot. Auton. Syst.* **2018**, *100*, 206–224. [CrossRef]
9. Han, R.; Li, W.F. Line-feature-based SLAM algorithm. *Acta Autom. Sin.* **2006**, *32*, 43–46.
10. Zhou, D.; Dai, Y.; Li, H. Ground-plane-based absolute scale estimation for monocular visual odometry. *IEEE Trans. Intell. Transp. Syst.* **2019**, *21*, 791–802. [CrossRef]
11. Yang, S.; Scherer, S. Monocular object and plane slam in structured environments. *IEEE Robot. Autom. Lett.* **2019**, *4*, 3145–3152. [CrossRef]
12. Cho, H.; Yeon, S.; Choi, H.; Doh, N. Detection and compensation of degeneracy cases for imu-kinect integrated continuous slam with plane features. *Sensors* **2018**, *18*, 935. [CrossRef]
13. Gomez-Ojeda, R.; Moreno, F.A.; Zuniga-Noël, D.; Scaramuzza, D.; Gonzalez-Jimenez, J. PL-SLAM: A stereo SLAM system through the combination of points and line segments. *IEEE Trans. Robot.* **2019**, *35*, 734–746. [CrossRef]
14. Zhang, X.; Wang, W.; Qi, X.; Liao, Z.; Wei, R. Point-plane slam using supposed planes for indoor environments. *Sensors* **2019**, *19*, 3795. [CrossRef] [PubMed]
15. Grant, W.S.; Voorhies, R.C.; Itti, L. Efficient Velodyne SLAM with point and plane features. *Auton. Robot.* **2019**, *43*, 1207–1224. [CrossRef]
16. Sun, Q.; Yuan, J.; Zhang, X.; Duan, F. Plane-Edge-SLAM: Seamless fusion of planes and edges for SLAM in indoor environments. *IEEE Trans. Autom. Sci. Eng.* **2020**, *18*, 2061–2075. [CrossRef]
17. Chen, X.; Cai, Y.; Tang, Y. A visual SLAM algorithm based on line point invariants. *Robot* **2020**, *42*, 485–493.
18. Li, H.; Hu, Z.; Chen, X. PLP-SLAM: A visual SLAM method based on point-line-plane feature fusion. *Jiqiren* **2017**, *39*, 214–220.
19. Simo-Serra, E.; Trulls, E.; Ferraz, L.; Kokkinos, I.; Fua, P.; Moreno-Noguer, F. Discriminative learning of deep convolutional feature point descriptors. In Proceedings of the IEEE International Conference on Computer Vision, Santiago, Chile, 7–13 December 2015; pp. 118–126.
20. Fu, K.; Liu, Z.; Wu, X.; Sun, C.; Chen, W. An Effective End-to-End Image Matching Network with Attentional Graph Neural Networks. In Proceedings of the 2022 IEEE 17th Conference on Industrial Electronics and Applications (ICIEA), Chengdu, China, 15–18 April 2022; pp. 1628–1633.
21. Zhang, J.; Marszałek, M.; Lazebnik, S.; Schmid, C. Local features and kernels for classification of texture and object categories: A comprehensive study. *Int. J. Comput. Vis.* **2007**, *73*, 213–238. [CrossRef]
22. Sarlin, P.E.; DeTone, D.; Malisiewicz, T.; Rabinovich, A. Superglue: Learning feature matching with graph neural networks. In Proceedings of the IEEE/CVF Conference on Computer Vision and Pattern Recognition, Seattle, WA, USA, 13–19 June 2020; pp. 4938–4947.
23. Tang, J.; Ericson, L.; Folkesson, J.; Jensfelt, P. GCNv2: Efficient correspondence prediction for real-time SLAM. *IEEE Robot. Autom. Lett.* **2019**, *4*, 3505–3512. [CrossRef]
24. Tang, J.; Folkesson, J.; Jensfelt, P. Geometric correspondence network for camera motion estimation. *IEEE Robot. Autom. Lett.* **2018**, *3*, 1010–1017. [CrossRef]
25. Pautrat, R.; Lin, J.T.; Larsson, V.; Oswald, M.R.; Pollefeys, M. SOLD2: Self-supervised occlusion-aware line description and detection. In Proceedings of the IEEE/CVF Conference on Computer Vision and Pattern Recognition, Nashville, TN, USA, 20–25 June 2021; pp. 11368–11378.
26. Li, H.; Yang, Y.; Chen, D.; Lin, Z. Optimization algorithm inspired deep neural network structure design. In Proceedings of the Asian Conference on Machine Learning, Beijing, China, 14–16 November 2018; pp. 614–629.
27. Vaswani, A.; Shazeer, N.; Parmar, N.; Uszkoreit, J.; Jones, L.; Gomez, A.N.; Kaiser, Ł.; Polosukhin, I. Attention is all you need. *Adv. Neural Inf. Process. Syst.* **2017**, *30*, 1–11.
28. Duan, K.; Bai, S.; Xie, L.; Qi, H.; Huang, Q.; Tian, Q. Centernet: Keypoint triplets for object detection. In Proceedings of the IEEE/CVF International Conference on Computer Vision, Seoul, Republic of Korea, 27 October–2 November 2019; pp. 6569–6578.
29. Zhang, H.; Luo, Y.; Qin, F.; He, Y.; Liu, X. ELSD: Efficient Line Segment Detector and Descriptor. In Proceedings of the IEEE/CVF International Conference on Computer Vision, Montreal, QC, Canada, 10–17 October 2021; pp. 2969–2978.
30. Hinton, G.; Vinyals, O.; Dean, J. Distilling the knowledge in a neural network. *arXiv* **2015**, arXiv:1503.02531.
31. Zhang, K.; Zhang, C.; Li, S.; Zeng, D.; Ge, S. Student network learning via evolutionary knowledge distillation. *IEEE Trans. Circuits Syst. Video Technol.* **2021**, *32*, 2251–2263. [CrossRef]
32. Valverde, F.R.; Hurtado, J.V.; Valada, A. There is more than meets the eye: Self-supervised multi-object detection and tracking with sound by distilling multimodal knowledge. In Proceedings of the IEEE/CVF Conference on Computer Vision and Pattern Recognition, Virtual, 19–25 June 2021; pp. 11612–11621.
33. Veličković, P.; Cucurull, G.; Casanova, A.; Romero, A.; Lio, P.; Bengio, Y. Graph attention networks. *arXiv* **2017**, arXiv:1710.10903.
34. Cuturi, M. Sinkhorn distances: Lightspeed computation of optimal transport. *Adv. Neural Inf. Process. Syst.* **2013**, *26*, 1–9.

35. Xie, Y.; Wang, X.; Wang, R.; Zha, H. A fast proximal point method for computing exact wasserstein distance. In Proceedings of the Uncertainty in Artificial Intelligence, Online, 3–6 August 2020; pp. 433–453.
36. Geiger, A.; Lenz, P.; Stiller, C.; Urtasun, R. Vision meets robotics: The kitti dataset. *Int. J. Robot. Res.* **2013**, *32*, 1231–1237. [CrossRef]
37. Huang, K.; Wang, Y.; Zhou, Z.; Ding, T.; Gao, S.; Ma, Y. Learning to parse wireframes in images of man-made environments. In Proceedings of the IEEE Conference on Computer Vision and Pattern Recognition, Salt Lake City, UT, USA, 18–22 June 2018; pp. 626–635.
38. Chen, B.B.; Gao, Y.; Guo, Y.B.; Liu, Y.; Zhao, H.H.; Liao, H.J.; Wang, L.; Xiang, T.; Li, W.; Xie, Z. Automatic differentiation for second renormalization of tensor networks. *Phys. Rev. B* **2020**, *101*, 220409. [CrossRef]
39. Kingma, D.P.; Ba, J.A.; Adam, J. A method for stochastic optimization. *arXiv* **2020**, arXiv:1412.6980.
40. Schubert, D.; Goll, T.; Demmel, N.; Usenko, V.; Stückler, J.; Cremers, D. The TUM VI benchmark for evaluating visual-inertial odometry. In Proceedings of the 2018 IEEE/RSJ International Conference on Intelligent Robots and Systems (IROS), Madrid, Spain, 1–5 October 2018; pp. 1680–1687.
41. Nistér, D.; Stewénius, H. Scalable Recognition with a Vocabulary Tree. In Proceedings of the Computer Vision and Pattern Recognition, New York, NY, USA, 17–22 June 2006.

Disclaimer/Publisher's Note: The statements, opinions and data contained in all publications are solely those of the individual author(s) and contributor(s) and not of MDPI and/or the editor(s). MDPI and/or the editor(s) disclaim responsibility for any injury to people or property resulting from any ideas, methods, instructions or products referred to in the content.

Article

A Spatial Location Representation Method Incorporating Boundary Information

Hui Jiang [1,*] and Yukun Zhang [2]

[1] School of Intelligent Manufacturing, Huainan Union University, Huainan 232038, China
[2] School of Electrical Engineering, Anhui Polytechnic University, Wuhu 241060, China
* Correspondence: aaa-jhui@163.com

Abstract: In response to problems concerning the low autonomous localization accuracy of mobile robots in unknown environments and large cumulative errors due to long time running, a spatial location representation method incorporating boundary information (SLRB) is proposed, inspired by the mammalian spatial cognitive mechanism. In modeling the firing characteristics of boundary cells to environmental boundary information, we construct vector relationships between the mobile robot and environmental boundaries with direction-aware information and distance-aware information. The self-motion information (direction and velocity) is used as the input to the lateral anti-Hebbian network (LAHN) to generate grid cells. In addition, the boundary cell response values are used to update the grid cell distribution law and to suppress the error response of the place cells, thus reducing the localization error of the mobile robot. Meanwhile, when the mobile robot reaches the boundary cell excitation zone, the activated boundary cells are used to correct the accumulated errors that occur due to long running times, which thus improves the localization accuracy of the system. The main contributions of this paper are as follows: 1. We propose a novel method for constructing boundary cell models. 2. An approach is presented that maps the response values of boundary cells to the input layer of LAHN (Location-Adaptive Hierarchical Network), where grid cells are generated through LAHN learning rules, and the distribution pattern of grid cells is adjusted using the response values of boundary cells. 3. We correct the cumulative error caused by long-term operation of place cells through the activation of boundary cells, ensuring that only one place cell responds to the current location at each individual moment, thereby improving the positioning accuracy of the system.

Keywords: boundary cells; grid cells; place cells; environmental characterization; brain-inspired computing

1. Introduction

Environmental cognition is a fundamental skill for mammalian foraging and survival. Physiological studies have indicated that mammals, when freely moving in unfamiliar environments, are capable of maintaining relative spatial relationships to nests or food through specific cognitive mechanisms. This provides them with positional information for navigation in unfamiliar environments and enables real-time updates based on changes in external environmental cues, thus endowing them with strong perceptual abilities in unknown surroundings [1–4]. However, existing mobile robot technologies fail to utilize distance information between themselves and obstacles or walls to update their current position when facing unexpected obstacles or barriers. Therefore, investigating and replicating the environmental cognition mechanisms observed in mammals holds significant importance in enhancing the environmental cognition capabilities of mobile robots and advancing our understanding of biological environmental cognition [5–7].

In 1971, O'Keefe et al. found, in the rat hippocampus, a cell with a selective firing to spatial locations. This cell undergoes firing activity only when the rat is in a spatially specific environmental location [8]. This cell is called a place cell and its corresponding spatial firing

Citation: Jiang, H.; Zhang, Y. A Spatial Location Representation Method Incorporating Boundary Information. *Appl. Sci.* **2023**, *13*, 7929. https://doi.org/10.3390/app13137929

Academic Editors: Luis Gracia and J. Ernesto Solanes

Received: 4 June 2023
Revised: 29 June 2023
Accepted: 1 July 2023
Published: 6 July 2023

Copyright: © 2023 by the authors. Licensee MDPI, Basel, Switzerland. This article is an open access article distributed under the terms and conditions of the Creative Commons Attribution (CC BY) license (https://creativecommons.org/licenses/by/4.0/).

area is called the place field [9,10]. In 2005, Hafting et al. identified another type of cell in the entorhinal cortex of rats that produces periodic firing to specific regions of space grid cells and whose hexagonal firing fields spread throughout the spatial environment with the movement of the rat [11]. Related studies have shown that when rats move freely in a two-dimensional space, grid cells in the entorhinal cortex undergo repetitive firing behavior at specific locations; furthermore, it was noted that their firing activity is highly stable and, as rats continue to explore the environment, the generated grid cells cover the entire environment and complete the spatial representation of the environment [12–14]. Barry et al. proposed an oscillatory interference (OI) to model the hexagonal firing structure of the grid cell. In the model, the self-motion information (direction and speed) of the mobile robot was used as the input of grid cells to update and maintain the grid field [15]. However, the verification of the model remained in the simulation stage and did not realize effective map construction in the real environment. In [16], the rat simultaneous location and mapping (RatSLAM) model, which was based on a rodent model, was investigated. This model centralizes path integration information and external visual scene information into the pose cell and is able to perform navigation and map construction tasks. However, this model does not incorporate the physiological characteristics of the hippocampal structures in the rat brain, which thus leads to a lack of accuracy and a low stability with respect to this model [17]. To address the problems of the insufficient physiological characteristics of the RatSLAM method, Oliver et al. proposed a grid cell to place cell competitive neural network models in a Hebb learning algorithm, based on the phenomenon of lateral inhibition in the rat hippocampus, which conforms to the physiological characteristics of the hippocampal navigation cells and can realize the information transfer and can also map from grid cells to place cells [18]. Yu Naigong et al. similarly used the Hebb learning algorithm in the work of constructing environmental cognitive maps by imitating the hippocampal cognitive mechanism in the rat brain. They also implemented the environmental cognitive map construction through a real physical platform and obtained better experimental results [19]. O'Keefe et al. found that the size of the place cell firing field changes somewhat when the rat moves to the environmental boundary; to explain this phenomenon in their experiments, O'Keefe et al. predicted the existence of a cell in the rat brain that responds to boundary information with a firing response and is able to use this response to correct for position errors in the position of the place cell [20]. In 2008, researchers discovered a new cell type in the rat internal olfactory cortex that fires when the animal approaches a wall or is separated by other obstacles; this new cell type was accordingly named boundary cells [21,22]. In order to investigate the effect of boundary cells on the distribution and localization accuracy of grid cells, Hardcastle et al. replaced the circular environment with a hexagonal environment that was rich in environmental boundary information. Furthermore, the grid cell distribution was rearranged, and the localization accuracy was improved [23].

Based on this, a spatial location representation method (SLRB) incorporating boundary information was proposed, inspired by the mammalian spatial cognitive mechanism, which obtains the boundary cell response values through the mutual excitation and inhibition of direction-aware information, as well as the distance-aware information between the mobile robot and the environment boundary. This method obtains the boundary cell response values by mutual excitation and through the suppression of direction and distance-sensing information between the mobile robot and the environment boundary. The method then maps the boundary cell response values and the self-motion information of the mobile robot to the input layer of LAHN, and then the output layer of LAHN is mapped to the grid cell response values. The grid cell response values are used as the main input source of the place cells and the response values of the place cells are obtained through the competitive Hebb learning network. At the same time, when the mobile robot runs to the boundary cell excitation zone through the activated boundary cells to correct the location information of the place cells, the mobile robot then learns and remembers the location points in a specific space, as well as constructs a spatial location representation map that can accurately express the current spatial characteristics. A block diagram of the overall system structure is shown in Figure 1.

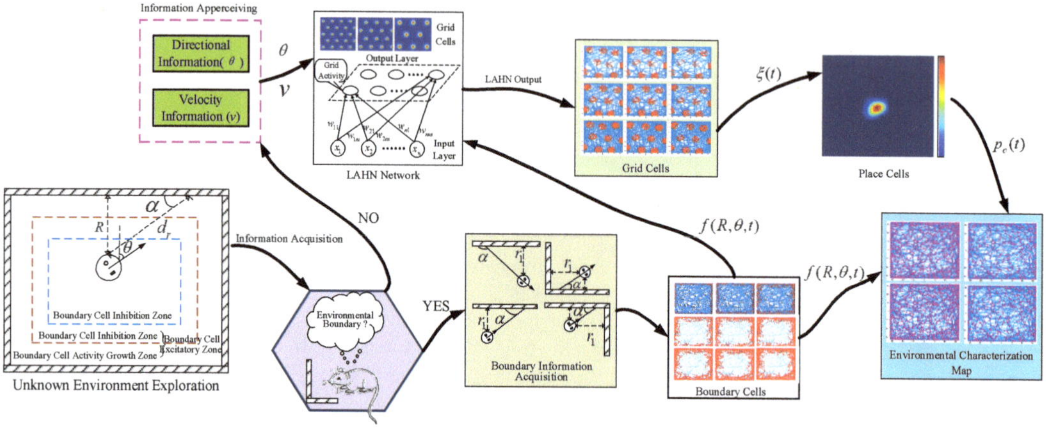

Figure 1. Block diagram of the overall system structure.

The main innovations of this paper are as follows:

(1) Inspired by the mammalian spatial cognitive mechanism, a new boundary cell model is proposed to establish boundary cell activity states in multiple scenarios by the mutual excitation and the inhibition of the direction-aware and distance-aware information that is acquired by mobile robots. The boundary cell model proposed in this paper can encode the boundary information in the environment and supplement the lack of environmental boundary perceptual information with path integration.

(2) The physiological phenomena indicate that the environmental boundary information can be used as the supplementary information of grid cells. The method in this paper maps the boundary cell response values to the input layer of LAHN, generates grid cells by LAHN learning rules, and uses the boundary cell response values to correct the grid cell distribution pattern, such that the grid cell firing response and distribution that is activated by the method are more consistent with the physiological characteristics.

(3) According to the problem that the mobile robot runs for a long time in an unknown environment, when the mobile robot reaches the boundary cell excitation zone, the accumulated error caused by the long running time of the position cell is corrected by the activated boundary cells, such that only one place cell responds to the current position at each time in order to improve the location accuracy of the system.

2. Spatial Navigation Cell Model

2.1. Boundary Cell Modeling

The boundary cells, which mainly exist in the entorhinal cortex, presubiculum, and parasubiculum tract of the rat hippocampus, are spatial navigation cells that respond to boundary information and can reflect the relative positions of rats at different distances and angles from the environmental boundary by encoding boundary information in the environment; these cells can be used to complement path integration information [24–26]. In this paper, the boundary cells are modeled by the mutual excitation and inhibition of direction-aware and distance-aware information of the mobile robot, and the construction process is shown below.

Step 1: The mobile robot explores in an unknown environment (its exploration schematic diagram is shown in Figure 2). The surrounding shaded part is the wall, the circular runner is the mobile robot, and the single black arrow is its movement direction.

The boundary response constant is set to divide the exploration area into the boundary cell activity inhibition zone, the attenuation zone, and the growth zone. The region division rules are as follows:

$$S(t) = \begin{cases} S_{inh}, & if\ R(t) > b \\ S_{excar}, & if\ b/2 < R(t) \leq b \\ S_{excgr}, & if\ R(t) \leq b/2 \end{cases} \quad (1)$$

where $S(t)$ denotes the region in which the mobile robot is located at the time t, b represents the boundary response constant, S_{excar} and S_{excgr} denotes the mobile robot is in the boundary cell inhibition zone, the attenuation zone, and the growth zone, respectively. Furthermore, the boundary cell activity attenuation zone and growth zone are subsets of the boundary cell excitation zone.

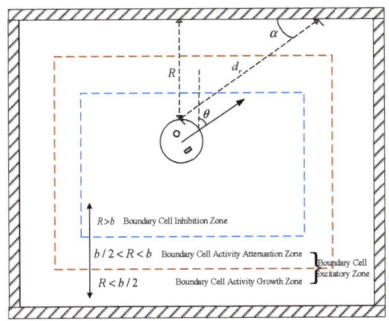

Figure 2. Schematic diagram of the mobile robot exploration in the environment.

Step 2: The mobile robot scenes are divided into six scenarios in the environment, as shown in Figure 3. Scenarios A and C depict the mobile robot moving towards and away from a wall, respectively. Scenarios B and D represent movements away from and towards a corner, respectively. Scenarios E and F illustrate movements away from and towards a curved wall, respectively. Where the shaded parts are walls and where the mobile robot updates the perceptual information during its movement:

$$\theta(t+1) = \theta(t) + \theta_s(t)T \quad (2)$$

$$[R(t), d_r(t)] = [\min(r_1(t), r_2(t) \cdots r_n(t)), \min(d_r(t), 50)] \quad (3)$$

$$\alpha = \gamma \arctan \frac{R(t)}{d_r(t)} - (\gamma - 1)(\pi - \arctan \frac{R(t)}{d_r(t)}) \quad (4)$$

where θ is the direction-aware information of the mobile robot, θ_s is the angular velocity-aware information of the mobile robot, and T is the sampling period. In this paper, it is set as 0.01 s, which represents the data collected by the mobile robot updated every 0.01 s, R is the distance-aware information of the mobile robot to the nearest environmental boundary, d_r is the distance-aware information between the current position and the environmental boundary directly in front of the mobile robot, r is the vertical distance between the mobile robot and the environmental boundary, and n is the number of environmental boundaries currently detected by the mobile robot. α is the angle information between the mobile robot and the nearest surrounding environmental boundary, γ is the regulatory factor of the angle information, and γ takes the value of 1 only when the robot's direction of motion is perpendicular to the wall—otherwise it takes the value of 0.

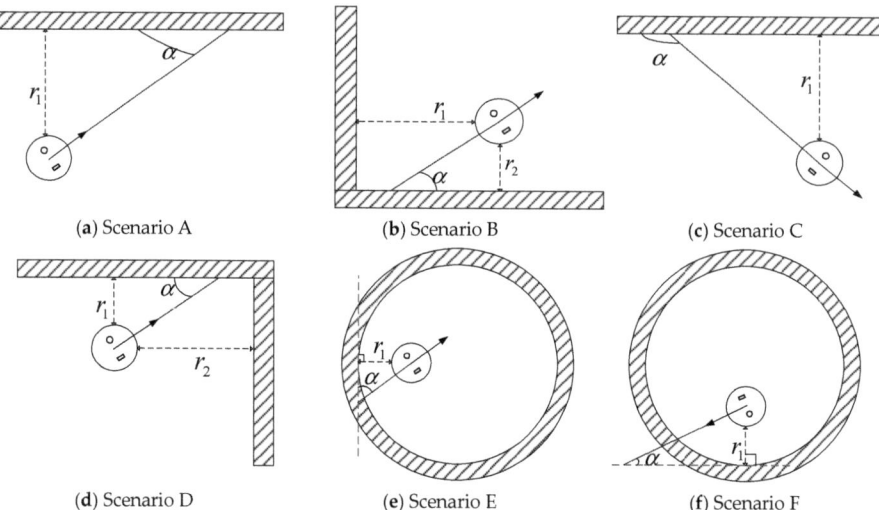

Figure 3. Diagram of the six scenarios of mobile robots in the environment.

When the mobile robot moves away from the wall, the boundary cells go through two processes, the activity growth zone and the attenuation zone. When they then reach the boundary cell inhibition zone their activity attenuates to zero. The rules for updating the activity state of boundary cell neurons are as follows:

$$h(t+1) = \begin{cases} h(t) + \tau \frac{b - d_r(t)}{b}, & if\ S(t) = S_{excgr} \\ 0, & if\ S(t) = S_{inh} \\ \left[h(t) - \tau \frac{b - d_r(t)}{b}\right]_+, & if\ S(t) = S_{excar} \end{cases} \quad (5)$$

where $h(t)$ is the current time boundary cell activity value, $h(t+1)$ is the next time boundary cell activity value, and τ is the activity factor (which is used to regulate the rate of change in boundary cell neuron activity and the value of 0.8 is taken for this factor in this paper). $[\bullet]_+$ indicates that the output value is non-negative.

Step 3: When the mobile robot runs into the boundary cell excitation zone, the boundary cell distance excitation value $b_{border}(t)$ is updated with the distance-aware information between the current position of the mobile robot and the environmental boundary.

$$b_{border}(t) = \exp\left(-\frac{h(t)(R(t) - d_r(t))^2}{2\sigma_{rad}^2 (d_r(t))}\right) \quad (6)$$

where $\sigma_{rad}(\bullet)$ is the boundary cell distance sensitivity function and the relationship between the sensitivity of the boundary cell to the environmental boundary. Moreover, the vertical distance from the mobile robot to the environmental boundary is expressed as per the following:

$$\sigma_{rad}(d_r(t)) = \delta_0 * (d_r(t)/\beta + 1) \quad (7)$$

where δ_0 is the boundary cell sensitivity enhancement constant, which is adapted to the complexity of the environmental boundary and which is set to 1.2 in this paper. β is the boundary cell distance perception correction factor, which avoids the boundary cell response value being too large due to the small distance information that is detected in the small environmental scenarios and which is taken as 0.8 in this paper.

Subsequently, the boundary cell angular excitation value $r_{border}(t)$ is updated based on the angular-aware information between the mobile robot and environmental boundary:

$$r_{border}(t) = \exp\left(-\frac{h(t)(\theta(t) - \alpha(t))^2}{2\sigma_{ang}^2}\right) \quad (8)$$

where σ_{ang} is the adjustment parameter for the angular excitation value of the boundary cell, which is used to regulate the effect of angle on the excitation value of the border cell, and is taken as 0.5 in this paper.

Step 4: The boundary cell response value is updated by the boundary cell distance excitation value and angular excitation value, and the boundary cell fire response $f(R, \theta, t)$ in the spatial environment is shown as per the following:

$$f(R, \theta, t) = \frac{b_{border}(t) \times r_{border}(t)}{\sqrt{2\pi\sigma_{rad}^2(d_r(t))}\sqrt{2\pi\sigma_{ang}^2}} \quad (9)$$

The rats explored freely in the experimental environment and the strain response was different from the environmental scene information, which were collected at different times. The six different boundary cell activation response maps in Figure 4 correspond one by one to the six different experimental scenarios in Figure 3, with the pentagram position as the starting point in Figure 4. As shown in Figure 4a, during the process of a rat running towards a wall, it gradually transitions from the boundary cell inhibition zone to the boundary cell activation zone, resulting in an increase in the number of activated boundary cells. Particularly when entering the boundary cell growth zone, the number of boundary cells rapidly rises. In the boundary cell decay zone, the number of boundary cells decreases accordingly. When reaching the boundary cell inhibition zone, the boundary cells will not be activated. In Figure 4b, the rat is currently moving away from the environmental boundary and the boundary cell activation frequency thus gradually decreases (i.e., the number of boundary cell activation increases slowly). The current movement posture of the rat in Figure 4c corresponds to Figure 3d, thereby showing a tendency to move away from the environmental corners and showing a gradual decrease in the boundary cell activation frequency. The transient movement posture of the rat shown in Figure 4d is similar to that in Figure 4c, but unlike Figure 4c, the rat is away from the corner of the environment at this time, and the binding force of the environment unilaterally on the movement of the rat decreases rapidly as the distance of the rat away from the boundary increases; as such, the number of boundary cell activations temporarily enters a low-rate growth phase. Similarly, the same is shown in Figure 4e,f, which show the boundary cell activation response maps of the rats in different scenarios, where the response maps are acquired by movement in a circular experimental environment, thereby corresponding to rats that are near and far from the environmental boundary in Figure 3e,f, respectively.

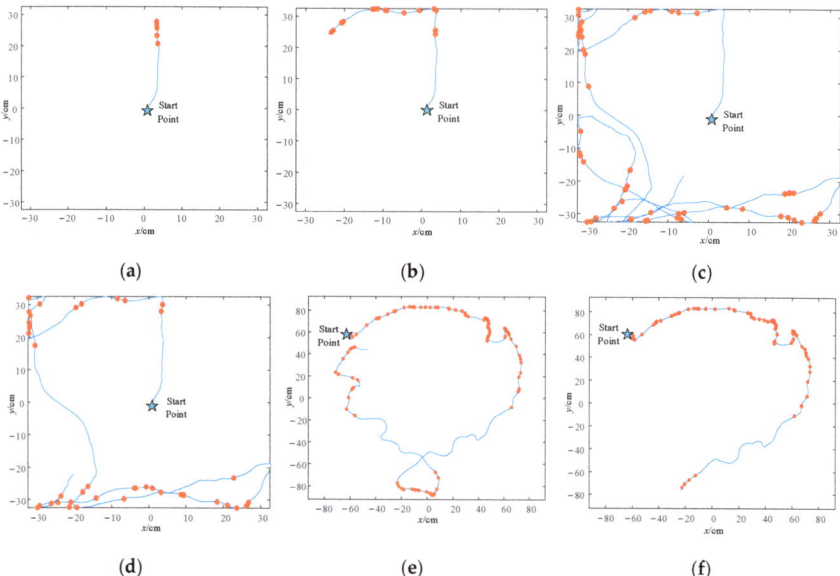

Figure 4. Activated boundary cells in different scenarios. (**a**) Activated boundary cells under scenario A. (**b**) Activated boundary cells under scenario B. (**c**) Activated boundary cells under scenario C. (**d**) Activated boundary cells under scenario D. (**e**) Activated boundary cells under scenario E. (**f**) Activated boundary cells under scenario F.

2.2. Grid Cell Update Model Based on Boundary Information

LAHN is designed as an unsupervised neural network that can obtain the best features from the input information [27]. The superiority of this network is also reflected in the fact that when the input information is limited by the external environment, the network itself can still update the output in real time by adjusting the lateral connections to adapt to the environmental changes [28]. When considering the influence of environmental boundary information on the distribution pattern of grid cells during the movement of the rat, LAHN is introduced in this paper to model the grid cell update mechanism. The self-motion information and boundary cell response values acquired by the encoder are mapped to the input layer of LAHN during the exploration of the environment by the mobile robot, while the excitation level and inhibition level of the grid cells are updated in real time with the movement of the mobile robot. The update rules of this are as follows:

$$\frac{d\left(\chi_j^{inh}\right)}{dt} = -\chi_j^{exc}\left[f(R,\theta) + vw\begin{bmatrix}\cos(\theta_s)\\ \sin(\theta_s)\end{bmatrix}\right] + \chi_j^{inh}\left[1 - \left(\chi_j^{inh\,2} + \chi_j^{exc\,2}\right)\right] \quad (10)$$

$$\frac{d\left(\chi_j^{exc}\right)}{dt} = \chi_j^{inh}\left[f(R,\theta) + vw\begin{bmatrix}\cos(\theta_s)\\ \sin(\theta_s)\end{bmatrix}\right] + \chi_j^{exc}\left[1 - \left(\chi_j^{inh\,2} + \chi_j^{exc\,2}\right)\right] \quad (11)$$

where θ_s is the angular velocity-aware information and W is the self-organizing mapping input weight matrix, θ represents the directional sensory information of the mobile robot. v is the current velocity of the mobile robot, where the value of χ_j^{inh} is a negative number indicating the inhibition level of the j-th grid cell. The value of χ_j^{exc} is a positive number indicating the j-th grid cell excitation level and $f(R,\theta)$ is the boundary cell response value.

LAHN uses a bipolar activation function and the dependent variable of the activation function takes values from -1 to 1, which is when the input and output of the activation function have the same sign and where the network connection weight is increased, otherwise the network connection weight is instead decreased. The network output value is the grid cell response value and the LAHN output value is shown in Equation (12):

$$\zeta_i(t) = \sum_{j=1}^{m} q_{ij}[\chi_j^{exc}(t) + \chi_j^{inh}(t)] + \sum_{k=1}^{n} w_{ik}\zeta_k(t-1) \quad (12)$$

where q_{ij} is the forward channel weight, w_{ik} is the lateral channel weight, $\zeta_k(t-1)$ is the grid cell response value at the previous time, m is the total number of neurons in the LAHN layer, and n is the number of grid cells.

The grid cell distribution maps and their corresponding grid cell firing rate maps were obtained by exploring in the trilateral, pentagonal, and nine-sided environments, respectively, as shown in Figure 5a,c. The control analysis shows that the grid cell clusters converge with the highest firing rate in the center, decreasing layer by layer toward the periphery. In this paper, we introduced the grid cell scoring mechanism, which is shown in Equations (13) and (14) [29–31]. This mechanism was constructed to score the distribution and activity of the grid cells that are obtained in the three different environments. This mechanism also allowed us to generate a grid cell score table, which is shown in Table 1. The trends of the grid cell scores in the three different environments showed that the grid cell scores gradually increased and eventually stabilized as the exploration time increased. This pattern of data change is due to the positive effect of the boundary cells that was activated by the rats visiting the boundary of the environment, which thus updated the grid cell distribution. The reason for the higher grid cell scores, which were obtained by exploring the nine-sided environment rather than the pentagonal and trilateral ones, is explained by the fact that the nine-sided environment provides richer boundary information.

$$r(\tau_x, \tau_y) = \frac{n\sum_{x,y}\lambda(x,y)\lambda(x-\tau_x, y-\tau_y) - \sum_{x,y}\lambda(x,y)\sum_{x,y}\lambda(x-\tau_x, y-\tau_y)}{\sqrt{\left[M\sum_{x,y}\lambda(x,y)^2 - \left[\sum_{x,y}\lambda(x,y)\right]^2\right]\left[n\sum_{x,y}\lambda(x-\tau_x, y-\tau_y)^2 - [\lambda(x-\tau_x, y-\tau_y)]^2\right]}} \quad (13)$$

$$HGS = \min\left[\cor\left(r, r^{60°}\right), \cor\left(r, r^{120°}\right)\right] - \max\left[\cor\left(r, r^{30°}\right), \cor\left(r, r^{90°}\right), \cor\left(r, r^{150°}\right)\right] \quad (14)$$

where n is the number of grid cells, HGS is the fraction of grid cells, r is the auto-correlation plot of grid cells, and $\lambda(x,y)$ is the firing rate of grid cells at position. Furthermore, τ_x and τ_y are the spatial lag coordinates corresponding to the x and y coordinates, and r^β is the auto-correlation plot rotated by β degrees. $\cor(r, r^\beta)$ is the correlation score of the auto-correlation plot r and the correlation score of the two plots after rotating the auto-correlation plot by β degrees.

Table 1. Grid cell scores in different geometric environments.

Time (s)	30	60	90	120	150	180	210	240	270	300	330	360
Trilateral environment	0.25	0.32	0.38	0.45	0.55	0.56	0.68	0.69	0.74	0.73	0.74	0.74
Pentagonal environment	0.24	0.35	0.41	0.51	0.62	0.68	0.72	0.75	0.78	0.78	0.78	0.78
Nine-sided environment	0.20	0.34	0.40	0.49	0.58	0.71	0.80	0.84	0.86	0.84	0.85	0.85

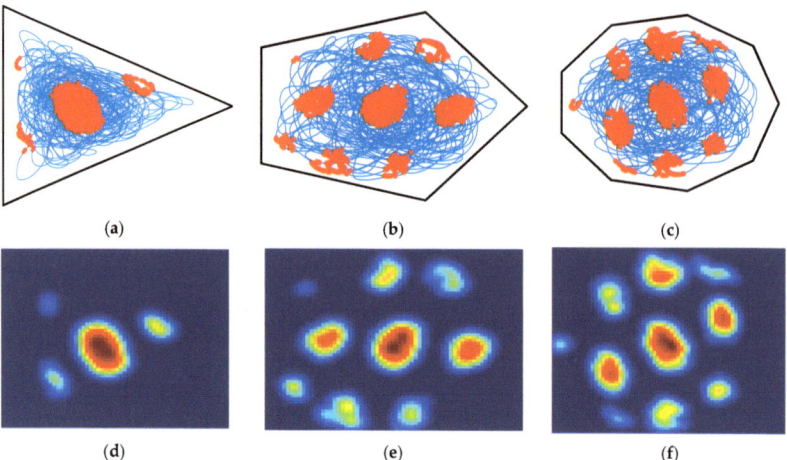

Figure 5. Cell distribution and firing rate in different geometric environments. (**a**) Cell distribution in a trigonal environment. (**b**) Cell distribution in a pentagonal environment. (**c**) Cell distribution in a nine-sided environment. (**d**) Cell firing rate in a trilateral environment. (**e**) Cell firing rate in a pentagonal environment. (**f**) Cell firing rate in a nine-sided environment.

3. Spatial Location Representation Map Construction

Based on the physiological properties of each the navigation cells mentioned above, it is known that boundary cells can fire specifically in response to the perception of the environmental boundary by the rat, i.e., the vectorial relationship between the rat and the boundary. Furthermore, the closer the rat is to the environmental boundary, the greater the value of the boundary cell firing response [32]. Grid cells are considered as a coordinate system for characterizing the environment due to their specific spatial metric properties, and when multiple grid cells fire aggregately the current position of the rat can be estimated [33,34]. A process schematic diagram of constructing a spatial location representation map, using the specific firing responses of these navigation cells and their mapping relationships with each other, is shown in Figure 6. The specific map construction steps are as follows:

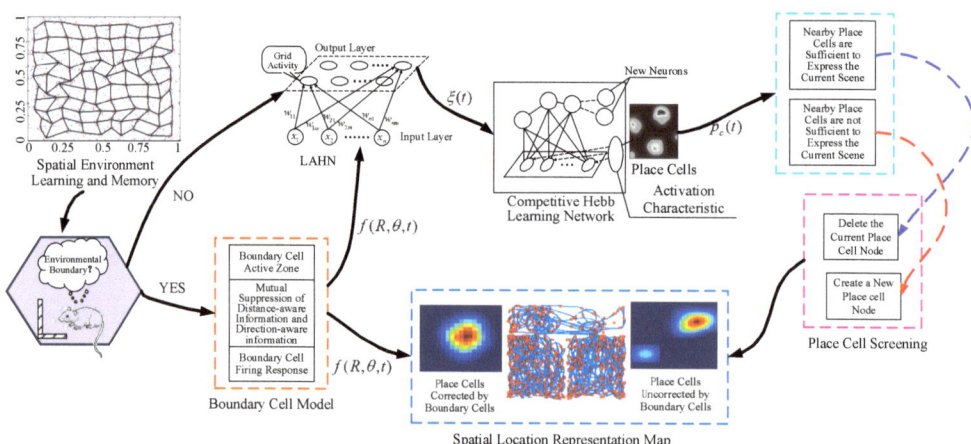

Figure 6. Schematic diagram of the spatial location representation map construction.

Step 1: As the mobile robot explores the environment, it collects the speed, direction, and distance-aware information needed to construct a spatial location representation map.

Step 2: The inputs of the direction and velocity-aware information to the input layer of LAHN are conducted. The output of the grid cell response value is obtained after the learning performed by LAHN.

Step 3: Grid cells undergo a competitive Hebb learning network in order to generate place cells that are capable of representing current location information [18]. The mobile robot explores the environment by continuously activating new place cells in response to new location scenarios and jointly constructs a spatial location cell representation map until the robot stops running. The algorithm for the construction of the spatial location representation map is shown in detail in Algorithm 1.

In order to avoid the undesirable situation where the number of place cell activations for the same scene is too many due to the small place cell spacing in the operation of the mobile robot (thus resulting in the waste of system computational resources) or the undesirable situation where the place cell spacing is too large (thus resulting in the poor accuracy of position estimation), this paper introduces the place cell distance threshold r_{th} in order to constrain the place cell activation response. Figure 7 shows the box plot of the localization accuracy of the mobile robot when constructing the spatial location representation map under different values of r_{th}. The localization error in Figure 7 fluctuates upward with the distance threshold, and the localization error is minimized when r_{th} is taken as 0.06 m, such that r_{th} is taken as 0.06 m in this paper.

Algorithm 1: Spatial location representation map construction algorithm

Input: Grid cell response value, place cell distance threshold r_{th}
Output: Spatial Location Representation Map
BEGIN:
FOR
Get grid cell response values
Updating winning place cells through competitive Hebb learning network
Calculate the Euclidean distance r_b between Current place cell and nearby place cell
    IF $r_b < r_{th}$
        The previous place cell can represent the current scene, continue run forward
        ELSE
        The previous palace cell is not enough to represent the current scene and construct a new place cell
    END IF
    IF the movement is not over
        Continue forward motion and update grid cell response value information
        ELSE
Output spatial location representation map
END IF
ND FOR

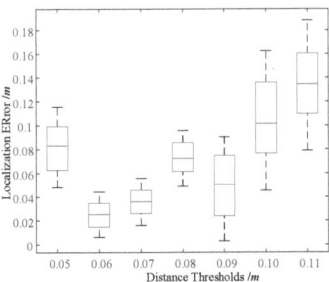

Figure 7. Comparison of the localization errors under different distance thresholds.

Step 4: When the mobile robot runs to the boundary cell excitation zone, the distance-aware information and angle-aware information of the mobile robot are relative to the environment boundary. They are mutually excited and inhibited in order to activate the boundary cells, which are used to correct the place cell response values and to eliminate the accumulated errors that are generated due to the long time running of the mobile robot. At the same time, the boundary cell response values are mapped to the input layer of LAHN, and the grid cell distribution law in the current scene is updated simultaneously. The place cell correction update rules are as follows:

$$p_{bc}(t) = \left[p_c(t) + \left(\prod_{i=1}^{n} f_i(R, \theta, t) / \max_x \right)^{\frac{1}{n}} \right]_+ \quad (15)$$

where $f_i(R, \theta, t)$ is the boundary cell firing response value, $p_{bc}(t)$ is the place cell response value after the boundary cell response correction, and $p_c(t)$ is the place cell response value before the boundary cell response correction. n represents the number of boundary cells. $[\bullet]_+$ indicates that the output value is non-negative.

Figure 8a depicts the pre-correction place cell response map, revealing the presence of an accumulated error resulting from prolonged operation of the mobile robot. This error is evident in the place cell response map, where a single place cell fails to generate a response to the current position. In Figure 8b, the post-correction position cell response map is presented. The comparison with Figure 8a demonstrates that the corrected place cell response map exhibits a solitary, distinct place cell response point, thereby enhancing the accuracy of current position estimation by eliminating interference caused by redundant place cell responses.

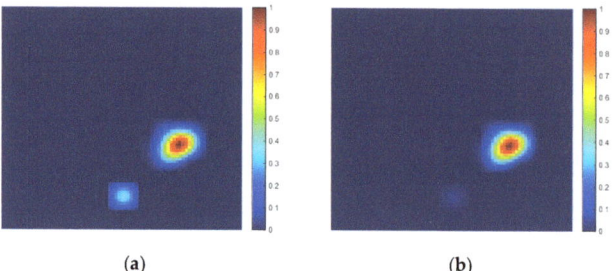

Figure 8. Place cell response maps. (**a**) Place cells corrected by boundary cells. (**b**) Place cells uncorrected by boundary cells.

4. Experimental Results and Analysis

The computer configuration used to test the experiments in this paper was as follows: i5-9400F CPU, 6-core processor, 2.9 GHz, 8 GB RAM. The method proposed in this paper was verified by the circular experimental datasets that were published in the Microstructure of a spatial map in the entorhinal cortex, published by Hafting et al. in Nature [11]. These datasets record the perceptual information, such as the movement direction, as well as the speed and distance of the rats at different times.

4.1. Boundary Cell Simulation Experiments

This paper further validates the method of this study using a larger Hafting circular experiment environment. The diameter of the circular experiment environment is 2 m and the rat also starts from the center of the experiment environment for the purposes of free exploration learning. The environmental plan diagram and the trajectory formed by the rat in completing the exploration are shown in Figure 9.

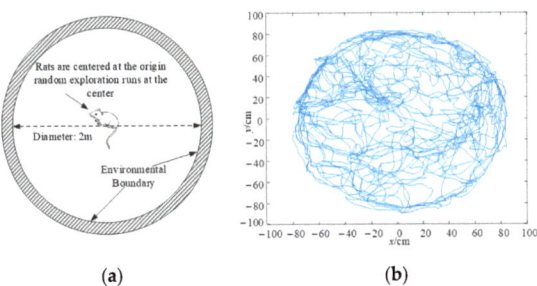

Figure 9. The environmental plan diagram and rat trajectory map. (**a**) The environmental plan diagram. (**b**) The rat trajectory map.

Figure 10 shows the intercepted boundary cell discharge response plots at different times. It can be seen that as the rat explores the environmental boundary gradually and comprehensively, the number of activated boundary cells in response to the environmental boundary increases. Table 2 shows the correlation data between the number of activated boundary cells and the mean localization error at different times. It can be seen that the number of activated boundary cells tends to increase rapidly before 1600 s, while after 1600 s, the number of activated boundary cells gradually slows down and stabilizes as the rat explores the environment more fully. At 1800 s, the activated boundary cells can adequately represent the environmental boundary and its number remains largely unchanged while the localization error is stable at about 0.037 m. It can be seen that the proposed method in this paper is also well adapted to larger circular environments.

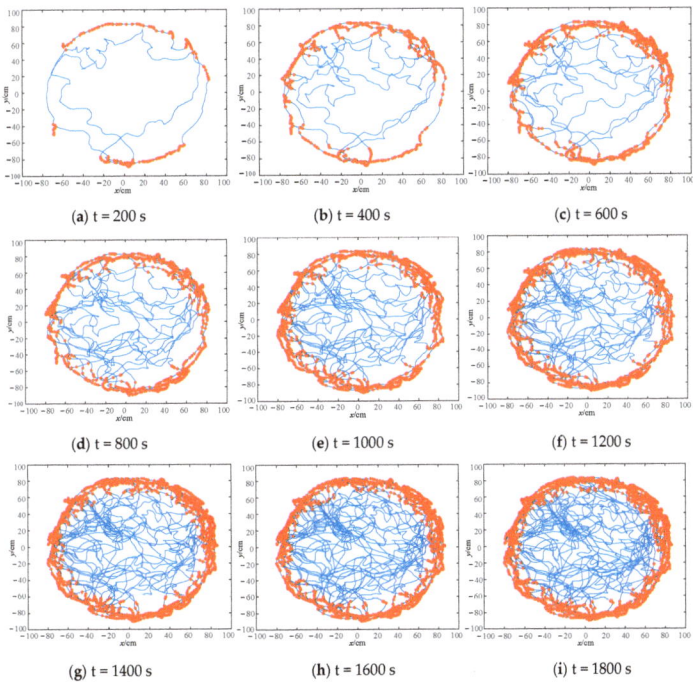

Figure 10. The boundary cell response maps at different times.

Table 2. The number of activated boundary cells at different times with the mean localization error.

Time (s)	200	400	600	800	1000	1200	1400	1600	1800
Number of boundary cells (pcs)	103	195	274	318	378	421	472	503	498
Mean localization error (m)	0.67	0.71	0.83	0.86	0.74	0.61	0.50	0.39	0.37

4.2. Grid Cell Simulation Experiment

The grid cell construction method proposed in this paper was validated by the Hafting circular experimental environment. Figure 11 shows the grid cell response maps obtained by the OI model, the CAN model, and the SLRB method at different times. The distribution of grid cells activated by the OI model after 30 min lacked physiological properties. In comparison, the grid cell distribution acquired by the CAN model has been improved, but the acquired grid cell clusters contain too many grid cells, posing a potential risk of computational time consumption for the construction of large-scale spatial location representation maps. Compared with the former two, the method in this paper obtained the vector information between the rat and the environment boundary, which was obtained by the rat in the process of exploring the environment and was performed to correct the grid cell distribution pattern. This meant that the method in this paper successfully achieved the goal of representing a circular experimental environment with fewer grid cells while maintaining the physiological characteristics of grid cells. Table 3 shows the number of activated grid cells and their corresponding grid cell fractions for the three compared methods in characterizing the above circular experimental setting. It is more intuitive to see from the data comparison of the three algorithms that the number of grid cells utilized by this method is lower. This was achieved under the premise of also achieving the purpose of characterizing the environment. Moreover, the fraction of the grid cells generated by this method is higher as the environment is gradually explored completely, which indicates that the grid cells activated by this method are highly active and reasonably distributed.

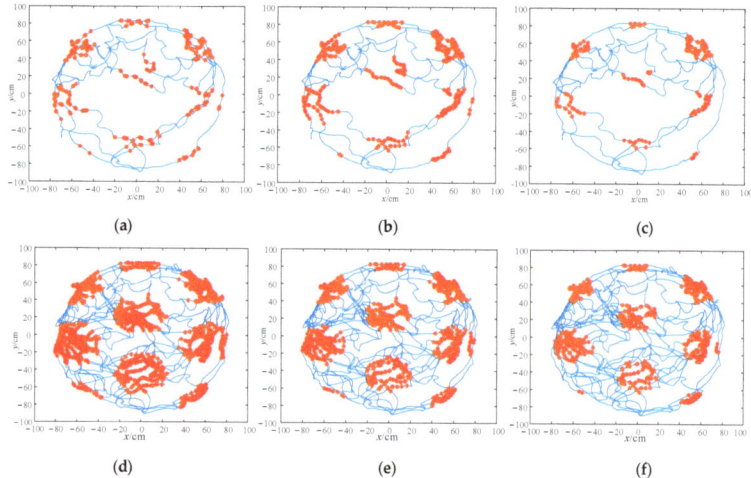

Figure 11. *Cont.*

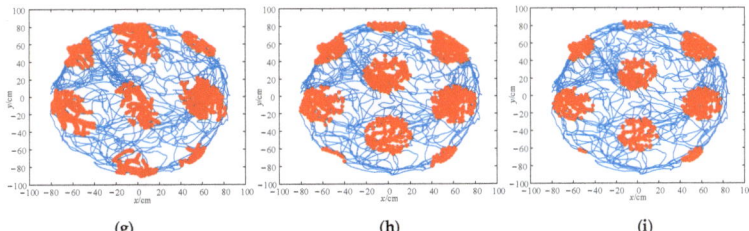

(g) (h) (i)

Figure 11. The grid cell response maps obtained by the OI and CAN models, as well as those obtained by the method used in this paper at different times. (**a**) 5 min for the OI model to obtain results. (**b**) 5 min for the CAN model to obtain results. (**c**) 5 min for this paper's method to obtain results. (**d**) 15 min for the OI model to obtain results. (**e**) 15 min for the CAN model to obtain results. (**f**) 15 min for this paper's method to obtain results. (**g**) 30 min for the OI model to obtain results. (**h**) 30 min for the CAN model to obtain results. (**i**) 30 min for this paper's method to obtain results.

Table 3. Comparison of the grid cell properties that were activated by the three algorithms.

Exploration Time (min)	Number of Activated Grid Cells (pcs)			Grid Cell Fraction		
	OI	CAN	SLRB	OI	CAN	SLRB
5	171	160	128	0.71	0.75	0.74
10	382	171	165	0.73	0.74	0.69
15	410	290	195	0.68	0.79	0.79
20	472	353	287	0.54	0.71	0.84
25	524	427	354	0.51	0.72	0.88
30	614	541	478	0.43	0.65	0.86

4.3. Spatial Location Representation Map Construction Experiment

The place cell properties obtained by the method in this paper were validated in a Hafting circular experimental environment. Figure 12 shows the firing response maps of the pose/place cells to the current location as acquired by RatSLAM, as well as by the competing Hebb learning networks and the method used in this paper at different times. In addition, the maps of their spatial location representations are generated after completing the environmental exploration. The RatSLAM method still did not perform well in the circular environment because the RatSLAM algorithm only integrated the rat's self-motion information to activate the pose cells in response to the rat's current location, without exhaustively considering the effect of the simple similarity boundaries on the firing pattern of the pose cells. At the same time, along with the increase in the environmental scene, the growth of the exploration time response leads to a gradual increase in the accumulated error, which renders the RatSLAM method unable to generate a single pose cell by which to respond accurately to the current location. Compared with the RatSLAM method, the competitive Hebb learning network can adjust the response values of the place cells via the connection weights between the place cells, which enables the system to maintain a better localization performance at the early stage of unknown environment explorations. However, as the exploration proceeds and the environment itself is characterized, the number of place cells gradually increases and the burden of adjusting the connection weights between the place cells increases, thus leading to the overlapping phenomenon of place cell responses, which then affects the accuracy of localization. In order to overcome the negative effects of environmental size and cumulative errors, this method introduces environmental boundary information to correct the place cell firing responses in real time, such that only one place cell responds to the current location at each individual time. By removing the interference of the other place cell firing responses, the accuracy of the location information estimation of this method is improved.

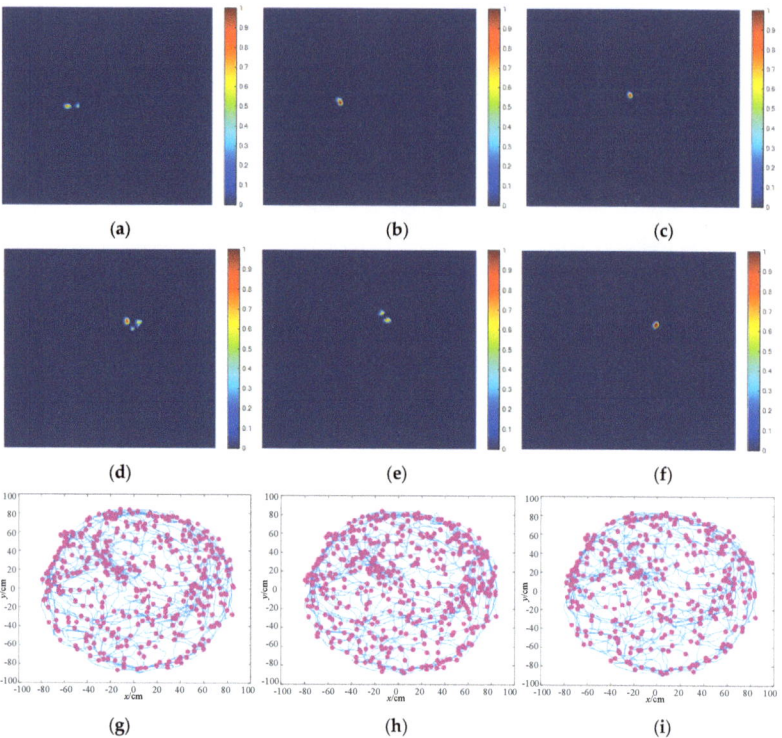

Figure 12. The process of constructing the spatial location representation maps by the three methods. (**a**) 5 min for the RatSLAM method to obtain results. (**b**) 5 min for the competitive Hebb learning network to obtain results. (**c**) 5 min for this paper's method to obtain results. (**d**) 30 min for the RatSLAM method to obtain results. (**e**) 30 min for the competitive Hebb learning network to obtain results. (**f**) 30 min for this paper's method to obtain results. (**g**) The RatSLAM spatial location representation map. (**h**) The competitive Hebb Learning network spatial location representation map. (**i**) The SLRB method spatial location representation map.

Figure 13 shows a comparison of the experimental data that was generated by the three methods for constructing spatial location representation maps. From Figure 13a, it can be seen that the number of place cells activated by all three methods in the early stage of the environmental information exploration grew rapidly with time, but with the completion of the environmental learning in the rats, the growth of grid cells in this method entered a stable interval after 20 min. Furthermore, the final number was stabilized at about 300, which was reduced by about half when compared with the other two methods. In terms of the absolute trajectory error shown in Figure 13b, the absolute trajectory error of the method in this paper at the end of the run is about 0.031 m, which is about 47.2% lower when compared to the competitive Hebb learning network and about 56.9% lower when compared to the RatSLAM algorithm. Additionally, in terms of the whole exploring time, the method in this paper shows a good performance in terms of the location estimation.

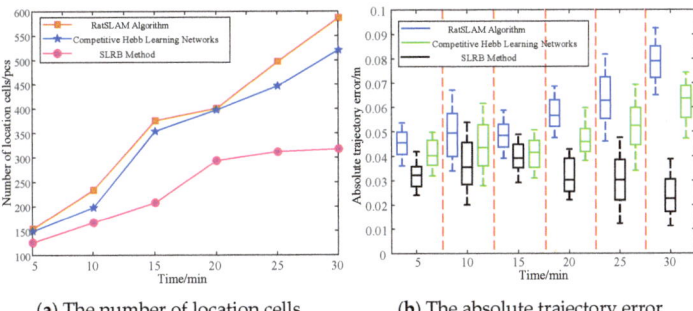

(a) The number of location cells (b) The absolute trajectory error

Figure 13. Comparison of the performance of the three methods in terms of their spatial location representation maps.

5. Analysis and Discussion

Discussion 1: Experiments on Activated Boundary Cells in Different Scenarios

In the experiments involving activated boundary cells in different scenarios, as the rat runs facing a wall, the number of activated boundary cells gradually increases, transitioning from the inhibition zone of boundary cells to the region of increased activity. When the rat moves away from the environmental boundary, the activation frequency of boundary cells gradually decreases (with a slower growth rate in the number of activated boundary cells). When the rat's motion corresponds to Figure 3d, exhibiting a trend of moving away from the environmental corner, the activation frequency of boundary cells gradually decreases. In an instantaneous motion similar to Figure 3d but with the difference that the rat is moving away from the environmental corner, and the restraining force from the environment decreases rapidly as the rat moves further from the boundary, the number of activated boundary cells temporarily enters a stage of slow growth. It can be observed that the activated boundary cells in different scenarios exhibit similar patterns as shown in Figure 4 (Activated Boundary Cells in Different Scenarios), aligning with the physiological observations. Furthermore, from the boundary cell response graphs at different time points in Figure 10, it can be observed that the proposed model can effectively model the boundary cells based on boundary information, regardless of the square or circular environment. As indicated by the boundary cell discharge response graphs captured at different time points in Figure 10, with the rat's comprehensive exploration of the environmental boundary, the number of activated boundary cells responding to the boundary continuously increases. Before 1600 s, the number of activated boundary cells exhibits a rapid increase, while after 1600 s, with the rat's comprehensive exploration of the environment, the growth rate of the number of activated boundary cells gradually slows down, approaching stability. At 1800 s, the activated boundary cells sufficiently represent the environmental boundary, and the number of activated boundary cells remains relatively stable, while the localization error stabilizes at around 0.37 m. This demonstrates the adaptability of the proposed method to larger circular environments, validating the effectiveness of the algorithm presented in this paper.

Discussion 2: Validation Experiment on the Public Hafting Dataset

The method proposed in this paper is validated using the square experiment dataset and the circular experiment dataset published by Hafting et al. in their paper "Microstructure of a spatial map in the entorhinal cortex" in Nature. The obtained position cell responses from the method proposed in this paper are compared with the position cell responses obtained from the competitive Hebbian learning network and the pose cell discharge response map obtained from RatSLAM. The RatSLAM algorithm only integrates self-motion information from the rat to activate pose cell responses at its current location, without fully considering the influence of simple geometric boundary cues on the discharge patterns of pose cells. Additionally, with the increase in exploration time response and the growing environmental scene, cumulative errors gradually accumulate, resulting in RatSLAM's inability to generate a single pose cell that accurately responds to the current location. Compared to RatSLAM, the competitive Hebbian learning network can adjust the response values of position cells through the connection weights between them, enabling the system to maintain good localization performance in the early stages of exploration in unknown environments. However, as exploration progresses and due to the characteristics of the overall environment, the number of position cells increases, and the burden of adjusting connection weights between position cells increases, leading to overlap in their response patterns and consequently affecting the accuracy of localization. The proposed method in this paper activates boundary cells when encountering boundaries, and the correction function of boundary cells on position cells enables real-time updating and constraint of position cell discharge responses, reducing position estimation uncertainty, and thereby improving the localization accuracy of the proposed method. At the end of the operation, the absolute trajectory error of the proposed method is approximately 0.031m, which is about 47.2% lower than that of the competitive Hebbian learning network, and about 56.9% lower than that of the RatSLAM algorithm.

6. Conclusions

In this paper, based on the understanding of the physiological properties of various spatial navigation cells and their role in autonomous navigation and localization, a spatial location representation method incorporating boundary information is proposed in order to construct a map of the unknown environment. The method improves the accuracy of autonomous localization and the robustness of map construction by activating the learning and memory of the spatial location of the unknown environment by navigation cells. The method presented in this paper belongs to an exploration of the mechanism of the brain operations that occur during the mammalian process of localization and map construction. It lays the foundation for further research on bionic localization and navigation algorithms for mobile robots. However, the method proposed in this paper only utilizes self-motion information such as rat's direction, velocity, and distance for mapping and does not consider the influence of visual perceptual information on mapping. This limitation results in the inability of the method to perform relocalization using familiar scenes. When fusing visual information with self-motion information, the difference in the sampling rates of the two signals can lead to joint initialization failure. Future work will propose a joint initialization method for visual and self-motion information to synchronize the two signals and overcome the challenges of joint initialization. By incorporating the obtained visual perceptual information into the proposed method, the stability and accuracy of spatial representation map construction will be improved.

Author Contributions: Conceptualization, H.J.; Funding acquisition, H.J.; Software, H.J.; Validation, Y.Z.; Writing—original draft, H.J.; Writing—review and editing, Y.Z. All authors have read and agreed to the published version of the manuscript.

Funding: This work is supported by Robotics Control Technology Research Center of Huainan Union University (LZX2201), and The cooperation R&D project of Anhui Sound Valley Intelligent Technology Co.

Institutional Review Board Statement: Not applicable.

Informed Consent Statement: Not applicable.

Data Availability Statement: The data related to this paper are available on request from the corresponding author.

Conflicts of Interest: The authors declare no conflict of interest.

References

1. Yu, H.-J.; Fang, Y.-C. A robot scene recognition method based on improved autonomous developmental network. *Acta Autom. Sin.* **2021**, *47*, 1530–1538.
2. Yu, F.; Wu, Y.; Ma, S.; Xu, M.; Li, H.; Qu, H.; Song, C.; Wang, T.; Zhao, R.; Shi, L. Brain-inspired multimodal hybrid neural network for robot place recognition. *Sci. Robot.* **2023**, *8*, 69–96. [CrossRef]
3. Sorscher, B.; Mel, G.C.; Ocko, S.A.; Giocomo, L.M.; Ganguli, S. A unified theory for the computational and mechanistic origins of grid cells. *Neuron* **2023**, *111*, 121–137. [CrossRef]
4. Zheng, J.; Huang, G. A novel grid cell–based urban flood resilience metric considering water velocity and duration of system performance being impacted. *J. Hydrol.* **2023**, *617-628*, 128911. [CrossRef]
5. Wu, Y.; Ruan, X.-G.; Huang, J.; Chai, J. An improved cortical network model for environment cognition. *Acta Autom. Sin.* **2021**, *47*, 1401–1411.
6. Ruan, X.-G.; Chai, J.; Wu, Y.; Zhang, X.-P. Huang Jing. Cognitive map construction and navigation based on hippocampal place cells. *Acta Autom. Sin.* **2021**, *47*, 666–677.
7. Tian, Y.; Chang, Y.; Arias, F.H.; Nieto-Granda, C.; How, J.P.; Carlone, L. Kimera-multi: Robust, distributed, dense metric-semantic slam for multi-robot systems. *IEEE Trans. Robot.* **2022**, *38*, 2022–2038. [CrossRef]
8. O'Keefe, J.; Doslrovsky, J. The hippocampus as a spatial map. preliminary evidence from unit activity in the freely-moving rat. *Brain Res.* **1971**, *34*, 171–175. [CrossRef] [PubMed]
9. Moser, E.I.; Kropff, E.; Moser, M.B. Place cells, grid cells, and the brain's spatial representation system. *Annu. Rev. Neurosci.* **2008**, *31*, 69–89. [CrossRef] [PubMed]
10. Jeffery, K.J.; Burgess, N. A metric for the cognitive map: Found at last? *Trends Cogn. Sci.* **2006**, *10*, 1–3. [CrossRef] [PubMed]
11. Hafting, T.; Fyhn, M.; Molden, S.; Moser, M.B.; Moser, E.I. Microstructure of a spatial map in the entorhinal cortex. *Nature* **2005**, *436*, 801–806. [CrossRef]
12. Krishna, A.; Mittal, D.; Virupaksha, S.G.; Nair, A.R.; Narayanan, R.; Thakur, C.S. Biomimetic FPGA-based spatial navigation model with grid cells and place cells. *Neural Netw.* **2021**, *139*, 45–63. [CrossRef] [PubMed]
13. Campbell, M.G.; Ocko, S.A.; Mallory, C.S.; Low, I.I.; Ganguli, S.; Giocomo, L.M. Principles governing the integration of landmark and self-motion cues in entorhinal cortical codes for navigation. *Nat. Neurosci.* **2018**, *21*, 1096–1106. [CrossRef] [PubMed]
14. Moser, E.I.; Roudi, Y.; Witter, M.P.; Kentros, C.; Bonhoeffer, T.; Moser, M.B. Grid cells and cortical representation. *Nuture Rev. Neuro Sci.* **2014**, *15*, 466–481. [CrossRef]
15. Barry, C.; Hayman, R.; Burgess, N.; Jeffery, K.J. Experience-dependent rescaling of entorhinal grids. *Nat Neurosci.* **2007**, *10*, 682–684. [CrossRef]
16. Milford, M.J.; Wyeth, G.F. Mapping a suburb with a single camera using a biologically inspired SLAM system. *IEEE Trans. Robot.* **2008**, *24*, 1038–1053. [CrossRef]
17. Yu, S.; Xu, H.; Wu, C.; Jiang, X.; Sun, R.; Sun, L. Bionic Path Planning Fusing Episodic Memory Based on RatSLAM. *Biomimetics* **2023**, *8*, 59–68. [CrossRef]
18. Shipston-Sharman, O.; Solanka, L.; Nolan, M.F. Continuous attractor network models of grid cell firing based on excitatory-inhibitory interactions. *J. Physiol.* **2016**, *594*, 6547–6557. [CrossRef]
19. Yu, N.G.; Yuan, Y.H.; Li, T.; Jiang, X.J.; Luo, Z.W. A cognitive map building algorithm by means of cognitive mechanism of hippocampus. *Acta Autom. Sin.* **2018**, *44*, 52–73.
20. O'Keefe, J.; Burgess, N. Geometric determinants of the place fields of hippocampal neurons. *Nature* **1996**, *381*, 425–428. [CrossRef]
21. Grieves, R.M.; Duvelle, E.; Dudchenko, P.A. A boundary vector cell model of place field repetition. *Spatial Cogn. Comput.* **2018**, *18*, 1–40. [CrossRef]
22. Bjerknes, T.; Moser, E.; Moser, M.B. Representation of geometric borders in the developing rat. *Neuron* **2014**, *82*, 71–78. [CrossRef] [PubMed]
23. Hardcastle, K.; Ganguli, S.; Giocomo, L.M. Environmental boundaries as an error correction mechanism for grid cells. *Neuron* **2015**, *86*, 827–839. [CrossRef] [PubMed]
24. Weber, S.N.; Sprekeler, H. Learning place cells, grid cells and invariances with excitatory and inhibitory plasticity. *Elife* **2018**, *7*, e34560. [CrossRef]
25. Gonzalez, M.; Marchand, E.; Kacete, A.; Royan, J. Twistslam: Constrained slam in dynamic environment. *IEEE Robot. Autom. Lett.* **2022**, *7*, 6846–6853. [CrossRef]
26. Kim, H.; Granström, K.; Svensson, L.; Kim, S.; Wymeersch, H. PMBM-based SLAM filters in 5G mmwave vehicular networks. *IEEE Trans. Veh. Technol.* **2022**, *71*, 8646–8661. [CrossRef]
27. Jayakumar, S.; Narayanamurthy, R.; Ramesh, R.; Soman, K.; Muralidharan, V.; Chakravarthy, V.S. Modeling the Effect of Environmental Geometries on Grid Cell Representations. *Front. Neural Circuits* **2019**, *12*, 120. [CrossRef] [PubMed]
28. Fldiák, P. Forming sparse representations by local anti-Hebbian learning. *Biol. Cybern.* **1990**, *64*, 165–170. [CrossRef] [PubMed]
29. Sargolini, F.; Fyhn, M.; Hafting, T.; McNaughton, B.L.; Witter, M.P.; Moser, M.B.; Moser, E.I. Conjunctive representative of position, direction, and velocity in entorhinal cortex. *Science* **2006**, *312*, 758–762. [CrossRef] [PubMed]
30. Soman, K.; Muralidharan, V.; Chakravarthy, V.S. A unified hierarchical oscillatory network model of head direction cells, spatially periodic cells and place cells. *Eur. J. Neurosci.* **2018**, *47*, 1266–1281. [CrossRef]

31. Jeewajee, A.; Barry, C.; O'Keefe, J.; Burgess, N. Grid cells and theta as oscillatory interference: Electrophysiological data from freely moving rats. *Hippocampus* **2010**, *18*, 1175–1185. [CrossRef] [PubMed]
32. Cong, M.; Zou, Q.; Liu, D.; Du, Y. Review of robot navigation inspired by the localization cells cognitive mechanism. *J. Mech. Eng.* **2019**, *55*, 1–12.
33. Knudsen, E.B.; Wallis, J.D. Hippocampal neurons construct a map of an abstract value space. *Cell* **2021**, *184*, 4640–4650. [CrossRef] [PubMed]
34. Guo, J.; Cheng, M.; Ren, J.; Ren, Q. A Bio-inspired SLAM System for a Legged Robot. In Proceedings of the 2022 IEEE 17th Conference on Industrial Electronics and Applications (ICIEA), Chengdu, China, 16–19 December 2022; pp. 1074–1079.

Disclaimer/Publisher's Note: The statements, opinions and data contained in all publications are solely those of the individual author(s) and contributor(s) and not of MDPI and/or the editor(s). MDPI and/or the editor(s) disclaim responsibility for any injury to people or property resulting from any ideas, methods, instructions or products referred to in the content.

Article

Enhancement of Robot Position Control for Dual-User Operation of Remote Robot System with Force Feedback

Pingguo Huang [1] and Yutaka Ishibashi [2,*]

[1] Faculty of Economics and Information, Gifu Shotoku Gakuen University, Gifu 500-8288, Japan; huangpg@gifu.shotoku.ac.jp
[2] Faculty of Business Administration, Aichi Sangyo University, Okazaki 444-0005, Japan
* Correspondence: ishibasi@asu.ac.jp

Abstract: We focus on dual-user operation, where two users control a single remote robot equipped with a force sensor using haptic interface devices. We employ a cooperative work in which the two users control the remote robot to collaborate with remote robot systems with force feedback to carry an object. By measuring the force acting upon the object, we aim to better understand the underlying mechanisms by which the user with lower network latency can help the other user, as observed in our previous work. We notice that with increasing network delays, the force exerted on the object tends to intensify, indicating that it becomes more challenging for users to operate the remote robot effectively as network delays increase. We also measure the force applied to the object by changing the network delays between the remote robot and the two users to clarify why the user with the lower network delay can assist the other user. We find that when the total network delay is the same, the average force magnitude and the average maximum force magnitude remain nearly identical. This is because, despite the challenges faced by the user with the larger network delay, the user with the smaller delay can operate the remote robot more easily and assist the other user. In order to reduce the force acting upon the object, we propose an enhancement method for the robot position control, which determines the position of the remote robot arm while accounting for network delay, and investigate the effects by experiment. Experimental results demonstrate that our proposed method is effective and can reduce the applied force. This is because the proposed method adjusts the ratio between the user with the lower delay and the user with the higher delay. The user with the lower delay can operate the remote robot more easily and respond to it more quickly. Our findings and proposed method can be useful in improving work accuracy and operability when designing a remote robot system with force feedback for applications.

Keywords: remote robot systems; force feedback; haptic interface device; dual-user operation; robot position control; network delay

Citation: Huang, P.; Ishibashi, Y. Enhancement of Robot Position Control for Dual-User Operation of Remote Robot System with Force Feedback. *Appl. Sci.* **2024**, *14*, 9376. https://doi.org/10.3390/app14209376

Academic Editors: Luis Gracia, J. Ernesto Solanes and Pedro Couto

Received: 7 August 2024
Revised: 22 September 2024
Accepted: 9 October 2024
Published: 14 October 2024

Copyright: © 2024 by the authors. Licensee MDPI, Basel, Switzerland. This article is an open access article distributed under the terms and conditions of the Creative Commons Attribution (CC BY) license (https://creativecommons.org/licenses/by/4.0/).

1. Introduction

Recently, there has been increasing interest among researchers in remote robot systems with force feedback [1–16]. In the systems, a user can remotely control a robot by manipulating a haptic interface device while perceiving the reaction force from an object touched or moved by a robot arm equipped with a force sensor. We can expect to significantly improve the efficiency and accuracy of remote operations, as the user is able to physically sense the shape, weight, and softness of the object [7–13]. Consequently, remote robot systems with force feedback can be utilized in environments that are hazardous or inaccessible to humans, such as disaster-stricken areas, nuclear power plants, deep-sea exploration, and outer space [11].

Nevertheless, when haptic data such as position and/or force information is transmitted over a non-guaranteed Quality of Service (QoS) [17] network, like the Internet, Quality of Experience (QoE) [18] might be greatly affected. Therefore, it is essential to clarify the influence of network delay, delay jitter, and packet loss on the operation and to study efficient QoS control [11,19,20].

On the other hand, Hagiwara et al. investigated the effects of two users controlling an avatar compared to one user controlling an avatar to move in a virtual space [21]. Their experimental results showed that the performance with two users was superior to that of one user. In [22], Kodama et al. proposed a "virtual co-embodiment" in which a virtual avatar is controlled by two users (one is a teacher, and the other is a learner) for motor skill learning. Experimental results indicated that using the proposed method enhances the efficiency of motor skill learning. Therefore, in order to clarify if dual-user operation is more effective than single-user operation for cooperation in a remote robot system with force feedback, the authors in [23] compare single-user and dual-user operations, where an object is collaboratively carried by two remote robot systems with force feedback. The results indicates that dual-user operation outperforms single-user operation regarding the force acting upon the object. Additionally, when two users experienced different network delays, the user with the lower network delay can help the other user [23].

However, the reasons why the user with the lower network delay can help the other user remain unclear, and it is necessary to clarify this mechanism. Additionally, in [23], the authors calculate the position vector of a robot by simply averaging the two position vectors of haptic interface devices in the robot position control, which is used to determine the position of the remote robot arm for dual-user operation. It is crucial to evaluate how varying the ratios of the two position vectors affects the calculation of the robot's position vector. Furthermore, from [23], it is observed that the force acting upon the object increases with the escalation of network delay. When the applied force becomes large, it may be difficult for the user to do collaborative work. Furthermore, if the force exerted is too large, the object could be damaged. It is important to reduce the applied force as network delay increases by considering enhancements to the QoS control employed in [23].

Therefore, in this paper, we focus on dual-user operation, which may be more efficient than single-user operation in remote robot systems. First, we examine the effects of network delays on dual-user operation and measure the force applied to the object by changing the network delays between the remote robot and the two users to clarify the underlying mechanisms. In the experiment, we use robot position control, which is a type of QoS control employed in [23] that adjusts the robot position using the positions of the two users' haptic interface devices. Next, we propose an enhancement method for the robot position control by taking network delays into account to reduce the applied force.

This paper makes the following key contributions:

(1) In order to understand the mechanism, we clarify the reasons why the user who experiences a small network delay can assist the user who experiences a large network delay by analyzing the force applied on the operating object in dual-user operation. It is the first time the reason is clarified, and this may help improve the work accuracy of the remote robot system with force feedback.

(2) To decrease the force exerted on the object, we propose an enhancement method for the robot position control as QoS control. Experimental results show the effectiveness of our proposed method. The proposed control can be widely used in remote robot systems with force feedback to improve operability.

(3) From the above, our findings and proposed method can be useful in improving work accuracy and operability when designing a remote robot system with force feedback for applications such as remote medical surgeries, remote control in deep-sea exploration, or outer space operations.

The remainder of this paper is structured as follows: Section 2 introduces the dual-user operation in remote robot systems with force feedback and details the robot position control for dual-user operation. Section 3 clarifies the mechanism by analyzing the applied force on an object in dual-user operation. In Section 4, we propose an enhancement method for the robot position control by taking network delays into account and investigate the effects of our proposed method. Lastly, Section 5 provides the conclusion of this- paper.

2. Dual-User Operation of Remote Robot System with Force Feedback

This section presents both single-user and dual-user operations of the remote robot system with force feedback. In single-user operation, one user manipulates a haptic interface device to control the movement of a remote robot. In dual-user operation, each of the two users uses their own haptic interface device to collaboratively control the movement of a remote robot.

2.1. Single-User Operation (Remote Robot System with Force Feedback)

Figure 1 illustrates the setup of single-user operation (remote robot system with force feedback). The system comprises a master terminal and a slave terminal [23]. Each terminal consists of two PCs connected through a switching hub. At the master terminal, one PC is linked to a haptic interface device (3D Systems Touch [24]) for haptic feedback, while the second PC is utilized to monitor the movements of the robot arm. At the slave terminal, one PC connects a web camera (manufactured by Microsoft Corp. (Redmond, WA, USA), with a video resolution of 1920 × 1080 pixels) to monitor the robot arm's movement, while the other PC controls the industrial robot. The industrial robot comprises a robot arm, a force sensor mounted on the arm's flange, a robot controller, and a force interface unit. The force interface unit is used to connect the force sensor to the robot controller.

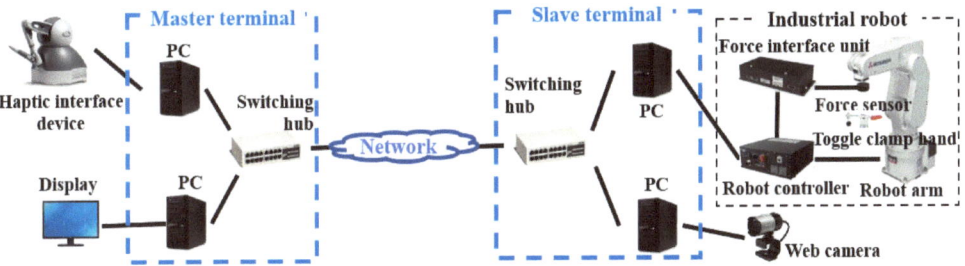

Figure 1. Setup of single-user operation (remote robot system with force feedback).

At the master terminal, by manipulating the haptic interface device, a user can control the robot arm remotely. As in [23], the reaction force $F_t^{(m)}$ exerted on the haptic interface device at time t ($t \geq 1$) is determined as follows:

$$F_t^{(m)} = K_{\text{scale}}^{(F)} F_{t-1}^{(s)} \quad (1)$$

where $F_{t-1}^{(s)}$ denotes the force transmitted from the slave terminal, and $K_{\text{scale}}^{(F)}$ represents a force mapping scale used to map forces between the haptic interface device and the force sensor of the industrial robot arm [23]. Additionally, because the maximum force that can be applied to the haptic interface device is 3.3 N [24], any calculated force exceeding 3.3 N is capped at 3.3 N. At the slave terminal, we use the same method as in [23] to determine the industrial robot's position vector S_t. The S_t outputted at time t ($t \geq 2$) is computed as follows:

$$S_t = K_{\text{scale}}^{(P)} M_{t-1} + V_{t-1} \quad (2)$$

where $K_{\text{scale}}^{(P)}$ is a scaling factor for workspace mapping, M_t is the haptic interface device's position vector transmitted from the master terminal at time t, and $V_{t-1} (= S_t - S_{t-1})$ represents the moving velocity of the robot arm at time t [23]. Additionally, $|V_t| \leq V_{\max}$, where $V_{\max}$ represents the maximum allowable movement velocity ($V_{\max}$ = 5 mm/ms [25] in this paper) to ensure safe operation of the robot arm.

To avoid instability phenomena, such as vibrations, we implement stabilization control with filters [25], originally proposed for single-user operation, for dual-user operation. Figure 2 shows one control loop of the enhanced stabilization control, which employs both a wave filter and a phase control filter. The wave filter consists of a cross component and a coefficient b, while the phase control filter includes $W_s(s)$ and $W_m(s)$ [26,27].

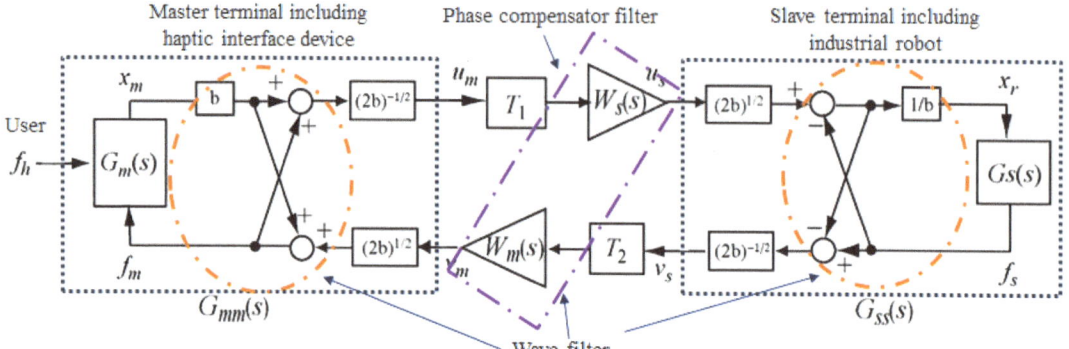

Figure 2. Block diagram of stabilization control with filter.

2.2. Dual-User Operation

The system configuration of dual-user operation is shown in Figure 3. As depicted in Figure 3, the system comprises two master terminals (referred to as *master terminals 1 and 2*, herein) and one slave terminal. Both users manipulate their respective haptic interface devices to collaboratively control the robot arm. The video captured by the web camera is multicast to both master terminals, allowing the two users to view the same video screen.

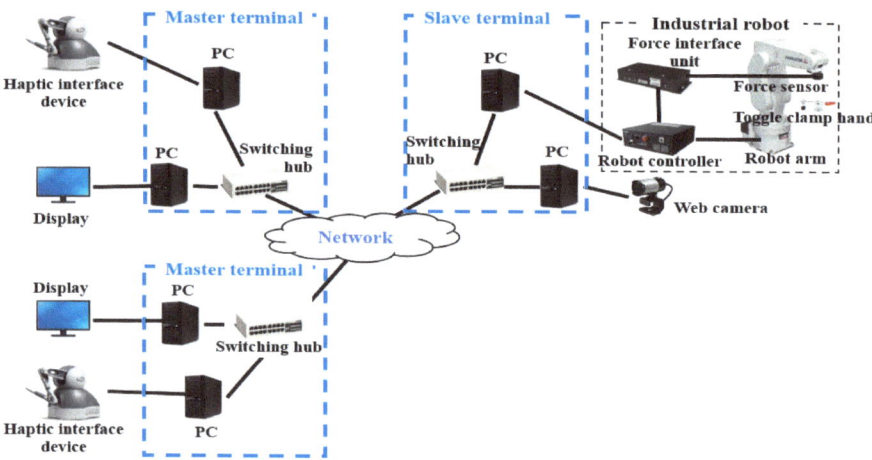

Figure 3. System configuration of dual-user operation.

As in [23], the reaction force exerted on the two haptic interface devices, denoted as $F_t^{(m_1)}$ and $F_t^{(m_2)}$, at master terminals 1 and 2 (the haptic interface devices are also called *haptic interface devices* 1 and 2, respectively) are calculated as follows:

$$F_t^{(m_1)} = F_t^{(m_2)} = K_{\text{scale}}^{(F)} F_{t-1}^{(s)} \qquad (3)$$

where $F_t^{(s)}$ represents the force transmitted from the slave terminal at time t, and $K_{\text{scale}}^{(F)}$ represents the mapping scale for force between the industrial robot and the haptic interface device. The position vector of the robot is determined by robot position control, which we will explain in Section 3. Please note that we use a three-dimensional coordinate system. The origin is at the center between the two remote robots, with the *x*-axis representing the left and right directions, the *y*-axis representing the front and back directions, and the *z*-axis representing the up and down direction (see Figure 4, right side). All vectors are calculated in this system. In addition, we implement the enhanced stabilization control for dual-user operation as follows: the wave filter $G_{mm}(s)$ and the phase control filter $W_m(s)$ are applied at each user's terminal; at the remote robot terminal, after calculating the position vector for the remote robot based on the position vectors received from two users' terminals, the wave filter $G_{ss}(s)$ and the phase control filter $W_s(s)$ are applied. Finally, the force is sent to both users' terminals. We find that this approach is effective in the dual-user context as well.

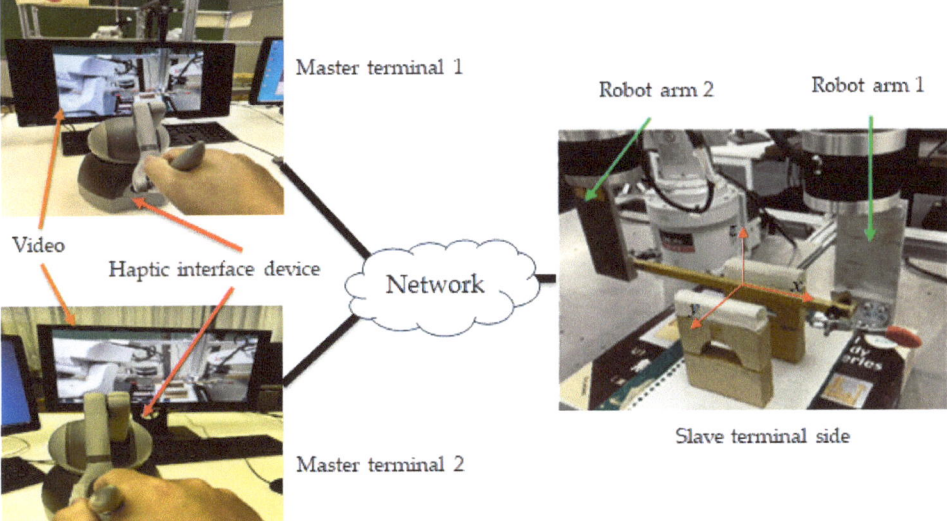

Figure 4. Appearance at master and slave terminals.

2.3. Robot Position Control

In the robot position control, the robot's position vector is determined by using the positions of both haptic interface devices [23]. By applying different ratios of the two position vectors when calculating the robot's position vector, we can obtain a different position vector for the industrial robot. In [23], the position vector of the robot is determined by averaging both haptic interface devices' positions:

$$S_t = \left(M_{t-1}^{(m_1)} + M_{t-1}^{(m_2)}\right)/2 + V_{t-1} \quad (4)$$

where $M_{t-1}^{(m_i)}$ represents the position vector of haptic interface device *i* (where *i* = 1 or 2) received from the master terminal at time *t*, and V_t is the movement velocity of robot arm at time *t* [23].

3. Analysis of Applied Force on Object in Dual-User Operation

As described previously, in dual-user operation, the reasons why the user with the shorter delay can support the other user remain unclear, and it is necessary to clarify this mechanism. In this section, we employ the same experiment system as in [23] to investigate the influences of network delays on dual-user operation. We measure the force applied to the object by changing the network delays between the remote robot and the two users to gain a better understanding of the underlying mechanisms.

3.1. Experiment Method for Clarifying Mechanisms

We employ a dual-user operation system to collaborate with a remote robot system to do cooperative work (see Figure 4) involving the movement of an object (a wooden stick) clamped by the two robot arms in the front–back direction, as in [23]. In this work, after moving the wooden stick from the initial position to the paper block (see Figure 5) at the front side, the wooden stick is moved backward to the paper block at the back side. The distance between the initial position and the paper block positioned at the front is approximately 40 mm and takes about 5 s, while the distance between the front paper block and the back paper block is about 80 mm and takes about 10 s. Since it is difficult to identify influencing factors if the robot arm (referred to as robot arm 1) of the remote robot system is also controlled by a human, robot arm 1 moves automatically at a constant speed of about 8 mm/s, ensuring consistent movement in each operation. To move robot arm 1 automatically, we calculate a new position based on the current position and movement speed (i.e., 8 mm/s) approximately every 3.5 ms, which is the position update cycle for the robot arm. The robot then updates its position based on the calculation result. The other robot arm (*robot arm 2*) is controlled by two users to move in the same manner as robot arm 1. The robot position control is implemented at the slave terminal of robot arm 2 to determine the position vector for robot arm 2.

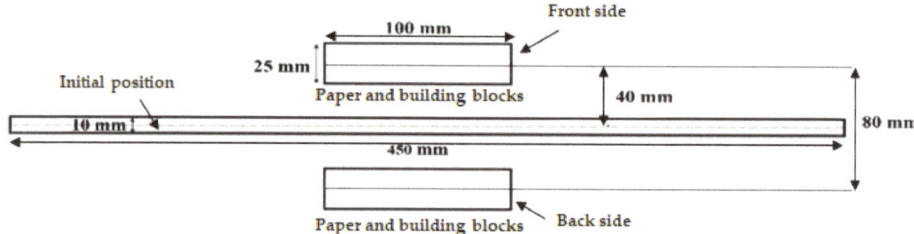

Figure 5. Plane view showing arrangement of the wooden stick, wooden blocks, and paper blocks.

In the experimental system, we use static IP addresses for each PC, and since the processing latency of each PC is only a few milliseconds, which is much shorter than the network delay, we ignore the processing latency in our experiment. A constant network delay is generated for packets transmitted between master terminals 1 and 2 and the slave terminal of robot arm 2 by a network emulator (NIST Net [28]). For one user, the constant delay ranges from 0 ms to 250 ms in 50 ms increments, whereas for the other user, the delay ranges from 0 ms to 600 ms in increments of either 50 ms or 100 ms.

The work was repeated 20 times for each set of network delay combinations. We measured the force of robot arm 2 approximately every 3.5 ms. Then, we averaged the force magnitude based on the output data and obtained the maximum force magnitude. Finally, we calculated the average force magnitude and the average maximum force magnitude over the course of the 20 trials.

3.2. Experiment Results for Clarifying Mechanisms

Figure 6 shows the average of average force magnitude and average of maximum force magnitude at robot arm 2. Additionally, the figure shows the 95% confidence intervals.

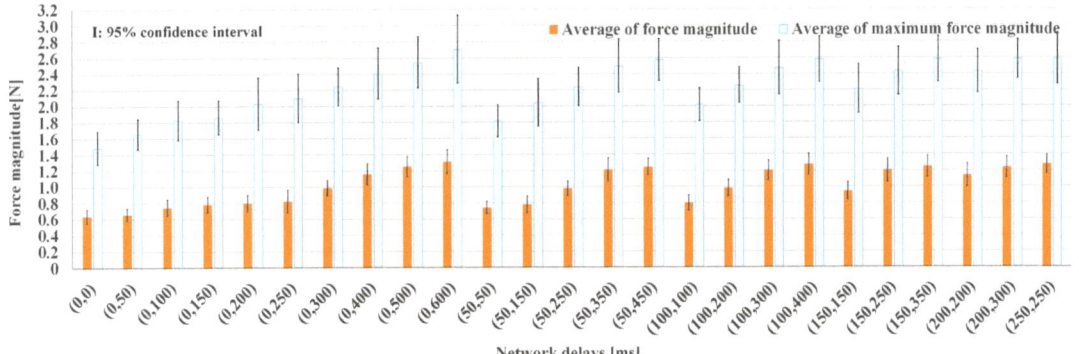

Figure 6. Average of average force magnitude and average of maximum force magnitude.

From Figure 6, we find that when the delay for one user is 0 ms and the delay for the other user increases, both the average force magnitude and the average maximum force magnitude tend to increase. In other words, the force exerted on the object rises as network delays become larger. A similar trend is observed when the delay for one user is 50 ms, 100 ms, or 200 ms. This indicates that as network delays increase, it becomes more challenging for users to operate the remote robot effectively. Additionally, the figure shows that when the total network delay is the same, for example, in the network delay combinations (0, 200), (50, 150), and (100, 100), the average force magnitude and the average maximum force magnitude are almost identical. This is because, despite the challenges faced by the user with the larger network delay, the user with the smaller delay can operate the remote robot more easily and assist the other user. As the smaller delay increases, it becomes more difficult for that user to control the robot, while the larger delay decreases, making it easier for the other user to operate the remote robot. Therefore, when the total network delay is the same, the average force magnitude and the average maximum force magnitude remain nearly identical.

We conducted a t-test to verify whether there are significant differences among different network delays. Figure 7 shows the results of the t-test between combinations of network delays (please note that the cells in blue color represent the combinations of network delays. The first value represents network delay 1, and the second represents network delay 2). Each cell contains two values: the upper value represents the p-value for the average of average force magnitude between network delay combinations, and the lower value is the p-value for the maximum force magnitude. For clarity, we have highlighted cells in which there is no significant difference (i.e., when at least one of the two p-values is greater than 0.05) in yellow.

From Figure 7, we observe that at least one p-value is smaller than 0.05 when the difference between the total network delay (i.e., the sum of network delay 1 and network delay 2) becomes large. However, when the total network delay is the same, both p-values exceed 0.05. This suggests that there is no statistically significant difference between these pairs of network delays. In simpler terms, the force of robot arm 2 is nearly identical when the total network delay is the same. Therefore, even though the force applied to each of the two dual-users may vary due to different network delays, the force of robot arm 2 remains the same. This observation can explain why the user with the shorter delay can support the other user.

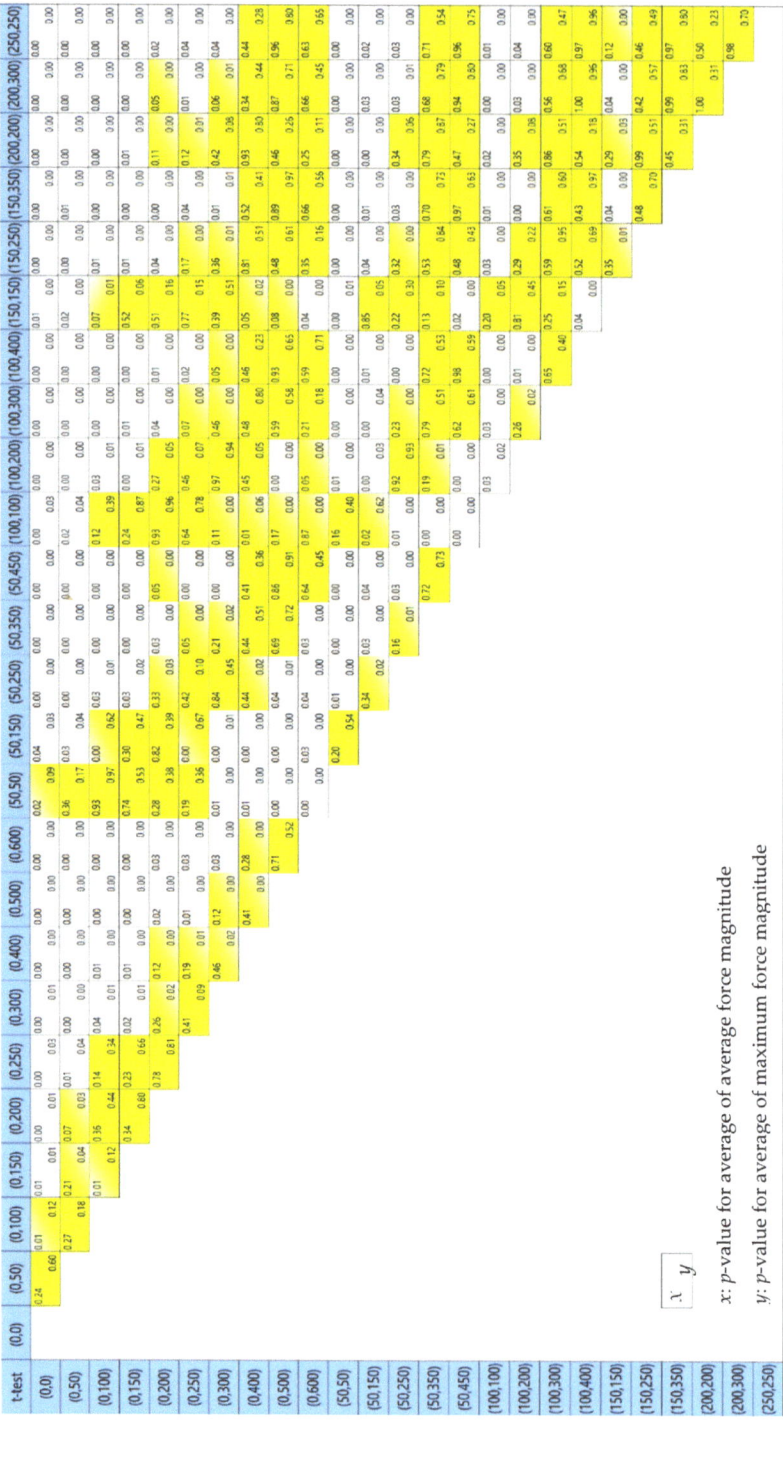

Figure 7. Results of *t*-test between combinations of network delays.

We further confirm the above results by grouping the averages with the same total network delay in Figure 8. It is evident that the force remains nearly identical when the total network delay is consistent. As previously mentioned, despite the challenges faced by the user with the larger network delay, the user with the smaller delay can operate the remote robot more easily and assist the other user.

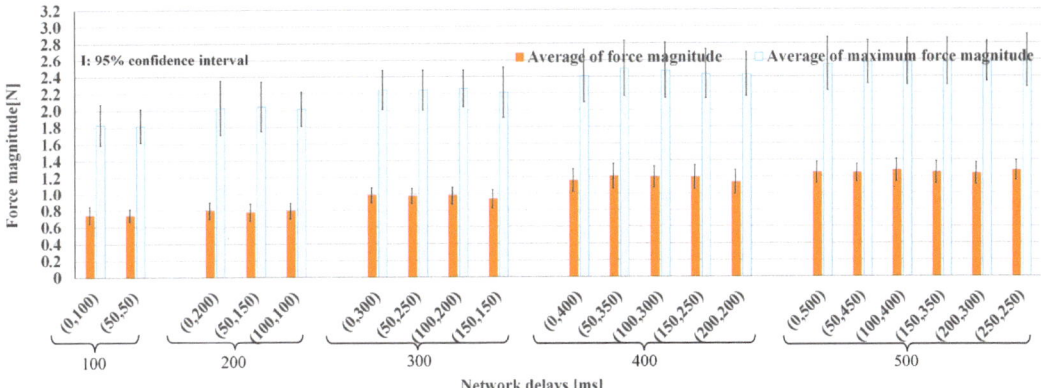

Figure 8. Average of average force magnitude and average of maximum force magnitude when the sum of network delay 1 and network delay 2 is same.

Furthermore, we also carry out subjective assessment to confirm the effect of dual-user operation by comparing single-user operation and dual-user operation for cooperative work in remote robot systems with force feedback. The assessment results also illustrated that dual-user operation outperforms single-user operation [29].

4. Enhancement of Robot Position Control

As outlined in the previous section, the force acting upon the object increases as the network delay grows. Therefore, it is necessary to consider different ratios of two haptic interface device's position vectors when calculating the robot's position vector and to reduce the applied force when the network delay is large. In this section, we enhance the robot position control by taking account of network delays to reduce the applied force.

4.1. Enhancement Method

To mitigate the applied force, we enhance the robot position control by considering network delay. The position vector of the robot is determined as follows (called *proposed method* 1 here):

$$S_t = \frac{d_{t-1}^{(m_2)} \times M_{t-1}^{(m_1)} + d_{t-1}^{(m_1)} \times M_{t-1}^{(m_2)}}{d_{t-1}^{(m_1)} + d_{t-1}^{(m_2)}} + V_{t-1} \tag{5}$$

where $d_t^{(m_1)}$ and $d_t^{(m_2)}$ represent the network delay between the robot and haptic interface devices 1 and 2 at time t, respectively. Note that we only consider cases where $d_{t-1}^{(m_1)} + d_{t-1}^{(m_2)} > 0$.

As will be described later, we found that it is challenging to assert that proposed method 1 is effective. Therefore, we conduct a preliminary experiment to investigate the effect by using fixed ratios (1:1 for the conventional method, 2:1, 3:1, 4:1, and 5:1) of $d_{t-1}^{(m_1)}$

to $d_{t-1}^{(m_2)}$ in Equation (5), and obtain the optimal fixed ratio for each network delay. Through regression analysis, we derive the following equations (called *proposed method* 2 here):

$$a = 0.0057 \times d_{t-1}^{(m_2)} + 0.5458 \tag{6}$$

$$S_t = \begin{cases} \left(M_{t-1}^{(m_1)} + M_{t-1}^{(m_2)}\right)/2 + V_{t-1} & (if\ a \leq 1) \\ \left(a \times M_{t-1}^{(m_1)} + M_{t-1}^{(m_2)}\right)/(a+1) + V_{t-1} & (otherwise) \end{cases} \tag{7}$$

where a is defined as the value when $d_t^{(m_1)} < d_t^{(m_2)}$ and the ratio of $d_t^{(m_1)}$ and $d_t^{(m_2)}$ is a:1.

4.2. Experiment

4.2.1. Experiment Method

We performed collaborative work of moving an object (i.e., a wooden stick) held by two robot arms along the *x*-axis (i.e., the front–back) direction, same as the cooperation work described in Section 4.1. The enhanced robot position control is implemented at the slave terminal of robot arm 2.

We generated a constant delay, known as the additional delay, for each packet transmitted between the master and slave terminals using NIST Net. Following the approach in [23], the additional delay for one user was configured to be either 0 ms or 50 ms, while for the other user, it was set to 100 ms, 200 ms, 250 ms, 300 ms, and 600 ms to investigate the effects of proposed method 1 (called *experiment 1* here). For proposed method 2, the additional delay for one user was configured to be either 0 ms or 50 ms, while for the other user, it varied from 0 ms to 600 ms in 100 ms increments (called *experiment 2* here).

As described in Section 3.1, we assessed the force exerted on the wooden stick and calculated the average of average force magnitude and average of maximum force magnitude during the work.

4.2.2. Experimental Results

Since the tendency of the average of maximum force magnitude is similar to that of the average of average force magnitude, as shown in Figures 6 and 7, we only show the average of average force magnitude here. Figure 9 illustrates the average of the average force magnitude of the robot arm controlled by two users in experiment 1, while Figure 10 presents the results of experiment 2. Additionally, the figures include the 95% confidence intervals.

From Figure 9, when the network delay for one user is 0 ms or 50 ms and the network delay for the other user is larger than 200 ms, the average of average force magnitude of proposed method 1 generally appears to be lower than those of the conventional method. However, when the network delay for one user is 0 ms or 50 ms and the network delay for the other user is 100 ms, the conventional method outperforms proposed method 1. Therefore, we can say that when the network delay is large, proposed method 1 is effective, but when the network delay is small, the conventional method is more effective. From the above, it is challenging to assert that proposed method 1 is consistently effective.

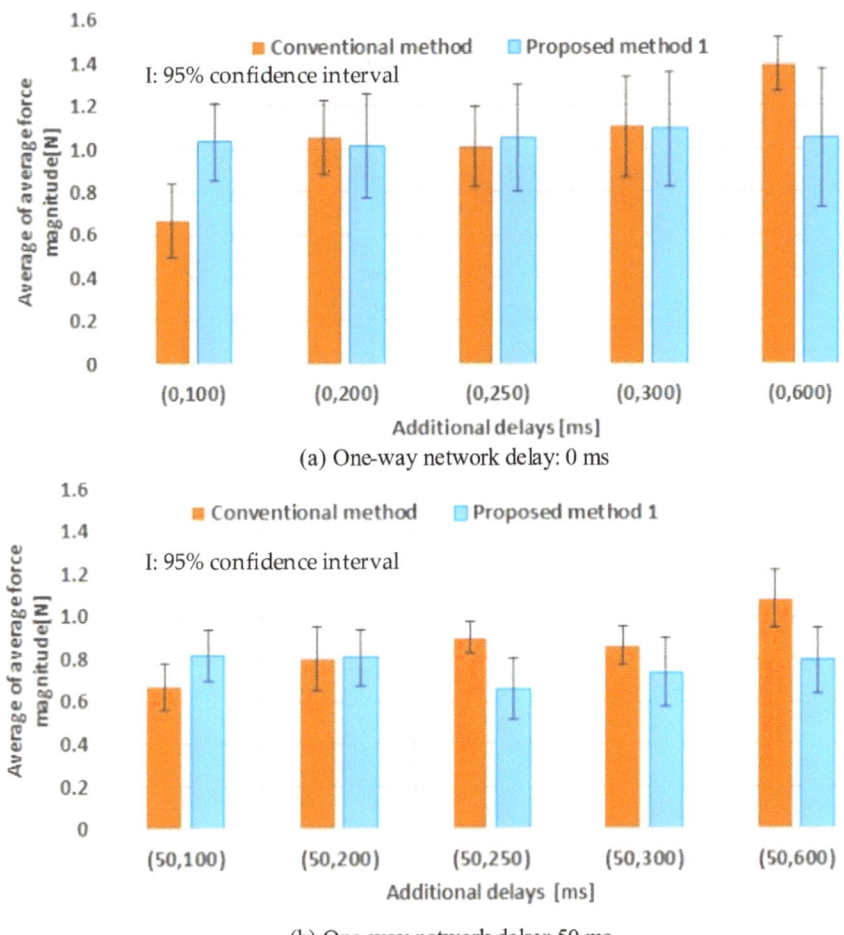

Figure 9. Average of average force magnitude in experiment 1.

On the other hand, from Figure 10, we can see that the averages of average force magnitude for proposed method 2 are generally smaller than those for the conventional method. By comparing Figure 9 with Figure 10, we also find that the averages of average force magnitude of proposed method 2 are smaller than those of proposed method 1. Thus, we can say that proposed method 2 is effective. This is because, in the proposed method, we account for network delays by adjusting the ratio between the user with the lower delay and the user with the higher delay. The user with the lower delay can operate the remote robot more easily and respond to it more quickly. This is why the user with the lower delay can assist the user with the higher delay. Therefore, the force exerted on the wooden stick using the proposed method is smaller than that with the conventional method.

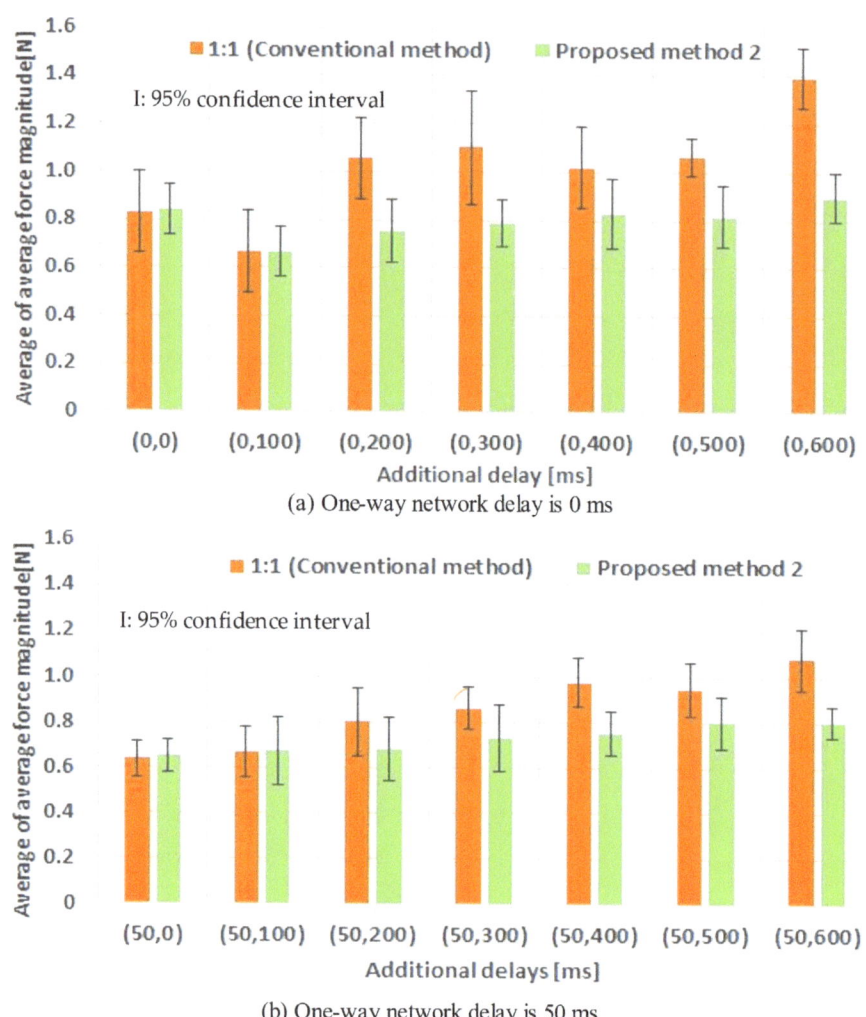

Figure 10. Average of average force magnitude in experiment 2.

5. Conclusions

In this paper, we dealt with dual-user operation, in which two users control a single remote robot equipped with a force sensor by using haptic interface devices for cooperative work of carrying an object between remote robot systems with force feedback. We measured the force applied to the object to clarify the underlying mechanisms explaining why the user with the shorter delay can support the other user with large network delay, as observed in our previous work. Consequently, we noticed that the force of the robot arm is nearly identical when the total network delay is the same. This is because, despite the challenges faced by the user with the larger network delay, the user with the smaller delay can operate the remote robot more easily and assist the other user. To decrease the force exerted on the object, we proposed an enhancement method for the robot position control by considering network delay and investigate the effects by experiments. The results of our experiments demonstrate that the proposed method effectively decreases the applied force. This is because the proposed method adjusts the ratio between the user with the lower delay and the user with the higher delay. The user with the lower delay can operate the remote robot more easily and respond to it more quickly. Our findings suggest that the proposed control method is likely to enhance the efficiency of remote robot collaborative work. Therefore, our findings and proposed method can be useful in improving work accuracy and operability when designing a remote robot system with force feedback for applications.

In future studies, it will be important to analyze the force and position information at both master terminals 1 and 2 to gain a deeper understanding of how the user with the shorter delay supports the other user. Additionally, we will investigate the effect of our proposed method by using different objects with different sizes, weights, and materials. Furthermore, we will carry out simulations and numerical analysis to clarify the proposed method's effect.

Author Contributions: Writing—original draft, P.H.; Supervision, Y.I.; Project administration, Y.I. All authors have read and agreed to the published version of the manuscript.

Funding: This work was supported by JSPS KAKENHI Grant Number 21K11865.

Institutional Review Board Statement: Not applicable.

Informed Consent Statement: Not applicable.

Data Availability Statement: The original contributions presented in the study are included in the article, further inquiries can be directed to the corresponding author.

Acknowledgments: The authors thank Chengying Li and Mizuki Inui for their help in the experiment.

Conflicts of Interest: The authors declare no conflict of interest.

References

1. Ohnishi, K. Real world haptics: Its principle and future prospects. *J. Inst. Electr. Eng. Jpn.* **2013**, *133*, 268–269. (In Japanese) [CrossRef]
2. Singh, J.; Srinivasan, A.; Neumann, G.; Kucukyilmaz, A. Haptic-guided teleoperation of a 7-DoF collaborative robot arm with an identical twin master. *IEEE Trans. Haptics* **2020**, *13*, 246–252. [CrossRef] [PubMed]
3. Haruna, M.; Kawaguchi, N.; Ogino, M.; Akino, T. Comparison of three feedback modalities for haptics sensation in remote machine manipulation. *IEEE Robot. Autom. Lett.* **2021**, *6*, 5040–5047. [CrossRef]
4. Duan, W.; Li, Z.; Omisore, O.; Du, W.; Akinyemi, T.O.; Chen, X.; Gao, X.; Wang, H.; Wang, L. Development of an intuitive interface with haptic enhancement for robot-assisted endovascular intervention. *IEEE Trans. Haptics* **2023**, *99*, 1–13. [CrossRef] [PubMed]
5. Huang, P.; Ishibashi, Y. QoS control in remote robot operation with force feedback. In *Robotics Software Design and Engineering*; IntechOpen: London, UK, 2021; pp. 1–13. [CrossRef]
6. Seminara, L.; Gastaldo, P.; Watt, S.; Valyear, K.; Zuher, F.; Mastrogiovanni, F. Active Haptic Perception in Robots: A Review. *Front. Neurorobotics* **2019**, *13*, 53. [CrossRef] [PubMed]
7. Rakhmatulin, V.; Cabrera, M.; Hagos, F.; Sautenkov, O.; Tirado, J.; Uzhinsky, I. Tsetserukou, CoboGuider: Haptic Potential Fields for Safe Human-Robot Interaction. In Proceedings of the IEEE International Conference on Systems, Man, and Cybernetics (SMC), Melbourne, Australia, 17 October 2021. [CrossRef]
8. Ueda, Y.; Miyahara, S.; Tokushi, K.; Sato, T. Impact of a pneumatic surgical robot with haptic feedback function on surgical manipulation. *Sci. Rep.* **2023**, *13*, 22615. [CrossRef] [PubMed]
9. Bong, J.; Choi, S.; Hong, J.; Park, S. Force feedback haptic interface for bilateral teleoperation of robot manipulation. *Microsyst. Technol.* **2022**, *28*, 2381–2392. [CrossRef]
10. Bergholz, M.; Ferle, M.; Weber, B. The benefits of haptic feedback in robot assisted surgery and their moderators: A meta-analysis. *Sci. Rep.* **2023**, *13*, 19215. [CrossRef] [PubMed]
11. Huang, P.; Ishibashi, Y. Cooperation among humans and robots in remote robot systems with force feedback. In *Human-Robot Interaction—Perspectives and Applications*; IntechOpen: London, UK, 2022. [CrossRef]
12. Masaki, R.; Kobayashi, M.; Motoi, N. Remote-controlled method with force and visual assists based on time to collision for mobile robot. *Appl. Sci.* **2022**, *12*, 3727. [CrossRef]
13. Fu, Y.; Lin, W.; Yu, X.; Andina, J.J.R.; Gao, H. Robot-assisted teleoperation ultrasound system based on fusion of augmented reality and predictive force. *IEEE Trans. Ind. Electron.* **2023**, *70*, 7449–7456. [CrossRef]
14. Nakadhamabhorn, S.; Pillai, B.; Chotivichit, A.; Suthakorn, J. Sensorless based haptic feedback integration in robot-assisted pedicle screw insertion for lumbar spine surgery: A preliminary cadaveric study. *Comput. Struct. Biotechnol. J.* **2024**, *24*, 420–433. [CrossRef]

15. Lukin, A.; Demidova, G.; Rassolkin, A.; Vaimann, T.; Roozbahani, H. Force-based feedback for haptic device of mobile assembly robot. In Proceedings of the 27th International Workshop on Electric Drives, Moscow, Russia, 27–30 January 2020. [CrossRef]
16. Alfaro, D.; Puente, S.; Ubieta, I. Trajectory generation using dual-robot haptic interface for reinforcement learning from demonstration. In *Lecture Notes in Networks and Systems*; Springer: Berlin/Heidelberg, Germany, 2023; Volume 976. [CrossRef]
17. ITU-T Rec. I. 350 General Aspects of Quality of Service and Network Performance in Digital Networks. 1993. Available online: https://www.itu.int/rec/T-REC-I.350-199303-I (accessed on 1 August 2024).
18. ITU-T Rec. G. 100/P. 10 Amendment 1, New Appendix I: Definition of Quality of Experience (QoE). 2007. Available online: https://www.itu.int/rec/T-REC-P.10-200701-S!Amd1 (accessed on 1 August 2024).
19. Hyodo, S.; Onnishi, K. A bilateral control system to synchronize with haptic and visual sense for teleoperation over network. *IEEJ J. Ind. Appl.* **2016**, *5*, 370–377. [CrossRef]
20. Santiago, D.; Slawinski, E.; Salinas, L.; Mut, V. Force and position coordination for delayed bilateral teleoperation of a manipulator robot. *Int. J. Dyn. Control* **2023**, *12*, 1679–1693. [CrossRef]
21. Hagiwara, T.; Ganesh, G.; Sugimoto, M.; Inami, M.; Kitazaki, M. Individuals prioritize the reach straightness and hand jerk of a shared avatar over their own. *iScience* **2020**, *23*, 101732. [CrossRef] [PubMed]
22. Kodama, D.; Mizuho, T.; Hatada, Y.; Narumi, T.; Hirose, M. Effects of collaborative training using virtual co-embodiment on motor skill learning. *IEEE Trans. Vis. Comput. Graph.* **2023**, *29*, 2304–2314. [CrossRef] [PubMed]
23. Ye, R.; Jasmin, S.; Ishibashi, Y. One user operation versus two users operation in cooperative remote robot systems. In Proceedings of the IEEE International Conference on Consumer Electronics, Taiwan, 17–19 July 2023. [CrossRef]
24. Available online: https://www.3dsystems.com/haptics-devices/touch (accessed on 1 August 2024).
25. Huang, P.; Miyoshi, T.; Ishibashi, Y. Enhancement of Stabilization Control in Remote Robot System with Force Feedback. *Int. J. Commun. Netw. Syst. Sci. (IJCNS)* **2019**, *12*, 99–111. [CrossRef]
26. Miyoshi, T.; Terashima, K.; Buss, M. A design method of wave filter for stabilizing non-passive operating system. In Proceedings of the 2006 IEEE Conference on Computer Aided Control System Design, 2006 IEEE International Conference on Control Applications, 2006 IEEE International Symposium on Intelligent Control, Munich, Germany, 4–6 October 2006; pp. 1318–1324. [CrossRef]
27. Miyoshi, T.; Imamura, T.; Terashima, K. Stability analysis via IQC for multilateral tele-control and application to multi-client/multi-coupling physical model system. In Proceedings of the 41st Annual Conference of the IEEE Industrial Electronics Society (IECON), Yokohama, Japan, 9–12 November 2015. [CrossRef]
28. Carson, M.; Santay, D. NIST Net: A Linux-based network emulation tool. *ACM SIGCOMM Comput. Commun. Rev.* **2003**, *33*, 111–126. [CrossRef]
29. Gassama, L.N.; Ishibashi, Y.; Huang, P. QoE assessment of single-user operation and dual-user operation in remote robot systems with force feedback. In Proceedings of the 9th International Conference on Computer and Communications (ICCC), Chengdu, China, 8–11 December 2023. [CrossRef]

Disclaimer/Publisher's Note: The statements, opinions and data contained in all publications are solely those of the individual author(s) and contributor(s) and not of MDPI and/or the editor(s). MDPI and/or the editor(s) disclaim responsibility for any injury to people or property resulting from any ideas, methods, instructions or products referred to in the content.

Review

A Review of Foot–Terrain Interaction Mechanics for Heavy-Duty Legged Robots

Hongchao Zhuang [1,*], Jiaju Wang [1], Ning Wang [2], Weihua Li [3,4], Nan Li [3], Bo Li [3,5] and Lei Dong [1]

1. School of Mechanical Engineering, Tianjin University of Technology and Education, Tianjin 300222, China; jiaju0919@163.com (J.W.); donglei_hit@163.com (L.D.)
2. School of Information Technology Engineering, Tianjin University of Technology and Education, Tianjin 300222, China; wangning811108@163.com
3. State Key Laboratory of Robotics and Systems, Harbin Institute of Technology, Harbin 150001, China; liweihua@hit.edu.cn (W.L.); lnlinanln@126.com (N.L.); 18222646720@163.com (B.L.)
4. School of Automotive Engineering, Harbin Institute of Technology (Weihai), Weihai 264209, China
5. Tianjin Institute of Aerospace Mechanical and Electrical Equipment, Tianjin 300458, China
* Correspondence: zhuanghongchao_hit@163.com; Tel.: +86-022-8818-1083

Abstract: Heavy-duty legged robots have played an important role in material transportation, planet exploration, and other fields due to their unique advantages in complex and harsh terrain environments. The instability phenomenon of the heavy-duty legged robots often arises during the dynamic interactions between the supporting feet and the intricate terrains, which significantly impact the ability of the heavy-duty legged robots to move rapidly and accomplish tasks. Therefore, it is necessary to assess the mechanical behavior of foot–terrain interactions for the heavy-duty legged robots. In order to achieve the above goal, a systematic literature review methodology is employed to examine recent technical scientific publications, aiming to identify both current and prospective research fields. The characteristics of supporting feet for different heavy-duty legged robots are compared and analyzed. The foot–terrain mechanical models of the heavy-duty legged robots are discussed. The problems that need further research are summarized and presented, which is conducive to further deepening and expanding the research on the mechanical behavior of foot–terrain interactions for heavy-duty legged robots.

Keywords: heavy-duty legged robot; terrain adaptability; supporting foot; foot–terrain interaction mechanics; sinkage

1. Introduction

In nature, there are various uneven and irregular terrains that have complex environmental surfaces, such as grassland, desert, mud pools, and mountains. The exploration of unknown terrain is dangerous for humans. Autonomous mobile robots can be the first to enter the detection before humans enter unfamiliar and dangerous environments, which greatly ensures the safety of human life and improves the efficiency of exploration work. With the continuous development of autonomous mobile robot technology, autonomous mobile robots have been widely used in multiple fields to protect human safety and improve production efficiency [1].

Considering the varying modes of contact between mobile robots and terrain, the broad classification of mobile robots includes wheeled robots, tracked robots, snake-like robots, spherical robots, and legged robots [2]. The currently widely researched and applied mobile robots are mainly wheeled robots. Wheeled robots have limitations in their use due to their high requirements for terrain environments, necessitating relatively wide, flat, or smaller rugged terrains. Compared to the harsh requirements of wheeled robots in the terrain environment, tracked robots have to some extent improved the high demand for the terrain. However, the large contact area of the tracks with the terrain also brings new

problems. The terrain adaptability of snake robots has significantly improved compared to the tracked robots, but these types of robots lack a load-bearing capacity and have relatively slow movement speed. They can only achieve the robot's own motion [3]. The spherical robots have good mobility performance. Although the spherical shape can effectively protect the fragile and moving parts of the robots from external damage, the contact mode between the spherical robots and the terrain is point contact, which is not conducive to control movement. The spherical robots have not been widely used [4]. The legged robots often use biomimetic technology to design their structures. They usually imitate humans walking on two legs, and mammals or insects walking on multiple legs. Their structures are more flexible and can maintain relative stability. Compared to wheeled robots and tracked robots, legged robots require only intermittent and discrete landing points to cross obstacles like legged animals. Therefore, walking mechanisms have stronger adaptability to walk on complex terrain. Compared to snake robots and spherical robots, the legged robots have a load-bearing capacity. The research on legged robots has received widespread attention in recent years due to their excellent terrain adaptability and motion flexibility. In fields such as interstellar exploration [5], humanitarian demining [6], logging [7], and nuclear industry [8], the legged robots have unique advantages and have been widely used.

Based on their load-bearing abilities, legged robots can be classified into two categories: heavy-duty legged robots and light-duty legged robots. It can be seen that heavy-duty legged robots have three characteristics compared to light-duty legged robots: large mass, large volume, and high payload–total mass ratio [1]. The heavy-duty legged robots may encounter various complex terrains in actual environments, which also makes the robots full of challenges when moving. Compared to the light-duty legged robots, the heavy-duty legged robots are more prone to foot sinkage occurring when traveling in soft and muddy terrains due to the lower pressure-bearing capacity of the soil. With the low adhesion of smooth surfaces such as ice and snow, heavy-duty legged robots are also more prone to foot slips occurring. The heavy-duty legged robots are more sensitive to foot–terrain interactions compared to the light-duty legged robots. When a heavy-duty legged robot interacts dynamically with complex terrain during movement, it is prone to the phenomenon of robot instability. It has a significant impact on achieving rapid robot movement and completing designated tasks. Studying the foot–terrain mechanical behavior of the heavy-duty legged robots and establishing an appropriate foot–terrain mechanical model are meaningful. The reasonable landing area of the heavy-duty legged robots is increased. The optimization of control strategies is achieved. The parameters selection of foot structure design is facilitated. By designing foot configurations for different working conditions, the mobility performance of the heavy-duty legged robots is improved. The area of some irregular feet in contact with the terrain is not equal to the overall size of the feet. An accurate area is essential in model design.

Compared to the light-duty legged robots, the heavy-duty legged robots have a larger leg mass. Both the supporting and the swinging legs can withstand greater torque during the movement, and that puts forward better technical requirements for maintaining the stability of the robots. Thus, it is particularly important to study the mechanical behavior of foot–terrain interactions of the heavy-duty legged robots. The forces acting on the robot's feet are divided into normal and tangential forces. In order to make the robot's walking smoother, the study of gait planning for heavy-duty legged robots also relies on the study of foot–terrain mechanics [9–11]. Bloesch and Voloshina have also pointed out that it is necessary to study foot–terrain mechanics of the legged robots to improve terrain adaptability [12,13]. Zhuang studied the multimodal information fusion of robots, which has a significant effect on improving their terrain recognition ability [14].

The supporting foot structures of the heavy-duty legged robots directly affect foot–terrain interactions. Based on the research process of the mechanical behavior of foot–terrain interactions in heavy-duty legged robots, the supporting foot structures and mechanical models of foot–terrain interactions are reviewed for the heavy-duty legged robots. In Section 2, the supporting foot structures of the heavy-duty legged robots are discussed.

The foot configurations and plantar pattern shapes of the heavy-duty legged robots' supporting feet are compared and analyzed. In Section 3, the key technologies related to the foot–terrain characteristics of the heavy-duty legged robots are provided. The development of foot–terrain mechanics is narrated. In Section 4, the challenging works in the study of terrain behavior mechanics for heavy-duty legged robots are described. In Section 5, the conclusions are presented. The future development trends are projected. The overall framework of the article is shown in Figure 1. The purpose of this paper is to ensure the terrain adaptability of heavy-duty legged robots by studying the foot–terrain mechanics mechanism.

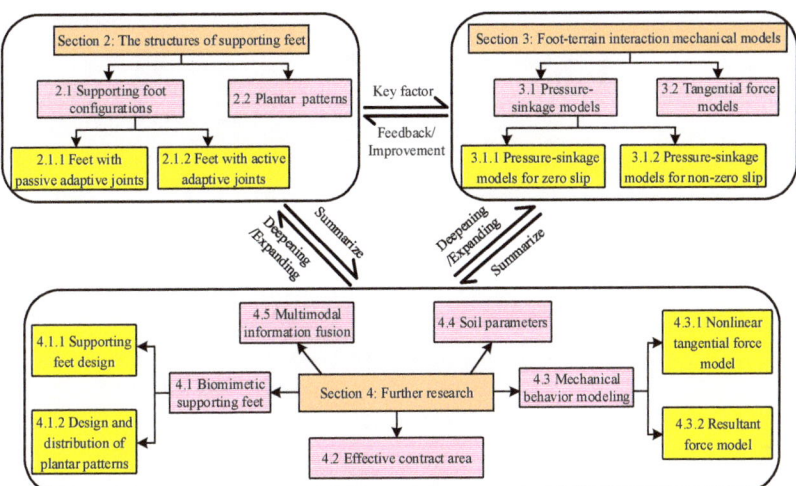

Figure 1. Overall framework of article.

2. Supporting Feet of Heavy-Duty Legged Robots

The heavy-duty legged robots are one of the basic forms of mobile robots. Unlike the wheeled and tracked robots, they can freely change the landing points during the actual walking. They adjust their posture at any time by changing the support between feet and terrain, which can ensure stability during the support process. The heavy-duty legged robots make direct contact with the terrain and need to adapt to different types and inclinations of terrain. It increases the requirements for the feet. The feet can play a supporting, load-bearing, and antiskid role. Also, they need to have multiple degrees of freedom to adapt to the forward and turning movements of the heavy-duty legged robots. The feet of the heavy-duty legged robots need to meet special requirements such as bearing heavy loads, adapting to different terrains, and having flexible degrees of freedom. The section briefly reviews two types of related work, namely the foot configurations and sole pattern shapes of different heavy-duty legged robots.

2.1. Supporting Foot Configurations of Heavy-Duty Legged Robots

2.1.1. Feet with Passive Adaptive Joints

Spheres, ellipsoids, and rectangles have been found to be the most common shapes of feet [15]. Common configurations such as cylindrical feet, semi-cylindrical feet, spherical feet, hemispherical feet, square feet, and special feet are summarized.

Cylindrical Supporting Foot Configurations

The Tokyo Institute of Technology has developed the TITAN series of robots. In 2002, the latest generation model machine called TITAN XI was developed, and the robot is shown in Figure 2a. It is a hydraulically driven quadruped robot. The robot can walk steadily and continuously on slopes covered with reinforced concrete frames. It can achieve intermittent crawling gait based on map information. Terrain adaptive gait makes the robot's motion more stable. The robot's feet are cylindrical [16]. TITAN IX is a quadruped robot with cylindrical foot shapes for humanitarian landmine detection missions [17]. TITAN III is a quadruped robot with cylindrical feet [18], as shown in Figure 2b.

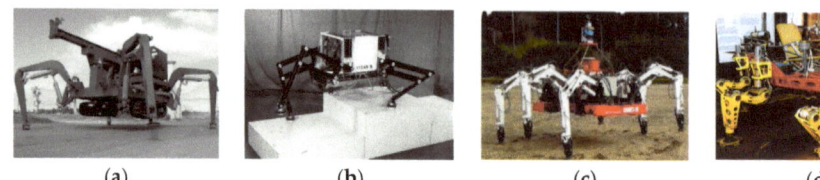

Figure 2. Robots of TITAN series, COMET-IV, and NMIIIA: (**a**) TITAN XI [16]; (**b**) TITAN III [18]; (**c**) COMET-IV [19]; and (**d**) NMIIIA [1].

The COMET-IV robot developed by Chiba University is a heavy-duty hexapod robot based on hydraulic drive, as shown in Figure 2c. The weight of the robot is approximately 2120 kg. Its load-bearing capacity is approximately 424 kg. The overall size is approximately 2.8 m × 3.3 m × 2.5 m. Each leg has four degrees of freedom (DOFs). It can walk on uneven terrain. The robot's feet are cylindrical [19].

The Dante II robot, designed for exploring planetary surfaces, operates semi-autonomously and is equipped with eight legs. It weighs 770 kg, has the capacity to carry a 130 kg payload, and is capable of navigating slopes up to 30 degrees. The feet of the robot are cylindrical [20].

The NMIIIA robot was successfully developed in 1985, as shown in Figure 2d. It is a crewed hexapod robot developed by the former Soviet Union during the implementation of lunar exploration activities. It is used for star surface exploration and load bearing. The robot has a mass of 750 kg, a load-bearing capacity of 80 kg, and a moving speed of 0.7 km/h. Its feet are cylindrical [1].

The SILO4 robot developed in Spain also has cylindrical feet [21]. The passive joint of the foot contains three rotational degrees of freedom (DOFs). The three-axis force sensors are installed on the robot's feet. The outdoor experiment and ankle joint are shown in Figure 3.

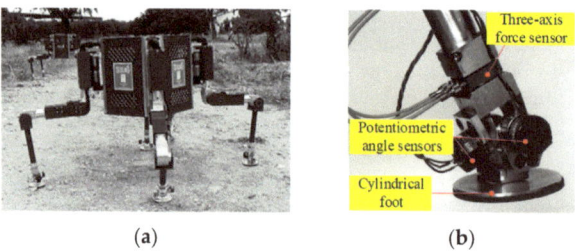

Figure 3. SILO-4 robot [21]: (**a**) outdoor experiment; (**b**) ankle-integrated sensor system.

Zhuang developed a terrain electric-driven hexapod robot with a high load ratio, ElSpider. Six supporting legs of the robot are uniformly distributed on the body of the central symmetric structure. A single leg adopts a structure with three active and four passive degrees of freedom. It has a weight of approximately 300 kg. The rated load of ElSpider is greater than 155 kg, as shown in Figure 4a. Its overall size is approximately 1.9 m × 1.9 m × 1.0 m. It can cross obstacles with a height greater than 0.3 m, cross trenches with a width greater than 0.3 m, walk regularly at a speed of 0.16 m/s, and climb a maximum slope of 35°. The robot's feet are cylindrical [22–24]. The six dimensions force sensors are also installed on the feet to measure the foot–terrain forces, as shown in Figure 4b.

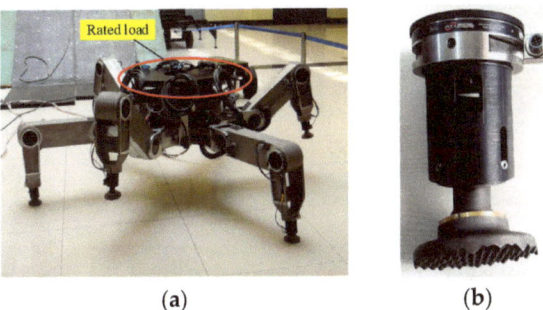

Figure 4. ElSpider robot [25]: (**a**) load experiment; (**b**) robot foot.

A P-P structured hexapod Octopus robot was developed by Professor Gao F's team from the School of Mechanical and Power Engineering at Shanghai Jiao Tong University. The robot's body adopts a symmetrical design. It always maintains three supporting legs to support the body during walking, with good stability and maneuverability. Its speed is 1.2 km/h, and its load-bearing capacity is 200 kg. The Octopus robot adopts cylindrical configurations at the feet. But unlike the other feet of heavy-duty legged robots, the middle of the cylindrical foot is hollow. Its structure can effectively reduce the mass of the robot's feet. And springs are installed above the feet to provide cushioning and shock absorption [26–28]. The indoor experiment is shown in Figure 5a. The load-bearing progress is shown in Figure 5b.

Figure 5. Octopus robot: (**a**) indoor walking experiment [26]; (**b**) load-bearing progress [29].

Researchers from Jilin University have designed a heavy-duty hexapod robot [30–32]. The feet are designed as ball joint structures, and force sensors are connected in series above the ball joints to detect whether the feet are firmly pressed against the terrain. There are reset springs parallel to the ball joints between the upper and the lower plates of the ball joints. They are used for feet to avoid sticking during the process of stepping on the terrain due to the large deflection angle of the foot bottom. Thick rubber pads are installed at the bottom of the feet to cushion the landing of the feet. The prototype of the heavy-duty hexapod robot and its foot are, respectively, shown in Figure 6a,b.

Figure 6. Heavy-duty hexapod robot of Jilin University: (**a**) prototype [30]; (**b**) foot [32].

On the basis of the investigation of the heavy-duty legged robot, researchers from Huazhong University of Science and Technology present a novel foot structure for the heavy-duty legged robot. Its highly adaptable foot system with significant adhesion can be utilized to navigate extreme roads and complex terrains, including mountainous areas and swamps. The foot design, inspired by mountain-dwelling creatures, has been crafted to ensure substantial adhesion and enhanced adaptability [33,34]. The feet are installed on the heavy-duty legged robot, as shown in Figure 7a. The robot foot and single leg are, respectively, shown in Figure 7b,c.

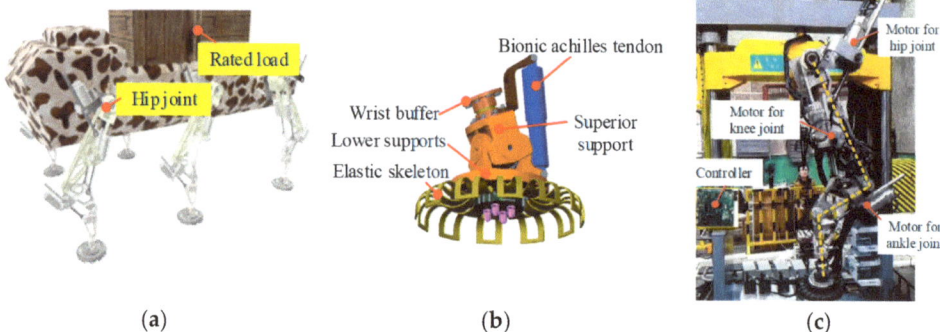

Figure 7. Heavy-duty six-legged robot from Huazhong University of Science and Technology: (**a**) robot model [33]; (**b**) robot foot [34]; (**c**) single leg [33].

The advantage of cylindrical feet is that they have a large contact area with the terrain. Large contact areas can provide greater adhesion to withstand heavy loads. At the same time, the heavy-duty legged robots equipped with cylindrical flat feet are suitable for long-distance transportation. The disadvantage is that it is necessary to design a swing structure, otherwise it cannot walk stably. The stress distribution model of the cylindrical foot of the heavy-duty legged robots is shown in Equation (1). Then

$$\begin{cases} F_N(t) = \sigma(t) \times A \\ F_T(t) = \tau(t) \times A \end{cases} \quad (1)$$

where F_N is the normal support force of the foot. F_T is the tangential driving force of the foot. A is the contact area between the foot and the terrain.

Semi-Cylindrical Supporting Foot Configurations

The Big Dog robot [35–37] developed by Boston Dynamics in the United States is a quadruped robot. The main components of the robot are shown in Figure 8a. It has full flexibility and can stand, squat, and move. The crawling speed is 0.2 m/s, the jogging speed is 1.6 m/s, and the jumping speed can reach 3.1 m/s in laboratory testing. The weight is approximately 109 kg, and the size is 1.1 m × 1 m × 0.3 m. The feet of the Big Dog robot are semi-cylindrical, as shown in Figure 8b. The Big Dog robot can pass through rock slopes up to 60° and has excellent adaptability to complex terrain.

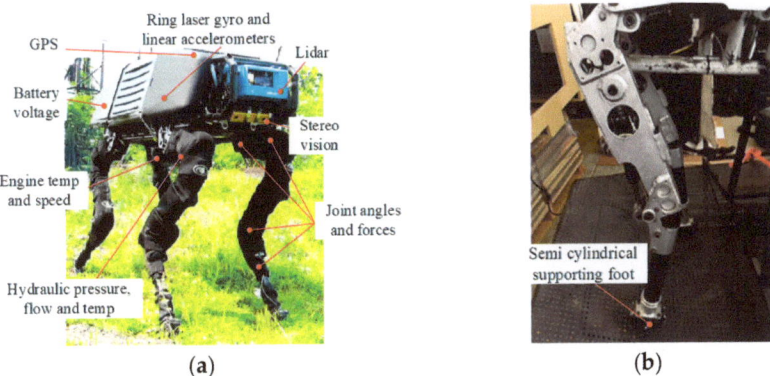

Figure 8. Big Dog robot: (**a**) main components of robot [1]; (**b**) foot.

Researchers at Huazhong University of Science and Technology have developed a hydraulic-driven quadruped robot, MBBOT [38,39]. Each leg of the robot includes four active degrees of freedom. The total mass of the robot is 140 kg. The feet of the four legs are also equipped with three-dimensional force sensors to detect the magnitude of the force between the legs and the external environment. The 3D model of the robot MBBOT is shown in Figure 9a. The prototype of the robot MBBOT is shown in Figure 9b.

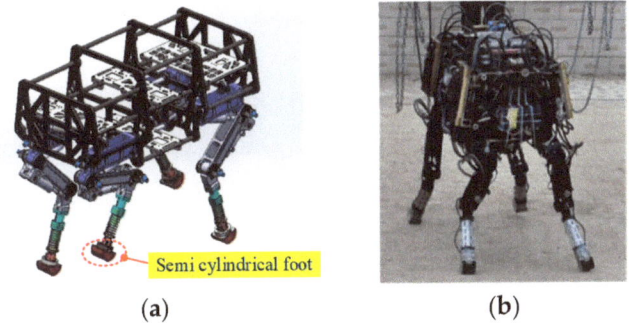

Figure 9. MBBOT robot: (**a**) 3D model [40]; (**b**) robot prototype [41].

Researchers from Shanghai Jiao Tong University have designed a disaster relief hexapod robot, HexbotIV [42–44]. The overall dimension of the robot is about 1.10 m × 0.72 m × 1.00 m. The robot has a total mass of 268 kg and can provide a load of 50 kg. In addition, to reduce the impact of the robot during movement, semi-cylindrical rubber cushions are installed at the end of the feet. The prototype of HexbotIV is shown in Figure 10a. The three-dimensional drawing of the parallel mechanism leg with an erect posture is shown in Figure 10b.

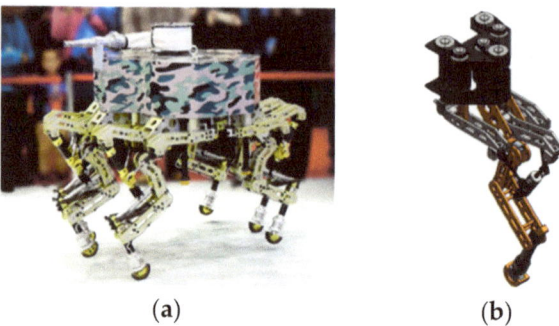

Figure 10. HexbotIV robot: (**a**) prototype [43]; (**b**) parallel mechanism leg [44].

LS3 is tailored for the Marine Corps to handle cargo, as shown in Figure 11a. It can bear a payload of approximately 182 kg, carry enough fuel to sustain for 24 h, and cover approximately 32.2 km. Its feet are semi-cylindrical [45].

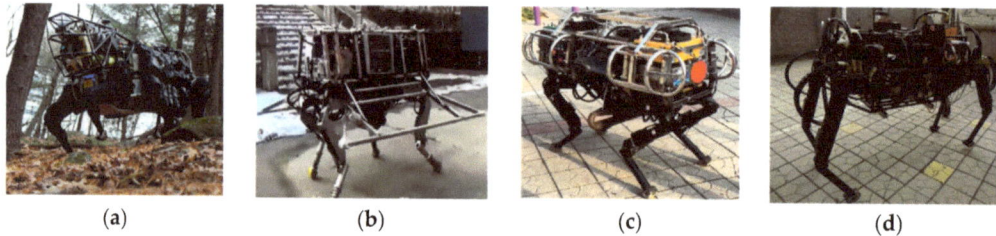

Figure 11. Robots of LS3 and SCalf series: (**a**) LS3 [45]; (**b**) SCalf-I Robot [46]; (**c**) SCalf-II Robot [47]; and (**d**) SCalf-III Robot [48].

The SCalf-I robot, SCalf-II robot, and SCalf-III robot developed by the research team of Shandong University are all quadruped hydraulic heavy-duty robots, as shown in Figure 11b–d, respectively. The payload–total mass ratio can reach 0.5. The feet are designed as semi-cylindrical shapes [46–48].

Compared with cylindrical feet, the semi-cylindrical feet of heavy-duty legged robots can effectively reduce the mass of the robot. However, the contact surface area between the semi-cylindrical feet and the terrain is relatively small for the cylindrical feet. Then, the stability of the heavy-duty legged robots is slightly worse than that of the cylindrical feet.

Spherical Supporting Foot Configurations

In 2010, the DFKI Robot Innovation Center at the University of Bremen designed a highly adaptable free-climbing robot (Space Climber) for the steep slopes of lunar craters. The robot feet are mechanisms similar to eagle claws, as shown in Figure 12a. The feet can effectively improve the terrain adhesion ability of the detector [49]. In 2012, to overcome the limited mobility of detectors in unstructured environments, such as obstacles, normal steep slopes, and steep slopes of fine-grained soil, the Space Climber feet were changed to spherical shapes [50]. The updated robot feet are shown in Figure 12b. The spherical feet can withstand collisions with hard surfaces or obstacles and provide an increased contact area when sinking into the soil. The spherical feet have the natural advantage of having the same tangential performance in different directions of motion.

Figure 12. Space Climber: (**a**) original robot [49]; (**b**) updated robot [50].

TITAN XIII is a quadruped robot, as shown in Figure 13a. Each leg has three degrees of freedom (DOFs). The body mass is 5.65 kg, and the load is 5.0 kg. Its feet shapes are spherical. It can move on rough and irregular terrains by selecting suitable footholds and changing the robot's posture [51]. Ohtsuka S invented terrain-adaptive feet for the TITAN XIII robot. Its feet can passively adapt to rough terrain, including bumps and tilts, while ensuring a stable foothold [52].

Figure 13. Robots of TITAN-XIII and SCOUT II: (**a**) TITAN-XIII [51]; (**b**) SCOUT II [53].

The SCOUT II robot [53] is a quadruped robot that can achieve a jumping gait, as shown in Figure 13b. Each leg has two degrees of freedom: a driving hip joint and a linear spring. The stable mobile control strategy can be achieved when it walks at a maximum speed of 0.9 m/s to 1.2 m/s. The dynamically stable legged robots lay greater emphasis on their terrain adaptability, making their movement more stable. The feet of the robot adopt hemispherical shapes to achieve the point contact between the foot and the terrain, which improves the stability of the robot in different terrains.

Based on the above statement, it can be very easy to come to a conclusion. The advantages of the spherical foot are that the mechanical structure design is simple, the tangential forces in all directions are equal, and it is very suitable for walking in soft soil or deserts. Meanwhile, the disadvantage of the spherical foot is that the contact between the foot and the terrain is point contact, with a relatively small contact area and low terrain friction, which is not conducive to the robot's smooth walking. When the velocity angle of the foot tip coincides with the attitude angle, the stress distribution models of the spherical foot can be obtained, as shown in Equations (2) and (3). Then

$$F_N = \left(K\delta^m(t) + C\delta^n(t)\dot{\delta}^p(t) \right) \sin \eta \qquad (2)$$

$$F_T = \begin{cases} \mu F_N \\ -\left(K\delta^m(t) + C\delta^n(t)\dot{\delta}^p(t)\right)\cos\eta \geq \mu F_N \end{cases} \quad (3a)$$

$$F_T = \begin{cases} -\left(K\delta^m(t) + C\delta^n(t)\dot{\delta}^p(t)\right)\cos\eta \\ -\left(K\delta^m(t) + C\delta^n(t)\dot{\delta}^p(t)\right)\cos\eta < \mu F_N \end{cases} \quad (3b)$$

where K is the spring coefficient, C is the damping coefficient, μ is the friction coefficient, m and q are the parameters to be identified, and n is the model parameter.

Hemispherical Supporting Foot Configurations

The SILO6 robot [54] is a hexapod robot system used for humanitarian demining missions. According to the static stability design, a triangular gait is adopted to achieve the maximum speed of the robot. The foot is fixed to the hemisphere of the ankle, with a simple structure and good performance on the hard terrain. But increasing the radius of the ball on the loose terrain will reduce the sinking amount. At the same time, on hard terrain, the radius of the ball is too large to make it attempt to rotate, changing the positions of the foot's support. The SILO-6 robot is shown in Figure 14a.

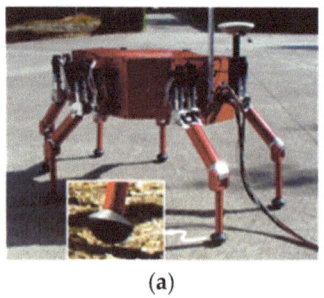
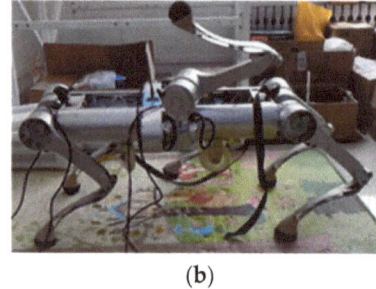

(a) (b)

Figure 14. Robots of SILO-6 and SDU Hex: (a) SILO-6 [54]; (b) SDU Hex [55].

The SDU Hex electric hexapod robot [55] designed by researchers from Shandong University in 2021 can achieve leg arm reuse and strong operation. The structure of the entire SDU Hex robot is shown in Figure 14b. The feet adopt hemispherical structures. And the feet are equipped with a high adhesion damping rubber pattern and air chamber, reducing the impact force during the interaction between the foot and the terrain.

The hemispherical feet and spherical feet have the same contact methods with the terrain, both of which are point contact. Therefore, the mechanical models of the two above can be generalized and will not be explained in detail here.

Square Supporting Foot Configurations

The Hydraulic Landmaster robot is a large hexapod robot that works on steep forest terrain, as shown in Figure 15. The weight of the robot is 3950 kg, with a rated load of 1000 kg. The size is 3.6 m × 2.3 m × 2.6 m, with a maximum height of 4.5 m, and a maximum height of 1.7 m when passing through obstacles. Electric Landmaster 3 is the previous generation of Hydraulic Landmaster. The electric Landmaster 3 robot has a weight of 82 kg and a rated load of 30 kg. Both robots have the same model structure with principle, and both have significant heavy-duty capacity. Square feet are used at the feet of robots [1].

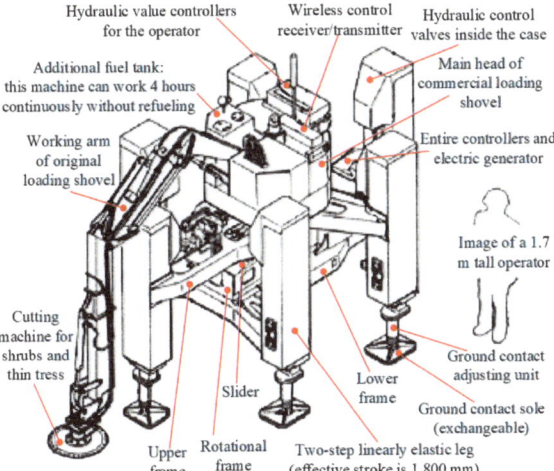

Figure 15. Hydraulic Landmaster robot [1].

The Petman robot [56] developed in the United States is a humanoid bipedal robot, as shown in Figure 16a. The maximum speed can reach 7.2 km/h. The robot's use of Big Dog's leg structure and electronic equipment enables faster design and testing experiments. When pushing moderately from the side while walking, it can restore its balance. Square feet are used at the feet. Another humanoid bipedal robot Altas [57] also adopts square foot structures, as shown in Figure 16b.

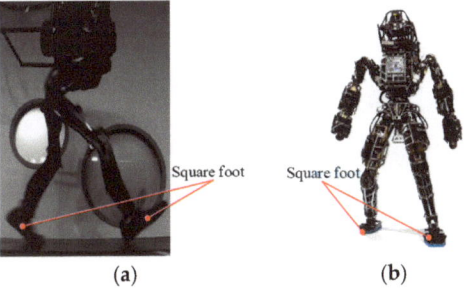

Figure 16. Robots of Petman and Altas: (**a**) Petman [56]; (**b**) Altas [57].

The advantages of square configuration are that the design is relatively simple, and no spiral structure design is required. The disadvantage is that it cannot adapt to more complex terrain. The rectangular foot–terrain mechanics models can be obtained by multiplying the average stress distribution with the plantar area. The rectangular foot–terrain mechanics models can be given in Equation (4). Then

$$\begin{cases} F_N(t) = (k_c \cdot a + k_\varphi \cdot a \cdot b)\delta^n \\ F_T(t) = a \cdot b \cdot c + F_N(t) \cdot \tan \varphi \end{cases} \quad (4)$$

where a, b, and c are the dimensions of the long side, wide side, and high side of the rectangular foot, respectively.

Special Supporting Foot Configurations

Charlie is a quadruped robot designed based on primitive humans. The feet of the front legs adopt curved structures [58,59]. The quadruped forward movement of the robot can be achieved. The Charlie robot can walk upright with both feet. The quadruped and bipedal walking postures are, respectively, shown in Figure 17a,b.

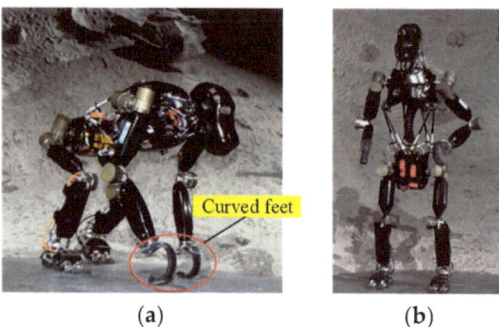

Figure 17. Charlie robot [58]: (**a**) quadruped walking posture; (**b**) bipedal walking posture.

In the 1960s, General Electric designed a quadruped walking truck for the US Army, as shown in Figure 18. The shape of the foot is curved [60]. The advantages of curved feet are that they have simpler structures and a lighter weight. Their disadvantage is that they cannot carry a larger mass.

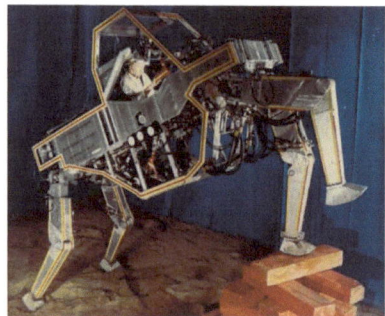

Figure 18. Walking truck [1].

Hirose proposed a passive terrain adaptive foot mechanism [61]. A sensor mechanism installed on the ankle and three fixed claws at the bottom of the foot are included. The effectiveness of these new mechanisms was verified through the TITAN VII robot walking experiment. The TITAN VII robot is shown in Figure 19.

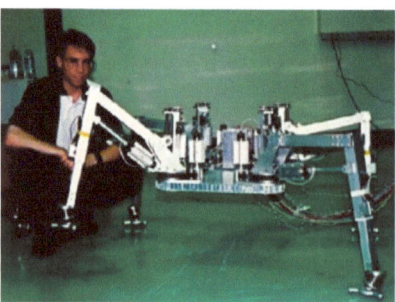

Figure 19. TITAN VII robot.

Researchers are inspired by the large surface area to volume ratio of X-shaped concrete piles in geotechnical engineering. An X-shaped foot with holes is designed and the relationship between sinkage and bearing capacity is analyzed. When subjected to an identical load, the sinkage experienced by an X-shaped foot with holes is less compared to that of other foot shapes [62,63]. It is beneficial for reducing the sinkage of the robot and improving walking stability.

Combining sinkage with multi-body dynamics, the characteristics of the circular foot, X-shaped foot, and improved X-shaped foot were analyzed for their sinkage and walking stability. It can be obtained that the improved X-shaped foot has the best capability of increasing the support length and lateral force of the robot. The horizontal cross-sectional shapes of the three types of feet are shown in Figure 20.

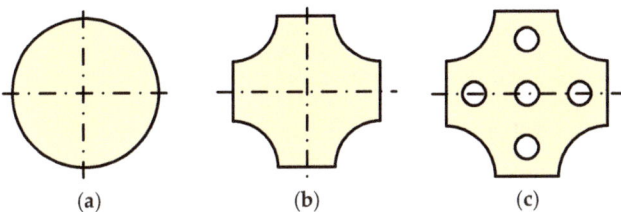

Figure 20. Horizontal section shapes [63]: (**a**) circle; (**b**) X-shaped; (**c**) improved X-shaped.

Chopra [64] proposed a foot design that can passively change shape and actively change stiffness to improve the robot's motion on the granular media. The foot is shown in Figure 21a. It has been proven that using a foot design with wrinkles is soft before falling and rigid during shearing. It can reduce foot acceleration at joints, traction force, and penetration depth, and obtain a greater resistance coefficient when the foot is at a certain displacement. The contact process between the foot and the terrain is shown in Figure 21b.

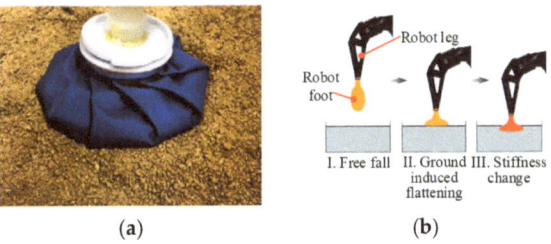

Figure 21. Passive and active shape-changing foot [64]: (**a**) foot to terrain contact; (**b**) contact process.

The advantages of robot feet with passive adaptive joints are their simple mechanical structures, simple mobility control policies, and the ability to adjust relative positions and angles according to changes in the environment. Robot feet with passive adaptive joints can be divided into cylindrical feet, semi-cylindrical feet, spherical feet, hemispherical feet, square feet, and special feet. The most widely used configuration for the supporting feet of heavy-duty legged robots is cylindrical. The performance indicators of the released heavy-duty legged robots with passive adaptive joints are shown in Table 1. The different foot configurations with the passive adaptive joints of heavy-duty legged robots are shown in Figure 22. Due to the reasons of technical confidentiality and copyright, the specific weight-bearing quality of heavy-duty robots that can be consulted is limited.

Table 1. Published performance indicators for heavy-duty legged robots with passive adaptive joints.

Robot	Length × Width × Height (m³)	Legs	Foot Shape	Driving Method	Mass (kg)	Payload (kg)	References
TITAN XI	5.0 × 4.8 × 3.0	4	Cylindrical	Hydraulic	6800	5200	[16]
TITAN IX	10 × 16 × 5.5	4	Cylindrical	Electric	170	-	[17]
TITAN III	-	4	Cylindrical	-	80	-	[18]
COMET-IV	2.8 × 3.3 × 2.5	6	Cylindrical	Hydraulic	2120	424	[19]
Dante II	3.7 × 2.3 × 3.7	8	Cylindrical	Electric	770	130	[20]
NMIIIA	1.5 × 0.5 × 1	6	Cylindrical	Electric	750	80	[1]
SILO 4	0.31 × 0.31 × 0.3	4	Cylindrical	Electric	30	-	[21]
ElSpider	1.9 × 1.9 × 1.0	6	Cylindrical	Electric	300	155	[22,23]
Octopus Robot	1.5 × 1.5 × 1	6	Cylindrical	Hydraulic	200	200	[24]
Hexapod Robot	-	6	Cylindrical	Hydraulic	3000	-	[30–32]
Legged Robot	-	6	Cylindrical	Electric	4200	-	[33,34]
Big Dog	1.1 × 0.3 × 1	4	Semi-cylindrical	Hydraulic	109	50	[25,26]
MBBOT	0.85 (Height)	4	Semi-cylindrical	Hydraulic	140	-	[40,41]
HexbotIV	1.0 × 0.72 ×1	4	Semi-cylindrical	Hydraulic	268	50	[43,44]
LS3	1.7 (Height)	4	Semi-cylindrical	Hydraulic	590	182	[45]
SCalf-I	1.0 × 0.4 × 0.68	4	Semi-cylindrical	Hydraulic	65	80	[46]
SCalf-II	1.1 × 0.45 (Length × Width)	4	Semi-cylindrical	Hydraulic	130	140	[47]
SCalf-III	1.4 × 0.75 (Length × Width)	4	Semi-cylindrical	Hydraulic	200	200	[48]
Space Climber$_1$	8.2 × 10 × 22	6	Special	Electric	185	-	[49]
Space Climber$_2$	8.5 × 10 × 22	6	Spherical	Electric	23	8	[50]
TITAN XIII	2.134 × 5.584 × 3.4	4	Spherical	Electric	5.65	5.0	[51,52]
SCOUT II	0.55 × 0.48 × 0.27	4	Spherical	Electric	20.86	-	[53]
SILO 6	0.88 × 0.45 × 0.26	6	Hemispherical	Electric	44.34	-	[54]
SDU Hex	0.98 × 0.4 × 0.1 to 0.6	6	Hemispherical	Electric	35	-	[55]
Landmaster	3.6 × 2.3 × 2.6	6	Square	Hydraulic	3950	1000	[1]
Landmaster 3	1.4 × 1.3 × 1.0	6	Square	Electric	82	30	[1]
Petman	1.5 (Height)	2	Square	Hydraulic	80	-	[56]
Altas	1.8 (Height)	2	Square	Electric	150	-	[57]
Charlie	8 × 4.4 × 5.4	4	Special	Electric	21.5	-	[58,59]
Walking Truck	4 × 3 × 3.3	4	Special	Hydraulic	1300	-	[60]
TITAN VII	-	4	Special	-	-	-	[61]

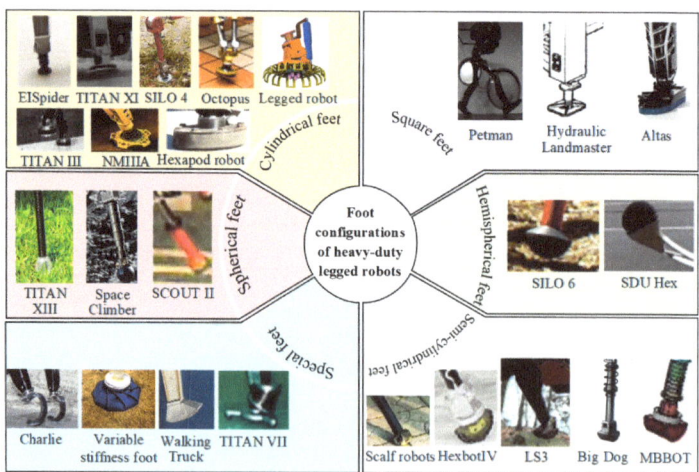

Figure 22. Foot configurations with passive adaptive joints for different heavy-duty legged robots.

In terms of configuration, the cylindrical shape is symmetrical in all directions, which can make the normal and the tangential forces on the robot's supporting feet more uniform. The robot's foot slip is effectively suppressed. It plays an irreplaceable role in the movement of heavy-duty legged robots on unstructured terrain. The cylindrical foot has a larger contact area with the terrain, which is compared to the smaller contact area of other feet. For the heavy-duty legged robots, increasing the area between feet and terrain in the process of operation can reduce the pressure on the foot per unit area and improve the support effect during the load-bearing period. However, the drawbacks of the robot feet with passive adaptive joints are also obvious. The structures cannot fully adapt to the changing terrain environment and actively control the foot posture.

2.1.2. Feet with Active Driving Joints

The mechanisms of feet with active driving joints in heavy-duty legged robots are generally more complex. Drive devices need to be installed to make them more difficult to control movement and more cost-effective compared to feet with passive adaptive joints. They have not been widely applied in current research on heavy-duty legged robots.

In 1996, Hong [65] from the South Korean University of Science and Technology was inspired by the structure of umbrellas and designed a point contact underactuated robotic foot. The oil in and out of the hydraulic cylinder in the middle of the foot will change the opening and closing state of the toes. The point contact between the feet and the terrain enhances the adaptability of the robot's feet to the rough terrain. This type of foot is applied by researchers to a quadruped robot, as shown in Figure 23a.

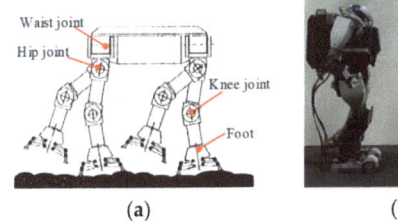
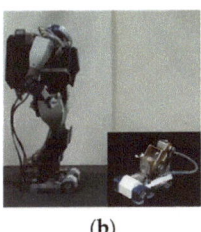
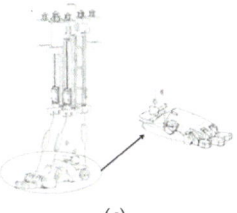

(a)　　　　　　　　(b)　　　　　　　(c)　　　　　　　(d)

Figure 23. Some feet with active driving joints: (**a**) quadruped legged walking robot Centaur [65]; (**b**) diagram of foot mechanism with toe joints [66]; (**c**) robot foot with active driving unit [67]; (**d**) Roboclimber robot performs climbing experiments outdoors [68].

In 2007, Yamamoto, Sugihara, Nakamura, and others from the University of Tokyo in Japan designed humanoid robot feet. The robot feet are installed on the UT-μ2 robot, as shown in Figure 23b. The characteristic of the robot's feet is that the toe mechanism does not use the commonly used hinge type rotating pair, but instead uses a parallel four-link mechanism. Through analysis, it is shown that the combined moment of force at the joints of the parallel four-link-type toe mechanism is smaller than that of the hinge-type toe joint during most motion periods [66].

In 2009, Borovac and Slavnic from the University of Novi Sad used motion analysis of human feet to design a humanoid robot foot. The type of robot foot not only has passive toe joints but also active toe joints, making humanoid robots able to walk more smoothly and improving their walking ability [67]. The robot foot with an active driving unit is shown in Figure 23c.

Nabulsi from the Polytechnic University of Madrid designed a mountain climbing robot called Roboclimber, as shown in Figure 23d. It adds hydraulic cylinders above the feet of the robot. Adjusting the foot–terrain force is carried out by changing the oil inlet and outlet quantities of the hydraulic cylinders. The friction force between the robot's feet and the terrain is adjusted. The mechanical performance of the foot–terrain contact surface is improved [68].

In 2010, Collins and Kuo from the University of Delft in the Netherlands designed a robotic foot that could utilize energy more effectively during walking. Because people usually waste a lot of beneficial energy when walking, they developed a micro-driven controlled humanoid foot [69]. Being able to more fully utilize the energy lost in human legs and ankle joints during walking, the energy utilization rate has increased by 23% compared to normal walking. The physical image of the robot foot is shown in Figure 24a. The 3D structure diagram of the robot foot is shown in Figure 24b.

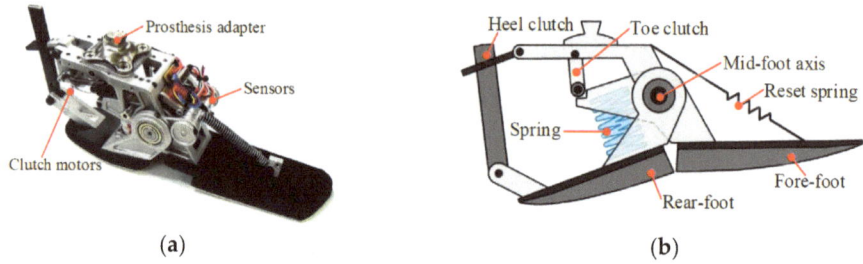

Figure 24. Foot with energy recovery [69]: (**a**) physical image; (**b**) 3D structure diagram of foot.

Compared with robot feet with passive adaptive joints, robot feet with active adaptive joints have certain advantages. They can actively adjust the configurations of their feet based on the shape of the terrain, thereby increasing the contact area between the feet and the terrain. When subjected to normal force from the vertical direction and tangential force from the horizontal direction, adjusting the feet to reach the positions where the force is most evenly applied improves the stability of the robot. Their significant drawbacks are a more complex structural design and high control difficulty compared to robot feet with passive adaptive joints. At present, there is little research on robot feet with active adaptive joints in heavy-duty legged robots.

2.2. Plantar Patterns of Supporting Foot of Legged Robots

The legged robots mainly rely on the friction force between their feet and the terrain when walking. When the friction force is high, the sliding phenomenon of the robot's feet will be reduced. Designing and installing some structures on the bottom of the robot's feet is carried out to improve their adhesion to the terrain. In current research, it has been found that the research on the foot patterns of heavy-duty legged robots is not yet in-depth enough.

Song [70] from the Harbin Institute of Technology conducted an analysis of the equivalent adhesion coefficient of typical foot patterns. The model of robot foot–terrain interaction attachment has been established. The equivalent adhesion coefficient of different foot configurations (flat foot, nail foot, single-baffle foot, and multi-baffle foot) can be calculated. The different feet used for testing in the experiment are shown in Figure 25. The higher the coefficient of adhesion, the better the adhesion characteristics of the robot. The conclusion is that the multi-baffle foot has the best adhesion performance, followed by the single-baffle foot, nail foot, and flat foot.

Zou [71] from the Dalian University of Technology designed a new plantar pattern. The middle part adopts horizontal stripes perpendicular to the robot's forward direction, while the remaining parts use 45° diagonal stripes to enhance the anti-slip ability of the foot. The design of the plantar pattern structure is to first establish a simulation model for the terrain action and an evaluation method for adhesion performance. On that basis, the plantar adhesion performance is the optimization objective, and the structural parameters of the plantar pattern are the optimization variables. The response surface method is used to optimize the design of the foot pattern. Simulation and experimental verification are conducted. Compared to the reference offroad tire design, the adhesion coefficient of the plantar pattern is increased by 7.41%. The optimized plantar pattern is shown in Figure 26a. The original plantar pattern is shown in Figure 26b.

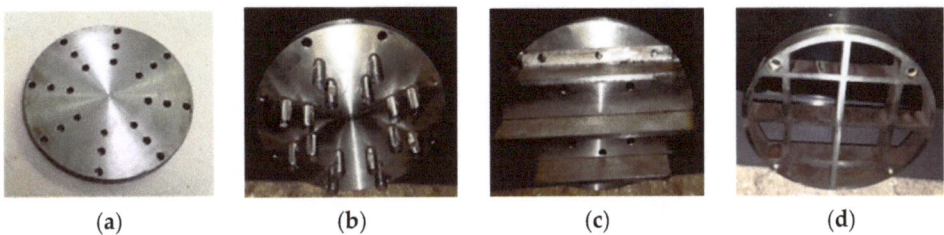

Figure 25. Some different feet [70]: (**a**) flat foot; (**b**) nail foot; (**c**) single-baffle foot; and (**d**) multi-baffle foot.

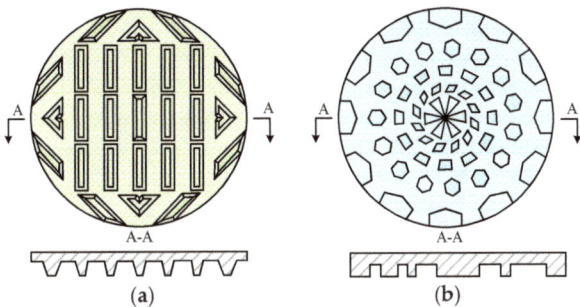

Figure 26. Comparison of plantar pattern shapes [71]: (**a**) optimized plantar pattern; (**b**) original plantar pattern.

Li [72] from the Dalian University of Technology designed the rubber feet of the heavy-duty robot. The plantar patterns of the feet adopt a mixed pattern design, with a crisscrossing pattern in the middle. The offroad patterns with wider grooves are evenly arranged around at an angle of 15°. The rubber feet can be designed with existing vehicle tire patterns as the research background. Considering the combination of the plantar patterns and the feet, it is equipped with patterned blocks, patterned grooves, and base glue. The calculation of the adhesion and climbing angle of the plantar patterns has also been carried out. Li [73–75] conducted in-depth research on the effects of plantar pattern depth, groove width, and pattern direction on the friction coefficient. The results show that on the wet terrain, the deeper the pattern, the higher the friction coefficient. Wide patterned grooves have a higher coefficient of friction. The friction coefficients of horizontal and 45° patterns are relatively high. Their anti-slip performance is good. The different groove designs of the plantar patterns are shown in Figure 27a–c.

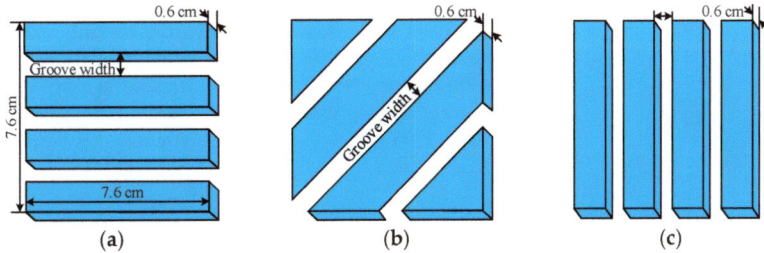

Figure 27. Groove designs of plantar patterns [74]: (**a**) groove orientation 0°; (**b**) groove orientation 45°; and (**c**) groove orientation 90°.

The heavy-duty legged robot relies on the reaction forces provided by the terrain to move. The foot serves as the only interface for direct contact with the terrain, which is a key component that ensures the excellent adaptability of the heavy-duty legged robots to unstructured terrain environments.

3. Dynamics Analysis of Robot

The robot foot–terrain interaction mechanics is a branch of contact mechanics. Studying the interaction process between the machinery and working terrain is of great significance when studying the design of foot mechanisms and the kinematic simulation of robot bodies. An accurate foot–terrain mechanics model is the basic condition for designing anti-sinkage, high-traction, and lightweight feet. At the same time, it can also optimize the path planning and motion control of the robots, thereby improving the terrain adaptability of the heavy-duty legged robots.

The current research on the terrain mechanics of wheeled robots has been very extensive. There is relatively little research on the terrain mechanics of legged robots [76,77]. The current research on the foot–terrain mechanical interactions of the legged robots will draw on the existing wheel–terrain mechanical models of the wheeled robots. Zhuang [78] believes that legged robots can flexibly walk on rough and uneven surfaces, but due to the presence of multiple driving joints, the power consumption of their mobile systems is often high. Therefore, studying the foot–terrain interaction mechanics of heavy-duty legged robots can also provide a reference for low-power research on robots.

The legged robots have the characteristics of discontinuous motion, large foot impact, and multiple degrees of control freedom. Each walk of the robot is equivalent to a collision between feet and terrain. The foot–terrain interaction models are used to analyze the relationship between terrain characteristic parameters and foot parameters of normal and tangential forces. In addition to the force from the normal direction, it is also subjected to tangential force including the horizontal direction. The normal force acting on a heavy-duty legged robot during movement is much greater than the tangential force, Liu [79] conducted a static analysis of the feet of an electrically driven heavy-duty hexapod robot under a tripod gait. A trend chart of the changes in the normal force of the feet is obtained. The walking method that can achieve the most average distribution of each foot force is determined.

During the walking process of the legged robot, the contact between the foot and the terrain not only exhibits normal relative motion but also tangential relative motion. It generates tangential relative motion and tangential friction. Taking into account both normal relative motion and tangential relative motion, analyzing the foot–terrain interactions generated by these two aspects is beneficial for further precise motion control and stable gait planning of the legged robots.

3.1. Models of Pressure–Sinkage for Mobile Robot

Regarding the study of terrain mechanics, the study of wheel–earth interaction mechanics started early and has been very extensive. The use of the wheel–terrain interactions of the wheeled robots as the basis for the study of foot–terrain mechanics of the legged robots has been recognized. When pressure continuously acts on the soil below through the contact surface, the part of the soil will diffuse towards the soil around the contact surface. When a compacted area is fully formed, the movement of surrounding soil particles becomes stable. The pressure–sinkage model is a representation of the pressure–sinkage relationship. For the convenience of elaboration, it is assumed that the depth of soil sinkage is uniform.

3.1.1. Models for Pressure–Sinkage at Zero Slip Conditions

A Theoretical Exploration of the Wheeled Robots

In 1913, Bernstein proposed the relationship between the pressure applied to the soil and the sinkage after conducting relevant experiments on the relationship between pressure and sinkage [80,81]. The updated model is shown in Equation (5). Then

$$p = kz^n \tag{5}$$

where n is the model parameter, and $n > 0$.

In the mid-19th century, Bekker conducted specialized research on the plasticity of soil subsidence and driving resistance [82–84] In classical soil mechanics, when considering the Bernstein model, the sinkage modulus k is bifurcated into two distinct components. One part represents the influence of the cohesion of the soil itself, while the other part represents the influence of the internal shear angle. The shear angle mentioned here is actually the friction angle. The Bekker model also considers the geometric shape of the contact surface. The Bekker model played an irreplaceable role in evaluating the motion performance of the wheeled robots, the tracked robots, and the legged robots [85]. The Bekker model is shown in Equation (6). Then

$$p = \left(\frac{k_c}{b} + k_\phi\right) z^n \tag{6}$$

where b is the smaller dimension of the contact patch. k_c is a sinkage modulus influenced by soil cohesion. k_ϕ is a sinkage modulus influenced by the soil friction angle.

Reece introduced two distinct pressure–sinkage models, each tailored to specific soil conditions. The first model, as shown in Equation (7), features model parameters whose dimensions remain constant regardless of the sinkage index, which stands in contrast to the Bekker model. On the other hand, the second equation, as shown in Equation (8), employs dimensionless model parameters and is primarily designed for highly compacted soil [86]. Reece's second model is particularly suited for very dense soil, showcasing its versatility. Then

$$p = (k_1 + k_2 b)(z/b)^n \tag{7}$$

Then

$$p = (ck_c + \gamma k_\phi b)(z/b)^n \tag{8}$$

where k_1 and k_2 are model parameters. c is the soil stickiness, and γ is the unit weight of the soil.

Notably, the Reece model proves highly effective for wheeled robots navigating frictionless clay and firm soil with minimal sinkage. It represents a substantial enhancement over the Bekker model. However, it is worth noting that the Reece model has not undergone extensive testing in softer clay soils, leaving room for further evaluation and refinement in these specific conditions.

Experimental curves showing pressure and sinkage are used to define the relationship between pressure and sinkage in soil. A semi-empirical hyperbolic law is established by Kacigin and Guskovt. By analyzing the compressive strength of the soil, two constants that can be utilized are proposed; they are the bearing capacity p_0 and the soil compression coefficient k. The relationship between pressure and sinkage can be obtained, as shown in Equation (9). Then

$$p = p_0 \frac{1 - \exp(-2kz/p_0)}{1 + \exp(-2kz/p_0)} \tag{9}$$

where p_0 is the bearing capacity of the soil.

Gottenland and Bonoit [87] selected three standard soils: a sand type is used for soils with frictional properties, a silt type for soils with cohesion, and a silty sand type for soils exhibiting both cohesive and frictional characteristics. A pressure–sinkage model N2M was proposed for the interaction between circular contact surfaces and soil. The N2M model is shown in Equation (10). It considers the mechanical behavior of the soil. Small vertical sinkage is similar to elastic behavior. For large sinkage, they are similar to plastic behavior. The initial linear function describes the linear relationship of sinkage pressure within the elastic and plastic areas of the sinkage pressure diagram. The subsequent composite function delineates the shift from the elastic to the plastic region. In the N2M model, distinct asymptotes in both the elastic and plastic sections differentiate the soil's elastic and plastic properties. The sinkage equipment for experimental equipment is shown in Figure 28. Then

$$p = \left(\frac{C_m}{A^m} + \frac{s_m}{A^{1-m}}z\right)\left(1 - \exp\left(-\frac{s_0}{C_m}\frac{z}{A^{1-m}}\right)\right) \quad (10)$$

where A is the diameter of the contact surface, C_m, and s_0, s_m, and m are model parameters.

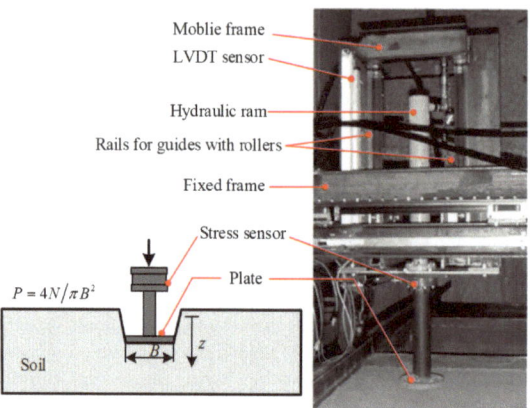

Figure 28. Sinkage equipment for experimental equipment [87].

The sinkage index N serves as a variable to represent the impact of terrain characteristics and various other factors. Ding formulated a model capable of mirroring the impact of normal load, the size of the plate or transmission, and slip on the relationship between pressure and sinkage [88]. The plate sinkage experiment is shown in Figure 29a. The pressure–sinkage relationship is shown in Figure 29b. The general form of the model that takes into account the influencing factors is shown in Equation (11). Then

$$p = k_S z \lambda_N \quad (11)$$

where k_S is the stiffness modulus of the terrain, which plays a leading role in determining the load-bearing performance of the terrain, in Pa/m. λ_N is a dimensionless function that reflects other key factors.

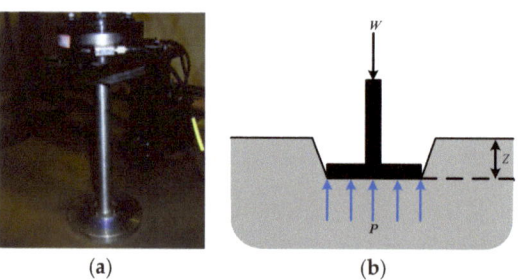

Figure 29. Sinkage experiment and pressure–sinkage relationship [88]: (**a**) plate sinkage experiment; (**b**) pressure–sinkage relationship.

A Theoretical Exploration of the Wheel-Legged Composite Robots

Hunt and Crossley proposed the Hunt–Crossley model. It describes the relationship between the equivalent stiffness and damping of the contact between the object and the terrain. The physical characteristics and the boundary conditions are fully revealed during the contact process [89]. The Hunt–Crossley model was applied by NASA to the study of the lunar hexapod robot ATHELETE. The wheels are modeled as three-dimensional springs to calculate reaction force and deformations [90]. The research results indicate that the model can accurately predict the sinking phenomenon of the robot and has sufficient accuracy for gait planning and execution. Future work can further improve the model to enhance prediction accuracy and apply it to more types of robots. NASA's ATHLETE robot is shown in Figure 30a. The reaction force and deformation are shown in Figure 30b. The Hunt–Crossley model is shown in Equation (12). Then

$$F_N = k_N \delta^{n_1} + C_N \dot{\delta}^m \delta^{n_2} \quad \dot{\delta} \geq 0 \tag{12}$$

where δ is the sum of foot and terrain deformations. C_N is the damping coefficient. n_1 and n_2 are the indicators of the stiffness terms. m is the exponent of the damping term, which can be set to 0 (the linear spring damping model) or n_1 (the simplified Hunt–Crossley model). k_N is the equivalent stiffness coefficient.

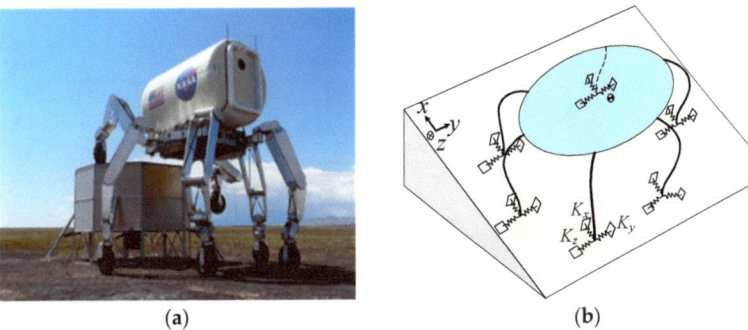

Figure 30. NASA's ATHLETE robot [90]: (**a**) outdoor experiment; (**b**) reaction force and deformation.

Then, the equivalent stiffness k_N can be obtained by Equation (13). Then

$$k_N = \frac{k_{FN} k_{TN}}{k_{FN} + k_{TN}} \tag{13}$$

A Theoretical Exploration of the Legged Robots

Youssef and Ali conducted comprehensive research on sandy soil and clay by integrating the bearing capacity model introduced by Terzaghi and Housel with the pressure–sinkage models of Bekker and Reece [91]. Considering the influence of the size and shape of the contact object, different parameters are provided for the shape of the contact surface, such as circular, square, rectangular, and elliptical. The geometric parameters of the flat plate are shown in Table 2. Through experimental verification, a new pressure–sinkage model is proposed, as shown in Equation (14). Then

$$p = (k_1 + \alpha b k_2)(\beta)^n (z/b)^n \tag{14}$$

where k_1 and k_2 are the soil shear strength values. α and β are dimensionless geometric constants.

Table 2. Geometric parameters of the flat plate.

Plate Shape	β
Circular	4
Square	4
Rectangular	$2(a+b)/a$
Elliptical	$\begin{cases} 2(a+b)/a, & \text{Max} \\ 4\sqrt{\frac{1}{2}(a^2+b^2)}/a, & \text{Min} \end{cases}$

Han from Jilin University designed and manufactured four typical structures of feet, namely hemispherical feet, semi-cylindrical feet, rectangular feet, and circular feet. Research has been conducted on how the size, shape, and density of quartz sand particles affect the matrix's physical characteristics and the mechanical performance of foot penetration. On the three types of quartz sand, the intrusion resistance and pressure of the hemispherical feet are lower than those of the other three mechanical feet. It was found that as the particle size of quartz sand increases, the invasion resistance of the mechanical foot first increases and then decreases. The revised model has been obtained [92]. The corrected integral equations are shown in Table 3. The mechanical feet and intrusion testing equipment are shown in Figure 31.

Table 3. Corrected integral equations.

Different Feet	Pressure–Sinkage Model
Foot with variable cross-sectional area	$\begin{cases} F = K' \times Z^{n+b}, \text{ where } K' = a \times K, \ Z \leq 0.035 \\ F = K'' \times Z^n, \text{ where } K'' = K \times A, \ Z > 0.035 \end{cases}$
Foot with constant cross-sectional area	$F = K'' \times Z^n$, where $K'' = K \times A$

Note: K' (MPa·m^{2-b-n}) and K'' (MPa·m^{2-n}) are both revised intrusion coefficients.

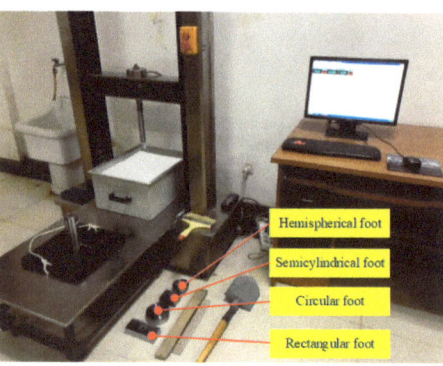

Figure 31. Mechanical feet and intrusion testing equipment [92].

Furthermore, Ding posited that in the normal direction, the interaction force typically resembles the force exerted on a spring and damper located at the foot. The spring damping model shows the interaction between the robot's foot and the terrain in the normal direction [93]. The foot–terrain interaction in the normal direction is shown in Figure 32. The mathematical model of spring damping can be shown in Equation (15). Then

$$F_N = F_{FN} = F_{TN} - m_F g + m_F \ddot{\delta}_T \tag{15}$$

where F_{TN} is the normal force exerted by the terrain on the foot. m_F is the mass of the foot. δ_T and δ_F represent the deformation of the terrain and feet, and δ is the sum of them.

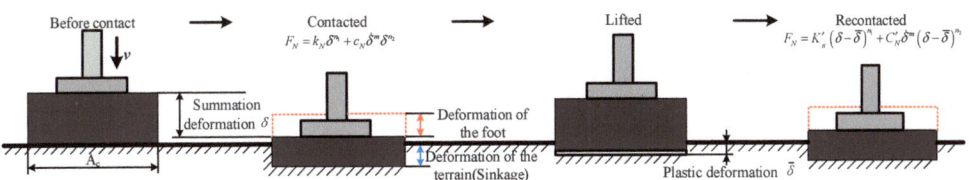

Figure 32. Foot–terrain interaction in normal direction [94].

If the damping is ignored and the spring is linear, the mathematical model of the normal force can be shown in Equation (16). Then

$$F_N = k_{FN}\delta_F = k_{TN}\delta_T \tag{16}$$

where k_{FN} is the normal stiffness coefficient of the foot. k_{TN} is the normal stiffness coefficient of the terrain.

When $\delta = \delta_F + \delta_T = F_N/k_{FN} + F_N/k_{TN}$, the equivalent equation for the mechanics of foot–terrain contact can be rewritten as follows:

$$F_N = \frac{\delta}{1/k_{FN} + 1/k_{TN}} \tag{17}$$

When a legged robot is in motion, the normal load on the foot is not constant. During the process of contact between the foot and the terrain, the deformation of the terrain and the speed of the foot are also in a state of change. Gao believes that during the foot–terrain interaction, the foot tip may shift multiple times and come into contact with the terrain again, including before contact, contact, departure, and recontact [94]. The first contact process can be represented by the Hunt–Crossley model, while the second contact process can be represented by an improved model. The improved model of normal force can be obtained and shown in Equation (18). Ding and Gao's research lays the foundation for improving the terrain stability of the heavy-duty hexapod robot ELSpider. The outdoor experiment of the robot on the interaction between the robot foot and the terrain is shown in Figure 33. Then

$$\begin{cases} F_N = k'_N(\delta - \bar{\delta})^{n_1} + C'_N \dot{\delta}^m (\delta - \bar{\delta})^{n_2} & \delta > \bar{\delta} \\ 0 & \delta \leq \bar{\delta} \end{cases} \tag{18}$$

Figure 33. Outdoor experiment on interaction between robot foot and terrain [94].

In light of the static force's continuity, an additional limitation is presented in Equation (19). Then

$$k_N \delta_{max}^{n_1} = k_N\prime(\delta_{max} - \bar{\delta})^{n_1} \tag{19}$$

However, considering the dynamic parameters of the robot's foot and the ultimate bearing capacity of the terrain, Yang [95] proposed a dynamic bearing capacity model. The model serves as a crucial indicator for determining the normal force boundary conditions essential for the interaction between the foot and the soft terrain. The dynamic bearing capacity model is shown in Equation (20). Then

$$F_N = \sum_{i=1}^{n} \sigma'_{mi} A_i \cos \alpha_i \quad (20)$$

where σ'_{mi} is the revised dynamic bearing capacity. A is the area of the foot.

The zero slip pressure–sinkage models applied to the wheeled robots, the wheel-legged robots, and the legged robots are summarized. The zero slip pressure–sinkage models provided in the literature are shown in Table 4.

Table 4. Zero slip pressure–sinkage models provided in the literature.

Model Name	Model Parameters	Equation Number	References
Bernstein	k, n	(5)	[80,81]
Bekker	k_c, k_Φ, b, n	(6)	[82–84]
Reece	$k_c, k_\Phi, k_1, k_2, b, n, c, \gamma$	(7), (8)	[86]
N2M	C_m, s_0, s_m	(10)	[87]
Ding	k_S, λ_N	(11)	[88]
Hunt–Crossley	$\delta, n_1, n_2, m, k_N, k_{FN}, k_{TN}$	(12), (13)	[89]
Youssef–Ali	$k_1, k_2, b, n, \alpha, \beta$	(14)	[91]
Gao	K_N', C_N', n_1, n_2, m	(17)	[93]

3.1.2. Models for Pressure–Sinkage at Non-Zero Slip Conditions

When the robot's foot slides on the terrain, a tangential force perpendicular to the normal pressure direction is generated. The tangential force can lead to tangential deformation, causing lateral soil loss and resulting in slip sinkage. Therefore, adding very little cohesive moist sandy soil to hard soil can also reduce slip sinkage. Reece discovered that the sinkage occurring when the robot is functioning on soil with non-zero slip can be described as a combination of static sinkage and sliding sinkage. The soil deformation model is shown in Equation (21). Then

$$z = z_o + z_j \quad (21)$$

where z_o represents static sinkage, and z_j represents dynamic sinkage.

The model for predicting soil sliding was proposed by Reece [86]. The Reece prediction model is shown in Equation (22). Then

$$z = z_o + h_{gr} i/(1-i) \quad (22)$$

where h_{gr} is the grouser height, and i is the slip ratio.

A new non-zero slip model was studied by Vasilev. This model can be used to represent the relationship between pressure and settlement [96]. The Vasilev model is shown in Equation (23). Then

$$z = z_o + iH_p \quad (23)$$

where H_p is the propagation depth of soil deformation that can only be evaluated through experiments.

Yeomans [97] considered the phenomenon of foot sinkage in the normal direction due to rotation. Through experimental verification of the hemispherical foot of the planetary exploration robot CREX, a semi-empirical formula for sinkage, rotation direction angle, and normal stress was established. The outdoor experiment of CREX and the rotating sinkage experimental device are shown in Figure 34. The lateral sinkage characteristics can be well described by Equation (24). Then

$$h_{\text{lateral}} = A(1 - \exp(B * slip)) \quad (24)$$

 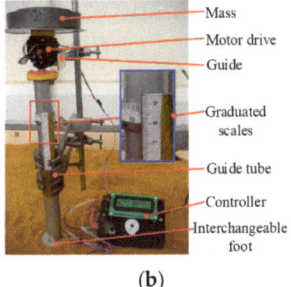

(a)   (b)

Figure 34. CREX robot [97]: (a) outdoor experiment; (b) rotating sinkage experimental device.

The rotational sinkage behavior can be described by Equation (25). Then

$$\text{Sinkage} = K * \text{Stress} * \text{footradius}^2 \left(1 - e^{B\theta}\right) \quad (25)$$

Overall, compared to the wheels of wheeled robots, the foot of the legged robot does not produce a significant rotation angle. Compared with zero slip, the pressure and sinkage caused by non-zero slip are smaller. When analyzing the normal force of heavy-duty legged robots, it is generally believed that the slip amount of foot sinkage is relatively small.

3.2. Tangential Force Models

The aim of integrating tangential interaction models is to illustrate that the shear displacement of the foot on the terrain induces an effect on the tangential plane. In traditional contact models, models that separately describe tangential forces often consider normal force and tangential relative motion position as common determining factors [98]. The heavy-duty legged robots generate tangential friction when performing the tangential relative motion.

In terms of the tangential mechanical models of the foot, the most classic tangential friction model is the Coulomb model [99,100]. As a static friction theory, the Coulomb model has a small computational complexity. Its mechanical parameters are easy to identify. The Coulomb model has been widely used [101,102]. The Coulomb model is shown in Equation (26). Then

$$F = \begin{cases} F_C + (F_S - F_C)e^{-|v/v_S|\delta_S} + F_v & \text{if } v \neq 0 \\ F_e & \text{if } v \neq 0 \text{ and } |F_e| < F_S \\ F_S \text{sgn}(F_e) & \text{otherwise} \end{cases} \quad (26)$$

The Hunt–Crossley model also describes the action model of tangential force, as shown in Equation (27). Then

$$F_T(t) = -f \times \text{sign}(v_T) \times F_N(t) - C_t \times v_T(t) \quad (27)$$

In the study of terrain mechanics, the spring damping system has been widely used in foot–terrain interactions. Liang [103] validated that a simple spring damping system can explain the characteristics of human walking by establishing models and conducting experiments. Conventional 3D models segment the deformation of feet or terrain into two perpendicular directions on a tangential plane, specifically the x and y axes. Significant errors are generated because the coupling effect of deformation is ignored.

In order to consider the coupling effect, Ding [93] proposed a new three-dimensional mechanical model of the foot–terrain interaction in combination with a spring damping system. The three-dimensional interaction mechanical model on a tangential plane is shown in Figure 35. The three-dimensional mechanical model of the foot–terrain interaction can be shown in Equation (28). Then

$$\begin{cases} F_z = F_N \\ F_x = F_T \cos \beta_F \\ F_y = F_T \sin \beta_F \end{cases} \quad (28)$$

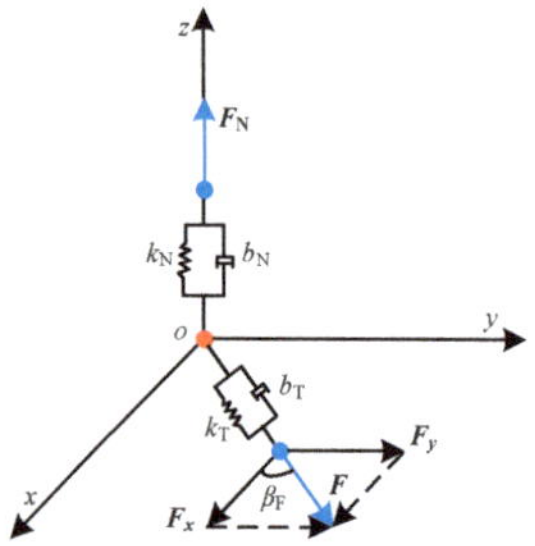

Figure 35. Three-dimensional interaction mechanical model on tangential plane [93].

The process of tangential interaction can also be seen as a normal interaction. As the foot slides across the terrain, the tangential force escalates in correspondence with the rising shear displacement and velocity. The tangential force quickly stabilizes as the shear speed decreases to a certain value. Contrary to the previous growth process, the tangential force suddenly drops to zero when the foot moves in the opposite direction.

The force in a specific tangent direction is usually represented by the Coulomb friction model. If the terrain is relatively hard, the tangential force model uses a modified form. When the direction of relative motion velocity changes, the friction force remains unchanged and does not meet the physical boundary conditions of the friction process, resulting in singular solutions in the simulation. When introducing the hyperbolic tangent function to establish a foot–terrain tangential force model, the value of $th(\delta)$ is infinitely close to 1 or -1 to describe the saturation of tangential friction. The foot–terrain interaction in the tangent direction is shown in Figure 36. The hyperbolic tangent mathematical model is shown in Equation (29). Then

$$th(\delta) = \frac{sh(\delta)}{ch(\delta)} = \frac{e^\delta - e^{-\delta}}{e^\delta + e^{-\delta}} \quad (29)$$

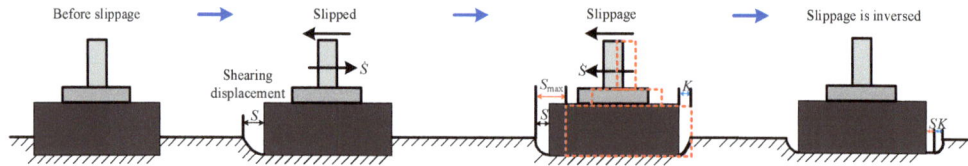

Figure 36. Foot–terrain interaction in the tangent direction [94].

For deformed soil [85], a modified model based on the Janosi equation is proposed; it can be shown in Equation (30). Then

$$F_r = -\frac{\exp(s/K') - \exp(-s/K')}{\exp(s/K') + \exp(-s/K')} \mu_f F_N K' = 1.5K \quad (30)$$

where s is the shearing displacement. K is the shear displacement modulus, affected by the physical characteristics of the feet and terrain. μ_f is the friction coefficient between hard terrain and foot materials. For deformable terrain, μ_f is related to the characteristics of the soil and feet.

However, when applying the new three-dimensional mechanical model to practical simulations, there is a lack of consideration for the damping effect between the feet and the terrain. The model is unstable when the feet interact dynamically with the terrain. Consequently, the force of interaction along the tangent direction is altered when the foot proceeds in a unidirectional movement. The interaction force in the tangent direction is shown in Equation (31). Then

$$\begin{cases} F_r = -\frac{\exp(s/K') - \exp(-s/K')}{\exp(s/K') + \exp(-s/K')} \mu_f F_N - c_T \dot{s} \sqrt{|s|} \\ 0 < s < s_{max} - \kappa \end{cases} \quad (31)$$

where μ_f is the friction coefficient. c_T is the tangential damping coefficient.

The suggested models are developed across three distinct categories: a flexible foot interacting with rigid terrain, a rigid foot on pliable terrain, and a flexible foot engaging with deformable terrain. The model proposes different mechanical models based on the geometric characteristics of different feet, which can accurately characterize the mechanical conditions of the feet in practical applications. The foot–terrain mechanics model parameters are shown in Table 5. An SVM method is proposed that uses two specific tactile movements of the heavy-duty legged robots to extract physical information features for effective terrain classification. Through the normal compression and tangential friction motion of legged robots, the representative interactive data is obtained to characterize the terrain features [104], which plays an important role in improving the accuracy of the model.

Table 5. Foot–terrain mechanics model parameters [93].

Foot Shape	k_{TN}	n_{TN}	μ	k_{TT}	n_{TT}
Flat circular	$k_c \pi r + k_\varphi \pi r^2$	n	$\pi r^2 c / F_{TN} + \tan \varphi$	$\mu F_N / 2K$	1
Flat rectangular	$k_c a + k_\varphi ab$	n	$abc / F_{TN} + \tan \varphi$	$\mu F_N / 2K$	1
Cylindrical	$\sqrt{2r}k_c + \sqrt{2r}bk_\varphi$	$(n+1)/2$	$\sqrt{2r}bc / \sqrt[(2n+1)]{\left(\sqrt{2r}k_c + \sqrt{2r}bk_\varphi\right) F_{TN}^{2n}} + \tan \varphi$	$\mu F_N / 2K$	1
Spherical	$\pi k_c + \pi R k_\varphi$	$n+1$	$\pi Rc / \sqrt[n+1]{(\pi k_c + \pi R k_\varphi) F_{TN}^n} + \tan \varphi$	$\mu F_N / 2K$	1

Yang fully considers the shape characteristics of the contact surface and slip surface under the assumptions of some classical soil mechanics for the limit-bearing theory. The normal and the tangential mechanical models of flat foot and sand, horizontal strip foot and sand, circular and sand, and rectangular flat foot and sand, as well as the interaction model of curved foot and sand, have been established [105]. It has a positive effect on calculating the foot mechanics of robots with different shapes. The tangential force models are shown in Table 6.

Table 6. The tangential force models provided in the literature.

Model Name	Model Parameters	Equation Number	References
Coulomb	μ	(26)	[99,100]
Hunt–Crossley	f, C_t	(27)	[89]
Ding	β_F	(28)	[93]
Ding–Janosi	$s, K', \mu_f, s_{max}, \kappa$	(30), (31)	[94]

The terrain mechanics models can establish a close connection between the parameters in soil mechanics and the foot contact mechanics of the robots. It is convenient to conduct a mechanical analysis of the foot–terrain interaction of the heavy-duty legged robots. However, there is still a long way to go in the research of foot–terrain mechanics for heavy-duty legged robots.

4. Further Research

The terrain mechanics characteristics are an effective supplement to the geometric characteristics of terrain. Taking into account the geometric and mechanical characteristics of the terrain comprehensively is an inevitable way to improve the adaptability of the heavy-duty legged robots to unstructured environments. There are still some issues that need further research regarding the mechanical behavior of terrain interaction for heavy-duty legged robots.

4.1. Configuration Research of Biomimetic Supporting Feet

4.1.1. Application of Bionic Technology in Supporting Feet Design

The common supporting feet of heavy-duty legged robots are feet with passive adaptive joints. Although there are currently cylindrical, spherical, rectangular, and other configurations, there is still a lack of feet that can be used for heavy-duty legged robots in the vast majority of scenarios. In further research, the feet design of the heavy-duty legged robots can adopt biomimetic technology. Biomimetic technology can help expand the application fields of heavy-duty legged robots. The feet of large legged animals in nature can be adopted, as shown in Figure 37. The characteristics and biomimetic design elements of the large legged animals' feet can be shown in Table 7.

(a) (b) (c) (d)

Figure 37. Large legged animals and their feet: (**a**) running ostrich; (**b**) camel walking in desert; (**c**) running horse; and (**d**) walking elephant.

Table 7. Characteristics and biomimetic design elements of large legged animals' feet.

Feet of Large Legged Animals	Walking Mode	Characteristics	Design Elements
Ostrich feet	Digitigrade	The didactyl foot structure of ostriches comprises only the 3rd and 4th toes. The 3rd toe has a larger contact area with the terrain than the 4th toe.	(1) A special arch is installed on the 3rd toe. (2) During walking or jogging, the 4th toe of an ostrich functions as an auxiliary element for load distribution, but it does not make contact with the terrain when the ostrich is running at high speeds.
Camel feet	Plantigrade	When camel feet walk in the sand, they come into contact with the terrain with a thick finger pillow (subcutaneous layer), which can play an elastic buffering effect and have less impact on the sand.	(1) The imitation camel walking can quickly expand the grounding area after landing on foot. The foot forms a concave grounding shape. (2) As the load increases, the boundaries around the foot of the camel like walking can generate circumferential adduction, strengthening the sand fixation effect.
Horse feet	Unguligrade	A horse's hoof usually has a curved shape, similar to an inverted U-shaped shape. The weight of a horse is mainly concentrated on the hoof wall, not the bottom of the hoof. The bottom of a horse's hoof is usually flat or slightly raised.	(1) The biomimetic horse hooves are usually curved in shape to provide stability. (2) They have anti-slip characteristics to provide better traction.
Elephant feet	Semiplantigrade	There is a thick fat foot pad beneath the root bone and metatarsal bone of an elephant's foot. During the weight-bearing process, the weight is distributed across the entire foot pad, giving the elephant's feet a stronger load-bearing structure.	(1) The foot configuration is cylindrical. (2) The bottom of the foot is equipped with thick cushioning pads.

4.1.2. Design and Distribution of Plantar Patterns of Supporting Feet

The plantar patterns of the heavy-duty legged robots also affect the process of foot–terrain mechanics. Therefore, it is essential to design plantar patterns for heavy-duty legged robots. The pattern shapes with better anti-slip performance need to be designed. Based on the previous research, the performance of the multi-baffle foot is good. A biomimetic foot plantar pattern with multi-directional braking stability is designed. The rubber plantar pattern can be fixed by bolts in grooves at the same latitude as the flat and spherical robot feet. The foot plantar pattern cannot undergo significant displacement after installation in the above way, as shown in Figure 38.

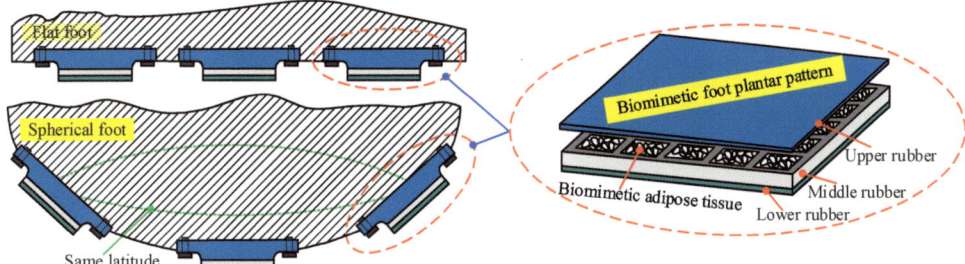

Figure 38. Biomimetic foot plantar pattern.

The direct contact between human feet and terrain is skin tissue, which also contains a large amount of adipose tissue on the inner side. The rubber foot plantar pattern consists of the upper, middle, and lower layers. The middle layer adopts a multi-baffle structure of biomimetic mesh fiber membrane. The rectangular gap in the middle of the baffle is filled with biomimetic adipose tissue.

4.2. Study of Effective Contact Area between Irregular Foot and Dynamic Deformable Terrain

The existing classical theories of pressure–sinkage do not include actual area parameters, as the area of the tested object in classical mechanical models is considered regular. Some robots carry patterns on their feet, and for different surfaces, it is not possible to calculate the actual contact area by substituting the total area of the foot contour into the model. K is considered as the ratio of the actual touchdown area to the outer contour area. In the design process of the model, determining the size of the ratio can consider the impact of the actual contact area on the model. ζ is the terrain coefficient affected by different mechanical properties. Its value is closest to 1 in muddy terrain, second in soft terrain, and smallest in hard terrain. The area evaluation mathematical model can be shown in Equation (32).

Then

$$K = \zeta \frac{S_0}{S} \tag{32}$$

where K is the ratio of the actual touchdown area to the outer contour area. ζ is the terrain coefficient affected by the different mechanical properties, and its value ranges from 0 to 1. S_0 is the actual contact area. S is the outer contour area.

The actual contact area is obtained by capturing images of the foot's contact with the terrain using a depth camera. The images are analyzed to measure the actual contact area by using computer vision techniques. The two sides of the robot's feet are equipped with the dividing rules to estimate the depth of sinkage. A depth camera is installed underneath the robot's foot to capture images of the foot's contact area with the terrain. The captured images undergo preprocessing to remove the noise, enhance the contrast, and improve the clarity. Image segmentation techniques are employed to separate the foot from the terrain in the images. In the segmented images, the contact area between the foot and the terrain can be detected and measured by counting pixels or using image processing libraries. Finally, the calibration is performed to relate the pixels in the images to the real-world physical dimensions based on the camera's parameters and the robot's position. The measurement of the actual contact area between the foot and the terrain is shown in Figure 39.

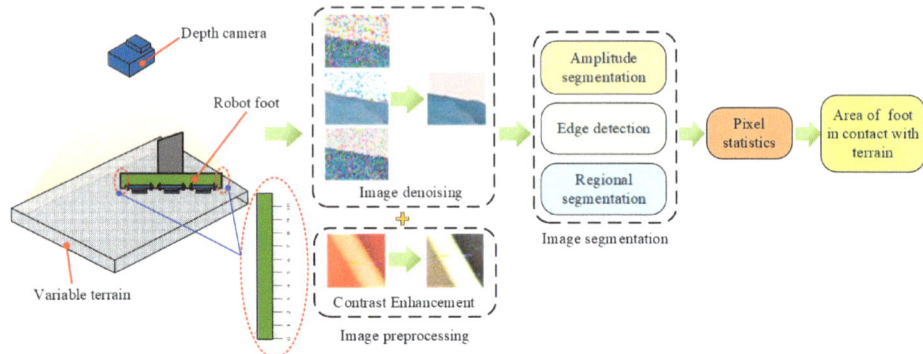

Figure 39. Measurement of actual contact area between foot and terrain.

4.3. Mechanical Behavior Modeling of Interaction between Supporting Feet and Extreme/Dynamic Environments

4.3.1. Construction of Nonlinear Tangential Force Mathematical Model

The tangential force models involving the heavy-duty legged robots still lack coefficients related to the material of the foot. Considering the effects of contact area, terrain, foot material, included angle, and displacement, a nonlinear mathematical model of tangential force is obtained, as shown in Equation (33). Then

$$F_T = F_T(S_0, N_1, N_2, \theta, \varphi, k, j) \tag{33}$$

where S_0 is the actual contact area, N_1 is the parameter related to the material of the foot, N_2 is the parameter related to terrain properties, θ is the angle between the foot and the terrain, φ is the friction angle inside the soil, k is the soil shear modulus, and j is the soil shear displacement.

It is necessary to include material performance parameters of the foot in the foot–terrain mechanics models. Hardness is the ability of the material to resist scratches and deformation, usually related to the frictional properties of the terrain. Strength is the ability of the material to resist fracture or deformation. Robot feet need sufficient strength to withstand the weight of the robot and external impact forces. The elastic modulus represents the elastic deformation ability of the material after being subjected to force. For the foot, an appropriate elastic modulus can provide the elasticity and shock absorption performance of the foot. Wear resistance refers to the ability of the material to withstand friction or wear conditions. The friction coefficient represents the friction performance between the material for robot feet and other surfaces. The robot foot needs an appropriate coefficient of friction to ensure stable terrain adhesion and movement.

4.3.2. Construction of Resultant Force Mathematical Model

The six-dimension force sensors are typically installed on the feet of the heavy-duty legged robots. The forces and moments in three directions are measured. When a robot travels on a slope, the proportion of normal and tangential forces acting on its foot in the resultant force is different. The difference in proportion is significant at a certain moment. Therefore, in model design, u is considered as the ratio of tangential force to normal force, as shown in Equation (34). A mathematical model for evaluating the resultant force on the foot is derived, as shown in Equation (35). Then

$$u = F_T/F_N \tag{34}$$

$$F_\Sigma = \begin{cases} F_N & u < 0.1 \\ F_T & u > 0.9 \\ (F_N + \tan\varphi F_T)(1 - \exp(-j/k)) & 0.1 \leq u \leq 0.9 \end{cases} \tag{35}$$

4.4. Parameterization Research of Soil Characteristics in Extreme/Dynamic Environments

The foot–terrain interaction behavior involves the configuration of feet and the dynamic terrain characteristics. In the future, in addition to optimizing the structural design of the foot, the various indicators of different soils can also be studied. Clarifying the properties of soil in an unstructured environment will be more conducive to the research on the mechanical properties of heavy-duty legged robots. The performance parameters of different soils on Earth are shown in Table 8.

Table 8. Performance parameters of different soils on Earth [106].

Terrain Mechanical Parameters	Dry Sand	Sandy Loam	Clayey Soil	Snow
n	1.1	0.7	0.5	1.6
c (kPa)	1.0	1.7	4.14	1.0
φ (°)	30.0	29.0	13.0	19.7
k_c (kPa/m^{n-1})	0.9	5.3	13.2	4.4
k_φ (kPa/m^n)	1528.4	1515.0	692.15	196.7
K (m)	0.025	0.025	0.01	0.04

The composition of Martian soil includes many complex organic compounds. The composition and performance vary from location to location [107–109]. Due to the limitations of rocket launch loads, current Mars rovers do not carry dedicated equipment for measuring the mechanical parameters of Martian soil, making it impossible to accurately obtain the mechanical parameters of Martian soil in real time. According to the theory of vehicle terrain mechanics and the mathematical models of the wheel–soil interaction, the mechanical parameters of the Martian soil under the wheel and around the rover can be identified. The Viking probe mainly includes two landers: Viking 1 and Viking 2 [110]. Viking 1 landed on the Chryse Planitia (22.48° N, 49.97° W) on 20 July 1976, and Viking 2 landed on the Utopia Planitia (47.97° N, 225.74° W) on 3 September 1976. The mechanical performance evaluation of the weathered materials at Viking 1 and Viking 2 landing sites is shown in Table 9. The captured images are shown in Figure 40. The properties of the Martian soil are indispensable for studying foot–terrain mechanical models in the Martian environment.

Table 9. Estimation of mechanical properties of weathered materials at Viking 1 and Viking 2 landing sites [110].

Property	Viking 1		Viking 2
	Sandy Flats	Rocky Flats	Bonneville and Beta
Bulk density (g/cm^3)	1 to 1.6	1.8	1.5 to 1.8
Particle size (surface and near surface)			
10 to 100 µm (%)	60	30	30
100 to 2000 µm (%)	10	30	30
Angle of internal friction (°)	20 to 30	40 to 45	40 to 45
Cohesion (kPa)	-	0.1 to 1	1
Adhesion (kPa)	-	0.001 to 0.01	-

(a)   (b)   (c)   (d)

Figure 40. Martian terrains [111]: (**a**) morning image of Viking 1's landing site (Chryse Planitia); (**b**) image of Viking 1's landing site (Chryse Planitia) at dusk; (**c**) morning image of Viking 2's landing site (Utopia Planitia); (**d**) image of Viking 2's landing site (Utopia Planitia) at dusk.

On the surface of the moon, due to the impact of meteorites and micro-meteorites, continuous bombardment by cosmic rays, solar wind, and changes in temperature differences between day and night, the lunar rocks undergo thermal expansion, contraction, and fragmentation, resulting in the formation of lunar soil with an average thickness of approximately 6–10 m. In addition, the lunar environment, which is completely different from that on Earth, such as anhydrous and biotic environments, low gravity, and almost zero atmospheric pressure, also results in significant differences in the physical and mechanical properties of lunar soil and Earth's soil [112].

Currently, the analysis of various physical parameters and mechanical properties of lunar soil mainly relies on two methods: in situ return and in situ detection. In situ detection is mainly achieved using uncrewed detection equipment. Many scholars aim to identify the mechanical parameters of lunar soil by studying the interaction between planetary detection wheels and sampling robotic arms with lunar soil. The mechanical parameters of lunar soil published by *Lunar Sourcebook* have been widely recognized [113], as shown in Table 10. The soil density is mainly obtained from density tests of samples retrieved from previous Apollo missions (US lunar landing program). The density of lunar soil is the accumulated mass of granular materials per unit volume in their natural state. The monthly soil density ranges of Apollo 11, 12, 14, 15, and 16, and Luna 16 and 20 are shown in Table 11. Other detailed physical and mechanical properties of lunar soil can be found in the literature [114].

Table 10. *Lunar Sourcebook* published mechanical parameters of lunar soil in United States [113].

Symbol	Meaning
n	1
k_c (kN/m^{n+1})	1.4
k_φ (kN/m^{n+1})	820
c (kPa)	0.17
φ (°)	35
K (m)	1.78

Table 11. Monthly soil density ranges of Apollo 11, 12, 14, 15, and 16, and Luna 16 and 20 [114].

Lunar Soil	Lunar Soil Density ρ (g/cm^3)
Apollo 11	1.36 to 1.8
Apollo 12	1.15 to 1.93
Apollo 14	0.89 to 1.55
Apollo 15	0.87 to 1.51
Apollo 16	1.1 to 1.89
Luna 16	1.115 to 1.793
Luna 20	1.040 to 1.798

The density of the lunar soil can be acquired using Equation (36). Then

$$\rho = \frac{m}{v_s + v_r} \tag{36}$$

where ρ is the bulk density, m is the total mass of lunar soil, v_s is the solid volume of lunar soil particles, and v_r is the pore volume of lunar soil particles.

4.5. Cross-Application of Multimodal Information Fusion and Foot–Terrain Interaction Mechanics

When heavy-duty legged robots are not equipped with effective sensing systems, the unstructured terrain features cannot be adequately extracted and analyzed. Then, the fundamental information of sufficient force distribution would be lacking, which would result in many uncertainties during the walking process of the heavy-duty legged robots. Based on the multimodal information fusion technologies, the appropriate mechanical models of the heavy-duty legged robots can be effectively selected through the analysis and extraction of the terrain information, which is helpful for the robot to complete the gait switching and reduce the danger of navigation in unknown environments. In addition, the combination of multi-sensor fusion and machine vision technology can effectively identify the model parameters and improve their accuracy. Thus, the cross-application of the multimodal information fusion and foot–terrain interaction mechanics would play an important role in the mechanical model selection. The process of choosing the appropriate mechanical model to use the multimodal information fusion is shown in Figure 41.

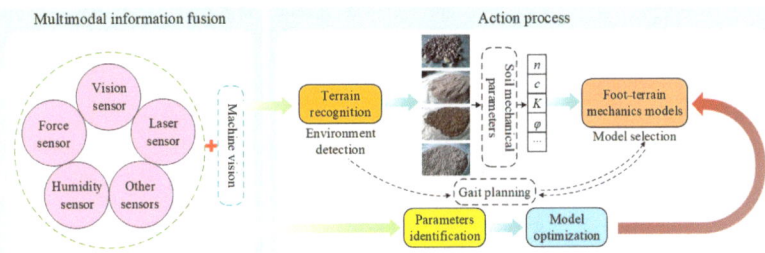

Figure 41. Process of choosing appropriate mechanical model to use multimodal information fusion.

5. Conclusions

(1) The factors influencing the terrain adaptability of the heavy-duty legged robots are explored. Various foot shapes, including cylindrical, semi-cylindrical, spherical, hemispherical, square, and special configurations, are examined, each presenting distinct advantages and disadvantages. When designing the mechanical structure of a robot, the selection of foot configurations and the design of appropriate foot patterns, tailored to specific needs, prove beneficial in enhancing the robot's adaptability to unstructured environments and improving its overall mobility. However, challenges persist as heavy-duty legged robots' feet encounter difficulties adapting to certain unstructured surfaces. Common terrains such as deserts, uneven lunar surfaces, and areas containing stones pose particular challenges for heavy-duty legged robots. Addressing these challenges will be crucial in further refining the design of heavy-duty legged robots for diverse terrains.

(2) The ultimate goal is to design feet for heavy-duty legged robots with enhanced anti-sinkage capabilities, increased traction, and a lightweight structure. To augment the terrain adaptability of heavy-duty legged robots, insights from the characteristics of large legged animals' feet have been distilled. Furthermore, the proposed design elements for biomimetic feet aim to emulate nature's solutions. The incorporation of biomimetic foot plantar patterns onto the sole of the foot proves particularly impactful, substantially amplifying the robot's adhesion capabilities.

(3) The mechanics of foot–terrain interactions encompass both normal and tangential forces occurring between the foot and the contact terrain. An accurate model detailing the mechanics of foot–terrain interaction plays a crucial role in investigating the terrain adaptability of robots. While research on wheel–terrain interaction models is relatively advanced, there is a noticeable gap in the exploration of mechanical models for foot–terrain

interactions. A comprehensive and fully established system for the mechanical model of heavy-duty legged robots' foot–terrain interactions is yet to be realized. The challenges in terrain mechanics for heavy-duty legged robots necessitate support from a systematic theoretical framework.

(4) To enhance the model's precision, an area evaluation parameter is introduced. Subsequently, a mathematical model incorporating the interaction between feet and terrain is proposed to calculate the tangential force. The resultant force equation on the robot's foot is predicted. The mechanical properties of the soil in contact with the foot–terrain interaction significantly influence performance. Investigating various soil parameters for the classification of unstructured terrain holds paramount importance in understanding the mechanics of foot–terrain interactions. Furthermore, exploring the soil on other planets is crucial for the future success of heavy-duty legged robots in interstellar exploration missions. This study includes mechanical performance parameters for real lunar soil, simulated lunar soil, and Martian soil. In future research, the integration of multimodal information fusion and foot–terrain interaction mechanics will be leveraged for cross-application purposes.

Author Contributions: Conceptualization, H.Z.; methodology, H.Z. and J.W.; formal analysis, N.W., W.L., N.L. and L.D.; data curation, H.Z. and J.W.; writing—original draft preparation, H.Z. and J.W.; writing—review and editing, H.Z.; visualization, J.W., N.W. and B.L.; supervision, H.Z.; funding acquisition, H.Z., W.L. and N.W. All authors have read and agreed to the published version of the manuscript.

Funding: This research was supported by the National Natural Science Foundation of China (Grant No. 51505335 and Grant No. 52175007), the Industry University Cooperation Collaborative Education Project of the Department of Higher Education of the Chinese Ministry of Education (Grant No. 202102517001), and the Doctor Startup Project of TUTE (Grant No. KYQD 1806). These supports are greatly acknowledged.

Conflicts of Interest: The authors declare no conflicts of interest.

Nomenclature

A	Contact area	δ	Sum of foot and terrain deformations
B	Geometric parameter of plate	λ_N	Dimensionless function
b	Smaller dimension of contact patch	v_T	Tangential sliding velocity
C_N	Normal damping coefficient	δ_T	Terrain deformation
C_T	Tangential damping coefficient	δ_F	Feet deformation
C_m	Model parameter	μ	Coefficient of friction
C_f	Shape coefficient of contact surface	F_N	Normal support force
c	Soil stickiness	F_T	Tangential driving force
α	Dimensionless geometric constant	Hp	Propagation depth of soil deformation
β	Dimensionless geometric constant	h_{gr}	Grouser height
i	Slip ratio	N_1, N_2	Model parameter
j	Soil shear displacement	p	Pressure
k	Sinkage modulus	p_0	Bearing capacity
k_N	Equivalent stiffness coefficient	s	Shearing displacement
k_{FN}	Stiffness coefficient of foot	s_0	Model parameter
k_{TN}	Stiffness coefficient of terrain	s_m	Model parameter
k_c	Sinkage modulus	v	Poisson's ratio
k_Φ	Sinkage modulus	v_s	Solid volume
k_S	Stiffness modulus of terrain	v_r	Pore volume
k_1	Model parameter	w	Dimensionless coefficient
k_2	Model parameter	z	Sinkage
m	Exponent of damping term	z_o	Static sinkage
m_F	Mass of foot	z_j	Dynamic sinkage
n	Model parameter	ρ	Bulk density
n_1, n_2	Indicators of stiffness terms		

References

1. Zhuang, H.; Gao, H.; Deng, Z.; Ding, L.; Liu, Z. A review of heavy-duty legged robots. *Sci. China Technol. Sci.* **2014**, *57*, 298–314. [CrossRef]
2. Biswal, P.; Mohanty, P.K. Development of quadruped walking robots: A review. *Ain Shams Eng. J.* **2021**, *12*, 2017–2031. [CrossRef]
3. Maity, A.; Majumder, S.; Ghosh, S. An experimental hyper redundant serpentine robot. In Proceedings of the 2010 IEEE International Conference on Systems, Man and Cybernetics—SMC, Istanbul, Turkey, 10–13 October 2010; pp. 3180–3185. [CrossRef]
4. Joshi, V.A.; Banavar, R.N.; Hippalgaonkar, R. Design and analysis of a spherical mobile robot. *Mech. Mach. Theory* **2010**, *45*, 130–136. [CrossRef]
5. Bartsch, S.; Manz, M.; Kampmann, P.; Dettmann, A.; Hanff, H.; Langosz, M.; von Szadkowski, K.; Hilljegerdes, J.; Simnofske, M.; Kloss, P.; et al. Development and Control of the Multi-Legged Robot MANTIS. In Proceedings of the ISR 2016: 47st International Symposium on Robotics, Munich, Germany, 21–22 June 2016; pp. 1–8.
6. Cobano, J.; Ponticelli, R.; de Santos, P.G. Mobile robotic system for detection and location of antipersonnel land mines: Field tests. *Ind. Robot. Int. J. Robot. Res. Appl.* **2008**, *35*, 520–527. [CrossRef]
7. Carbone, G.; Ceccarelli, M. *Legged Robotic Systems*; Intech Open Access Publisher: London, UK, 2005.
8. Zhang, Q.; Zhao, W.; Chu, S.; Wang, L.; Fu, J.; Yang, J.; Gao, B. Research Progress of Nuclear Emergency Response Robot. *IOP Conf. Ser. Mater. Sci. Eng.* **2018**, *452*, 042102. [CrossRef]
9. Zhuang, H.C.; Wang, N.; Gao, H.B.; Deng, Z.Q. Autonomous fault-tolerant gait planning research for electrically driven large-load-ratio six-legged robot. In Proceedings of the 12th International Conference on Intelligent Robotics and Applications (ICIRA 2019), Shenyang, China, 8–11 August 2019; pp. 231–244. [CrossRef]
10. Zhuang, H.-C.; Gao, H.-B.; Deng, Z.-Q. Gait Planning Research for an Electrically Driven Large-Load-Ratio Six-Legged Robot. *Appl. Sci.* **2017**, *7*, 296. [CrossRef]
11. Zhuang, H.-C.; Gao, H.-B.; Deng, Z.-Q. Analysis Method of Articulated Torque of Heavy-Duty Six-Legged Robot under Its Quadrangular Gait. *Appl. Sci.* **2016**, *6*, 323. [CrossRef]
12. Bloesch, M.; Gehring, C.; Fankhauser, P.; Hutter, M.; Hoepflinger, M.A.; Siegwart, R. State estimation for legged robots on unstable and slippery terrain. In Proceedings of the 2013 IEEE/RSJ International Conference on Intelligent Robots and Systems (IROS 2013), Tokyo, Japan, 3–7 November 2013; pp. 6058–6064. [CrossRef]
13. Voloshina, A.S.; Kuo, A.D.; Ferris, D.P.; Remy, D.C. A model-based analysis of the mechanical cost of walking on uneven terrain. *bioRxiv* **2020**. [CrossRef]
14. Zhuang, H.; Xia, Y.; Wang, N.; Li, W.; Dong, L.; Li, B. Interactive method research of dual mode information coordination integration for astronaut gesture and eye movement signals based on hybrid model. *Sci. China Technol. Sci.* **2023**, *66*, 1717–1733. [CrossRef] [PubMed]
15. Saraiva, L.; da Silva, M.R.; Marques, F.; da Silva, M.T.; Flores, P. A review on foot-ground contact modeling strategies for human motion analysis. *Mech. Mach. Theory* **2022**, *177*, 105046. [CrossRef]
16. Hodoshima, R.; Doi, T.; Fukuda, Y.; Hirose, S.; Okamoto, T.; Mori, J. Development of a Quadruped Walking Robot TITAN XI for Steep Slope Operation—Step Over Gait to Avoid Concrete Frames on Steep Slopes. *J. Robot. Mechatron.* **2007**, *19*, 13–26. [CrossRef]
17. Hirose, S.; Yokota, S.; Torii, A.; Ogata, M.; Suganuma, S.; Takita, K.; Kato, K. Quadruped Walking Robot Centered Demining System—Development of TITAN-IX and its Operation. In Proceedings of the 2005 IEEE International Conference on Robotics and Automation, Barcelona, Spain, 18–22 April 2005; pp. 1284–1290. [CrossRef]
18. Hirose, S.; Fukuda, Y.; Kikuchi, H. The gait control system of a quadruped walking vehicle. *Adv. Robot.* **1986**, *1*, 289–323. [CrossRef]
19. Irawan, A.; Nonami, K. Compliant Walking Control for Hydraulic Driven Hexapod Robot on Rough Terrain. *J. Robot. Mechatronics* **2011**, *23*, 149–162. [CrossRef]
20. Bares, J.E.; Wettergreen, D.S. Dante II: Technical Description, Results, and Lessons Learned. *Int. J. Robot. Res.* **1999**, *18*, 621–649. [CrossRef]
21. A Galvez, J.; Estremera, J.; de Santos, P.G. A new legged-robot configuration for research in force distribution. *Mechatronics* **2003**, *13*, 907–932. [CrossRef]
22. Zhuang, H.C. Electrically Driven Large-Load-Ratio Six-Legged Robot Structural Design and Its Mobile Characteristics Research. Ph.D. Dissertation, Harbin Institute of Technology, Harbin, China, 2014. (In Chinese)
23. Zhuang, H.; Wang, N.; Gao, H.; Deng, Z. Quickly Obtaining Range of Articulated Rotating Speed for Electrically Driven Large-Load-Ratio Six-Legged Robot Based on Maximum Walking Speed Method. *IEEE Access* **2019**, *7*, 29453–29470. [CrossRef]
24. Liu, Y.; Ding, L.; Gao, H.; Liu, G.; Deng, Z.; Yu, H. Efficient force distribution algorithm for hexapod robot walking on uneven terrain. In Proceedings of the 2016 IEEE International Conference on Robotics and Biomimetics (ROBIO), Qingdao, China, 3–7 December 2016; pp. 432–437. [CrossRef]
25. Xu, P.; Ding, L.; Li, Z.; Yang, H.; Wang, Z.; Gao, H.; Zhou, R.; Su, Y.; Deng, Z.; Huang, Y. Learning physical characteristics like animals for legged robots. *Natl. Sci. Rev.* **2023**, *10*, nwad045. [CrossRef]
26. Pan, Y.; Gao, F. A new six-parallel-legged walking robot for drilling holes on the fuselage. *Proc. Inst. Mech. Eng. Part C J. Mech. Eng. Sci.* **2014**, *228*, 753–764. [CrossRef]

27. Yang, P.; Gao, F. Kinematical Model and Topology Patterns of a New 6-Parallel-Legged Walking Robot. In Proceedings of the ASME 2012 International Design Engineering Technical Conferences and Computers and Information in Engineering Conference, Volume 4: 36th Mechanisms and Robotics Conference, Parts A and B, Chicago, IL, USA, 12–15 August 2012; pp. 1197–1205. [CrossRef]
28. Pan, Y.; Gao, F. Payload capability analysis of a new kind of parallel leg hexapod walking robot. In Proceedings of the 2013 International Conference on Advanced Mechatronic Systems (ICAMechS), Luoyang, China, 25–27 September 2013; pp. 541–544. [CrossRef]
29. Yang, P.; Gao, F. Leg kinematic analysis and prototype experiments of walking-operating multifunctional hexapod robot. Proc. Inst. Mech. Eng. Part C J. Mech. Eng. Sci. 2013, 228, 2217–2232. [CrossRef]
30. Zhang, H.Y. Analysis of the Structure and Stability of a Large and Highly Adaptable Hexapod Robot. Master's Thesis, Jilin University, Changchun, China, 2021. (In Chinese)
31. Zhai, C. Research on Motion Trajectory Planning of Heavy-Load Hydraulic Driven Hexapod Robots. Master's Thesis, Jilin University, Changchun, China, 2023. (In Chinese)
32. Gao, J. Leg Mechanism Design and Simulation Analysis for a Heavy-Duty Hydraulic Hexapod Robot. Master's Thesis, Jilin University, Changchun, China, 2017. (In Chinese)
33. Xu, Z.; Yi, H.; Liu, D.; Zhang, R.; Luo, X. Design a Hybrid Energy-Supply for the Electrically Driven Heavy-Duty Hexapod Vehicle. J. Bionic Eng. 2023, 20, 1434–1448. [CrossRef]
34. Xu, Z.; Chen, X.; Liu, Y.; Wang, L.; Zhou, L.; Yi, H.; Bao, C. Design and Implementation of a Novel Robot Foot with High-adaptability and High-adhesion for Heavy-load Walking Robots. In Proceedings of the 2019 IEEE 9th Annual International Conference on CYBER Technology in Automation, Control, and Intelligent Systems (CYBER), Suzhou, China, 29 July–2 August 2019; pp. 1509–1514. [CrossRef]
35. Raibert, M.; Blankespoor, K.; Nelson, G.; Playter, R. BigDog, the rough-terrain quadruped robot. IFAC Proc. Vol. 2008, 41, 10822–10825. [CrossRef]
36. Wooden, D.; Malchano, M.; Blankespoor, K.; Howardy, A.; Rizzi, A.A.; Raibert, M. Autonomous navigation for BigDog. In Proceedings of the 2010 IEEE International Conference on Robotics and Automation (ICRA 2010), Anchorage, AK, USA, 3–7 May 2010; pp. 4736–4741. [CrossRef]
37. Meng, X.; Wang, S.; Cao, Z.; Zhang, L. A review of quadruped robots and environment perception. In Proceedings of the IEEE 35th Control Conference (CCC), Chengdu, China, 27–29 July 2016; pp. 6350–6356. [CrossRef]
38. Zang, H.; Zhao, D.; Shen, L. Theoretical Study of Global Scale Analysis Method for Agile Bionic Leg Mechanism. Robotica 2020, 38, 427–441. [CrossRef]
39. Han, B.; Yi, H.; Xu, Z.; Yang, X.; Luo, X. 3D-SLIP model based dynamic stability strategy for legged robots with impact disturbance rejection. Sci. Rep. 2022, 12, 5892. [CrossRef]
40. Zhong, J.F. Design, Control of Hydraulical Actuators for Quadruped Legged Robot. Master's Thesis, Huazhong University of Science and Technology, Wuhan, China, 2014. (In Chinese)
41. Cheng, P. Research, Design of Control System for Bionic Quadruped Robot. Master's Thesis, Huazhong University of Science and Technology, Wuhan, China, 2014. (In Chinese)
42. Qi, C.; Gao, F.; Sun, Q.; Chen, X.; Xu, Y.; Zhao, X. A foot force sensing approach for a legged walking robot using the motor current. In Proceedings of the 2015 IEEE International Conference on Robotics and Biomimetics (ROBIO), Zhuhai, China, 6–9 December 2015; pp. 1078–1083. [CrossRef]
43. Sun, Q.; Gao, F.; Chen, X. Towards dynamic alternating tripod trotting of a pony-sized hexapod robot for disaster rescuing based on multi-modal impedance control. Robotica 2018, 36, 1048–1076. [CrossRef]
44. Qiao, S. Design, Dynamic Gait Control of the Rescue Hexapod Robot with Erect Posture and Parallel Mechanism Leg. Ph.D. Dissertation, Shanghai Jiaotong University, Shanghai, China, 2018. (In Chinese)
45. Michael, K. Meet Boston Dynamics' LS3—The Latest Robotic War Machine; University of Wollongong: Wollongong, NSW, Australia, 2012.
46. Rong, X.; Li, Y.; Ruan, J.; Li, B. Design and simulation for a hydraulic actuated quadruped robot. J. Mech. Sci. Technol. 2012, 26, 1171–1177. [CrossRef]
47. Chen, T.; Rong, X.; Li, Y.; Ding, C.; Chai, H.; Zhou, L. A compliant control method for robust trot motion of hydraulic actuated quadruped robot. Int. J. Adv. Robot. Syst. 2018, 15, 1729881418813235. [CrossRef]
48. Yang, K.; Zhou, L.; Rong, X.; Li, Y. Onboard hydraulic system controller design for quadruped robot driven by gasoline engine. Mechatronics 2018, 52, 36–48. [CrossRef]
49. Bartsch, S.; Birnschein, T.; Cordes, F.; Kuehn, D.; Kampmann, P.; Hilljegerdes, J.; Planthaber, S.; Roemmermann, M.; Kirchner, F. Spaceclimber: Development of a six-legged climbing robot for space exploration. In Proceedings of the ISR 2010 (41st International Symposium on Robotics) and ROBOTIK 2010 (6th German Conference on Robotics), Munich, Germany, 7–9 June 2010; pp. 1–8.
50. Bartsch, S.; Birnschein, T.; Römmermann, M.; Hilljegerdes, J.; Kühn, D.; Kirchner, F. Development of the six-legged walking and climbing robot SpaceClimber. J. Field Robot. 2012, 29, 506–532. [CrossRef]
51. Kitano, S.; Hirose, S.; Horigome, A.; Endo, G. TITAN-XIII: Sprawling-type quadruped robot with ability of fast and energy-efficient walking. ROBOMECH J. 2016, 3, 8. [CrossRef]

52. Ohtsuka, S.; Endo, G.; Fukushima, E.F.; Hirose, S. Development of terrain adaptive sole for multi-legged walking robot. In Proceedings of the 2010 IEEE/RSJ International Conference on Intelligent Robots and Systems (IROS 2010), Taipei, Taiwan, 18–22 October 2010; pp. 5354–5359. [CrossRef]
53. Talebi, S.; Poulakakis, I.; Papadopoulos, E.; Buehler, M. Quadruped robot running with a bounding gait. In *Experimental Robotics VII*; Springer: Berlin/Heidelberg, Germany, 2001; pp. 281–289. [CrossRef]
54. de Santos, P.G.; Cobano, J.; Garcia, E.; Estremera, J.; Armada, M. A six-legged robot-based system for humanitarian demining missions. *Mechatronics* **2007**, *17*, 417–430. [CrossRef]
55. Chen, T.; Li, Y.; Rong, X.; Zhang, G.; Chai, H.; Bi, J.; Wang, Q. Design and Control of a Novel Leg-Arm Multiplexing Mobile Operational Hexapod Robot. *IEEE Robot. Autom. Lett.* **2022**, *7*, 382–389. [CrossRef]
56. Nelson, G.; Saunders, A.; Neville, N.; Swilling, B.; Bondaryk, J.; Billings, D.; Lee, C.; Playter, R.; Raibert, M. PETMAN: A Humanoid Robot for Testing Chemical Protective Clothing. *J. Robot. Soc. Jpn.* **2012**, *30*, 372–377. [CrossRef]
57. Kuindersma, S.; Deits, R.; Fallon, M.; Valenzuela, A.; Dai, H.; Permenter, F.; Koolen, T.; Marion, P.; Tedrake, R. Optimization-based locomotion planning, estimation, and control design for the atlas humanoid robot. *Auton. Robot.* **2016**, *40*, 429–455. [CrossRef]
58. Kuehn, D.; Schilling, M.; Stark, T.; Zenzes, M.; Kirchner, F. System Design and Testing of the Hominid Robot Charlie. *J. Field Robot.* **2017**, *34*, 666–703. [CrossRef]
59. Fondahl, K.; Kuehn, D.; Beinersdorf, F.; Bernhard, F.; Grimminger, F.; Schilling, M.; Stark, T.; Kirchner, F. An adaptive sensor foot for a bipedal and quadrupedal robot. In Proceedings of the 2012 4th IEEE RAS & EMBS International Conference on Biomedical Robotics and Biomechatronics (BioRob 2012), Rome, Italy, 24–27 June 2012; pp. 270–275. [CrossRef]
60. Mosher, R. Test and evaluation of a versatile walking truck. In Proceedings of the Off-Road Mobility Research Symposium, Washington, DC, USA, 1968; pp. 359–379.
61. Hirose, S.; Yoneda, K.; Tsukagoshi, H. TITAN VII: Quadruped walking and manipulating robot on a steep slope. In Proceedings of the International Conference on Robotics and Automation, Albuquerque, NM, USA, 25 April 1987; pp. 494–500. [CrossRef]
62. He, G.; Xu, J.; Jiang, J.; Cao, Z.; Zhu, D. Soil arching effect analysis and structure optimization of a robot foot sinking in soft soil. *Adv. Mech. Eng.* **2017**, *9*, 1687814017727940. [CrossRef]
63. He, G.; Cao, Z.; Li, Q.; Zhu, D.; Aimin, J. Influence of hexapod robot foot shape on sinking considering multibody dynamics. *J. Mech. Sci. Technol.* **2020**, *34*, 3823–3831. [CrossRef]
64. Chopra, S.; Tolley, M.T.; Gravish, N. Granular Jamming Feet Enable Improved Foot-Ground Interactions for Robot Mobility on Deformable Ground. *IEEE Robot. Autom. Lett.* **2020**, *5*, 3975–3981. [CrossRef]
65. Hong, Y.; Yi, S.; Ryu, S.; Lee, C. Design and experimental test of a new robot foot for a quadrupedal jointed-leg type walking robot. In Proceedings of the 5th IEEE International Workshop on Robot and Human Communication. RO-MAN'96 TSUKUBA, Tsukuba, Japan, 11–14 November 1996; pp. 317–322. [CrossRef]
66. Yamamoto, K.; Sugihara, T.; Nakamura, Y. Toe joint mechanism using parallel four-bar linkage enabling humanlike multiple support at toe pad and toe tip. In Proceedings of the 2007 7th IEEE-RAS International Conference on Humanoid Robots (Humanoids 2007), Pittsburgh, PA, USA, 29 November–1 December 2007; pp. 410–415. [CrossRef]
67. Borovac, B.; Slavnic, S. Design of Multi-segment Humanoid Robot Foot. In Proceedings of the Research and Education in Robotics—EUROBOT 2008: International Conference, Heidelberg, Germany, 22–24 May 2008; pp. 12–18. [CrossRef]
68. Nabulsi, S.; Sarria, J.F.; Montes, H.; Armada, M.A. High-Resolution Indirect Feet–Ground Interaction Measurement for Hydraulic-Legged Robots. *IEEE Trans. Instrum. Meas.* **2009**, *58*, 3396–3404. [CrossRef]
69. Collins, S.H.; Kuo, A.D. Recycling Energy to Restore Impaired Ankle Function during Human Walking. *PLoS ONE* **2010**, *5*, e9307. [CrossRef]
70. Song, Y. The Analysis and Test of the Robot Foot-Ground Adhesion Properties. Master's Thesis, Harbin Institute of Technology, Harbin, China, 2014. (In Chinese)
71. Zou, Y.Y. Landing Point Planning and Foot Pattern Design of Hexapod Robot. Master's Thesis, Dalian University of Technology, Dalian, China, 2019. (In Chinese)
72. Li, J. The Design and Research of Heavy-Duty Robot High Adaptability Foot. Master's Thesis, Dalian University of Technology, Dalian, China, 2016. (In Chinese)
73. Li, K.W.; Wu, H.H.; Lin, Y.-C. The effect of shoe sole tread groove depth on the friction coefficient with different tread groove widths, floors and contaminants. *Appl. Ergon.* **2006**, *37*, 743–748. [CrossRef]
74. Li, K.W.; Chen, C.J.; Lin, C.-H.; Hsu, Y.W. Relationship between measured friction coefficients and two tread groove design parameters for footwear pads. *Tsinghua Sci. Technol.* **2006**, *11*, 712–719. [CrossRef]
75. Li, K.W.; Chen, C.J. Effects of tread groove orientation and width of the footwear pads on measured friction coefficients. *Saf. Sci.* **2005**, *43*, 391–405. [CrossRef]
76. Irani, R.; Bauer, D.; Warkentin, A. A dynamic terramechanic model for small lightweight vehicles with rigid wheels and grousers operating in sandy soil. *J. Terramechanics* **2011**, *48*, 307–318. [CrossRef]
77. Ding, L.; Yang, H.; Gao, H.; Li, N.; Deng, Z.; Guo, J.; Li, N. Terramechanics-based modeling of sinkage and moment for in-situ steering wheels of mobile robots on deformable terrain. *Mech. Mach. Theory* **2017**, *116*, 14–33. [CrossRef]
78. Zhuang, H.; Wang, N.; Gao, H.; Deng, Z. Power Consumption Characteristics Research on Mobile System of Electrically Driven Large-Load-Ratio Six-Legged Robot. *Chin. J. Mech. Eng.* **2023**, *36*, 26. [CrossRef]

79. Liu, Z.; Zhuang, H.-C.; Gao, H.-B.; Deng, Z.-Q.; Ding, L. Static Force Analysis of Foot of Electrically Driven Heavy-Duty Six-Legged Robot under Tripod Gait. *Chin. J. Mech. Eng.* **2018**, *31*, 63. [CrossRef]
80. Bernstein, R. Problems of the experimental mechanics of motor ploughs. *Der Motorwagen* **1913**, *16*, 1–10.
81. Saakyan, S.S. Vzaimodeistrie vedomogo kolesa i pochvi. 1959.
82. Comin, F.J.; Saaj, C.M. Models for Slip Estimation and Soft Terrain Characterization with Multilegged Wheel–Legs. *IEEE Trans. Robot.* **2017**, *33*, 1438–1452. [CrossRef]
83. Komizunai, S.; Konno, A.; Abiko, S.; Uchiyama, M. Development of a static sinkage model for a biped robot on loose soil. In Proceedings of the 2010 IEEE/SICE International Symposium on System Integration (SII 2010), Sendai, Japan, 21–22 December 2010; pp. 61–66. [CrossRef]
84. Bekker, M.G. Land Locomotion on the Surface of Planets. *ARS J.* **1962**, *32*, 1651–1659. [CrossRef]
85. Patel, N.; Scott, G.; Ellery, A. Application of Bekker Theory for Planetary Exploration Through Wheeled, Tracked, and Legged Vehicle Locomotion. In Proceedings of the Space 2004 Conference and Exhibit, San Diego, CA, USA, 28–30 September 2004; p. 6091. [CrossRef]
86. Reece, A.R. Principles of Soil-Vehicle Mechanics. *Proc. Inst. Mech. Eng. Automob. Div.* **1965**, *180*, 45–66. [CrossRef]
87. Gotteland, P.; Benoit, O. Sinkage tests for mobility study, modelling and experimental validation. *J. Terramechan.* **2006**, *43*, 451–467. [CrossRef]
88. Ding, L.; Gao, H.; Deng, Z.; Li, Y.; Liu, G. New perspective on characterizing pressure–sinkage relationship of terrains for estimating interaction mechanics. *J. Terramechan.* **2014**, *52*, 57–76. [CrossRef]
89. Hunt, K.; Crossley, F.R.E. Coefficient of Restitution Interpreted as Damping in Vibroimpact. *J. Appl. Mech.* **1975**, *42*, 440–445. [CrossRef]
90. Wheeler, D.D.; Chavez-Clemente, D.; Sunspiral, V.K. FootSpring: A compliance model for the ATHLETE family of robots. In Proceedings of the 10th International Symposium on Artificial Intelligence, Toronto, ON, Canada, 20–21 June 2010.
91. Youssef, A.-F.A.; Ali, G.A. Determination of soil parameters using plate test. *J. Terramechan.* **1982**, *19*, 129–147. [CrossRef]
92. Han, D.; Zhang, R.; Zhang, H.; Hu, Z.; Li, J. Mechanical Performances of Typical Robot Feet Intruding into Sands. *Energies* **2020**, *13*, 1867. [CrossRef]
93. Ding, L.; Gao, H.; Deng, Z.; Song, J.; Liu, Y.; Liu, G.; Iagnemma, K. Foot–terrain interaction mechanics for legged robots: Modeling and experimental validation. *Int. J. Robot. Res.* **2013**, *32*, 1585–1606. [CrossRef]
94. Gao, H.; Jin, M.; Ding, L.; Liu, Y.; Li, W.; Yu, X.; Deng, Z.; Liu, Z. A real-time, high fidelity dynamic simulation platform for hexapod robots on soft terrain. *Simul. Model. Pract. Theory* **2016**, *68*, 125–145. [CrossRef]
95. Yang, C.; Ding, L.; Tang, D.; Gao, H.; Deng, Z.; Wang, G. Analysis of the normal bearing capacity of the terrain in case of foot-terrain interaction based on Terzaghi theory. In Proceedings of the 2016 IEEE International Conference on Robotics and Biomimetics (ROBIO), Qingdao, China, 3–7 December 2016; pp. 443–448. [CrossRef]
96. Vasilev, A.V.; Dokychaeva, E.N.; Utkin-Lubovtsov, O.L. *Effect of Tracked Tractor Design Parameters on Tractive Performance*; Mashinostroenie: Moscow, Russia, 1969.
97. Yeomans, B.; Saaj, C.M. Towards terrain interaction prediction for bioinspired planetary exploration rovers. *Bioinspiration Biomim.* **2014**, *9*, 016009. [CrossRef] [PubMed]
98. Awrejcewicz, J.; Olejnik, P. Analysis of Dynamic Systems with Various Friction Laws. *Appl. Mech. Rev.* **2005**, *58*, 389–411. [CrossRef]
99. Olsson, H.; Åström, K.; de Wit, C.C.; Gäfvert, M.; Lischinsky, P. Friction Models and Friction Compensation. *Eur. J. Control* **1998**, *4*, 176–195. [CrossRef]
100. Haddadi, A.; Hashtrudi-Zaad, K. A New Method for Online Parameter Estimation of Hunt-Crossley Environment Dynamic Models. In Proceedings of the 2008 IEEE/RSJ International Conference on Intelligent Robots and Systems, Nice, France, 22–26 September 2008; pp. 981–986. [CrossRef]
101. Zapolsky, S.; Drumwright, E. Inverse dynamics with rigid contact and friction. *Auton. Robot.* **2017**, *41*, 831–863. [CrossRef]
102. Senoo, T.; Ishikawa, M. Analysis of sliding behavior of a biped robot in centroid acceleration space. *Robotica* **2017**, *35*, 636–653. [CrossRef]
103. Liang, H.; Xie, W.; Zhang, Z.; Wei, P.; Cui, C. A Three-Dimensional Mass-Spring Walking Model Could Describe the Ground Reaction Forces. *Math. Probl. Eng.* **2021**, *2021*, 6651715. [CrossRef]
104. Ding, L.; Xu, P.; Li, Z.; Zhou, R.; Gao, H.; Deng, Z.; Liu, G. Pressing and Rubbing: Physics-Informed Features Facilitate Haptic Terrain Classification for Legged Robots. *IEEE Robot. Autom. Lett.* **2022**, *7*, 5990–5997. [CrossRef]
105. Yang, C.; Ding, L.; Tang, D.; Gao, H.; Niu, L.; Lan, Q.; Li, C.; Deng, Z. Improved Terzaghi-theory-based interaction modeling of rotary robotic locomotors with granular substrates. *Mech. Mach. Theory* **2020**, *152*, 103901. [CrossRef]
106. Iagnemma, K.; Kang, S.; Shibly, H.; Dubowsky, S. Online Terrain Parameter Estimation for Wheeled Mobile Robots with Application to Planetary Rovers. *IEEE Trans. Robot.* **2004**, *20*, 921–927. [CrossRef]
107. Wu, C. Space exploration: Secrets of the martian soil. *Nature* **2007**, *448*, 742–744. [CrossRef] [PubMed]
108. Yen, A.S.; Gellert, R.; Schröder, C.; Morris, R.V.; Bell, J.F.; Knudson, A.T.; Clark, B.C.; Ming, D.W.; Crisp, J.A.; Arvidson, R.E.; et al. An integrated view of the chemistry and mineralogy of martian soils. *Nature* **2005**, *436*, 49–54. [CrossRef]

109. Hecht, M.H.; Kounaves, S.P.; Quinn, R.C.; West, S.J.; Young, S.M.M.; Ming, D.W.; Catling, D.C.; Clark, B.C.; Boynton, W.V.; Hoffman, J.; et al. Detection of Perchlorate and the Soluble Chemistry of Martian Soil at the Phoenix Lander Site. *Science* **2009**, *325*, 64–67. [CrossRef]
110. Shorthill, R.W.; Moore, H.J.; Hutton, R.E.; Scott, R.F.; Spitzer, C.R. The Environs of Viking 2 Lander. *Science* **1976**, *194*, 1309–1318. [CrossRef]
111. Moore, H.J.; Hutton, R.E.; Clow, G.D.; Spitzer, C.R. *Physical Properties of the Surface Materials at the Viking Landing Sites on Mars*; United States Government Printing Office: Washington, USA, 1987. Available online: https://pubs.usgs.gov/publication/pp1389 (accessed on 1 July 2024).
112. Ding, L.; Zhou, R.; Yuan, Y.; Yang, H.; Li, J.; Yu, T.; Liu, C.; Wang, J.; Gao, H.; Deng, Z.; et al. A 2-year locomotive exploration and scientific investigation of the lunar farside by the Yutu-2 rover. *Sci. Robot.* **2022**, *7*, eabj6660. [CrossRef] [PubMed]
113. Heiken, G.H.; Vaniman, D.T.; French, B.M. *Lunar Sourcebook: A User's Guide to the Moon*; Cambridge University Press: Cambridge, UK, 1991.
114. Slyuta, E.N. Physical and mechanical properties of the lunar soil (a review). *Sol. Syst. Res.* **2014**, *48*, 330–353. [CrossRef]

Disclaimer/Publisher's Note: The statements, opinions and data contained in all publications are solely those of the individual author(s) and contributor(s) and not of MDPI and/or the editor(s). MDPI and/or the editor(s) disclaim responsibility for any injury to people or property resulting from any ideas, methods, instructions or products referred to in the content.

MDPI AG
Grosspeteranlage 5
4052 Basel
Switzerland
Tel.: +41 61 683 77 34

Applied Sciences Editorial Office
E-mail: applsci@mdpi.com
www.mdpi.com/journal/applsci

Disclaimer/Publisher's Note: The title and front matter of this reprint are at the discretion of the Guest Editors. The publisher is not responsible for their content or any associated concerns. The statements, opinions and data contained in all individual articles are solely those of the individual Editors and contributors and not of MDPI. MDPI disclaims responsibility for any injury to people or property resulting from any ideas, methods, instructions or products referred to in the content.